Jewish Backgrounds
of the New Testament

Jewish Backgrounds of the New Testament

J. Julius Scott Jr.

Baker Academic
a division of Baker Publishing Group
Grand Rapids, Michigan

© 1995 by J. Julius Scott, Jr.

Published by Baker Academic
a division of Baker Publishing Group
P.O. Box 6287, Grand Rapids, MI 49516-6287
www.bakeracademic.com

Previously published by Baker Book House as *Customs and Controversies: Intertestamental Jewish Backgrounds of the New Testament*

Printed in the United States of America

Library of Congress Cataloging-in-Publication Data
Scott, J. Julius.
   [Customs and controversies]
   Jewish backgrounds of the New Testament / J. Julius Scott, Jr.
      p.   cm.
   Originally published : Customs and controversies. Grand Rapids, Mich.: Baker Books, c1995.
   Includes bibliographical references and indexes.
   ISBN 10: 0-8010-2240-1 (pbk.)
   ISBN 978-0-8010-2240-1 (pbk.)
   1. Judaism—History—Post-exilic period, 586 B.C.–210 A.D.   I. Title.
BM176.S38 2000
296′.09′014—dc21   00-030407

Pseudepigraphical quotations are from *Old Testament Pseudepigrapha*, ed. James H. Charlesworth, 2 vols. (Garden City, N.Y.: Doubleday, 1983, 1985). Quotations from Josephus are from Josephus, *Works*, trans. H. St. J. Thackeray, Ralph Macus, Allen Wikgren, and Louis H. Feldman, 9 vols., Loeb Classical Library (Cambridge, Mass.: Harvard University Press, 1926–65). Quotations from Philo are from Philo, *Works*, trans. F. H. Colson, G. H. Whitaker, and Ralph Marcus, 10 vols. with two suppls., Loeb Classical Library (Cambridge, Mass.: Harvard University Press, 1929–62). Mishnaic material is from *The Mishnah*, trans. Herbert Danby (Oxford: Oxford University Press, 1933). For the Dead Sea Scrolls I have used *The Dead Sea Scrolls in English*, trans. Geza Vermes, 3d ed. (New York: Viking Penguin, 1990).

With Love and Appreciation

to the two Mrs. J. Julius Scotts

In Memory of
LaVerne
who bore me

and

For
Florence
who bears with me

Contents

Illustrations

Figures

Maps

Tables

Preface

During the Christmas season of 1963 I was in my first year of college teaching. My brother David, a devout, thoughtful Christian businessman, accompanied me when I gave a brief survey of "The Jewish Backgrounds of Christmas" to a Sunday school class. Later he asked, "Why isn't that type of information available to laypersons?" Thus was sown in my mind the seed for my "David book." David may not always be pleased with what follows; it may seem a bit too technical. I am comforted when I remember that he too gets a bit technical when explaining his business; this is, I fear, inevitable in every area.

In 1963 I did not tell my brother that I actually had in hand a brief complete manuscript on the subject. I wanted to flesh it out. Subsequently there has been an explosion of both discovery and writing about Intertestamental Judaism. Since 1963 new translations and editions of the Apocrypha, Pseudepigrapha, and Dead Sea Scrolls have appeared. In addition, several major secondary sources have become available. I refer especially to the new edition of Emil Schürer's great work, *The History of the Jewish People in the Age of Jesus Christ,* the massive, multivolume *Compendia Rerum Iudaicarum ad Novum Testamentum,* Robert Kraft and George Nickelsburg's *Early Judaism and Its Modern Interpreters,* and Lester Grabbe's two-volume *Judaism from Cyrus to Hadrian.* I have gained much help from articles in Gerhard Kittel and Gerhard Friedrich's *Theological Dictionary of the New Testament.* As this study drew toward its conclusion, the *Anchor Bible Dictionary* became available; I have often consulted it with much profit. Acknowledgments in notes cannot begin to indicate my debt to these and numerous other studies.

One of the major pleasures of completing a project such as this is to acknowledge and thank many of those to whom the writer is indebted. Although this list is long it is not complete. Four mentioned here are no longer with us, but in the presence of him who is now their Rewarder.

My interest in Intertestamental Judaism was first kindled by my mother through a little book on customs of the biblical world. During my doctoral study at the University of Manchester it was fanned into a fire by F. F. Bruce, Arnold A. T. Ehrhardt, and especially Robert A. Kraft (now of the University of Pennsylvania). Enthusiasm for the subject has been kept alive and has grown by the interest of students who have studied it with me at Belhaven College (Jackson, Miss.), Western Kentucky University, the Wheaton College Graduate School, and the ECWA Theological Seminary (Evangelical Church of West Africa—Igbaja, Nigeria).

I have enjoyed the encouragement of and opportunity to talk through issues with such colleagues as Norman E. Harper, John N. Akers, J. Knox Chamblin, E. Margaret Howe, Ronald A. Veenker, Walter A. Elwell, Herbert M. Wolf, C. Hassell Bullock, and New Testament archaeologist John R. McRay. I have frequently turned for assistance with both content and editorial matters to my good friend Robert D. Carlson.

Far too many years ago Allan Fisher, now director of publications at Baker Book House, began to prod me gently to get serious about this project. His friendship and persistent encouragement have never wavered, even in the face of my well-practiced procrastination. Jim Weaver, editor of academic and reference works at Baker and a kindred spirit with me in the appreciation of bluegrass music, has been a pleasant and helpful person with whom to work. Wholehearted thanks and admiration go to Ray Wiersma, senior editor of academic and reference books, for his work on the manuscript. His patient, meticulous, and expert work has gone far beyond what most think of as the task of an editor. Others in the Baker Book House organization deserve both credit and praise. To each I say, "Thank you, lots!"

Although through the years I tried to work on this project in spare moments here and there, I made little substantial progress. I needed long uninterrupted periods of time for research, contemplation, and writing. This was made possible during sabbatical leaves from Wheaton College in 1985 and 1993–95. Again, "thank you" seems so inadequate for expressing the depth of my gratitude.

Before their deaths, my mother and father showed much interest in my studies on the Jewish backgrounds of the New Testament. My sister Mary S. Ward and her husband Jack have shown encouraging attention, as have my children Mary S. Smith, Julia S. Fox, and James J. Scott III. My brother David, having planted the seed for this book, has watched over and cultivated its growth. While reading through the entire manuscript, he weeded out numerous mistakes in spelling and phraseology. To all these whom I have named, and to countless others who, in one way or another, have helped, I say, "Thank you."

Prefaces frequently acknowledge the contribution of the author's wife. That is not sufficient here. She has listened, talked through issues, asked provocative questions, made suggestions, and helped me to keep going. I am a gifted creative speller with my own grammatical innovations; Florence has labored long to conform the manuscript to the more traditional kind. She has worked with my grammar and writing style to make the rough places plain and the crooked straight. Without Florence, this project would never have been completed.

The lot of the writer is a lonely one. I have had the frequent company of Syd, a diminutive, brainless, but lovable K-9. He has dozed near me day after day. They also serve who lie and sleep!

In putting this volume together, I kept in view that few laypersons, students, and ministers have a proficient command of the linguistic and literary studies that are of help in reading and studying the Bible. On the other hand, I am convinced that some understanding of the historical, social, cultural, and religious backgrounds of the Bible is within the grasp of many such people. Off and on for more than thirty years I have been an academic resident in Intertestamental Judaism. I hope that acquaintance with that distant time, place, and culture, made available through this book, will do for others what it has done for me, namely, provide a better understanding of the New Testament.

I am grateful for the opportunity to have undertaken this study. Ultimately this opportunity was made possible by him who chose Intertestamental Judaism as the stage and environment to break into history in a unique way, as the Word become flesh! My ultimate desire is that in some way this labor will bring glory to God.

Wheaton, Illinois
November 1994

*   *   *   *   *

I am pleased that there has been sufficient demand for a second printing of this book. It is especially gratifying to know that a number of fellow teachers on this continent have found it useful in the classroom. I have also received word of its usefulness in Africa and Japan, where a translation is underway.

Though I would like to offer a thorough revision, there is no opportunity to do so at this time. Since the original title, *Customs and*

Controversies, was not immediately recognizable as a work on Jewish backgrounds of the New Testament, we have retitled the book accordingly. We have also taken the opportunity to make a few corrections in spelling and the like.

I am especially concerned that readers be aware that the present section on the Dead Sea Scrolls was completed in late 1993, just after the release of the final group of those documents. To advance their knowledge, readers should consult books on the Scrolls published after 1996, but they should do so cautiously. A number of sensational claims have been made about this material that have not been substantiated by the scholarly community as a whole. While I cannot endorse all of the author's conclusions, I commend Hartmut Stegemann, *The Library of Qumran* (Grand Rapids: W. B. Eerdmans; Leiden: E. J. Brill, 1998), as an adequate report of recent developments and a plausible analysis of them.

Wheaton, Illinois
February 2000

Abbreviations

Scripture Versions

KJV	King James Version
NASB	New American Standard Bible
NIV	New International Version
NRSV	New Revised Standard Version
RSV	Revised Standard Version

Dead Sea Scrolls

CD	Covenant of the Damascus Community (Zadokite Document)
1QH	Psalm Scroll
1QM	War Scroll
1QpHab	Commentary (*Pesher*) on Habakkuk
1QS	Manual of Discipline
1QSa	Rule of the Congregation
4Q169	Commentary (*Pesher*) on Nahum
4Q ʿAmram	Vision of Amram
4QFlor	Florilegium
4QMMT	*Miqsat Ma'ase ha-Torah* ("Some of the Precepts of Torah")
4QPBless	Patriarchal Blessings
4QpNah	Commentary (*Pesher*) on Nahum
4QPsDan	Pseudo-Daniel
4QSirShabb	Angelic Liturgy
4QTest	Testimonia
11QMelch	Melchizedek Scroll
11QTemp	Temple Scroll

Introduction
and Definitions

- The Contemporary Christian and Intertestamental Judaism
- Intertestamental Judaism: A Distinct Period
- The New Consensus on Intertestamental Judaism
- The Basic Principles Shaping This Study
- A Note on Some Terms

The Contemporary Christian
and Intertestamental Judaism

As the apostle Paul stood before King Agrippa II, he expressed gratitude that he could speak to one "familiar with all the customs and controversies of the Jews" (Acts 26:3). He assumed that to understand his case, and by implication Christianity as a whole, it was necessary to have some awareness of Intertestamental Judaism. That situation has not changed.

In moving from the Old to the New Testament, the reader is plunged into a radically different world. The original language is no longer Hebrew or Aramaic but Greek. Persian political dominance has given way to that of Rome. "Jew," a term found throughout some books covering the end of the Old Testament Era (Jeremiah, Ezra, Nehemiah, Esther) but only rarely elsewhere in the Old Testament, is a common name for the descendants of Abraham, Isaac, and Jacob. The word *king* no longer designates an absolute monarch, and new administrative titles such as ethnarch, tetrarch, and governor (or procurator) appear for the first time or take on a new significance. The Jewish priesthood is more prominent and its role broadened to include administration of civil as well as ceremonial affairs. One senses an increased degree of hostility in the attitude of the people of Israel toward their foreign rulers. Centurions and publicans appear.

New Testament writers assume the readers will know the locations and significance of such geographical areas as Galilee, Samaria, Perea (literally, the region "beyond" the Jordan), Idumea, Judea, Decapolis, and more. For the first time we meet the Jewish council or Sanhedrin, and find worship being carried on in the synagogue as well as the temple. Groups such as Pharisees, Sadducees, Herodians, rabbis, and Zealots have recently come on the scene; scribes have taken on new importance and altered roles. A different cultural influence is present, one toward which Jewish feelings are ambivalent.

In the religious life of the times, Old Testament law continues to occupy a central place but is interpreted and observed with new emphases. Written Scripture seems to share authority with customs or tradition ("tradition of the elders" or "human tradition" as it is called in Mark 7:5, 8). Concern for Jewish separateness from other peoples is heightened as is the determination to protect the Hebrews' unique place before God. Some of Jesus' contemporaries are preoccupied with questions related to life after death, the resurrection, immortality—subjects only barely touched upon in the Old Testament. Other terms and ideas only seldom mentioned in the Old Testament—kingdom of God, Messiah, Son of man—have become prominent; the spheres of thought with which they are associated are now of extreme importance to many of the general populace. There is apparently an air of frustration, restiveness, longing, hope, and expectation among many Jews living during New Testament times in what we now call Palestine or the land of Israel (*Eretz Israel*).

Clearly, significant changes have taken place. The Old Testament is *not* the immediate historical, cultural, or religious setting for the life and ministry of Jesus, the apostles, and their associates. While the New Testament writers assume knowledge of the Old Testament, the middle phase of Jewish history is their immediate background and setting. The influences of Greece and Rome are, of course, considerable. But, at least in the beginning, even these were mediated through the Jewish setting.

Students of this historical period have become increasingly aware of its distinctiveness, not only from the Old Testament but also from the form of Judaism which followed it. What caused the differences? The answer is simple, its implications are complex. In 586 B.C. the Babylonians destroyed Jerusalem and its temple, thus bringing to a close the period of Hebrew history within the Old Testament. In A.D. 70 Jerusalem and the temple were again destroyed, this time by the Romans, and again Jewish life and culture underwent change. Between these two devastating events the Jews faced other significant crises, but none more significant than the incursion of Hellenistic (Greek) culture following the conquests of Alexander the Great in the fourth century B.C.

This book is written from the conviction that the Bible must be interpreted within its original grammatical and historical context. "Grammatical" has traditionally been understood to refer to linguistic features; I would like to expand this category to include literary forms and features. Similarly, "historical" must include more than the recounting of the chronological sequence. Geography, cultural and sociological phenomena, differing ways of looking at life and the world, and the particular circumstances of the author and readers of a biblical document are also part of the historical context.

The world conditions that prevailed when the events recorded in Scripture took place and the inspired writers did their work are the setting for what Christians believe to be unique divine revelation. The writers assumed that the original reader was familiar with this setting or that a few words would bring sufficient clarity (see, e.g., Mark 7:3–4). We serious modern readers must not take the first-century background lightly. We need to undertake a journey into a land in which we are strangers, the land of those to whom the gospel first came. Then we may return to our time and place, better understanding and better prepared to live and proclaim.

Although this volume deals with certain aspects of Jewish history and thought, it is a Christian book. The focus is not to present Judaism, even Intertestamental or Second Temple Judaism, per se. Rather, this volume selects and interprets those parts of a total body of information which the writer believes will be of special help to his fellow Christians in understanding the New Testament. I have sought to deal honestly and fairly with the relevant Jewish data. It is my hope to correct some misimpressions about Judaism of the period in view and Judaism in general.

In describing Intertestamental Judaism from a Christian perspective, I want to make it clear that in no way do I see the differences between Judaism and Christianity providing even the slightest support for anti-Semitism, the darkest blot on the face of the church. Anti-Semitism is a fact of Christian history, but one of which I am ashamed. I believe all vestiges of it must be purged from our midst. Even anti-Semitic feelings are, in the Christian sense, a sin—a sin from which we must repent with that true repentance which produces radical change in our minds, emotions, and actions. We must seek forgiveness from both God and the Jewish people.

Intertestamental Judaism: A Distinct Period

It is difficult to know what to call the period that is the subject of this book. Jewish writers seem to prefer "Second Temple" or "Second Commonwealth Judaism." At times such names as "Early Judaism," "Middle Judaism," "Greco-Roman Judaism," and "Judaism of the Late Hellenistic Period" are employed. We shall call it "Intertestamental Judaism" because this is more likely to have a familiar ring to most readers of this book. We use the term with apologies to our Jewish friends who may find it difficult because they cannot recognize the legitimacy of a new or second testament.

All too often the unique character of Intertestamental Judaism goes unrecognized. Students frequently have proceeded on the assumption that the background of the New Testament can be determined by supplementing the Old Testament with information from rabbinic writings (e.g., the Talmud, midrashim, etc.) which, in their present form, actually came into being after the New Testament Era. The result has been to risk anachronistically reading into the New Testament setting conditions, practices, and ideas which arose or were modified after A.D. 70.

Our assertion that Intertestamental Judaism is distinct is the result of both fresh material discoveries and renewed study of all that is known from that period. The catalyst for contemporary investigations was undoubtedly the discovery of the Dead Sea Scrolls in 1947. These documents provided not only new evidence but also new perspectives from which to interpret previously available information. With the additional evidence came new and improved techniques and methods for understanding and interpretation. In the next phases of scholarly work the newly discovered information was made readily available. The results of these studies are now being utilized in revised portrayals of the era in part or in whole.

As these new pieces are added to the puzzle and as better techniques sharpen the focus, the picture of Intertestamental Judaism becomes progressively clearer. Current knowledge of the period certainly exceeds that which has been available since shortly after Intertestamental Judaism faded into the pages of history. There are now accessible to the specialist and nonspecialist alike information and perspectives essential to better understand the background of numerous New Testament features and tensions, customs and controversies.

The New Consensus on Intertestamental Judaism

More than thirty years have passed since the writing of the first draft of this study. I then sought to demonstrate and utilize a number of assumptions about Intertestamental Judaism. These assumptions were recognized by only a few individuals involved in the more technical aspect of the study of the New Testament and related literature. Since then, investigation into the nature of the post–Old Testament Jewish world has moved rapidly. Most of the assumptions with which I originally worked are now firmly fixed as part of a growing scholarly consensus. These include at least eight broad, but very important points.

First, Intertestamental Judaism is a descendant of the Old Testament Hebrew faith and culture, but is not identical with it. At the same time it must be distinguished from Rabbinic Judaism, which developed after the destruction of Jerusalem, the temple, and the Jewish state by the Romans in A.D. 70.

Second, the society, culture, and faith of Intertestamental Judaism were not a monolithic whole but a conglomerate. They contained diverse elements which both individually and together must be taken into account in attempting to understand the period.

Third, the traditional ways of distinguishing between Jewish (or Hebraic) and Hellenistic elements in intertestamental Jewish life are too simplistic. These elements (as they appear, e.g., in Acts 6:1) refer to more than linguistic preferences. It is also incorrect to equate Hebraic culture exclusively with Palestine, and Hellenism with the form of Intertestamental Judaism found among Jews in the Dispersion.

Fourth, the four-sect division of Judaism (Pharisees, Sadducees, Essenes, and the fourth philosophy) of the first-century historian Josephus is an inadequate description of the diversities of the time. There were divisions within each of these sects; there were also other groups. Furthermore, we must recognize that the majority of Jesus' contemporaries, the average Jews, belonged to none of these sects or parties. _revelation or prophecy_

Fifth, the apocalyptic movement and eschatology of the time are important for understanding the outlook of significant numbers of people within Intertestamental Judaism. While eschatology and the apocalyptic are closely related, they are not identical; nor can it be assumed that all eschatology is apocalyptic, nor that apocalyptic is always primarily eschatological.

Sixth, there was no separation of church and state in Intertestamental Judaism. Nationalistic and religious thinking, actions, and aspirations were usually inseparable.

Seventh, Intertestamental Judaism was a dynamic civilization which faced and responded to genuine tensions arising from political, cultural, sociological, existential, and religious situations and issues. It was shaped by both commitment to its nationalistic-religious heritage, as then understood, and the need to face realistically the changing circumstances of the world.

Finally, the diverse cultures, groups, concerns, ways of life, and aspirations of Intertestamental Judaism, its customs and controversies, played a significant part in the formative period of the two major groups which emerged from it—early Rabbinic Judaism and primitive Christianity. Thus, an understanding of the major tensions and trajectories within Intertestamental Judaism is essential for understanding properly the literature and nature of both groups.

The Basic Principles Shaping This Study

This book seeks to provide the reader with an intermediate understanding of those features of Intertestamental Judaism which will be of most value in interpreting the New Testament. Most of the elementary books for the New Testament student, such as textbooks for courses in biblical survey, provide overviews of basic features of intertestamental history, government and religion, groups and sects, and a little about the messianic expectation. There are, of course, many single-volume works dealing with the events of intertestamental Jewish history.[1] It is our purpose to go beyond them. We will seek to take into account information which might not be so readily available but may help the reader get a feel for the time. In this way we hope to make available to college or seminary students, busy pastors, and inquiring laypersons some of the results of the recent discoveries and scholarly conclusions

---

1. There are numerous single-volume studies of Intertestamental Judaism. The list is too long to mention all of those I have consulted, always with profit. The following titles represent some which I have found particularly helpful: Edwyn R. Bevan, *Jerusalem under the High-Priests* (London: Edward Arnold, 1918); Charles Guignebert, *The Jewish World in the Time of Jesus,* trans. S. H. Hooke (London: Kegan Paul, Trench, Trubner, 1939); D. S. Russell, *Between the Testaments* (London: SCM, 1960) and *From Early Judaism to Early Church* (Philadelphia: Fortress, 1986); Elias Bickerman, *From Ezra to the Last of the Maccabees: Foundations of Post-Biblical Judaism* (New York: Schocken, 1962); F. F. Bruce, *Israel and the Nations* (Grand Rapids: Eerdmans, 1963) and *New Testament History* (Garden City, N.Y.: Doubleday, 1972); Werner Foerster, *From the Exile to Christ* (Philadelphia: Fortress, 1964); Bo Reicke, *The New Testament Era: The World of the Bible from 500 B.C. to A.D. 100,* trans. David E. Green (Philadelphia: Fortress, 1968); Eduard Lohse, *The New Testament Environment,* trans. John E. Steely (Nashville: Abingdon, 1976); H. L. Ellison, *From Babylon to Bethlehem: The People of God between the Testaments* (Grand Rapids: Baker, 1984); Martin McNamara, *Palestinian Judaism and the New Testament* (Wilmington, Del.: Michael Glazier, 1983); H. Jagersma, *A History of Israel from Alexander the Great to Bar Kochba,* trans. John Bowden (Philadelphia: Fortress, 1986); Jacob Neusner, *From Testament to Torah: An Introduction to Judaism in Its Formative Age* (Englewood Cliffs, N.J.: Prentice Hall, 1988); Frederick J. Murphy, *The Religious World of Jesus* (Nashville: Abingdon, 1991); and Gabriele Boccaccini, *Middle Judaism: Jewish Thought, 300 B.C.E. to 200 C.E.* (Minneapolis: Fortress, 1991).

about which we have been speaking, particularly those which are most helpful in understanding the New Testament.

I have a definite interpretive stance; namely, that the differing customs and controversies which make Intertestamental Judaism unique in Jewish history were the result of certain historical, social, and psychological dynamics of the time. More specifically, I suggest that a highly significant reason for the rise of distinctive customs and controversies was the variety of reactions to two major crises, the destruction of the Jewish state and temple by the Babylonians in the sixth century B.C. and the arrival of Hellenistic culture in the fourth century B.C.[2] Individuals and groups reacted differently to these crises. From these reactions developed most of the features which made Intertestamental Judaism a clearly distinguishable phenomenon within the history of the race and nation.

This book falls into three sections. The first, "The Background and Setting of Intertestamental Judaism," identifies the major sources of information, outlines the geography, and sketches the historical framework of both the Old Testament and intertestamental periods. The second section, "The Crises and Responses of Intertestamental Judaism," focuses upon the crises of the sixth and fourth centuries and attempts to portray the results of the more important reactions to them. Chapter 12, "Common Life in First-Century Israel," is really an intrusion into the nature and outline of the book. I have included it because it may be of both interest and help to those attempting to better understand the world of Intertestamental Judaism.

Finally, the section "The Religious Thought of Intertestamental Judaism: A Background for Christian Customs and Controversies" reflects my conviction that intertestamental views about the nature and results of the final age are of special importance for the New Testament reader. The earliest Jewish Christians believed the final age already to be a present reality. This, along with their convictions about the person and role of Jesus of Nazareth in relation to the final age, made them distinct from other intertestamental Jewish groups. Along with the Old Testament it provided the setting within which they interpreted and worked out the implications of commitment to Jesus. The issues and diversity which were a part of contemporary Jewish views about the final age and related mat-

---

2. Well after coming to the conclusion that Intertestamental Judaism developed in reaction to two crises, I was gratified to find that Jacob Neusner uses the concept of crises as the organizing foci for his study *From Testament to Torah*. He too sees the destructions of the Jewish state in 586 B.C. and A.D. 70 as formative crises and adds the conversion of Constantine in A.D. 312 as a third.

ters are reflected in the life, faith, and struggles of the original disciples and followers of "the Way" (Acts 9:2; 19:9, 23; 22:4; 24:14).

We will not go into depth with any feature covered in this study. The reader desiring to continue the study should explore the primary sources listed in chapter 1. Fortunately all of the major ones are now available in convenient English translations.[3] The major recent volumes mentioned in the preface are also essential for work in this field. Lester Grabbe's study is a valuable guide to the historical and critical debates related to this period—an important area upon which I have barely touched. Individual studies of various topics and issues abound.

During the course of our study I will make reference to some specific New Testament passages and issues. This will usually be done for illustration or clarification. Providing specific background for particular passages or issues is beyond our purpose. Our primary task is to paint the general scene with broad strokes. This, I trust, will be of maximum assistance to those desiring to better understand the New Testament and to apply more accurately in the modern world the implications of the revelation of God's person and will which was originally given in that other time, place, and culture.

A Note on Some Terms

The use of four terms needs to be explained. The first has to do with the personal name for God.[4] With most modern translators of the Old Testament I will render the sacred personal name of God as "the Lord," and I will use "Lord" as the translation for *Adonai*, a more generic reverential term. In a few cases, where the context seems to demand it, I use "Yahweh," the most probable pronunciation of God's personal name.

The second word is *Torah*, the Hebrew word used for the five books of Moses or those sections of them which prescribe behavior, worship, and the like. The Greek versions of the Old Testament translate *Torah* as *nomos* (law), and this is followed by New Testament writers. *Torah* is not exactly "law," however; "instructions" might be better. It involves precise requirements but also contains promises and blessings. It is the instructions for those in special,

3. The data for these translations can be found in the bibliography (p. 375). I have used the multivolume Loeb Classical Library editions of Josephus and Philo, which contain both Greek texts and English translations. Readers should also be aware of the less expensive, single-volume updated translations of these writers published by Hendrickson.

4. For an explanation of the issue involved here, see p. 268.

favorable relationship with the LORD. I will usually use "law," but may use "instructions" or *Torah*, depending on the context.

Third, "eschatology" is a term we cannot avoid using. Its root is the Greek *eschaton*, which means "last" or "end." Discussions of eschatology traditionally deal with such topics as the end of all things and the fate of the individual. Hence, discussions of Christian eschatology are concerned with physical death, the events preceding the second coming of Christ, including the last struggle(s) with evil forces, and then the second coming of Christ itself. They also may consider the millennial issue, intermediate state and immortality, resurrection(s), and judgment(s). Such studies will also deal with the end of nature (the cosmic order) and of humanity, rewards and punishments (heaven and hell), the new heaven and earth, and the final state of the universe. These are but some of the topics that might be considered in traditional eschatology.

Much contemporary theology focuses attention upon other issues under the heading of eschatology.[5] It may, for an example, discuss the final stage of moral, social, intellectual, physical, and spiritual developments. The result, it is assumed, is utopia on earth, brought about by (largely) naturalistic processes. Even more widespread, since "end" often means "goal" or "purpose," is the view that the subject matter of eschatology is the attainment of meaning, purpose, self-awareness, and the authenticity of the individual.[6]

Finally, what do we call the land promised by God to Abraham and his descendants? Frequently in the Old Testament, and in Acts 13:19, it is called "the land of Canaan," after its original inhabitants (Gen. 10:15–19). "Palestine" means "land of the Philistines," and is used neither by biblical writers nor by modern Jews to refer to the Promised Land. I follow the convention of employing the translation of *Eretz Israel*, "the land of Israel" (with apologies to modern Palestinian Arabs who share at least parts of it with modern Israelis).

5. Most nonevangelical theology proceeds on assumptions which de-emphasize or deny the supernatural and the claims of the end of the material world.

6. Note the way Rudolf Bultmann uses the term within his existential interpretation of the New Testament in "The New Testament and Mythology," in Rudolf Bultmann, *The New Testament and Mythology and Other Basic Writings*, trans. Schubert M. Ogden (Philadelphia: Fortress, 1984), 1–43.

Part 1

The Background
and Setting
of Intertestamental Judaism

1

Sources of Information

- A Catalog of General Sources
- Jewish Writers of the First Century A.D.
  - + Flavius Josephus
  - + Philo Judaeus

A Catalog of General Sources

An essential element in any historical study is the identity and character of the primary sources of information.[1] The contribution of archaeology to the study of Intertestamental Judaism has often been minimized or overlooked. The purpose of archaeology is to reconstruct life as it was. Few recognize that Palestinian archaeology as a science is virtually a twentieth-century development. The light it has shed on individual locations contributes immensely to our understanding of the period as a whole.[2]

The major written sources for Intertestamental Judaism are unevenly spread over the period. Outside the Old Testament our knowledge of the first two hundred years is slight; the vast majority of our sources come from 200 B.C. onwards. They fall into a number of categories:

1. For a detailed discussion of sources see Emil Schürer, *The History of the Jewish People in the Age of Jesus Christ*, ed. Geza Vermes et al., 3 vols. (Edinburgh: T. and T. Clark, 1973–87), 1:17–122; 3.1:177–703; 3.2:705–889; *The Jewish People in the First Century*, ed. S. Safrai, M. Stern et al., in *Compendia Rerum Iudaicarum ad Novum Testamentum*, 7 vols. (Philadelphia: Fortress, 1974–92), 1:1–61; and Lester L. Grabbe, *Judaism from Cyrus to Hadrian*, 2 vols. (Minneapolis: Augsburg Fortress, 1991–92), 1:1–73 and *passim*.

2. See John McRay, *Archaeology and the New Testament* (Grand Rapids: Baker, 1991).

1. The Hebrew Old Testament was the starting point for Intertestamental Judaism. The Pentateuch held a special place as unquestioned authority. By the end of the period all thirty-nine books of the Hebrew canon were regarded as the Holy Word of God.

2. The Greek translation of the Old Testament, the Septuagint (LXX), has some emphases and content that differ from the Hebrew text. Where these differences appear, the Septuagint is essentially a separate source.

3. The Apocrypha of the Old Testament, books found in the Septuagint but not in the Hebrew Old Testament, constitutes a separate collection. (For a list of the titles usually recognized as belonging to the Apocrypha see Appendix A, p. 357.)[3]

4. The so-called Pseudepigrapha of the Old Testament is a rather open-ended category of Jewish works coming from roughly 200 B.C. to A.D. 200.[4] They represent diverse viewpoints. Some have their origin in the strictly Hebraic world; others come from Hellenistic (or Greek-oriented) Judaism. Collections of pseudepigraphal writings may contain a wide variety of literary types and titles. Some of the major literary classifications include history, expansions of the Hebrew Scriptures, stories and legends, prayers, odes and psalms, testaments, wisdom literature, and apocalyptic literature. Some of these categories overlap; there is disagreement as to where some writings should be assigned.

The preservation and transmission of pseudepigraphal books have sometimes been less careful than we might wish. Parts of some documents are lost. The way in which the sections of some books have been arranged is puzzling. Although representatives of intertestamental Jewish thought, virtually all of these documents were preserved not by Jews, but by early Christians. Save for a few fragments, they are available only in ancient translations from which all modern translations have been made.

Our knowledge of the pseudepigraphal writings has been greatly expanded by recent discoveries. R. H. Charles's 1913 translation of the Pseudepigrapha contained seventeen titles.[5] The 1983–85 translation edited by James H. Charlesworth gives sixty-three doc-

3. For a description of the apocryphal books see Bruce M. Metzger, *An Introduction to the Apocrypha* (New York: Oxford University Press, 1957). George W. E. Nickelsburg, *Jewish Literature between the Bible and the Mishnah* (Philadelphia: Fortress, 1981), and Leonhard Rost, *Judaism outside the Hebrew Canon: An Introduction to the Documents*, trans. David E. Green (Nashville: Abingdon, 1976), discuss both the apocryphal books and some pseudepigraphal writings.

4. For an introduction see James H. Charlesworth, *The Pseudepigrapha and Modern Research* (Missoula, Mont.: Scholars, 1976).

5. *The Apocrypha and Pseudepigrapha of the Old Testament*, ed. R. H. Charles, 2 vols. (Oxford: Clarendon, 1913), vol. 2.

uments (not including two titles in the older edition [Pirke Aboth and Fragments from a Zadokite Work] which are now assigned to other categories).[6] We list here the categories and titles of the pseudepigraphal books most frequently cited in this study (for a complete list see Appendix B, pp. 358–59):

a. History and legends: Jubilees, the Letter of Aristeas, Life of Adam and Eve, Martyrdom and Ascension of Isaiah, Pseudo-Philo, and Joseph and Aseneth.
b. Apocalypses: 1 Enoch, Sibylline Oracles, 2 (Syriac) Baruch, and 4 Ezra.[7]
c. Testaments: the Testaments of the Twelve Patriarchs; the Testament (Assumption) of Moses.
d. Psalms and prayers: Psalms of Solomon; Odes of Solomon.

5. Of the writings of the Jewish sectarians of Intertestamental Judaism the famous Dead Sea Scrolls are the most significant. However, it should be remembered that similar or identical documents were found in the Cairo genizah (a synagogue storage room) and at Masada, the ancient desert fortress in the land of Israel. We list here by category some of the most important manuscripts:[8]

a. Old Testament texts: Isaiah (1QIsa); Exodus in paleo-Hebrew script (4QEx.α); Exodus in Jewish script (4QEx.a); Leviticus; Deuteronomy 32 (4QDeut.32); 1 and 2 Samuel (4QSam.a); 1 and 2 Samuel—a second manuscript (4QSam.b).
b. Apocrypha and Pseudepigrapha: the Testament of Levi (from the Testament of the Twelve Patriarchs) (4QT.Levi); fragments of Enoch.
c. Sectarian or community rules: the Manual of Discipline (1QS); the Rule of the Congregation (or Messianic Rule)

6. *The Old Testament Pseudepigrapha,* ed. James H. Charlesworth, 2 vols. (Garden City, N.Y.: Doubleday, 1983, 1985). Note also *The Apocryphal Old Testament,* ed. H. F. D. Sparks (New York: Oxford University Press, 1984); the title is deceiving, since this volume is actually a separate translation of the more important pseudepigraphal writings.

7. Also called 2 Esdras, 4 Ezra is included in many collections of the Apocrypha.

8. The individual documents of the Dead Sea Scrolls are frequently identified by standard abbreviations. Those documents assumed to be associated with Qumran were discovered in eleven different caves, some manuscripts were discovered elsewhere, the origin of others is unknown. The number in the abbreviation identifies the particular cave. The following letter indicates the place of discovery, Q if from a Qumran cave, some other symbol for another location, or no symbol if the origin is unknown. Then come an abbreviation of the name of the document and, if there is more than one copy, a lowercase letter to so indicate. The standard abbreviation 1QSa, for example, has in view a document from the first (1) Qumran (Q) cave, namely, the second copy (a) of the sect's Manual of Discipline (S).

(1QSa); the Covenant of the Damascus Community (or the Zadokite Document) (CD or CDC); a papyrus exemplar of the Rule of Discipline (pap4QSa); *Miqsat Ma'ase ha-Torah* ("Some of the Precepts of Torah") (4QMMT).

d. Worship materials: the Psalm Scroll (1QH).

e. Eschatological speculations: the War of the Sons of Light against the Sons of Darkness (1QM); Florilegium (or Midrash on the Last Days or Eschatological Midrashim) (4QFlor[ilegium] or 4QEschMidr).

f. Testimonia (4QTest).

g. Biblical interpretations: Genesis Apocryphon (1QApoc or 1QapGen); Prayer of Nabonidus (4QPrNab); Commentary (*Pesher*) on Hosea (4QpHos); Commentary (*Pesher*) on Micah (1QpMic); Commentary (*Pesher*) on Nahum (4QpNah or 4Q169); Commentary (*Pesher*) on Habakkuk (1QpHab); Patriarchal Blessings or Messianic Anthology (4QPBless); Words or Sayings of Moses (1QDM); Biblical Laws or Essene Halakah (4QOrd).

h. Miscellaneous: Copper Scroll (3Q15); Temple Scroll (11QTemp); Melchizedek Scroll (11QMelch); the Angelic Liturgy (4QSirShabb).

6. Many students forget to include the New Testament in a list of sources for Intertestamental Judaism, even though it is among the most significant. On the other hand, it is heartening to note the seriousness with which some contemporary writers, including Jewish ones, take the New Testament as an important source from which to learn about the intertestamental period.[9]

7. The lives as well as the writings of two first-century writers—Philo (c. 20 B.C.–A.D. 50), the Jewish philosopher from Alexandria, and Flavius Josephus (c. 37–100), the soldier-traitor-scholar-historian from Palestine—are of special significance.

8. During the 1950s and early 1960s explorations were carried on in the Judean desert caves on the Nahal Hever near the southwestern shore of the Dead Sea. They yielded documents and other information from the period of the Jewish revolt of the second century of the Common Era (132–35). These documents included letters written by the leader Bar Kosiba himself and provide insights into the afterglow period of Intertestamental Judaism. Other caves in the deserts south and east of Bethlehem have provided additional information about this period.

9. E.g., the editors of *Compendia Rerum Iudaicarum ad Novum Testamentum* (*CRINT*).

9. The writings of the rabbinic Jewish period (from A.D. 90 onward) constitute a massive corpus that is difficult for nonexperts to use and evaluate.[10] Most of the religious and related traditions of Intertestamental Judaism were circulated orally. Only after the A.D. 70 destruction of Herod's temple was a concerted effort made by the rabbis to collect and reduce this material to writing. The process involved much more than preservation of tradition. Material was collected selectively, abridged, expanded, adapted, and partly created to meet the needs of post–70 situations. The result was collections such as the Mishnah (codified by the Tannaim, A.D. 90–200), Gemara (codified by the Amoraim, A.D. 200–500 [the Mishnah and Gemara together make up the Talmud]), the Tosephta, targums, and midrashim.

The rabbinic writings may, at places, reflect the intertestamental Jewish period. However, this first-century information stands side by side and is often intertwined with records that reflect situations and practices that arose after that era. Accordingly, those using rabbinic writings as a source for the intertestamental period must do so with caution and critical skill. (For a list of the titles in the Mishnah, which are also the titles in the Talmud and Tosephta, see Appendix C, pp. 360–63.)

10. Christian collections, including the New Testament Apocrypha, ante-Nicene fathers, heretical writers (e.g., the Gnostic books found at Nag Hammadi, Egypt, in 1945), and a few later writers like Eusebius, Jerome, and Epiphanius, provide limited information about Jews and Judaism.

11. The Greco-Roman writers make references to Jews and their customs. Pliny the Elder, Tacitus, Juvenal, and Dio Cassius are among the more important for our purposes. Various texts about Jews by non-Jewish, classical authors have been collected by Menahem Stern.[11]

12. Numerous papyri coming from the beginning to the end of the intertestamental period have been discovered. Most are fragmentary but still often informative. Three important papyrus collections, not particularly well known, deserve special note and explanation:

a. Elephantine Papyri: Sometime during the sixth century B.C., a Persian military colony consisting of Hebrews was estab-

10. For an introduction to this material see H. L. Strack and G. Stemberger, *Introduction to the Talmud and Midrash*, trans. Markus Bockmuehl (Edinburgh: T. and T. Clark, 1991).

11. *Greek and Latin Authors on Jews and Judaism*, ed. Menahem Stern, 3 vols. (Jerusalem: Israel Academy of Sciences and Humanities, 1989); see also Menahem Stern, "The Greek and Latin Literary Sources," in *Jewish People*, ed. Safrai et al. (*CRINT*), 1:18–35.

lished on the island of Elephantine in southern Egypt. Archaeological and written (Aramaic) records have revealed the cultural, business, social, and religious life of this Diaspora community during a period from which very little else is known. Of particular interest is the fact that the documents mention the name *Sanballat,* which may or may not refer to Nehemiah's adversary. Another interesting feature is that the Elephantine community had their own temple and appealed to Jerusalem when faced with a crisis.[12]

b. Wadi Daliyeh or Samaritan Papyri: Skeletons, jewelry, household goods, coins as well as fragmentary Aramaic documents were discovered in 1962–64 in a cave near the Wadi Daliyeh about nine miles north of Jericho. They are probably the remains of some upper-class Samaritans who fled from but were massacred by Alexander the Great about 332 B.C. In addition to general information about the times, the documents are helpful in reconstructing the situation in Samaria, including the list of governors of the area. Although the books of Ezra and Nehemiah were probably written earlier, information from this cave is important for understanding the background and situation assumed in them.

c. The Zeno Papyri: Much of the correspondence of Zeno, an administrator under Apollonius, a treasury official of Ptolemy II Philadelphus (285–246 B.C.) of Egypt, was discovered in 1915. About a fourth of the documents relate to Palestine and surrounding areas and include information reflecting life and conditions while Zeno was on a personal journey through those areas from 260 to 258 B.C.

13. Numerous inscriptions from tombs, public buildings, and other monuments cast light on the culture and history of the intertestamental period.

14. Some scholars might wish to create separate categories for documents reflecting Gnostic, magical, and mystical intertestamental Jewish literature.

The interpretation of the literary works coming from or pertaining to Intertestamental Judaism is fraught with difficulties. At times we cannot be completely sure of the meaning of some of the

12. See A. E. Cowley, *Aramaic Papyri of the Fifth Century B.C.* (New York: Oxford University Press, 1929); Bezalel Porten, *Archives from Elephantine: The Life of an Ancient Jewish Military Colony* (Berkeley: University of California Press, 1968); *Corpus Papyrorum Judaicarum,* ed. Victor Tcherikover and Alexander Fuks, 3 vols. (Cambridge, Mass.: Harvard University Press, 1957–64).

concepts and words they use. There are times when we cannot identify the persons, events, or institutions of which they speak.

Another problem is that the ancients' handling of documents was very different from modern methods. Their standards of accuracy were very unlike ours. Also, the ways documents assumed their present forms were varied and sometimes confusing. Three ancient literary practices identified by modern scholars are evident in some of the written sources of information for Intertestamental Judaism: (1) Bringing together materials written in different places and times has resulted in what may be called evolved documents. (2) Interpolation is the practice of inserting into a document material that clearly comes from a later period or different provenance, and that often is of a different viewpoint. (3) More difficult (and often impossible) to distinguish are a later editor's redactions, that is, additions, subtractions, rewriting, rewording, reorganizing in order to accomplish his purposes. Thus we must often ask not only the intent of the original writer, but also what the present form tells us about later collectors and editors. It is little wonder that these and other critical considerations inevitably lead to differences of opinion about a document and hence to differing interpretations and assessments of it.

Jewish Writers of the First Century A.D.

Two non-Christian Jewish writers from the first century are so significant to our purpose that we need to sketch them briefly. In their own ways they were Hellenistic Jews. Josephus gives information about the life and history of the land of Israel in his day. Philo lived in Alexandria, Egypt. His primary concerns were intellectual pursuits, biblical exposition, philosophy, and the like. For the most part, Philo gives but glimpses of himself and the world about him. Coupled with his description of events in which he was involved at the end of his life, they are major sources of information about the Jewish backgrounds of the New Testament.

Flavius Josephus

Through his father Mattathias, Josephus was of the priestly nobility.[13] He was related to the royal Hasmonean house through his mother. Originally named Joseph, he later called himself Flavius Josephus, Flavius being the name of the family of Roman emperors who were his patrons, and Josephus the romanized form of

13. The following discussion is a condensation and revision of my article "Josephus," in *Dictionary of Jesus and the Gospels*, ed. Joel B. Green, Scot McKnight, and I. Howard Marshall (Downers Grove, Ill.: Inter-Varsity, 1992), 391–94.

his Hebrew name. Between his birth and death (c. 37–100) Josephus was a student, sectarian, statesman, military officer, traitor, historian, and apologist for the Jews.

The life and times of Josephus are closely entwined. Shortly before his birth Pontius Pilate was recalled from Judea to face charges of mismanagement. Gaius Caligula became emperor in A.D. 37, released his friend Herod Agrippa from prison, and made him king of the Jews. In 40–41 all Jewry was thrown into consternation and Judea pushed to the brink of war when Caligula threatened to erect his own statue in the Jerusalem temple.

By age fourteen, Josephus claims, his learning was so highly regarded that rabbis consulted him. A couple of years later he began a study of the three primary national sects, Sadducees, Pharisees, and Essenes. For three years, he says, he lived as an ascetic in the wilderness with Bannus, a hermit. He then became a Pharisee. In 64 Josephus visited Rome and obtained freedom for some priests who had been imprisoned there. In that city Josephus was impressed with the grandeur and power of the empire.

Back in Judea Josephus found his country headed for war with Rome. Realizing the folly, he sought to steer his nation in other directions. But when only twenty-nine years of age Josephus was placed in charge of preparing Galilee for the anticipated Roman invasion.

In the autumn of 67 the Romans arrived in Galilee. Josephus's efforts to stop their advance were futile. He and his forces made their last stand against the Romans at Jotapata. Because his soldiers preferred death with honor to surrender and servitude, Josephus proposed a plan of mass suicide. After all the others had killed themselves, however, Josephus and a companion surrendered to the Romans. When brought before Vespasian, Josephus predicted the general would one day become emperor. Josephus continued to be held as a captive.

Roman military operations in Palestine were halted during 68–69 to await the outcome of the struggle for the throne following Nero's death. Eventually, Vespasian's army proclaimed him emperor. He liberated Josephus, who accompanied his benefactor as far as Alexandria and then returned to assist Vespasian's son Titus in the final siege of Jerusalem. Josephus acted as an interpreter and mediator between the combatant forces, was wounded, and witnessed the overthrow of the nation and city in 70.

After the war Josephus was taken to Rome by Titus, who himself eventually succeeded to the imperial throne. Under Vespasian and Titus, Josephus lived as a ward of the court. Granted a stipend and a villa, he spent much of his time in writing. His fortunes may not have fared quite so well after the death of Titus (81). With regard to the length of his life, we know that Josephus outlived Herod Agrippa II, who died in 100.

The writings of Josephus were preserved by Christians who recognized their contribution toward establishing the historical origins of their faith. These writings provide the major (virtually the only) contemporary Jewish account of the history and conditions of the periods leading up to and including the New Testament Era. From his pen come also the oldest non-Christian references to Christianity in the form of brief comments about John the Baptist, Jesus, and the death of James the brother of Jesus.

Although Josephus mentions other works that he had written or planned, only four of his writings survive.[14] His first writing, *The History of the Jewish War,* is most important. It focuses on the struggle against the Romans (66–70) in which he played a part (on both sides!). The first two books provide an introduction which traces those events and attitudes which Josephus considers led to the Jewish revolt. Throughout the work the writer describes the geography of Palestine (including Jerusalem and its temple) and Jewish history, life, customs, and thought. These descriptions provided necessary background for Roman readers not acquainted with the region and people. Josephus's objective was to praise his Roman patrons and to quiet anti-Jewish feelings by shifting blame for the war from the Jewish people as a whole to a minority of unwise leaders and radical parties or sects, especially the Zealots.

The Antiquities of the Jews appeared in twenty books in 93–94. The almost twenty-year interval between *Jewish War* and *Antiquities* was probably spent in research and writing. This period encompassed the reign of Domitian, whose dislike of literature, especially history, silenced such writers as Tacitus, Pliny the Younger, and Juvenal. The *Antiquities* (or *Archaeology,* as Josephus calls it) traces Jewish history from the creation of the world to his own day. For the biblical portions of history he employs the structure of the Greek translation of the Old Testament, the Septuagint, into which he inserts Jewish stories, legends, and embellishments. For his account of the centuries immediately following Old Testament

14. Josephus, *Works,* trans. H. St. J. Thackeray, Ralph Marcus, Allen Wikgren, and Louis H. Feldman, 9 vols., Loeb Classical Library (Cambridge, Mass.: Harvard University Press, 1926–65); *The Works of Josephus,* trans. William Whiston (Peabody, Mass.: Hendrickson, 1987); the latter is a resetting and slightly updated edition of Whiston's 1736 translation.

There are two major methods of referring to the writings of Josephus. Whiston's original translation divided each book into chapters and paragraphs. For example, the account of the death of James appeared in *Antiquities* XX:9, 1. The Loeb edition divides each book into sections; here the death of James appears in *Antiquities* 20.200. The updated edition of Whiston employs both systems. For the convenience of the reader we will also combine the two: *Antiquities* 20.9.1 (200).

history, he has but scanty information. He briefly mentions, for example, Jewish and Samaritan conflicts, the arrival of Alexander the Great in Jerusalem, the subsequent Egyptian (Ptolemaic) control of Palestine, the translation of the Septuagint, and conflicts over the priesthood. He then begins covering the same material found in the first and second books of *Jewish War* up to the outbreak of the war with Rome, but often with different detail, form, and emphases.

With regard to his own life, at the end of *Jewish War* Josephus tells of charges against himself. His *Life of Josephus* is not so much an autobiography as a defense against continuing criticisms of his conduct and position during the war. *Against Apion*, Josephus's final surviving writing, is a defense of Judaism against its detractors, especially Apion, a contemporary anti-Semite.

The accuracy of Josephus's writings has often been called in question. He is self-serving in his accounts, overly gracious and generous in his presentation of the Romans, and he molds the facts of Jewish history to suit his own ends. He is notorious in his exaggeration of numbers. Parallel sections of different works have unreconcilable variants. Nevertheless, although the point is still debated, recent data, such as provided by the excavations of Masada during the 1960s, appear to add some credibility to Josephus's handling of at least the major features of his accounts.

Josephus's greatest value to a study of the New Testament and early Christianity lies in the background information he provides. Without his writings moderns would be left to try to put together a history of the first century in Palestine from bits and pieces. In spite of his limitations, as Josephus conducts us through that strange time and world which was home to Jesus and the apostles, he enables us better to understand the era in which the Word appeared.

Philo Judaeus

The Jewish community in Alexandria was the largest outside the land of Israel. Philo was a member of a prominent, wealthy family in that city. His brother Alexander held responsible governmental positions. From his own resources Alexander lent money to the Jewish king Agrippa I, and made a gift of gold and silver doorplates to the Jerusalem temple. Alexander's son Tiberius Julius Alexander renounced Judaism and followed a political career. He was procurator (governor) of Judea from 46 to 48, and from 66 to 70 the Roman prefect of Egypt, the highest position there. Tiberius Julius Alexander was Titus's chief of staff during the siege and overthrow of Jerusalem in 70.

Little is known of Philo's life. He was obviously very well educated in Greek learning; he was proficient in Greek philosophy, especially that of Plato and the Stoics. Although he took part in Alexandrian social life, he remained a deeply committed Jew, holding to monotheism, the inspiration of the Scriptures, and other basic tenets of his religion. Philo mentions making a pilgrimage to the Jerusalem temple. His writings show a deep religious interest and life.

Philo tells of having to leave his intellectual pursuits at one point to take part in civic affairs during a time of turbulence. This may have been during the time of anti-Semitic riots in Alexandria, which began about 38, while Flaccus was prefect, events which Philo describes. Though elderly, Philo headed a Jewish delegation to Rome to appeal to the emperor Gaius Caligula to rescind his order to have his statue placed in the Jerusalem temple. The embassy to Caligula failed; it is the last glimpse we have of Philo. It is usually assumed that he died about 50.

Philo's writings are voluminous.[15] They can be classified as philosophical, apologetic, historical, and expository. Such categories can be deceptive since Philo deals with the biblical text in the vast majority of his writings.

Philo employed the allegorical interpretive method that was popular in the world of his day, especially in Alexandria. However, he criticized the extreme use of it that ignored the literal meaning of the text. With allegory he sought to synthesize Jewish and Greek thought. This included demonstration that the essential ideas of Plato were already present in Moses (in the ancient world the antiquity of concepts validated their truth). His studies of Abraham depict the patriarch as an example of a virtuous life "according to nature," that is, without the law. Abraham thus portrays the journey of every soul that seeks God.

Philo's place in the total spectrum of Judaism is debated (he has been called everything from a follower of a Greek mystery religion to an adherent of a form of Pharisaism). It seems accurate to recognize him as a thoroughly Hellenistic Jew who remained true to his faith. For our purposes Philo is valuable as an example of a form, probably the highest form, of Hellenistic Judaism and of an intellectual Diaspora (non-Palestinian) Jew. He was well versed in Jewish thought as a whole and will make important contributions to our study of Intertestamental Judaism.

15. Philo, *Works*, trans. F. H. Colson, G. H. Whitaker, and Ralph Marcus, 10 vols. with two suppls., Loeb Classical Library (Cambridge, Mass.: Harvard University Press, 1929–62); *The Works of Philo*, trans. C. D. Yonge (Peabody, Mass.: Hendrickson, 1993); the latter is an update of Yonge's 1854–55 translation.

2

The Geography
of the Land of Israel

- The Physical Features
- Political Divisions in New Testament Times
- The City of Jerusalem
- The Temple Complex

The Physical Features

An appreciation of the physical features of the land of Israel is helpful for understanding its history. We can here give only a brief sketch of some of the more important of these features.[1] To the east of Israel is the Arabian Desert, the Mediterranean (or Great) Sea is its western border. In both the ancient and modern worlds Lebanon (the land of Tyre and Sidon) and Syria lie at the northern border of the land of Israel, desert at the southern. A bit further south and west is Egypt.

Israel's strategic importance is far greater than her size. For those wishing to avoid either sea or desert travel this area offered the only passages between, on the one hand, the lands of the great civilizations of Mesopotamia and of what is now modern Turkey to the north and, on the other, Egypt and Ethiopia to the south. Much of the history of the area, including biblical history, took place

1. For more comprehensive studies of biblical geography see Yohanan Aharoni, *The Land of the Bible: A Historical Geography*, rev. ed. (Philadelphia: Westminster, 1979); and George Adam Smith, *The Historical Geography of the Holy Land* (New York: Harper and Row, 1966 reprint).

along the trade routes which gave passage (not always easy passage) through the country. Control of trade, including the rights to collect tariffs, made Israel a highly sought prize. It is not surprising that Israel has historically been surrounded by enemies.

The modern land of Israel is different from the ancient in a number of ways. Much of the modern area is without substantial vegetation, especially trees, causing one to wonder if this is really "a land flowing with milk and honey" (Exod. 3:8, 17; 13:5; 33:3; Lev. 20:24; Num. 13:27; 14:8; Deut. 6:3; 11:9; 26:9, 15; 27:3; 31:20). The reader should know that after biblical times governing powers sometimes charged a special tax on trees, and so unnecessary ones were cut down, with disastrous ecological results. Similarly, the large number and variety of animals mentioned in the Bible are not now present. Israel is not the only land whose living creatures have paid dearly for the onrush of civilization.

Some things do not change, however. The terrain remains varied. First-time visitors to the land are impressed by how quickly the topography changes, how close together significant biblical sites are, and how strategic water is. Several features of the terrain must be noted before we continue. A glance at a map reveals a small promontory, about three-fourths of the way up the coastline, jutting out into the Mediterranean Sea. This is Mount Carmel, where Elijah had his famous contest with the prophets of Baal (1 Kings 18:20–40). At the northeast foot of Carmel begins a wide plain, running southeastward, that virtually cuts across the country. The hills of Galilee are on its north and those of Ephraim and Judah to the south. This is the Plain of Esdraelon with the Valley of Megiddo (Armageddon) at the west and the Valley of Jezreel at its eastern extremity. Esdraelon is the most fertile part of the land of Israel, a major thoroughfare for travelers, and the scene of numerous decisive battles.

Another major feature is the inland bodies of water. The Jordan River, with its several headwaters in the Mount Hermon region, runs the length of the country. About ten miles south of Dan, which is in the north, the waters of the Jordan are collected into Lake Huleh (or Semechonitis) and then proceed to the Sea (or Lake) of Galilee (or Chinnereth). This roughly teardrop-shaped, freshwater body is up to 13 miles (21 km.) in length and 6.8 miles (11 km.) at its widest point. At the time of Jesus it supported a thriving fishing industry, of which some of his disciples were a part. Towns which Jesus visited along the lake include Bethsaida, Gennesaret, Magdala, and Capernaum, which became his headquarters. The Jordan continues southward and eventually empties into the Dead Sea (Salt Sea). This sea has no outlet; its waters have a high con-

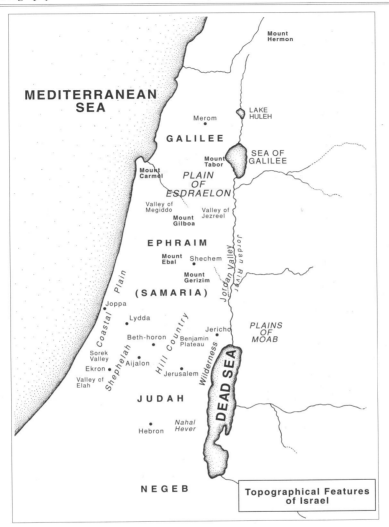

Mount
Hermon

MEDITERRANEAN
SEA

Merom

LAKE
HULEH

GALILEE

Mount
Tabor

SEA OF
GALILEE

Mount
Carmel

PLAIN
OF
ESDRAELON

Valley of
Megiddo

Valley of
Jezreel

Mount
Gilboa

EPHRAIM

Mount
Ebal

Shechem

Jordan River

Mount
Gerizim

Jordan Valley

(SAMARIA)

Coastal Plain

Joppa

Lydda

Jericho

PLAINS
OF
MOAB

Beth-horon

Benjamin
Plateau

Hill Country

Sorek
Valley

Ekron

Aijalon

Shephelah

Jerusalem

Wilderness

DEAD SEA

Valley of
Elah

JUDAH

Hebron

Nahal
Hever

NEGEB

**Topographical Features
of Israel**

centration of minerals, especially salt, and support no life (because
of the sea's buoyancy a person can float without effort).

We are speaking of a small land. From Dan, the traditional
northern border, to Beer-sheba in the south is only about 150 miles
(242 km.). From the Sea of Galilee to the Dead Sea is approximately 65 miles (105 km.). East-west distances vary from about 28
miles (45 km.) from the Sea of Galilee to the Mediterranean to
some 54 miles (87 km.) from the Dead Sea to the Mediterranean.

The differences in elevation are dramatic. The summit of Mount
Hermon, in the north, is about 9,200 feet (2,804 meters); the Sea

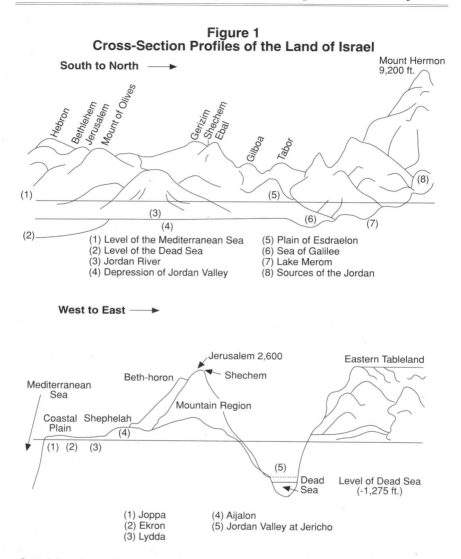

Figure 1
Cross-Section Profiles of the Land of Israel

South to North ⟶

Mount Hermon 9,200 ft.

Hebron
Bethlehem
Jerusalem
Mount of Olives
Gerizim
Shechem
Ebal
Gilboa
Tabor

(1)
(2)
(3)
(4)
(5)
(6)
(7)
(8)

(1) Level of the Mediterranean Sea
(2) Level of the Dead Sea
(3) Jordan River
(4) Depression of Jordan Valley
(5) Plain of Esdraelon
(6) Sea of Galilee
(7) Lake Merom
(8) Sources of the Jordan

West to East ⟶

Jerusalem 2,600
Eastern Tableland
Beth-horon
Shechem
Mediterranean Sea
Mountain Region
Coastal Plain Shephelah
(4)
(1) (2) (3)
(5)
Dead Sea
Level of Dead Sea (-1,275 ft.)

(1) Joppa
(2) Ekron
(3) Lydda
(4) Aijalon
(5) Jordan Valley at Jericho

of Galilee lies about 685 feet (211 meters) below sea level. The elevation of Jerusalem is 2,593 feet (790 meters) above sea level, while only some 15 miles east, the Dead Sea, the lowest spot on earth, is 1,275 feet (388 meters) below sea level.[2]

It is important to note the several general geographical areas. In predicting future restoration and blessing, Jeremiah mentions or

2. Note that the drop in elevation from Jerusalem to the Dead Sea is almost 3,900 feet (1,187 meters) in a distance of about 15 miles.

alludes to several of them: "In the towns of the hill country, of the Shephelah, and of the Negeb, in the land of Benjamin, the places around Jerusalem, and in the towns of Judah, flocks shall again pass under the hands of the one who counts them, says the LORD" (Jer. 33:13).

A systematic listing of these areas from west to east would begin at the Mediterranean Sea. Along the sea the coastal plain is a flat, fertile area. Although there were at least three other major north-south trade routes, the easiest to travel was in this plain; accordingly, its inhabitants were subject to frequent contact with foreigners. In the south, in the western part of the territory of Judah, lie rolling foothills, the Shephelah, which rise from the plain.

The backbone of Israel is the hill country, which runs from Esdraelon southward. The hills are high and rugged, cut by deep valleys. Successful agriculture requires development of the natural terracing, means for preserving water, and careful selection of crops and flocks. The residents of the hill country had minimum contact with outsiders.

A second major north-south trade route ran along the tops of the hills. It is sometimes referred to as the Ridge Route. Because Abraham and his descendants traveled this route, it is also known as the Way of the Patriarchs. The east-west valleys in the hill country are particularly important because they provide access to the interior and beyond. Samson's home near Zorah in the Sorek Valley gave him easy access to Philistine lands; David's defeat of Goliath thwarted a Philistine attempt to invade the hill country through the Valley of Elah.

The western side of the hills receives a reasonable amount of rain. Not so the eastern slopes. Jerusalem, for example, has an annual rainfall of about twenty-four inches; Jericho, less than 20 miles to the east, gets only four inches. Hence, along the eastern side of the hills is the hot, dry, rough, barren wilderness of Judah where the Maccabean forces hid during the intertestamental period, where John the Baptist preached, and Jesus was tempted.

The desert of the eastern hill country falls away suddenly into the Jordan Valley, part of a great rift that continues into Africa.[3] Most of this deep escarpment has the same type of landscape found in the wilderness just above it. Occasional oases, such as

3. Deuteronomy, Joshua, and a number of other Old Testament books refer to the Arabah. Technically the Arabah is the region from the south of the Dead Sea to the Gulf of Aqaba. But the term, which means "depression," is often expanded to cover other areas: (1) the whole Jordan Valley (Josh. 11:2, 16; 12:1, 3); (2) the area around the Dead Sea (Deut. 1:7; 2:8); and (3) the possessions of the Transjordanic tribes ("The Arabah also, with the Jordan and its banks, from Chinnereth down to the Sea of the Arabah, the Dead Sea," Deut. 3:17).

Jericho, make habitation possible and even desirable; the favorite palace of Herod the Great was near Jericho. Along the floor of the valley runs the twisting Jordan River. Just south of Jericho it empties into the Dead Sea. A third north-south trade route ran alongside the Jordan.

On the east of the Jordan Valley rise the Plains of Moab, the Transjordan Plateau (the modern Hashemite Kingdom of Jordan). This is the area Moses divided between the tribes of Reuben, Gad, and half of Manasseh. The Highway of the Kings, the fourth north-south trade route, began at Damascus and continued through this Transjordan territory. These plains gradually merge with the Arabian Desert.

As if the west-to-east terrain were not complicated enough, we also have to contend with that which runs from the north to the south. The towering heights of the Mount Hermon range feed into the less rugged hills of the Upper and Lower Galilee (or Chinnereth) areas. These drop very steeply into the broad Esdraelon Valley.

South of this central plain the land ascends into the hill country, first the hills of Ephraim (or Samaria), then the hill country of Judah. Between them, just north of Jerusalem, is a relatively flat area, the Benjamin Plateau, around which lay such towns as Bethel, Ai, Ramah, Gibeon, Gibeah, Michmash, and others which played major roles in the early history of Israel. The Beth-horon pass provides access from this plateau to the coastal plain on the west; along this road Joshua chased the confederation of five kings who had attacked Gibeon and Israel (Josh. 10:10).

A bit south of Hebron begins the Negeb. This desertlike region is the extreme southern part of the country. It is virtually barren in the dry summer months but fertile in the wet seasons.[4] Beer-sheba is its major city, but other biblical sites, such as Arad, lie within its borders.

Political Divisions in New Testament Times

Political divisions of the land of Israel changed from time to time. Before the conquest under Joshua it seems to have been divided into numerous city-states. After the conquest the Israelites settled into a federation in which each tribe was virtually autonomous. During the monarchy the land was first a unified political whole, then divided into two sections. Judah, after the return from captivity, was a tiny temple-state which began at the Jordan on the

---

4. Ezekiel 20:46–47 speaks of "the forest land in the Negeb"; modern reforestation projects are slowly restoring parts of this area.

east but did not extend as far west as the coastal plain; it included neither Bethel on the north nor Hebron on the south.

Boundaries were constantly subject to change during the intertestamental period. Our concern is with the political situation during New Testament times. At first, Herod the Great ruled the whole area as a kingdom. At his death it was divided into several sections. At first some of these were ruled by his descendants; other arrangements, including rule by Roman governors, later prevailed in some locations.

Only three sections of the country were populated primarily by Jews. These included Judea (and Idumea) in the south, Perea to the east of the Jordan, and Galilee in the north. Although Samaria was politically a part of Judea, its inhabitants were not Jews, and there was ill will between the two peoples.

Three sections were primarily Gentile in population and government. Phoenicia (the land of Tyre and Sidon) lay along the Mediterranean coast, north and a bit west of Galilee. Inland from Phoenicia was the northeast territory, which included the regions of Gaulanitis, Iturea, and Trachonitis, as well as the city of Caesarea Philippi. The Decapolis, a federation of ten Greek-speaking cities, was primarily a Transjordanic area to the north and east of Perea. It crossed the Jordan and occupied a bit of territory in Israel proper just south of the Sea of Galilee.

The City of Jerusalem

The importance of Jerusalem can hardly be overstated. Even at the height of its expansion, however, the biblical city, called today the Old City, was minuscule by modern standards. Its origins are lost in history. Its strategic location even today is obvious. It sits high in the Judean hill country, within sight of the Ridge Route. Its dominant features are deep valleys, the Kidron on the east and the Hinnom on the west, which circles to join the Kidron in the south. In ancient times these valleys were the foundation of the city's fortifications. A more shallow valley, the Central Valley (also called the Tyropoeon or Cheesemakers' Valley), goes through the city. The Mount of Olives rises above Jerusalem from the eastern side of the Kidron Valley. It figures prominently in both the skyline and history of the city, but has never been an official part of it.

The biblical city eventually spread over five hills between the Kidron and Hinnom valleys. David built his city on a small kidney-shaped rise called Ophel on the southeastern hill. Mount Moriah, the site of the temple, was included in the city by Solomon. The city began to spread to the large southwestern hill during the monarchy; this area is called Zion today.[5] Archaeological evidence indicates that Hezekiah probably extended the city walls to include this area. Some think that Psalm 122:3, "Jerusalem—built as a city that is bound firmly together," may commemorate that event.

The exact location of the walls of the New Testament city is a major problem for archaeologists and historians. Evidently an area just west of the temple and north of the southeastern hill was developed as a marketplace (agora) and site for public buildings and

5. The term *Zion* was formerly used of the whole city.

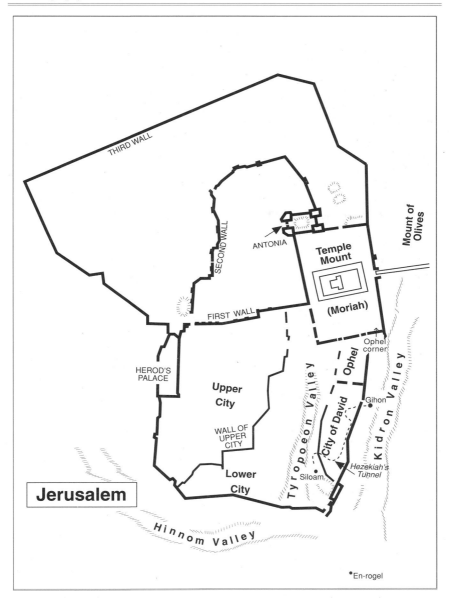

The following labels appear on the map: THIRD WALL, SECOND WALL, ANTONIA, FIRST WALL, HEROD'S PALACE, Upper City, WALL OF UPPER CITY, Lower City, **Jerusalem**, Temple Mount, (Moriah), Mount of Olives, Ophel corner, Ophel, City of David, Gihon, Tyropoeon Valley, Kidron Valley, Hezekiah's Tunnel, Siloam, Hinnom Valley, En-rogel

palaces during the intertestamental period. The location of the wall which lay to the west of this area is crucial in determining the probable site of the crucifixion and burial of Jesus.

The northern section of the city has no valley or other natural form of protection. Militarily, it is the most vulnerable part of

Jerusalem. Several ancient walls protected it. After the ministry of Jesus, Herod Agrippa I began the construction of a long wall to surround on the north and west the northern suburbs of Jerusalem. The Roman emperor ordered him to halt the project before it was completed.

Water supply has always been a major concern in Jerusalem. The ancient city was supplied by two major springs. The Gihon, below the City of David in the Kidron Valley, was the primary water supply. En-rogel was to the south of the city and not so frequently used. Throughout the history of Jerusalem numerous aqueducts and cisterns were built to transport and store water. The best known is the tunnel built by Hezekiah (2 Kings 20:20; 2 Chron. 32:30) to connect the Gihon spring with the Pool of Siloam (John 9:7) in the Central Valley. It was dug through 1,749 feet of solid rock beneath the Ophel. The project was part of the preparations for an anticipated siege by the Assyrians. An inscription found in the tunnel tells of the midpoint meeting of two teams of diggers that had started from different ends.[6] Another pool, Bethesda (or Beth-zatha), is mentioned in John 5:2; it probably lay just north of the temple, but its exact location is uncertain.

The Temple Complex

The physical features of the temple complex in New Testament times are fairly well known, but the exact details of a reconstruction are in dispute. Descriptions of the physical layout of the temple are given by Josephus and, with some deviations, in *Middoth*, a tractate of the Mishnah.[7]

The location of the New Testament temple was the same as that of previous temples. Its floor plan and essential furniture were modeled after those of the tabernacle. However, when Herod the Great undertook to rebuild the construction of Zerubbabel, he decided to surpass it in size and beauty.

To meet the need for adequate space for the worshipers who flocked to the temple during festival occasions, Herod enlarged the platform on which it stood. This he accomplished by an extension, supported by arches, over the Kidron Valley. This platform, the

6. ". . . was being dug out. It was cut in the following manner . . . axes, each man towards his fellow, and while there were still 3 cubits to be cut through, the voice of one man calling to the other was heard, showing that he was deviating to the right. When the tunnel was driven through, the excavators met man to man, axe to axe, and the water flowed for 1,200 cubits from the spring to the reservoir. The height of the rock above the heads of the excavators was 100 cubits" (see D. J. Wiseman, "Siloam," in *New Bible Dictionary*, ed. J. D. Douglas et al., 2d ed. [Downers Grove, Ill.: Inter-Varsity, 1982], 1113–14).

7. Josephus *Jewish War* 5.5.1–8 (184–247); idem, *Antiquities* 15.11.3–7 (391–425).

Figure 2
The Basic Plan of Herod's Temple

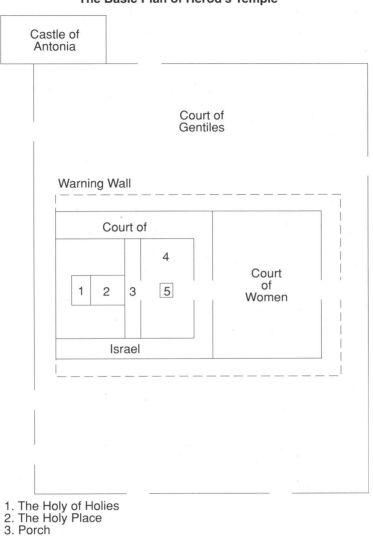

1. The Holy of Holies
2. The Holy Place
3. Porch
4. Court of Priests
5. Altar

Court of Gentiles, occupies some 35 acres. Herod enclosed the platform with porticos (porches, stoas). Solomon's Portico (John 10:23; Acts 3:11; 5:12) was probably the eastern stoa, overlooking the Kidron Valley. Several gates led to the platform; the main one was probably the triple-arched gate at the top of a large stairway on the south. Different suggestions have been made for the location of the pinnacle of the temple (Luke 4:9); it may have been the highest point of the temple structure proper, or the southeast corner of the platform (the Ophel corner), which overlooks the Kidron Valley.

Within the confines of the platform was the temple structure itself. It was surrounded by a low wall warning Gentiles to go no further.[8] Three open-air divisions lay within the temple, the Court of the Women, the Court of Israel (of the Men), and the Court of the Priests. Sacrifices and other acts of worship were conducted in the last-named area.

The enclosed structure was of magnificent construction. Like the tabernacle, this structure comprised the Holy Place and the Holy of Holies. Evidently the ark of the covenant had been lost when the Babylonians destroyed the first temple. Because the ark had not been replaced, the Holy of Holies of the New Testament temple was empty. Nevertheless, it remained the focal point of the Israelite religion.

8. Josephus mentions this wall in *Jewish War* 5.5.2 (193–94); 6.2.4 (124–26); *Antiquities* 15.11.5 (417). Archaeologists have found two occurrences of the inscription. It read, "No foreigner is to enter within the forecourt and the balustrade around the sanctuary. Whoever is caught will have himself to blame for his subsequent death."

3

A Survey of the Old Testament

1. Beginnings (–c. 2000 B.C.; Genesis 1–11)
2. The Patriarchs (c. 2000–1650 B.C., Middle Bronze Age; Genesis 12–50)
3. The Exodus: The Wilderness and the Birth of the Nation (c. 1445–1405 or 1290–1250, Late Bronze Age; Exodus, Leviticus, Numbers, Deuteronomy)
4. Conquest and Occupation of Canaan (c. 1400–1350 or 1250–1200, Late Bronze Age; Joshua)
5. The Judges (c. 1350– or 1200–1050, Iron Age I; Judges, Ruth)
6. United Kingdom (1050–931, Iron Age I; 1 Samuel, 2 Samuel, 1 Kings 1–11, 1 Chronicles 10–29, 2 Chronicles 1–9)
7. Divided Kingdom (931–586, Iron Age II; 1 Kings 12–22, 2 Kings, 2 Chronicles 10–36)
8. The Exile or Captivity of Judah (586–538, Iron Age III or Persian Age)
9. Postexilic Period (538–c. 400, Persian Age; Ezra and Nehemiah)

Intertestamental Jewish writers assume the reader is familiar with the Old Testament. It is therefore imperative to review the major periods of its history. In the next chapter we will survey some of its more important institutions, ideas, and customs.

Old Testament history is religious history. Although it deals with events and people in the real world, it is concerned primarily with God and human beings' relationship to him. It covers real persons and events which are significant for this religious purpose. Hence, items which are of grave importance in world history may be passed over quickly or completely omitted by the biblical writers,

Figure 3
Time Line of the History of Israel

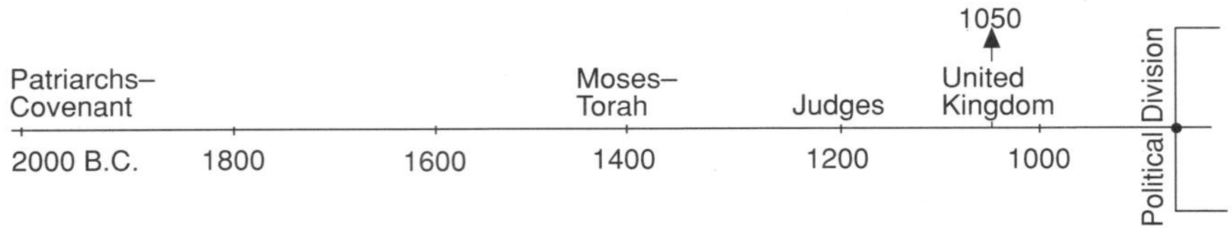

Patriarchs–Covenant			Moses–Torah	Judges	1050 ▲ United Kingdom	Political Division
2000 B.C.	1800	1600	1400	1200	1000	

whose telling or review of history is always for theological purposes. Typical is Micah, who mentions a number of events in Israel's national experience and then calls the reader to remember them, "that you may know the saving acts of the LORD" (6:5). It is through Israel's history that God works redemption and makes himself and salvation known.

We will summarize Old Testament history in nine divisions. Although they are presented in chronological order, there are gaps in this sequence. In particular, about four hundred years intervene between the end of the period of the patriarchs and the period of the exodus. Although this was an important time in the history of Egypt, the land where the Hebrews were living, nothing in the divine-human relationship was significant enough to be recorded. On the other hand, some of the activities recorded in the Book of Judges may well overlap; various judges may have lived at the same time but were active in different parts of the country.

1. Beginnings (–c. 2000 B.C.; Genesis 1–11)

The first period of biblical history set the stage for the drama of redemption. The writer shows that all things came into being as a result of the initiative and action of God, and that the universe was created good. The writer then relates that it was through human disobedience, sin, that evil entered the creation, causing confusion, disharmony, alienation, and death. Events are cited which demonstrate that God punishes sin, but rewards and blesses those who seek him. The record of this period ends with a summary of the beginning of national and ethnic groups. The major persons and events of the period of beginnings are the creation, Adam and Eve, the fall and entrance of sin, Noah and the flood, and the birth of nations.

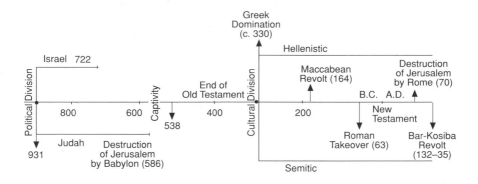

2. The Patriarchs (c. 2000–1650 B.C., Middle Bronze Age; Genesis 12–50)

As nations developed, God acted to found one nation that would be related to him in a special way and through which he would act upon the earth in a unique manner. He selected Abraham, a citizen of the city of Ur in Mesopotamia, to bring this nation into existence. God offered Abraham a covenant in which he was promised fatherhood of a nation, a geographical possession (the land of Canaan, later called the land of Israel or Palestine), and a spiritual relationship and mission (God promised, "I will . . . be God to you and to your offspring" and "in you all the families of the earth shall be blessed" [Gen. 17:7; 12:3]). To demonstrate his faith in the trustworthiness and promises of God and to show his acceptance of the offer made in the covenant, Abraham traveled from Mesopotamia to the land of Canaan.

Although Abraham had a number of children, only Isaac was selected to continue the covenant line, to receive the promises of God. And only one of Isaac's sons, Jacob (also called Israel), continued that line. All of Jacob's twelve sons participated in this national-spiritual tradition and became the heads of the subdivisions (or tribes) of the Hebrew nation. A famine drove Jacob and his family to Egypt where one of their number, Joseph, had risen to an important position in the government.

The major events of the patriarchal period are the giving of the covenant, Abraham's demonstrations of faith, and the move to Egypt. Abraham, Isaac, Jacob, and Joseph are the most significant persons.

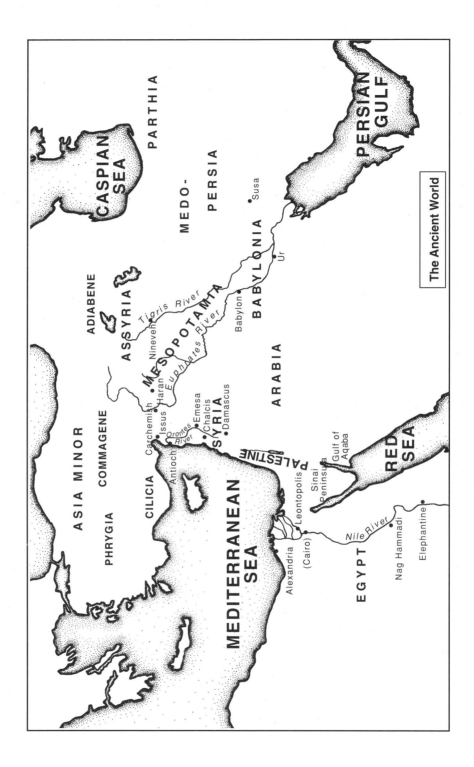

The Ancient World

3. The Exodus: The Wilderness and the Birth of the Nation (c. 1445–1405 or 1290–1250, Late Bronze Age; Exodus, Leviticus, Numbers, Deuteronomy)

The descendants of Abraham, Isaac, and Jacob, now grown to a clan of considerable number, were forced into slavery by the Egyptians. At length God (the LORD, Yahweh) appointed Moses as leader of the Hebrews. With the aid of divine signs (plagues) and guidance, he led the people out of Egypt and slavery (the exodus) into the wilderness of the Sinai Peninsula (the exact date of the exodus is a matter of controversy).

At Mount Sinai the LORD made a series of appearances to Moses, the national leaders, and all the people. In addition to renewing the covenant made earlier with Abraham, he gave instructions (Torah or the law) for the political, social, and religious organization of the nation. These instructions (including the Ten Commandments) were intended to guide every aspect of the lives of those in covenant relation with the LORD. At Sinai the tabernacle (a tent) was constructed to serve as the worship center for the nation.

On the trip from Sinai toward Canaan, discontent, impatience, and fear led to rebellion, disobedience, and sin against God. As a consequence the Hebrews were forced to wander in the wilderness for forty years until the generation that had been adults at the time of the exodus from Egypt died. Moses too, because of sin, was forbidden to enter Canaan, the Promised Land.

Moses is considered the greatest of Hebrew leaders, the lawgiver, and God's spokesman who talked with the LORD face to face. "He was unequaled" (Deut. 34:11; the Revised Standard Version says there was "none like him"). His brother Aaron was the first high priest. We also meet Joshua, Moses' assistant and later his successor, during this period.

Events of the exodus period center in Israel's bondage and deliverance from Egypt, the events at Mount Sinai (the giving of the law, the organization of the nation, the building of the tabernacle, and establishment of worship). The final phases of this period include Israel's wanderings in the wilderness as punishment for her disobedience, Moses' preparations on the Plains of Moab for the nation's entry into the Promised Land, and his death.

4. Conquest and Occupation of Canaan (c. 1400–1350 or 1250–1200, Late Bronze Age; Joshua)

Moses was succeeded by his assistant Joshua, who led the Hebrews across the Jordan River into Canaan. In a series of military campaigns the land was subdued by the Hebrews. However, contrary to God's directive, many of the original inhabitants were allowed to remain in the land.

Joshua divided the land among the twelve tribes. Each settled in its own territorial possession. The tabernacle was set up at Shiloh, in the middle of the country.

The major events during this period were Joshua's leading Israel in the conquest, occupation, and division of the land the LORD had promised to Abraham many years before.

5. The Judges (c. 1350– or 1200–1050, Iron Age I; Judges, Ruth)

After the conquest and settlement each tribe existed as virtually an independent entity, united with the others only by racial ties and a common place of worship. There was virtual anarchy in the land ("all the people did what was right in their own eyes" [Judg. 17:6]).

The history of the Hebrews during this period followed a frequently repeated cycle: (1) the Hebrews fell into sin—often the idolatry of the native tribes who had not been expelled during the conquest; (2) punishment came, usually in the form of defeat or oppression by an enemy; (3) Israel repented and called upon the Lord for deliverance; (4) deliverance came when God anointed a judge (a charismatic, that is, a nonhereditary leader) to lead the oppressed Hebrews to victory over their enemies. The judge usually remained as administrator or governor after the military victory was secure. Some of the more important judges were Deborah and Barak, Gideon, Jephthah, and Samson.

The Book of Judges ends with the record of some events which illustrate the sin and evil characteristics of life during the period. The Book of Ruth, in sharp contrast, gives an account of faithfulness and devotion and serves as a transition to the life of David.

6. United Kingdom (1050–931, Iron Age I; 1 Samuel, 2 Samuel, 1 Kings 1–11, 1 Chronicles 10–29, 2 Chronicles 1–9)

A number of factors, especially the military-economic threat from the Philistines, caused the Hebrews to seek to unite under a king. Samuel, the last of the judges, reluctantly anointed Saul as the first king of the twelve tribes. Disobedience brought a loss of the LORD's favor, and Saul eventually lost his life in battle with the Philistines.

Samuel also anointed Israel's second king, David. David, in spite of numerous personal sins, was repentant and faithful to the LORD and consequently blessed by him. David succeeded in establishing the Hebrews as the major power of the world of his day. The LORD promised David that his family would reign "forever" (2 Sam. 7:13). This promise, the basis for a hereditary kingship within David's family, was later looked upon as assurance that the coming anointed king and leader (Messiah) would be a descendant of David.

Solomon continued to expand his father David's kingdom. His building projects included a temple for the LORD. However, his administrative and financial policies, coupled with major flaws in his personal and religious life, led the country to the brink of ruin.

Persons of special note are the three kings, Saul, David, and Solomon. This was the time of transition from a loose tribal confederation to a monarchy, from occasional gifted rulers to a settled leadership in one family. During the united monarchy the Hebrews were the superpower of the ancient world. Israel enjoyed her political, social, financial, and religious heyday. Later generations remembered this period as a golden age, the pattern for the future time of glory. It marked the zenith of Hebrew geographical control, influence, and grandeur.

7. Divided Kingdom (931–586, Iron Age II; 1 Kings 12–22, 2 Kings, 2 Chronicles 10–36)

In spite of his wisdom Solomon permitted the worship of pagan deities in the land of Israel (primarily brought in by his many wives, most of whom he married for political reasons). God decreed punishment in the form of a split in the kingdom after Solomon's death. Solomon's expensive building projects and policies of high taxation, conscription for military service and forced labor, and the centralization of power brought widespread opposition and hostility toward the royal family. These factors became the impetus for the division of the kingdom. That division came at the coronation of Solomon's son Rehoboam. The northern tribes rebelled against the house of David; the southern tribes remained under the rule of the Davidic kings.

The northern kingdom, called Israel (sometimes Ephraim or Samaria), was composed of approximately ten of the Hebrew tribes and occupied the larger portion of the geographical area. Eventually Samaria was built as her capital. Various forms of idolatry or paganism mixed with the worship of the LORD prevailed as the popular and sometimes official religion of Israel. Some of the nineteen kings (e.g., Omri and Jeroboam II) were credible political or military rulers. The Bible, however, evaluating all from the spiritual point of view, pronounces all kings of the north evil in the sight of God.

The southern kingdom, called Judah, occupied the area held by approximately two-and-a-half tribes. Her population was enlarged by numbers of the priestly tribe of Levi who moved into the area after the political division. Jerusalem, the city established as the capital by David and the location of the temple erected by Solomon, remained the political, religious, and cultural center in Judah. Although the influence of idolatry and pagan religions was felt with increasing strength in Judah, its progress was much slower than in Israel. The onslaught of spiritual and moral decay was occasionally checked by revivals of devotion to the law and worship of the LORD led by certain kings (especially Asa, Joash, Hezekiah, and Josiah). All of the twenty rulers of Judah were descended from David. Only eight of them received commendation for doing "what was right in the sight of the LORD" (Asa, Jehoshaphat, Joash, Amaziah, Uzziah, Jotham, Hezekiah, and Josiah), and two of those went into apostasy in their latter days (Joash and Amaziah).

Throughout the history of the divided kingdom, the Hebrew people were caught in interplay with the affairs of other nations. At the beginning of the period the Egyptians, Moabites, Edomites, Philistines, Syrians, and others brought political, economic, and social pressure upon one or both of the kingdoms. Later, the larger empires of Assyria, Babylonia, and Medo-Persia played decisive roles in determining the fortunes of the Hebrews.

Assyria invaded and made vassal states of both Hebrew kingdoms. Eventually the Assyrians completely destroyed Israel in 722. The Bible records that only the miraculous intervention of God saved Judah from a similar fate. The Assyrians deported most of the people of Israel and repopulated the area with foreigners. These foreigners intermarried with the surviving native Hebrews; the Samaritans of the New Testament were their descendants.

Judah survived until 586. At that time she lost her independence; the city of Jerusalem and the temple were destroyed by the Babylonian Empire (successor to Assyria as the dominant world power).

8. The Exile or Captivity of Judah (586–538, Iron Age III or Persian Age)

After the defeat of Judah by Babylonia, the surviving leadership and the influential families were deported to Babylon, where the

Hebrews lived in exile for approximately seventy years (the first deportation may have occurred as early as 605). These captives were allowed considerable freedom and engaged in the political and economic life of Babylon. Other Hebrews fled and settled in Egypt. Still others seem to have been scattered throughout various parts of the world. Some Hebrews, mainly the poor and those groups considered insignificant by the Babylonians, were allowed to remain in Judah but exerted no political influence.

No historical books in the Bible relate the events of this period. Of the prophetical books Jeremiah 40–44, Ezekiel 25–48, Obadiah, and Daniel come from and reflect the period of the captivity.

9. Postexilic Period (538–c. 400, Persian Age; Ezra and Nehemiah)

The postexilic period is both the end of Old Testament history and the beginning of the Intertestamental Era. The precise dividing line between the two cannot be established. After the initial part of the period it becomes increasingly difficult to date persons and events precisely. Josephus says that biblical history came to a close with the reign of "Artaxerxes, who succeeded Xerxes as king of Persia";[1] this would be Artaxerxes I Longimanus (464–424).

The Medo-Persians wrested world domination from the Babylonians and inaugurated a new policy toward captured peoples. In consequence the Hebrews were allowed to return to their homeland and to establish a small vassal state. Although Hebrews from many areas migrated back, the Bible gives attention only to formal returns by some of those who had lived in Babylon. Four distinct trips to Judah are mentioned. The first was led by Zerubbabel and Sheshbazzar, the second by Ezra the scribe, and the final two by Nehemiah. From the reconstructed Hebrew state there gradually emerged an adapted form of the Hebrew religion which placed special emphasis upon the development and observance of legal and ceremonial traditions.

After her defeat by Assyria, the northern kingdom of Israel was never reestablished as a nation. Some individuals filtered back and were probably absorbed into the renewed state of Judah. Before Judah's defeat by the Babylonians, King Josiah had annexed to Judah the northern section of the territory of Israel (later called Galilee). As a result of the extended reach of Josiah's reforms and developments during the intertestamental period, this area maintained close ties with Judah during the New Testament period.

1. Josephus *Against Apion* 1.8 (39).

The historical books of Chronicles, Ezra, Nehemiah, Esther, and the prophecies of Haggai, Zechariah, and Malachi come from this period. Zerubbabel, Sheshbazzar, Ezra, and Nehemiah were major players during the postexilic period. The rebuilding of the walls and temple of Jerusalem, conflict with the Samaritans, and moral and religious reform were among the more important events.

4

Old Testament Ideas and Institutions

- Theology
- Old Testament Worship
  + The Place of Worship
  + Leaders for Worship
  + Sacrifices
  + Feasts and Festivals
  + Ritual Cleanliness (Kosher Laws)
  + Vows
- Prophets and Kings

Theology

In neither the Old Testament nor intertestamental writings is what Westerners call theology of first concern. Although abstract religious concepts and content are not unimportant, the major attention is upon more concrete concerns. Nevertheless, certain beliefs and convictions are clearly central to the entirety of Israel's religious life and experience. The first of these is monotheism, belief in and worship of only one God. Not only do the Hebrews worship but one God (Yahweh, the LORD), they also hold that only one God exists.

The Old Testament refers to the Hebrew deity with terms like *El* (or *Elohim*), the generic name for deity, and *Adonai,* which means something like "Lord" or "Master." However, in Exodus 3:13–15, in answer to the question "What is [God's] name?" God said to Moses: "'I AM WHO I AM.' He said further, 'Thus you shall say to the Israelites,

"I AM has sent me to you."' God also said to Moses, 'Thus you shall say to the Israelites, "The LORD, the God of your ancestors, the God of Abraham, the God of Isaac, and the God of Jacob, has sent me to you": This is my name forever, and this my title for all generations.'" The name revealed to Moses is represented in Hebrew by the letters *YHWH*, sometimes referred to as the "tetragrammaton" (four letters). Eventually the Hebrews totally abstained from ever pronouncing this name. The proper pronunciation was probably forgotten. The closest we can now come is something like "Yahweh." Wherever the term appears, the American Standard Version (1901) has "Jehovah." It has, however, become the common practice in recent English translations (e.g., the Revised Standard, the New American Standard Bible, the New International Version, and the New Revised Standard) to follow the King James in representing the four letters as "the LORD," thus distinguishing this name from the reverential title *Adonai* ("the Lord").

The Hebrews, as we said, held fast to their conviction that Yahweh, the LORD, a single being, was not only their God, but the only God who existed. Pagan idols, the gods of other nations, were not only false, but deficient in the all-important area of existence. They simply did not exist; those who worshiped them had been deceived by demonic powers.

A second cardinal principle of the Hebrew faith is belief in the creation of the universe: God made all things out of nothing. Closely associated with this is the belief in providence, that activity of God by which he continues to be involved in the affairs of the universe as he preserves, governs, and provides for the needs of all creation. The psalmists, finding strength and confidence in their conviction that this personal God, the LORD, created and is still at work in the universe, frequently proclaim that fact.

A third area essential to the Hebrew faith is belief in the unique status of the nation Israel. They regard themselves as the people of God, a favored nation. The covenant, of which we spoke in our survey of history (p. 55), is the basis for this belief. The word *covenant*, in the Semitic mind, refers to an agreement instituted and defined by only one party. The potential recipient must either accept or reject that which is offered, including all its provisions and conditions. Like a person's last will and testament, it is nonnegotiable.

We noted that the essential core of the covenant was God's promise to Abraham, "I will . . . be God to you and to your offspring" and "in you all the families of the earth shall be blessed" (Gen. 17:7; 12:3). The import of this promise can be understood only within the context of the God-human relationship depicted in Scripture prior to the making of the covenant with Abraham. In the covenant the holy God, who has been offended by sin, takes the initiative and identifies himself with sinners, those who have offended him. Here he identifies himself with a particular group, but also states his desire to work through them for the benefit of other groups and individuals. The covenant exemplifies the essence of grace—undeserved, unmerited favor and acceptance by God. Although later provisions will broaden and expand the covenant, its essential core remains the same. It is the framework for redemption throughout the salvation history depicted in the Bible.

Abraham and later his descendants, both physical and spiritual, responded to the offer of the covenant by accepting and acting on its promises.[1] In the case of Old Testament Israel, circumcision was involved as an outward sign or seal. Abraham demonstrated his acceptance by obeying God's instructions to move into the land of Canaan and to worship and serve the LORD only.[2] At Mount Sinai the covenant was renewed—God identified himself as "the LORD your God" (Exod. 20:2), and a formal covenant ceremony was conducted (Exod. 24:1–8). There again God gave instructions which were to be obeyed as the nation's way of accepting and keeping covenant.

The Hebrew word *Torah* is usually translated "law." By the time of Intertestamental Judaism the emphasis upon law was certainly paramount. However, the meaning is broader; "instructions" would often be a better translation. At Mount Sinai the LORD gave Israel the instructions for those who were in covenant relationship with him. The concept of Torah-law is the fourth essential area of the Hebrew faith.

The biblical books of Exodus, Leviticus, Numbers, and Deuteronomy contain 613 written laws or instructions to direct every facet of the life of the Hebrews. These laws include injunctions and directives in several broad areas. Later writers (mostly Christian) divided the Old Testament law into ceremonial (religious ritual), civil, and moral (including the Ten Commandments). Such a division may be helpful in identifying the areas covered by the Old Testament instructions, but it can also be misleading. To the Hebrews the law was one, and all parts were of equal importance.

1. On the spiritual descendants of Abraham see Gal. 3:11–14, 23–29.
2. Before the covenant was offered, Abraham and his family were pagans; they "served other gods" (Josh. 24:2, 14–15). But in Canaan, Abraham began to worship the LORD; "he built there an altar to the LORD, who had appeared to him" (Gen. 12:7–8; 13:4).

Old Testament Worship

Many of the instructions given at Mount Sinai had to do with worship. God thereby informed his people that the means of worship were not to be of their choosing but of his.

The Place of Worship

Considerable attention is given in Exodus 25–40 to the construction of a place of worship. At first, in the wilderness and through the periods of conquest and the judges, the place of worship was a tabernacle or a tent. Later, Solomon, Zerubbabel and Sheshbazzar after the captivity, and, at the beginning of the New Testament Era, Herod the Great built temples as the place of worship. Although these were large, elaborate, permanent structures, their floor plans and furniture were generally the same as in the original tabernacle.

The tabernacle consisted of three parts. The outer court was an uncovered area enclosed by curtains. Just inside the single entrance was an altar of bronze upon which various kinds of offerings were burned. Behind the altar stood a basin or laver also of bronze. It contained water with which the priests washed themselves.

Inside the outer court was an enclosed rectangular structure made of poles, panels, and several layers of curtains. The first two-thirds of this structure was the Holy Place. Here were three pieces of furniture, a table upon which loaves of bread were replaced weekly, a lampstand with seven branches for holding lamps (of either clay or brass), and a small altar upon which only incense was burned. Finally there was the Holy of Holies, separated from the rest of the structure by a heavy curtain or veil. Here rested a gold-covered box, the ark of the covenant. Its lid was ornate and called the mercy seat. At each end of the ark was the form of a cherub with wings overshadowing the mercy seat. Within the ark was the covenant (Exod. 25:16, 21; 40:20), usually assumed to be the stone tables of the law (Exod. 24:12).

This floor plan was symbolic. The Holy of Holies and the ark of the covenant represented the presence of God in the midst of his people. He was separated from them (by the veil), and approach to him required washings and sacrifice by the priests, whom he had chosen to be the representatives from Israel. Nevertheless, God was in fact present with those to whom he had said, "I will take you as my people, and I will be your God" (Exod. 6:7).

Leaders for Worship

Moses was Israel's unique human leader (Deut. 34:10–12). In addition, the books of Exodus through Deuteronomy designated the tribe of Levi to be leaders in community life and worship. The men of one Levitical clan, that of Moses' brother Aaron, were appointed priests. Priests were representatives of the people before God. Their primary responsibility had to do with ceremonies, sacrifices, and other religious duties associated with the tabernacle or temple. The priests were led by the high (or chief) priest, originally Aaron, and then the oldest son in each succeeding generation.

The function of the Levites is more difficult to determine. During the period of the exodus they moved the tabernacle from place to place. Later they lived in special towns and cities scattered throughout the land of Israel and served as representatives of religion, possibly gave religious instructions, and, when necessary, assisted the priests in their duties.

Sacrifices

The most obvious of Israel's means of worship were the prescribed sacrifices. An offering, in the broadest sense, is anything presented to God. The term *sacrifice* is usually reserved for gifts presented at the altar. A sacrifice could be offered by either the nation or individuals for a variety of reasons, as an atonement[3] in seeking forgiveness for sin, as an expression of thanksgiving, or as a regular part of the rituals of worship. The usual sacrifice was a ceremonially clean domestic animal or bird which was killed and then burned in whole or in part on the altar. Oil, wine, incense, or grain could, under some circumstances, be offered in sacrifice. In some cases part of the sacrifice was eaten by the priest or the worshiper.

There were five major types of sacrifices. They differed in motive, material, and method:

1. The burnt offering, which called for a domestic animal or bird, was the regular evening and morning sacrifice. It was entirely consumed on the altar and always accompanied by a grain offering.
2. The peace offering ("fellowship offering," NIV; "sacrifice of well-being," NRSV), which involved an animal, was a voluntary offering in which family and friends participated. There were three kinds, depending on the motive of the worshiper: the

---

3. "Atonement" is an Anglo-Saxon word which means, literally, "a making at one." In the Old Testament it is usually the translation for the Hebrew root *kpr*, which carries such meanings as to "cover," "pacify," and "make propitiation." This Hebrew root occurs about eighty times in Exodus through Numbers alone.

thank (praise) offering recognized God's unmerited or un-
expected blessing; the votive offering was made in payment of
a vow; and the freewill offering was an expression of love for
God. Each type of peace offering was accompanied by a prescribed grain offering.

3. Sin offerings were made for sin committed unwittingly or for
   ceremonial defilement (there was no offering for a willful sin).
   Both the ritual and the victim (domestic animal or bird) varied
   according to the prominence and economic state of the one
   who had sinned.

4. Trespass (guilt) offerings were required for ritual infraction or
   for wrongdoing to another person. These wrongs required
   both correction or restitution and presentation of an offering.

5. The grain (meal, cereal, food ["meat," KJV]) offering was the
   only sacrifice which did not involve animal life; instead the
   products of the soil were offered. These could be oil or frank-
   incense, parched or roasted grain, unleavened bread, cakes,
   or wafers. The grain offering usually accompanied some other
   form of offering, especially the burnt or peace offering.

Old Testament sacrifices and offerings represent the God-
ordained means whereby a person could approach and be received
by God. The pattern of Hebrew religion involved (1) election
through the covenant, and (2) either obedience or repentance and
atonement as the condition for remaining in the covenant. Hence
God's requirement of sacrifices emphasizes that disobedience, sin,
is an offense to him. Although an individual act might be directed
against another person, it also affects God; sin is primarily against
him. Furthermore, the need for sacrifices indicates the seriousness
of sin: it separates a person from God and is a barrier to acceptance, favor, and fellowship. Sacrifices show that with God sin is a
life-and-death matter; it must be atoned by shedding blood. Human beings cannot by their own efforts obtain forgiveness and thus
regain access to God. Because of the nature of sin and human
helplessness, atonement for and forgiveness of sin must be on
God's terms and involve extrahuman means.

Feasts and Festivals

Feasts, festivals, and special seasons of the Jewish year were regular parts of the worship of the LORD. They centered on, respectively, aspects of the lunar year, seasonal agricultural events, or the
remembrance of important historical and religious moments. The
biblical description and prescriptions are general. Some of the

feasts and festivals survived and even took on additional meanings during the intertestamental period. The more detailed instructions found in rabbinic literature (the Mishnah) represent some of these later developments.[4]

All feasts had certain basic elements in common. Their purpose was to remind the people that every area of life is controlled by and must be in subjection to the LORD. Two themes, sorrow for sins and joy in the LORD, ran concurrently through all special seasons. Thus, fasting, mourning, and sacrifices for sin accompanied feasting, joy, blowing trumpets, and presenting thank offerings.

Numbers 28:11–15 mentions a special sacrifice on the day of the new moon. Elsewhere the Old Testament confirms some sort of observance on the occasion of the new moon during the monarchy and postexilic periods (1 Sam. 20:5–34; 2 Kings 4:23; Ezra 3:5; Ps. 81:3; Isa. 1:13; 66:23; Ezek. 46:1, 6; Amos 8:5). This was hardly a major feast.

Of the major special seasons or feasts the most frequent was the Sabbath. Every seventh day all work ceased. This commemorated God's creative work and his resting from it. Observance of the Sabbath was also a sign of covenant relationship with the LORD. Through Moses God said, "You shall keep my sabbaths, for this is a sign between me and you throughout your generations, given in order that you may know that I, the LORD, sanctify you" (Exod. 31:13).

The Passover, the Feast of Unleavened Bread (the fourteenth of Nisan, late March or early April), lasted for seven days (Exod. 12:1–13:16; 23:15; 34:18, 25; Lev. 23:4–8; Num. 28:16–25; Deut. 16:1–8). In it Israel remembered her deliverance from Egypt and the entire exodus experience. Although it was one of the three pilgrimage feasts in which all males were required to participate (ideally with a trip to Jerusalem), it was also a family celebration. Leaven was removed from homes during the feast; as a reminder of the night of deliverance, only unleavened bread was consumed. The Passover feast itself consisted of a special meal of prescribed foods and a rehearsal of the events of the exodus, often in the form of questions from children and answers by the adults.

Pentecost (the Feast of Weeks) came fifty days after Passover and signaled the end of the grain harvest and the beginning of the season for offering firstfruits. As another pilgrimage feast it provided opportunity for presenting tithes of grain and firstfruits in the central sanctuary (Exod. 23:16; 34:22; Lev. 23:15–21; Num. 28:26–31; Deut. 16:9–12).

4. For a description of observances in modern Judaism see Theodor H. Gaster, *Festivals of the Jewish Year: A Modern Interpretation and Guide* (New York: Sloane, 1952).

With the first of Tishri (late September to early October) came the blowing of Trumpets to mark the beginning of the civil year. It was celebrated by a cessation of work and a "holy convocation" (Lev. 23:23–25).

The Festival of Trumpets preceded by only ten days the most solemn special occasion, Yom Kippur, the Day of Atonement (literally, "the day of coverings" or "propitiation") (Lev. 16; 23:26–32; 25:9). Of it the LORD said, "On this day atonement shall be made for you, to cleanse you; from all your sins you shall be clean" (Lev. 16:30). Special sacrifices were offered. The day included the ceremony of the scapegoat or the "goat for Azazel": by lot one of two goats was chosen to be sacrificed as a sin offering, and the other to be released in the wilderness (Lev. 16:7–10, 15–22). This was the one day of the year on which the high priest, bearing blood first for himself and then for the people, entered the Holy of Holies.

The third pilgrimage feast was the Feast of Tabernacles or Booths, which lasted a week with additional observances on the eighth day (Exod. 23:16; 34:22; Lev. 23:33–36, 39–43; Num. 29:12–38; Deut. 16:13–16). To commemorate the wilderness wanderings, all Hebrew males lived in tents or booths during the week. Special ceremonies were observed and sacrifices offered. This festival also marked the end of the harvest.

Two other special seasons of the Old Testament, the Sabbatical Year and the Year of Jubilee, had economic as well as religious implications.[5] They made provision for the land to rest, that is, to lie uncultivated for a year while the people lived off the bounty of the previous years' produce and whatever grew without cultivation. Also required were the cancelation of debts, the return of real estate to its original owner, and the freeing of Hebrew slaves. The Sabbatical Year, occurring every seventh year, and the Jubilee, every fiftieth year, prevented the accumulation of too much wealth and the oppression of the poor.

Ritual Cleanliness (Kosher Laws)

Personal cleanliness was important in the ancient Near East. Many groups and religions had their own taboos related to foods, hygienic conditions, and so forth. The Hebrew practices were rooted firmly in the directives of the LORD and were connected with the concept of holiness. Leviticus 10:10 says, "You are to distinguish between the holy and the common, and between the unclean and the clean."

---

5. There is a difference between the two main biblical descriptions of these special seasons, Lev. 25 and Deut. 15; see also Exod. 23:10–11.

God was here instructing the people of Israel about a ceremonial (religious) condition in which a specific person, animal, food, or object was considered unclean.[6] A person contacting defilement was unacceptable and could not associate with one's coreligionists. Such a person and some objects could be cleansed by submitting to a ceremony, usually involving water; sometimes cleansing also required a sacrifice. Frequently an unclean person had to wait for a period before being considered clean. There was no disgrace, sin, or guilt associated with becoming unclean; the difficulty came when someone could not or would not seek cleansing through the prescribed ceremonies.

Noah was told to make a distinction between clean and unclean animals (Gen. 7:2), but it is in the Mosaic law that the requirements are clearly spelled out. Leviticus 11 and Deuteronomy 14:3–20 list unclean land animals, fish, birds, and reptiles which must not be eaten. Other causes of uncleanness include contact with a dead human body, certain reproductive functions, and some diseases. Certain physical deformities excluded persons, especially priests or Levites, from conducting religious rituals.

Vows

A vow was a voluntary oblation assumed by a group or an individual. It could involve a promise to do something, abstain from something, make an offering, present a gift, or the like. Vows were usually made verbally and were considered binding (except in the case of a woman whose vow was nullified by her father or husband [Num. 30:3–15]).

It was no sin to vow or not to vow. One usually did so to express gratitude for God's favor (e.g., Num. 21:1–3) or to express zeal and devotion to God (Ps. 22:25). On fulfilling a vow, the individual was obligated to offer certain sacrifices (Lev. 22:17–25).

Particular importance was placed upon the Nazarite vow, which prescribed strict regulations. During the period the vow was in effect the Nazarite was to abstain from strong drink, from cutting his hair, and from touching a dead body (even of a family member) (Num. 6:1–8). Prescriptions for the termination of a Nazarite vow were particularly precise (Num. 6:13–20).

Prophets and Kings

Later in the Old Testament we meet another group of religious leaders, the prophets. Their task was the opposite of that of the

---

6. In addition to detailed treatments like Lev. 11–15, regulations for ceremonial cleanliness are found throughout the books of Exodus through Deuteronomy.

priest; they were representatives of God before his people. Prophets (whose authorization was simply a call from God) could come from any tribe or section of society. Their primary function was to call God's people back to the LORD when the regular institutions of religion were not functioning properly. Their call to Israel was to return to the LORD and to worship, service, and conduct appropriate for those in covenant relationship with him. Hence, prophets usually appeared during periods of apostasy and spiritual decay.

Although the prophets were primarily concerned with the Hebrews' relation to their God, they frequently spoke to political, social, and moral issues as well. These they considered symptomatic of the more fundamental problem of failure to maintain a proper religious attitude toward the LORD and his law.

Many of the prophets left no written message. The best known of these nonwriting prophets are Elijah and Elisha, who preached to the northern kingdom during the middle part of her history. The writing prophets, men whose messages in part or in whole are found in the Old Testament, first appeared in the latter part of the divided kingdom. Portions of Jeremiah, of Ezekiel, possibly of Isaiah, and all of Obadiah and Daniel are set in the period of exile. Haggai, Zechariah, and Malachi prophesied during the reconstruction period.

Most of the writing prophets addressed themselves to one of the Hebrew kingdoms, Israel (Amos and Hosea) or Judah (Isaiah, Jeremiah, Ezekiel, Daniel, Habakkuk, Zephaniah, Haggai, Zechariah, and Malachi). Micah and maybe Joel (a book virtually impossible to place either historically or geographically) were written to both. Three books were addressed to foreign nations: Obadiah to Edom; Jonah and Nahum to Nineveh, the Assyrian capital.

The final Old Testament institution that we need to mention is the Hebrew monarchy. Although one normally thinks of kings as political, judicial, and military leaders, in the Hebrew community they were religious leaders as well. The Hebrew king was not an absolute monarch. He was the representative of God, the ultimate king. He was to carry out the policies and to enforce the laws of God.

5

A Survey of the History of Intertestamental and New Testament Judaism

From 586 B.C. to the Second Revolt against Rome (A.D. 132–35)

- The Persian Period (539–331 B.C.)
- The Hellenistic Period (331–164)
  + Alexander the Great
  + Ptolemaic Period (320–198) *Macedonian dynasty*
  + Seleucid Period (198–164)
- The Hasmonean (Maccabean) Period (164–63)
  + Judas Maccabeus (164–160)
  + Jonathan (160–143)
  + Simon (143–134)
  + John Hyrcanus (134–104)
  + Aristobulus I (104–103)
  + Alexander Jannaeus (103–76)
  + Salome Alexandra (76–67)
  + Hyrcanus II, Aristobulus II, and Antipater
- The Roman Period (63 B.C.–A.D. 135)
  + A Quick Overview of the Roman Empire
  + Key Local Institutions
    - The High Priesthood
    - The Sanhedrin

73

+ Political Rulers
  - Herod the Great
  - Sons of Herod the Great
  - Roman Procurators (Governors)
  - Herod Agrippa I
  - Roman Procurators
  - Herod Agrippa II
+ The Roman Period from the First through the Second Revolt

A second exodus! So Jeremiah (16:14–15; 23:7–8) described the return and restoration which would follow the Babylonian captivity. The first exodus, under Moses, had marked God's direct intervention into the history of the Hebrews to reveal himself, to deliver them from slavery in Egypt, to provide the necessities of life, and to give protection and guidance through the wilderness. At Mount Sinai God gave directions for life and worship and later established his people in the Promised Land. The prophet looks toward the second exodus similarly, as a time of divine deliverance, supernatural provision, and a new national beginning—complete with a new (or renewed) covenant (Jer. 31:31–34).

Such was doubtless the expectation of the first wave of returnees who accompanied Sheshbazzar the prince from Babylon to Jerusalem in 538 B.C. (Ezra 1:8). The glamour of the first exodus had been quickly dulled by the reality of wars with the Canaanites, the laborious drudgery of building towns, cultivating farms, and other tasks necessary to the routine of daily life. Those who followed Joshua into Canaan found the temptation always strong to stray from the LORD their God, to disobey or ignore his instructions, and to make accommodations with other religious systems. Although the time and external conditions were different, the returnees from Babylon were to face the same sort of experience. Little did they realize that their new beginning would change their lives as much as the first exodus changed the lives of those former slaves who had followed Moses.

We know only little about the captivity. The Hebrews spent the period of captivity in scattered locations. Their experiences were diverse. Many never returned to the land of Israel. In fact, from this time forward the majority of Hebrews, at every point in history, have lived in the Dispersion or Diaspora, that is, outside the boundaries of the land of Israel.

The trauma of the captivity must not be underestimated. We will later examine some of its social, cultural, and religious ramifications. It is enough to note here that, positively, it extracted the people from conditions which promoted physical, cultural, intellectual, and spiritual inbreeding, and it subsequently awoke in them a sense of oneness not possible while the old tribal ties and rivalries remained strong. The exile provided the seedbed from which grew the new order.

The events of intertestamental political history may be neatly summarized under the headings of the four major groups who succeeded one another to power in the land of Israel—the Persians, the Greeks or Hellenists (including Alexander the Great, the Ptolemies of Egypt, and the Seleucids from the north), the Maccabees or Hasmoneans, and finally the Romans. Our information prior to the beginning of Seleucid rule (c. 200 B.C.) is slight. Events from that point moved rapidly, and the number of available sources increases. Accordingly, some modern writers begin their study of the intertestamental period at that point. But, as is always the case in history, the latter stage emerges from the former; the Persian and early Greek periods cannot be ignored.

The Persian Period (539–331 B.C.)

The Persian period was both the last phase of Old Testament history and the first of Intertestamental Judaism. Until recently, little was known about this period. The latter part of the twentieth century, however, has seen new data and a better understanding of the Hebrews under Persian rule.[1]

Almost all we know of the history of the Hebrews under the Persians comes from the writings of the Chronicler—the author(s) of 1 and 2 Chronicles and Ezra-Nehemiah (possibly Ezra himself)—the Book of Esther, some Psalms, and the postexilic prophets of the Old Testament (Haggai, Zechariah, and Malachi).[2] Archaeology, occasional inscriptions, and especially the artifacts and writings from Elephantine in Egypt and the Wadi Daliyeh cave near Jericho provide additional tidbits of information.

1. See A. T. Olmstead, *History of the Persian Empire* (Chicago: University of Chicago Press, 1948); *Cambridge History of Judaism*, vol. 1, ed. W. D. Davies and Louis Finkelstein (New York: Cambridge University Press, 1984); Edwin M. Yamauchi, *Persia and the Bible* (Grand Rapids: Baker, 1990); Jon L. Berquist, *Judaism in Persia's Shadow: A Social and Historical Approach* (Minneapolis: Fortress Press, 1995). The major rulers of the Persian Empire were:

Cyrus, 559–530 B.C.	Darius II Nothus, 424–404
Cambyses, 530–522	Artaxerxes II Mnemon, 404–358
Darius, 522–486	Artaxerxes III Ochus, 358–338
Xerxes (Ahasuerus), 486–465	Darius III Codomannus, 336–330
Artaxerxes I Longimanus, 464–424	Persia conquered by Alexander the Great, 330

2. Note that originally 1 and 2 Chronicles constituted a single book as did Ezra and Nehemiah. Both are a part of the Writings (*Kethubim*), the third division of the Hebrew Old Testament. The close relationship between Chronicles and Ezra-Nehemiah is evident in the virtual identity of 2 Chron. 36:22–23 and Ezra 1:1–3.

The Assyrian and Babylonian policy of deporting captives was not an attempt to amalgamate or assimilate peoples and cultures. Rather, it sought to destroy the sense of oneness and to make rebellion difficult by scattering ethnic and national groups and intermingling them with others. Almost immediately after defeating Babylon in 539, Cyrus (559–530) reversed this policy. The Persians believed that their subjects would be easier to manage if allowed to live in their own lands and practice their own religions (it was assumed that a religion could not be practiced outside the territorial domain of its gods). Thus, dispersed Hebrews who so desired were permitted to return and rebuild Jerusalem and its temple. Judea, comprising only a small area around Jerusalem, seems to have been little more than a temple-state.

The sequence and significance of the events in Ezra-Nehemiah are much debated. The following survey reconstructs the history in accordance with the four phases implied in the biblical documents.

1. Following the decree of Cyrus in 538 (2 Chron. 36:22–23; Ezra 1:2–4), groups of Jews from Babylon returned to Jerusalem (possibly at different times) under the leadership of Sheshbazzar, Zerubbabel, and Jeshua the priest. Sacrifices were reinstated (Ezra 3:1–6), and work begun toward rebuilding the temple (vv. 6–13).

Some local groups (probably inhabitants of the Samaritan region, the area formerly occupied by the northern kingdom) offered their assistance in constructing the temple. They were rebuffed and became bitter adversaries of the returnees and their building projects in Jerusalem. This local opposition, combined with Jewish apathy (Hag. 1:1–11), was successful in temporarily halting work on the temple (Ezra 4).

More than a decade later, the prophets Haggai and Zechariah stirred the people to action, and royal permission for work on the temple was again secured, this time from Darius I (522–486). The project was completed in 516, and the ceremonial worship was reinstated (Ezra 5–6).[3]

2. Ezra, a priestly scribe, arrived in Jerusalem with a commission from Artaxerxes.[4] He instituted organizational, ceremonial, and moral reforms; in particular, he forced the dissolution of mixed marriages (Ezra 7–10). Though Ezra is not mentioned in the first seven chapters of Nehemiah, he reappears in chapter 8. He may

3. It is difficult to calculate the exact duration of the exile. Jer. 25:11–12; 29:10 had predicted seventy years of captivity. From Nebuchadnezzar's first invasion of Palestine and the first deportation (605) until the first return (538) was approximately sixty-seven years. From the destruction of the temple (586) until the dedication of the second temple (516) was seventy years.

4. Probably Artaxerxes I (464–424), although some scholars have suggested Artaxerxes II Mnemon (404–358).

have left Judea (presumably to return to the Persian king in Susa) and come back later.

3. Nehemiah was appointed governor of Judea and evidently arrived in Jerusalem about 445 (Neh. 1–2). In spite of continuing opposition from Sanballat the Horonite, Tobiah the Ammonite, and others (Neh. 2:10, 19; 4–6), Nehemiah rebuilt the walls of the city, reorganized the economy, and carried out cultic reforms.

Of particular importance is Nehemiah 8 (the only context where Ezra and Nehemiah act together [v. 9]). Ezra read the law, and the Levites explained it to the people. This was followed by a renewed attempt to implement the law in the lives of individuals and society.

4. Nehemiah visited Artaxerxes and returned to Jerusalem about 432 (Neh. 13). In his absence foreigners, including the archadversary Tobiah, had been permitted to enter the temple. A grandson of Eliashib the high priest had married the daughter of Tobiah's confederate Sanballat, and Eliashib had even made living space for Tobiah in the sacred precinct. Upon his return Nehemiah excluded the foreigners from the temple, reinstated the tithe as the means of supporting the Levites, enforced sabbatical regulations, and again dealt with the problems of mixed marriages.

Some Jewish traditions associate the Samaritans' building of a temple on Mount Gerizim with Nehemiah's expulsion of Tobiah from the Jerusalem temple. Others ascribe the building of the Samaritan temple to the time of Alexander the Great (see pp. 197–98). Undoubtedly, the controversy between Samaritans and Jews over the place of worship and other matters was aggravated (if not begun) when both Samaria and Judea were parts of the Persian province called Beyond the River.

While the Book of Esther describes events among Jews outside the land of Israel, probably about the time of Ezra, we know little of specific events in the land of Israel during the last century of Persian reign. The Aramaic language, which was known by some Jews at least as early as the time of Hezekiah (2 Kings 18:26), became the common tongue of the region. Essentially, the Hebrews in their homeland constituted a small, insignificant, ignored vassal state on the fringes of the empire. The prophet Malachi suggests that the returnees were lethargic and apathetic in carrying out religious observances and obligations.

In general, the Persian period saw the development of distinctive religious and nationalistic outlooks among the Hebrews. These were to be among the hallmarks of the characteristic forms of Judaism which were arising. They included special emphases and interpretations relating to the temple and the law, and the growth of practices to protect ethnic, national, cultural, and religious identity. The Persian period saw too the growth of new tension with neighbors, especially those just to the north of Judea. The Samaritans would be a source of conflict for centuries to come.

This is the historical period from which come traditions about a political-religious body called the Great Synagogue. It is mentioned in the Mishnah (*Aboth* 1:1–2) and by talmudic writers.[5] Few details about it are available; even its existence is uncertain. Nehemiah 8–10 may describe its origin. According to the tradition, the Great Synagogue was founded by Ezra, who was its first president. It is said to have been composed of either 85 or 120 men who controlled Jewish affairs, especially religious ones, between 450 and 200 B.C. Even if it did not in fact exist in the form suggested by the sources, the traditions about it did have profound effects in subsequent history.

While living under the Persians, at least some Jews came into contact with a religion now known as Zoroastrianism. Scholars disagree as to whether or not Zoroastrianism influenced Intertestamental Judaism, and if so in what ways. It is sufficient for us to note that Zoroastrianism illustrates the influences to which at least some of the Jews were exposed in the greater world of the day.

It was not only the cultures of the East to which the Hebrews were exposed during the Persian period. Archaeologists have found pre-Alexander Greek pottery in the land of Israel. This indicates contact with Greek culture even before the invasion of Alexander the Great. The oldest Greek texts on ostraca come from 277 B.C., the Ptolemaic period.[6] Traces of Greek culture are especially evident in cities along the coastal plain. It was inevitable that some of this influence should find its way into the hill country and to Jerusalem itself.

The Hellenistic Period (331–164)

"Hellenism" is a term used to describe the period and culture stemming from the conquests of Alexander the Great. While the term refers literally to "Greek" civilization, it should be distinguished from the classical Greek civilization which preceded it. Hellenism is the legacy of one of history's most remarkable men.

5. See Louis Finkelstein, "The Men of the Great Synagogue (*circa* 400–170 B.C.E.)," in *Cambridge History of Judaism*, vol. 2, *The Hellenistic Age*, ed. W. D. Davies and Louis Finkelstein (New York: Cambridge University Press, 1989), 229–44.

6. Lester L. Grabbe, *Judaism from Cyrus to Hadrian*, 2 vols. (Minneapolis: Augsburg Fortress, 1991–92), 1:73, 149; Elias Bickerman, *From Ezra to the Last of the Maccabees: Foundations of Post-Biblical Judaism* (New York: Schocken, 1962), 14–16.

Alexander the Great

Alexander's career was brief but his movements rapid. He was really Greek only by training, not birth. His father Philip had galvanized the Macedonian tribes (in the northern part of modern Greece) and become king of Greece by force. Alexander succeeded his father and in 334 set out on his career of conquest. That year he defeated the Persian generals at the river Granicus and liberated the Greek cities along the western coast of Asia Minor (modern Turkey). The following year, at Issus, Alexander met and defeated the Persian king Darius III Codomannus (336–330) and then entered Syria. In 332 he moved down the eastern seaboard of the Mediterranean toward the land of Israel. After difficult battles Tyre and Gaza fell; the Samaritans and inhabitants of Judea voluntarily switched allegiance from Persia to Alexander and apparently were left virtually undisturbed.

During the next year the Macedonian subdued Egypt, where he built the city of Alexandria. He then returned through the land of Israel and Syria, crossed the Euphrates and Tigris rivers, again defeated Darius, and occupied the great Persian capitals of Babylon and Susa.

From 330 through 326 Alexander fought his way through Persia, Afghanistan, and as far as the Indus River in India. When his troops became restless (homesick), Alexander turned back westward and began suffering losses. In 323, while laying plans for future expeditions, he suddenly died of fever in Babylon at the age of thirty-three.

The career of Alexander marked the beginning of a new phase of world history. In his campaigns we meet, perhaps for the first time, the desire for ideological as well as military conquest. Hellenistic influences remain imbedded in Western culture. The Jews, especially those in Judea, because of their ready acceptance of Greek rule and their remote location were initially little affected by Hellenism. This was not long to be. No group could escape encounter with this new world force.

Ptolemaic Period (320–198)

Following the death of Alexander, his generals fought for control of the empire. It was eventually divided into four parts, each governed by one of his four generals (the *Diadochi* [Successors]). As the dust cleared, the land of Israel in 320 found herself annexed to the Ptolemaic Empire of Egypt. Unfortunately, she was strategically located between the Ptolemaic Empire to the south and the Seleucids, who ruled Syria and Persia to the north and east. The major trade routes between the two lay along her coast and within her hills. So the Jews could not escape involvement in the rivalry between the two powers. In the following centuries the land of Israel became a major battlefield in several wars between the Seleucids and the Ptolemies.

Early in the period Ptolemy I (323–285) settled many Jews in Alexandria.[7] They became the nucleus of the Jewish community, which constituted one of the city's five wards and was to play an important part in the history of succeeding centuries (the biblical Apollos came from Alexandria [Acts 18:24–28]). According to the oldest tradition, Ptolemy II Philadelphus (285–246) ordered the Septuagint, the Greek rendering of the Hebrew Scriptures.

We have little information about affairs in Judea while it lay under Egyptian rule. Two families, the Oniads and the Tobiads, struggled for both political influence and control of the priesthood, a conflict which increased in significance in the following period. The Zeno Papyri attest that Hellenistic culture was widespread in the Jewish countryside outside Jerusalem. Some scholars see in such writings as Ecclesiasticus (the Wisdom of Jesus the Son of Sirach) and parts of 1 Enoch evidence of negative Jewish reactions to Hellenism prior to the crisis which led to the Maccabean revolt.

Seleucid Period (198–164)

With the arrival of the second century B.C. came also the passing of political power in the land of Israel from the Ptolemies to the Seleucids (often called Syrians). Both ideological reasons and practical political considerations prompted the Seleucids to forcefully accelerate the insertion of Hellenistic culture into all aspects of Jewish life.

At Alexander's death his general Seleucus had gained control of Babylon.[8] He and his heirs expanded their dominion both eastward as far as India, and westward to include Syria and Asia Minor. Antioch on the Orontes River in northern Syria became their most prominent city—a city destined to become the first major non-

---

7. The kings of Egypt after Alexander the Great were:
   Ptolemy I Lagi (or Soter), 323–285   Ptolemy IV Philopator, 221–203
   Ptolemy II Philadelphus, 285–246   Ptolemy V Epiphanes, 203–181
   Ptolemy III Euergetes, 246–221   Ptolemy VI Philometor, 181–145
                          Ptolemy VII Physcon, 145–117
8. The Seleucid kings were:
   Seleucus I Nicator, 312–280   Antiochus II Theos, 261–247
   Antiochus I Soter, 280–261   Seleucus II Callinicus, 247–226

Jewish center of Christianity (Acts 11:19–26) and the headquarters from where Paul left for his missionary journeys.

In 198 B.C. Antiochus III the Great (223–187) defeated Ptolemy V Epiphanes (203–181) at Paneas (later Caesarea Philippi) near the headwaters of the Jordan River. Some Jews welcomed Seleucid control. Antiochus confirmed Jewish privileges, reduced tribute, and made contributions to the temple. Amicable relations were not to last, however.

When Antiochus IV Epiphanes (175–163) came to the Seleucid throne, the Jews faced a ruler determined to spread Hellenism throughout his empire. He had to deal with two international problems. On his southern border Ptolemy VI Philometor (181–145) sought to regain the land of Israel; for his part Antiochus desired to control Egypt. Furthermore, he was compelled to seek funds with which to pay a staggering settlement imposed by the Romans when they defeated Antiochus III.

The tax burden of the Jews became much heavier. Antiochus plundered the temple for its gold. When the Jews resisted, they suffered military defeat and the slaughter of many of their countrymen. The walls of Jerusalem were razed, and troops friendly to the king were stationed in the newly constructed Acra, a Seleucid military stronghold in the city. Most severe of all was Antiochus's determination to create a loyal ideological-cultural boundary with Egypt by completely hellenizing Jewish society.

As previously noted, Palestinian Judaism had been exposed to Greek culture from the Ptolemaic period and before. Many, especially from the upper class, had embraced the new world spirit. One prominent family, the Tobiads (descendants of Nehemiah's adversary Tobiah), was particularly strong in supporting Hellenism. Equally intent in opposition was the high-priestly family, the Oniads (with roots running through the noteworthy Simon the Just back to Zadok, priest during David's reign [2 Sam. 15:24–29]).[9]

During the latter years of Ptolemaic rule an Oniad priest, Onias II, had failed to fulfil the obligation to present tribute money to the king. The Tobiads took advantage of the situation to gain the

---

Seleucus III Soter Ceraunos, 226–223	Demetrius I Soter, 162–150
Antiochus III the Great, 223–187	Alexander Balas, 150–145
Seleucus IV Philopator, 187–175	Demetrius II Nicator, 145–138
Antiochus IV Epiphanes, 175–163	(Antiochus VI Epiphanes Dionysus, 145–142)
Antiochus V Eupator, 163–162	Antiochus VII Sidetes, 138–129
Demetrius II (again), 129–125	

9. On Simon the Just (died c. 200 B.C.) see Sirach 50; Mishnah *Aboth* 1:2; Josephus *Antiquities* 12.2.5 (43); 12.4.1 (157).

profitable and prestigious right to collect taxes and to present the tribute, a right they retained under the Seleucids. Later, under Antiochus Epiphanes, Onias III lost his priestly office to his brother Jason, who used bribery and the promise (contrary to family policy) to promote Hellenism in Jerusalem. Jason himself was later outbid for the high-priestly office by Menelaus, a Tobiad. Thus, important precedents were set that removed the Zadokite family's exclusive right to the high priesthood and placed bestowal of the office in the hands of the ruler. Consequently, succeeding priests generally supported both the ruling power and Hellenism.

At this point the written sources first introduce a group called the Hasidim (Pious Ones). They seem to have resisted Hellenism. They were appalled at the transfer of the priesthood from Onias to Jason, and horrified when it left the clan of Aaron and particularly the family of Zadok—the legitimacy of the Zadokite priesthood was later a prominent issue for the writers of the Dead Sea Scrolls.

Jason kept his promise to hellenize Jerusalem. He built a gymnasium, established Greek-type social organizations, and installed other Greek customs. Menelaus, his successor, furthered the process and even assisted Antiochus in confiscating the temple wealth.

Interpreting as a rebellion Jason's efforts to retake the high priesthood from Menelaus, Antiochus in 168 attempted to eliminate Jewish religion, which he saw to be at the heart of resistance to Hellenism. Temple ritual was stopped, the Scriptures ordered destroyed, observance of the Sabbath, festival days, food laws, and circumcision prohibited. A new altar, dedicated to Olympian Zeus, was erected in the Jerusalem temple, and a pig offered on it.[10] There was probably a statue of Zeus as well, whose manifestation Antiochus thought himself to be ("Epiphanes" means "God Manifest"). Shrines and altars were erected throughout the land, and the populace was commanded to offer sacrifice as token of their acceptance of the new religion. Noncompliants were punished with torture and death.[11]

10. Josephus *Antiquities* 12.5.4 (253) attests that, contrary to Jewish law, swine were offered in sacrifice; cf. 2 Macc. 6:5.

11. Josephus Antiquities 12.5.4 (256) says that the Jews who refused to obey Antiochus's orders were "maltreated daily, and enduring bitter torments, they met their death. Indeed, they were whipped, their bodies were mutilated, and while still alive and breathing, they were crucified, while their wives and sons whom they had circumcised in spite of the king's wishes were strangled, the children being made to hang from the necks of their crucified parents. And wherever a sacred book or copy of the Law was found, it was destroyed; as for those in whose possession it was found, they too, poor wretches, wretchedly perished."

The Hasmonean (Maccabean) Period (164–63)

Judas Maccabeus (164–160)

Antiochus Epiphanes' assault on Jewish religion resulted in an armed revolt. Resistance and martyrdoms are recorded in 1 and 2 Maccabees and other writings. At Modein, in the Judean foothills, an aged priest, Mattathias (from the family of Hasmon), killed a Seleucid officer and an apostatizing Jew and sounded the cry, "Let every one who is zealous for the law and supports the covenant come out with me!" (1 Macc. 2:27). He and his supporters then withdrew to the Judean desert.

Mattathias died shortly after the beginning of the revolt, but his five sons, of whom Judas Maccabeus was the leader, carried on a guerrilla struggle.[12] They were joined by many, including some of the Hasidim, who were loyal to the traditional religion and way of life. Judas displayed extraordinary skills as a leader, military tactician, and diplomat. The unstable international situation kept the Seleucids from devoting their full energies to crushing the Jewish revolt. Eventually they were forced to withdraw to regroup their forces. In 164, three years after the altar to Zeus had been set up, the temple was cleansed, the daily burnt offering and other religious ceremonies resumed. That rededication of the temple is still commemorated each December as Hanukkah, the Feast of Lights. In 163, the Seleucids offered terms to Judas and his followers, including removal of the ban on Jewish worship.

The Maccabees had won their struggle for religious liberty, but the Seleucids remained their overlords, Hellenism was still a threat, Menelaus continued as high priest, and Jews outside Jerusalem and Judea lived in constant danger of attack. Judas and his followers, except some of the Hasidim who were content with gaining religious freedom, now turned their sights toward political independence. Battle followed battle, periods of peace and compromise came and went. Judas's brother Eleazer was killed in battle just south of Jerusalem less than a year after the temple had been secured.

12. The Hasmonean (or Maccabean) rulers were:

Judas Maccabeus, 164–160	Alexander Jannaeus, 103–76
Jonathan, 160–143	Salome Alexandra, 76–67
Simon, 143–134	Aristobulus II, 67–63
John Hyrcanus, 134–104	Hyrcanus II, 63–40
Aristobulus I, 104–103	Antigonus Mattathias, 40–37

The Seleucids eventually replaced Menelaus with Alcimus, a descendant of Aaron but not of the Zadok-Oniad family. About this time Onias IV fled to Egypt and obtained permission from Ptolemy VI Philometor (181–145) to build a temple on Egyptian soil. For the next 230 years, until it was closed by the Romans in A.D. 73, a Jewish temple at Leontopolis, which was under the leadership of Zadokite priests, duplicated the Jerusalem ritual. Archaeological remains at Araq el-Emir in Transjordan, unearthed in the early 1960s, reveal what some have thought to be the remains of another Jewish temple, which a member of the Tobiad family may have begun about this same time.[13]

Jonathan (160–143)

In 160 Judas was killed in battle at the strategic Beth-horon pass and was succeeded by his brother Jonathan, a man of prudence and great skills. Early in Jonathan's tenure, their brother John was killed by robbers on the other side of the Jordan. Although the Seleucids still sought to impose their will on the Jews, their kingdom was torn by internal strife. Jonathan possessed diplomatic as well as military skills. He exploited the internal Seleucid situation to great advantage, succeeding in expanding Jewish-held territory and acquiring virtual independence. Although the Hasmonean family were ordinary priests rather than from the high-priestly line of Zadok, in 152 Jonathan became high priest; the position was to remain in the family until Roman occupation. Jonathan was eventually murdered by the Seleucids in 143.

Josephus's description of the reign of Jonathan makes mention of three groups that were to play important roles in later days, the Pharisees, Sadducees, and Essenes.[14] Although he has not mentioned them before, Josephus seems to imply that they were already well established by that time.

Simon (143–134)

On Jonathan's death, leadership immediately went to Simon, the second and only surviving son of Mattathias. The Seleucid king, Demetrius II Nicator, was faced with both the strength of Simon's military forces and the need for Simon's help in his struggle against other claimants to the Seleucid throne. Consequently, he freed the Jews from payment of tribute. This was virtually the charter of independence for which the Jews had so long sought.

---

13. Some scholars hold that this structure was probably a fortress surrounded by a moat; see Grabbe, *Judaism*, 1:188, 193.

14. Josephus *Antiquities* 13.5.9 (171–73).

"The yoke of the Gentiles was removed from Israel" (1 Macc. 13:41). The enemy was expelled from their long-term stronghold in Jerusalem, the hated Acra. Simon and his followers entered Jerusalem "with praise and palm branches, and with harps and cymbals and stringed instruments, and with hymns and songs, because a great enemy had been crushed and removed from Israel" (1 Macc. 13:51).[15]

Both political and religious leadership were given to Simon and his descendants: "The Jews and their priests have resolved that Simon should be their leader and high priest forever, until a trustworthy prophet should arise, and that he should be governor over them and that he should take charge of the sanctuary . . . and that he should be obeyed by all" (1 Macc. 14:41–43; see also 13:42). From time to time the Seleucids still sought to involve themselves in Jewish affairs. Nevertheless, for all practical purposes they no longer posed a real threat. A renewal of treaties with Sparta and Rome further strengthened the position of the Jews. Like his brothers, Simon met a violent end (134), but his assassin was a member of his own family, Ptolemy son of Abubus.

John Hyrcanus (134–104)

Ptolemy had intended to seize leadership for himself, but Simon's son John Hyrcanus, having escaped Ptolemy's attempt to murder him as well, was acclaimed his father's successor. During the first five or six years of Hyrcanus's rule the Seleucids once again invaded and assumed temporary control of the land of Israel, but by the seventh year the Jews were once again independent.

Hyrcanus then set out on a policy of conquest, using mercenaries as well as Jewish soldiers. He added areas east of the Jordan, Idumea to the south, and the Samaritan lands as far as Scythopolis (Beth-shan) to the north. The Idumeans were forced to accept circumcision and to live under the Jewish law. Hyrcanus destroyed the Samaritan temple on Mount Gerizim circa 108 and, later, the city of Samaria.

---

15. Triumphal processions were common in the ancient world. Simon's may reflect Hellenistic influence, but could also have Hebrew roots (1 Chron. 13:5–8; Ps. 24:7–10). One wonders whether this display may have been influenced by the prophecy of Zech. 9:9: "Rejoice greatly, O daughter Zion! Shout aloud, O daughter Jerusalem! Lo, your king comes to you; triumphant and victorious is he, humble and riding on a donkey, on a colt, the foal of a donkey." Of course, Simon certainly employed no means of transportation as humble as a donkey.

The parallels between Simon's triumphal entry and that of Jesus (Matt. 21:1–11; Mark 11:1–11; Luke 19:28–40; John 12:12–19), more than a century and a half later, are striking. The messianic aura of Jesus' entry is heightened when considered alongside this episode in Simon's career, and especially alongside the Zechariah passage.

Josephus includes an account of John Hyrcanus's changing his allegiance from the Pharisees to the Sadducees.[16] At first Hyrcanus favored the Pharisees, but turned from them to the Sadducees when one of the Pharisees, Eleazer, urged him to give up the high priesthood and be content with political and military power. The reason given was the (probably unfounded) rumor that his mother had been a captive and hence was defiled; it is also possible that theological objections to the union of the offices of ruler and priest in a single individual may have been involved. From this time onward, with the sole exception of Salome Alexandra, the Pharisees were enemies of the Hasmonean dynasty; there grew a strong relationship between the Hasmoneans and the Sadducees.

It is possible, though far from certain, that this period saw the beginning of the Qumran community (writers of the Dead Sea Scrolls), a group whose withdrawal from society was stimulated by their assessment of social, political, and religious evils in the land. They also rejected the leadership of the then reigning priestly family.

Hyrcanus did not claim the title of king, but acted as if he occupied that position. His primary attention was upon external concerns, and his reign was marked by increasing secularization (although rabbinic sources describe liturgical activities and changes in which he was involved). The geographical boundaries of Jewish territory and the prestige and strength of the state were virtually as great as the Hebrews had enjoyed at any time since the division of the kingdom following Solomon. Most later writings (some of the Dead Sea Scrolls being a possible exception) render a favorable evaluation of his reign.

Aristobulus I (104–103)

Aristobulus, who was to reign but a year, consolidated his power at the cost of imprisoning his closest relatives, including his mother, whom he allowed to die of starvation. He continued the program of territorial expansion begun by his father and brought Iturea, in the Lebanese foothills, and Galilee (the area which was to be the scene of most of the life and activity of Jesus) under Jewish control.

Unlike his predecessors, Aristobulus openly claimed the title of king. Josephus records that this great-grandson of Mattathias also bore another title, *Philhellene* (Lover of things Greek).[17]

16. Josephus *Antiquities* 13.10.5–6 (288–98).
17. Ibid., 13.11.3 (318).

Alexander Jannaeus (103–76)

Aristobulus's widow, Salome Alexandra, released his brothers from prison and offered herself in marriage to one of them, Alexander Jannaeus. This enabled him to become both king and high priest. His devotion to Hellenism is evident in his use of two names, one Greek (Alexander) and the other Hebrew (Jannaeus = Yannai = Jonathan), and in his inscribing his coins in the two languages.

Jannaeus was involved in either foreign or domestic military conflict during most of his career (usually with the aid of Greek mercenary troops). Early on he suffered defeat at the hands of the Egyptians and Nabateans. Jannaeus also faced mounting opposition from sectarian groups and other Jews concerned with religious affairs. At one point, while officiating in the temple, he was pelted with fruit by worshipers who disapproved of the way he carried out a part of the ritual for the Feast of Tabernacles. Relations with the Pharisees deteriorated to the point that some of their number called in the Seleucid king Demetrius III Eukairos against him. However, the sight of a Jewish king fleeing from the Seleucids caused even his enemies to turn to his aid, and the Seleucids were expelled. This event marked the turning point in Jannaeus's fortunes. He retaliated against the Pharisees by crucifying eight hundred of them in Jerusalem and having their wives and children killed before their eyes at the same time.[18] This and other acts of atrocity caused eight thousand of his opponents to flee the country. Thereafter his military campaigns were largely successful. He extended the boundaries of Jewish-held territory beyond those reached under Hyrcanus; of special note were his acquisitions on the other side of the Jordan and along the coastal plain from Egypt to Mount Carmel (where only the city of Ashkelon remained outside his control).

Alexander Jannaeus modeled neither the ideals of the priestly Maccabean movement nor the higher values of Hellenistic culture. He was more of a hellenized Asian despot. His personal life was characterized by debauchery of the worst kinds. His death left the country badly divided; the kingdom passed to Salome Alexandra, the widow of both Jannaeus and his predecessor Aristobulus.

18. Ibid., 13.14.2 (380). Reference to this event is probably intended in the Nahum Commentary of the Dead Sea Scrolls (4QpNah), which speaks of "the furious young lion [who executes revenge] on 'the seekers after smooth things' [Pharisees?] and hangs men alive, [a thing never done] formerly in Israel." For more information on crucifixion see Appendix D, pp. 364–65.

Salome Alexandra (76–67)

Josephus says that on his deathbed Jannaeus advised Salome to conceal his death until she had seized the fortresses and then, upon returning to Jerusalem, to share power with the Pharisees.[19] Whether or not this is true, the Pharisees were virtually in complete control during her reign. Josephus says, "If she ruled the nation, the Pharisees ruled her."[20] Later rabbinic writings picture her reign as a golden age.

Alexandra's elder son, Hyrcanus II, a quiet and peaceful man, became high priest. His brother, Aristobulus II, a more dominant personality and ambitious for power, became leader of the military forces.

In foreign affairs there was little of significance during Alexandra's reign. Internally, the old Sadducean-aristocracy coalition was not completely broken and had the advantage of being closely allied with Aristobulus. In 67 the Pharisees, with the queen's permission, sought to move against their enemies. For their part Aristobulus and his associates were poised not only to defend themselves but also to seize power. At that point Alexandra died and civil war was inevitable.

Hyrcanus II, Aristobulus II, and Antipater

Aristobulus's forces immediately defeated Hyrcanus. In return for permission to retire peacefully to his estate, Hyrcanus yielded the high priesthood as well as civil authority to his brother. The days of the Maccabean/Hasmonean rulers were all but over. Although priests, they had proved to be as corrupt as any pagan overlord. They were not able to weld the country into a strong unit.

After Aristobulus had become king, Antipater, whose father (also named Antipater) had been appointed governor of the area south of Judea (Idumea) by Alexander Jannaeus, set himself to gain power through the weak Hyrcanus. Eventually he persuaded Hyrcanus to seek support from the Nabatean king Aretas. With this aid Hyrcanus defeated Aristobulus, who in 65 fled to the temple area and fortified himself against a siege by his brother and the Nabateans.

To the north the Roman general Pompey had subdued Asia Minor and Syria. Pompey's lieutenant Scaurus was charged with settling the affairs in the former Seleucid possessions. Word of the strife in Jerusalem took him to that city, where both parties offered money in exchange for Roman support. Aristobulus's party was successful. The Nabateans were ordered to raise their siege and, as

19. Josephus *Antiquities* 13.15.5 (399–404).
20. Josephus *Jewish War* 1.5.2 (112).

they sought to return home, suffered a humiliating defeat by Aristobulus and his army. Pompey eventually became suspicious of Aristobulus's later activities and turned against him. After another siege and battle centered in the temple area, on a Sabbath day in 63 the temple fortress was breached, Aristobulus's forces were defeated, and Jerusalem was claimed by the Romans. As the battle raged, priests calmly went about their regular acts of sacrifice and worship; many died at their posts.

Probably made curious by rumors within the Gentile world, Pompey forcibly entered the Holy of Holies in the temple. To him the act was nothing more than exercising the privilege of a conqueror. To his surprise, he found it empty. To the Jews his action represented the ultimate sacrilege. They did not soon forget, and the incident initiated the atmosphere of mistrust, misunderstanding, and hostility that was to mark future Jewish-Roman relations.

The Roman Period (63 B.C.–A.D. 135)

The beginning of Roman rule in the land of Israel saw a continuation of the internal conflicts begun in the Maccabean period. In fact, the same characters who had brought that era to its end were still involved—Aristobulus II, Hyrcanus II, who was reappointed high priest, and the Idumean Antipater, who, having ingratiated himself with the Romans, held the power. In addition to the Romans, other new faces emerged, including Antipater's sons, Joseph, Phasael, and Herod, and Aristobulus's son Antigonus.

The events and intrigues were numerous and complex. Antigonus, the last Maccabean ruler, was locked in a bitter struggle for control with Herod and his brother Phasael until the invasion of the Parthians in 40 B.C. In response to promises by Antigonus, the Parthians captured Phasael and Hyrcanus II. They then enthroned Antigonus as king and high priest of the Jews. Herod, however, gained Roman assistance and was given authority in the land of Israel. A return of the Parthians in 38 briefly restored the rule to Antigonus. By 37 Herod emerged the victor, theoretically an independent monarch, but in fact a puppet of Rome. It is he whom history has labeled King Herod (Matt. 2:1) and Herod the Great. The execution of Antigonus ended the Hasmonean dynasty.

A Quick Overview of the Roman Empire

The Roman Empire was the world of the New Testament. Until 27 B.C. Rome was technically a republic governed by two

consuls and the senate. However, only the patricians (the upper class) had full legal rights to participate politically. The
equestrians (business class) and plebeians (lower-class citizens) had only limited rights; foreigners, freedmen, and slaves
had virtually none. The aspirations of these underprivileged
classes led to revolution and movement toward more centralized government (thus to break the power of the ruling families). Toward this end, in 49 Julius Caesar established himself
as sole ruler, but he was assassinated (44) by supporters of pa-
trician republicanism. The defeat of the conspirators (Brutus
and Cassius) led to the ascendancy of Octavian (great-nephew
and adopted son of Caesar). In 27 Octavian took the name Augustus (see Luke 2:1) and ruled as emperor. Throughout the
New Testament period, although the titles and governmental
forms of the republic were maintained, Rome was actually an
absolute monarchy.

Augustus divided the empire into thirty-two provinces. The
older, more stable ones were designated as senatorial provinces.
They were governed by a proconsul, who was answerable to the
senate and had no military authority. Imperial provinces were usually more difficult to govern and often contained revolutionary elements. Their rulers held both civil and military authority and were
answerable directly to the emperor. Legates were placed over the
larger imperial provinces, prefects over the smaller. Procurators
(governors) were civil servants who administered a specific area
under the supervision of a proconsul or legate. There were also a
number of semi-independent kingdoms presided over by native rulers called kings; they held office at the pleasure of Rome. Other
petty subject princes were called tetrarchs or ethnarchs (a slightly
higher title). Additional types of government officials and titles
were found in specific locations.

The affairs of each province were strictly regulated by Roman
law. However, the provisions of Roman law were often interpreted
quite differently by individual rulers. Anyone who had the status
of Roman citizen, whether through birth, particular grant, or pur-
chase, enjoyed special rights and privileges not available to others.[21] The whole system, unfortunately, was open to abuses and

21. The exact rights of Roman citizens are not fully known. It seems that at least they (1)
held preferential positions in the army, (2) may have been taxed at lower rates than were noncitizens, (3) could not, if arrested, be beaten or otherwise tortured, (4) had the right to appeal
legal cases to the imperial court, and (5) could not be executed by crucifixion, except in the case
of desertion from the army. See A. N. Sherwin-White, *The Roman Citizenship*, 2d ed. (New
York: Oxford University Press, 1973), and *Roman Society and Roman Law in the New Testament*
(Oxford: Clarendon, 1963), 144–85.

injustice, as illustrated by the popular distrust of publicans, who were charged with collecting taxes for Rome.[22]

Three Roman emperors are mentioned in the New Testament: Augustus (27 B.C.–A.D. 14), who ruled when Jesus was born (Luke 2:1); Tiberius (14–37), who ruled when John the Baptist and Jesus began their ministries (Luke 3:1); and Claudius (41–54)—Acts 11:28 mentions a worldwide famine during the reign of Claudius, and Acts 18:2 notes that Aquila and Priscilla had left Rome because of an edict of Claudius expelling Jews from that city.

There were other emperors, not mentioned in the New Testament, during whose reigns events occurred which profoundly affected the Jews. Caligula (37–41) ordered his statue placed in the temple in Jerusalem. The whole of Jewry was thrown into consternation. Attempts by Jewish groups, including the one led by Philo, to persuade the emperor to rescind his order proved futile. Disaster was averted by the delaying tactics of Petronius, the legate of Syria, and the death of the emperor. During the reign of Nero (54–68), James the brother of Jesus was martyred in Jerusalem by Jewish authorities (62). Nero unleashed the first official imperial persecution of Christians in Rome (64–66); this occasioned the death of Peter and probably of Paul as well.

Jewish revolt broke out during the final years of Nero's emperorship and was put down under Vespasian (69–79). Domitian (81–96) persecuted Jews and possibly Christians as well, as did Trajan (98–117). The second Jewish revolt (132–35) broke out under Hadrian (117–38).

The stability of the empire and the maintenance of the famous *pax Romana* (Roman peace) depended upon the army. Officers were named from the roll of citizens; other soldiers were freedmen and sometimes mercenaries. The New Testament mentions several centurions, officers who commanded a hundred foot soldiers. In Roman military organization there were six centurions in a cohort and ten cohorts in a legion.

Key Local Institutions

Whenever possible, the Romans ruled through local channels. With two exceptions, when procurators were appointed, this policy was followed in the land of Israel during the intertestamental period.

---

22. Publicans often subdivided their territory, giving authority to other publicans who worked under them. A chief publican was required to raise a specified amount for Rome; each publican under him was required to raise his share. Each tax collector along the way collected added amounts, which were his profit. Rome seems to have had no regulations for publicans except that they meet their prescribed quota. Obviously, this system was open to much suspicion and abuse. Since the publicans were usually local citizens (non-Romans), they were often regarded as traitors; this was especially true in the land of Israel.

This the Romans did primarily through the family of Antipater, and especially through his son Herod the Great and his heirs, who became the Romans' loyal surrogates. In addition the Romans utilized the Jewish institutions of the high priesthood and the Sanhedrin.

The High Priesthood

As we have seen, the politicizing of the high priesthood began during the Ptolemaic period with the conflict between the Oniads and Tobiads. Later the Maccabean rulers obtained the office for themselves. Thus the Old Testament ordinance that the office was to reside within a single family was set aside. The brothers Aristobulus II and Hyrcanus II acrimoniously exchanged the high priesthood between themselves.

Herod the Great and other Roman rulers following him saw the high-priestly office as far too important to leave it to the chance of generational succession. They set aside the provision that a high priest serve for life. Instead, they installed and deposed chief priests at their pleasure. Josephus lists twenty-eight different persons who held the office between 37 B.C. and the suppression of the revolt in A.D. 70. These, it seems, essentially came from only a few aristocratic families.

The most influential high-priestly family was that of Annas, son of Seth; Annas held the office from A.D. 6 to 15.[23] A total of eight members of his family filled the office. The best known is the son-in-law of Annas, Joseph Caiaphas (18–36), who presided at the trial of Jesus.[24] The frequent turnover of high priests explains why Annas, who was not then the high priest, participated in the trials of Jesus (John 18:13, 24) and of Peter and John (Acts 4:6), and why Caiaphas is described as "high priest that year" (John 11:51).

When Paul stood before the Sanhedrin, the high priest was Ananias, son of Nebedaeus (Acts 23:2; 24:1). Well known for his oppressive political activities, he held the office from 47 to 58. At one point during his reign he was charged with stirring up disorders in Judea and was sent to Rome in chains.[25] He was acquitted, however, and his power and influence increased.[26] Even after

23. Luke 3:2 speaks of "the high priesthood of Annas and Caiaphas" at the beginning of the ministries of John the Baptist and Jesus. Annas remained active and his influence extended far beyond the nine years of his rule as high priest. Even after he left office he was frequently the power behind the throne.

24. The probable tomb of Joseph Caiaphas has been discovered in Jerusalem; see Zvi Greenhut, "Burial Cave of the Caiaphas Family," *Biblical Archaeology Review* 18.5 (Sept.-Oct. 1992): 29–31; John McRay, "High Priest Caiaphas' Tomb Found South of Jerusalem," *Messianic Times* 3.2 (Fall 1992): 10.

25. Josephus *Jewish War* 2.12.6 (243); *Antiquities* 20.6.2 (131).

26. Josephus *Antiquities* 20.9.4 (213).

he left office, he continued to wield considerable influence. At the outset of the Jewish revolt against the Romans, the house of Ananias was burned;[27] the next month he was killed.[28]

The final high priest was Phinehas, son of Samuel (68–70). He was installed by the people during the revolt after they had assassinated his predecessor, Mattathias, son of Theophilus and grandson of Annas (65–68).

The Sanhedrin

The Sanhedrin was the supreme Jewish council, the body which governed the Jews after the monarchy had been destroyed. In the latter part of the intertestamental period its prominence and authority rose and waned. Technically, a description of the Sanhedrin should not be subsumed under the larger topic of Roman rule in the land of Israel, for it predated that period. Nevertheless, New Testament readers need to be particularly aware of the form in which it existed during the early part of Roman control. Sources of information about the Sanhedrin are numerous but not always consistent.[29] The New Testament and sometimes Josephus, for example, present a much more negative view than do most of the others.

A number of Greek terms are used to refer to the primary institution of postexilic Jewish government.[30] In sources which come from the Persian and Seleucid periods the body is customarily called the *gerousia*. From the Maccabean period onward its name is usually Sanhedrin. Antecedents of the first-century Sanhedrin can be traced back to the earliest days of Israel's nationhood. While in the wilderness during the exodus, seventy or seventy-two elders were appointed to assist Moses (Num. 11:10–17). In the Old Testament through the captivity, however, there are only a few vague references to any body similar to the Sanhedrin. From the return onward the institution becomes increasingly prominent.

After the exile, in the community of those who returned to the land of Israel, the elders of the Jews seem to have gained more and more influence in all areas of Jewish life (see, e.g., Ezra 5:5, 9; 6:7–8, 14; 10:8, 14). The rulers of the Hasmonean dynasty enlisted the support of experts in the interpretation of the law, including priests. Gatherings of these experts frequently became

27. Josephus *Jewish War* 2.17.4 (426); see also *Antiquities* 20.9.3 (208–10).

28. Josephus *Jewish War* 2.17.9 (441–42).

29. The primary sources are the apocryphal literature (especially Judith, 1, 2, and 3 Maccabees), Josephus, early rabbinic writings, and the New Testament.

30. In addition to *synedrion* (the high council, Sanhedrin), the Greek terms include *gerousia* (assembly), *boulē* (council), *presbyterion* (gathering of the elders, the synod), and *to koinon tōn Ierosolymitōn* (the common council of Jerusalem), a title found only in Josephus. Other names include the great court in the chamber of hewn stone, the court of one-and-seventy (judges), the elders of the court, elders and sages, and occasionally the Great Sanhedrin.

scenes of conflict between Pharisees and Sadducees. During the Roman period the power and significance of the Sanhedrin fluctuated greatly. Herod the Great began his reign by executing at least the more prominent members of the body.[31] By eliminating the old nobility and intimidating the surviving and newly appointed members, he curtailed the Sanhedrin's authority to its lowest point.

The Sanhedrin is said to have consisted of seventy or seventy-one members (the number probably depends on whether or not the presiding officer was counted). The membership of the Sanhedrin was drawn primarily from the priestly nobility; the Sadducees were in the majority or most influential. The high priest was the president and convener.[32] Later, as Pharisees became increasingly popular among the people, they too were included in the number of the council. The presence of the Pharisees is evidenced by the New Testament references to Nicodemus (John 3:1) and Gamaliel (Acts 5:34; cf. 22:3) as members of the Sanhedrin, and by the conflict recorded in Acts 23:6–10. Josephus says that by the first century, the Sadducees, who controlled the Sanhedrin, had to conform to the formulae of the Pharisees or else "the people would not tolerate them."[33] Even later, scribes and elders became a part of the Sanhedrin. The membership of Joseph of Arimathea shows that the body was not restricted to men from Jerusalem (Luke 23:50). We do not know how members were selected; the lack of a democratic process of popular election is one of the major differences between the Jewish council and those of Hellenistic cities. It is assumed that new members were inducted or ordained by the laying on of hands.[34]

There were, of course, similar councils in other cities, towns, and regions. The exact relation between them and the Great Sanhedrin of Jerusalem is not always clear. Certainly in matters of interpretation of religious law the Jerusalem body had the final say.

As already stated, the function and authority of the Sanhedrin varied, depending upon the will and strength of the sitting political

31. Josephus *Antiquities* 14.9.4 (175) says that Herod executed "all" of the members of the body; *Antiquities* 15.1.2 (6) says he executed forty-five of Antigonus's supporters.

32. Emil Schürer, *The History of the Jewish People in the Age of Jesus Christ,* ed. Geza Vermes et al., 3 vols. (Edinburgh: T. and T. Clark, 1973–87), 2:215, regards as completely unfounded the claims of later rabbinic writings that the heads of the Pharisaic schools were the presidents of the Sanhedrin.

33. Josephus *Antiquities* 18.1.4 (17). This claim is also made in rabbinic writings; see Mishnah *Yoma* 1:5; *Sukkah* 4:9.

34. This practice is in keeping with the pattern of Moses' passing his leadership on to Joshua (Num. 27:18–23; Deut. 34:9); see also Schürer, *History*, 2:211 (esp. n. 41).

ruler. In general, its responsibilities were both religious and civil. Of course it supervised the established national religion, had oversight of the temple, and carried out such religious duties as fixing the date of the new moon and inserting an extra month into the lunar year. It had legislative duties as well as executive-administrative and judiciary; it also was an academic institution. As a law-enforcement body it had its own police force and served as a court of law. There is continuing debate as to its authority to carry out capital punishment. John 18:31 is the lone ancient source to indicate clearly that it did not have such authority. Other evidence indicates that the Sanhedrin was not completely limited in capital cases.[35]

After the destruction of Jerusalem in 70, Jamnia and a few other cities became centers of rabbinic discussions and study. They served as focal points as Judaism reorganized itself. They had virtually no political influence, however.

Political Rulers

Herod the Great

Herod the Great, who was king of all the land of Israel from 37 to 4 B.C., was a man of powerful body and by nature wild, passionate, harsh, arrogant, calculating, and ruthless.[36] The suspicion, scheming, and cruelty implied in Matthew's account of his dealing with the Magi and of the slaughter of the babies of Bethlehem are in complete harmony with what is known of his character from other sources.

As an Idumean, Herod's Jewishness was suspect in the eyes of many. He was sensitive to Jewish concerns and usually went out of his way not to offend. But at heart he was thoroughly Hellenistic, and probably completely pagan, in outlook—a fact reflected in his style of life, in his activities, and even in the architecture of the crowning achievement of his building projects, the reconstructed Jerusalem temple.

It is customary to divide Herod's rule into three parts: the periods of (1) consolidation of power (37–25), (2) prosperity (25–13), and (3) domestic strife (13–4). On the whole he was an able ruler, and his achievements were considerable. In particular, Herod's

---

35. Schürer, *History*, 2:221–22, notes the Sanhedrin seems to have been competent to try and execute various capital cases: (1) the entry of anyone into the Holy of Holies, even the high priest on any occasion other than the Day of Atonement; (2) the entry of a Gentile, even a Roman citizen, into the inner court of the temple; (3) Stephen; (4) Paul; (5) James the brother of Jesus; and (6) a priest's daughter convicted of adultery.

36. On the Herodian family see Harold W. Hoehner, *Herod Antipas* (Grand Rapids: Zondervan, 1980); Stewart Perowne, *The Life and Times of Herod the Great* (Nashville: Abingdon, 1956); idem, *The Later Herods* (Nashville: Abingdon, 1958).

friendship and cooperation with Rome were of real value to the Jews of the land of Israel. Politically he brought stability and a reasonable amount of prosperity to the region.

Herod's building projects were vast; the remnants of some remain to this day. They included whole cities such as Samaria (renamed Sebaste) and Caesarea Maritima with its magnificent artificial harbor. Many cities were beautified and received pagan temples, sport facilities, and other important buildings. He virtually rebuilt Jerusalem with all the features expected in a Hellenistic city. His own palace was magnificent and well fortified. The Antonia, the military citadel he built at the northwest corner of the temple mount, is mentioned in connection with Paul's arrest (Acts 21:31–40), and was possibly the location of part of the trial and torture of Jesus. A series of fortress palaces provided places of luxurious refuge for Herod and his family—best known are Herodium near Bethlehem, and Machaerus and Masada on the eastern and western sides of the Dead Sea respectively.

Herod's work on the temple of Jerusalem deserves special note. The structure erected by Zerubbabel was old, had been damaged in wars, and was too small for the crowds that flocked to the city during pilgrimage feasts. It was not in keeping with the new character Herod envisioned for the city. A thousand Levites were trained and dedicated to the task of rebuilding, which was begun about 20 or 19 B.C. The platform on the temple mount was expanded. The major structure was completed in about a year and a half; additional work continued until almost A.D. 70, when it was destroyed by the Romans.[37] Its size and magnificence were renowned throughout the ancient world.

Herod's enemies were many. He was never fully accepted by his Jewish subjects. The uncertainties of Roman politics required constant vigilance and adaptation. To the south Cleopatra, the Egyptian queen and lover of several Romans of power and influence, schemed to have Herod's kingdom added to her own. Herod's personal and family life were tragic, almost beyond imagination. He exiled, imprisoned, or executed children, wives, other relations, and friends whom, often with good reason, he suspected of plotting against him.[38] When death finally found him in his beloved palace in Jericho (4 B.C.), Herod the Great was a diseased, crazed, broken, pathetic figure.

37. Hence the statement in John 2:20 that the temple had been under construction for forty-six years.

38. Augustus, mindful of the Jewish aversion to eating pork, once said it was safer to be Herod's pig than his son. This is a play on two similar-sounding Greek words, *hys* (pig) and *huios* (son).

Sons of Herod the Great

Herod's will divided his kingdom among three of his sons. When his wishes were confirmed by the Romans, Archelaus was designated ethnarch of Samaria and Judea.[39] Because of his incompetence and the severity of his rule Jewish and Samaritan officials appealed to Caesar for relief. Archelaus was deposed in A.D. 6 and the area placed under procurators appointed by the emperor.

Philip received lands northeast of the Sea of Galilee and the title of tetrarch (Luke 3:1). He was a just and conscientious ruler. After his death in A.D. 34 his territory was briefly added to the province of Syria and then given to Herod Agrippa I, grandson of Herod the Great.

Herod Antipas, Herod the tetrarch, as he is called in the New Testament, received Galilee in the north and Perea, the region east of the Jordan River. Like his father he carried on ambitious building projects, including the cities of Sepphoris and Tiberias.

While visiting his half brother Herod Philip (not the tetrarch), Antipas became infatuated with Herod Philip's wife Herodias, daughter of another half brother, Aristobulus, and mother of Herod Philip's daughter Salome (Mark 6:22–28). Although marriage to the wife of a living brother was contrary to levirate law (Lev. 18:16; 20:21), Antipas married her. In order to do so he divorced the daughter of Aretas IV, the Nabatean king (who later, in retaliation, inflicted a military defeat upon Antipas). It was the denunciation of this union (Matt. 14:4; Mark 6:18; Luke 3:19) that brought about the imprisonment of John the Baptist in the Herodian fortress Machaerus and eventually his death.[40]

Herod Antipas seems to have possessed the less desirable of his father's qualities but not his ability to rule. It is not without cause that, upon hearing of the tetrarch's plot against him, Jesus referred to Antipas as "that fox" (Luke 13:32). We know also that Antipas had earlier desired to see Jesus (Luke 9:7–9). A meeting between the two did in fact take place during Jesus' trial (Luke 23:7–12).

When Caligula became emperor (37), he gave to his friend Agrippa, Herodias's brother, both the territory that had until three years earlier been ruled by Philip the tetrarch and the title of king. Herodias persuaded Antipas to request the same title from the emperor. However, Agrippa proceeded to bring charges against Antipas of plotting insurrection, which resulted in his being exiled to Gaul (modern France) in 39; he was accompanied by Herodias.

39. Matt. 2:22; Josephus *Antiquities* 17.9.3–7 (213–49); 17.11.1–5 (299–323).
40. Josephus *Antiquities* 18.5.2 (116–19).

Figure 4
Herod the Great and His Descendants

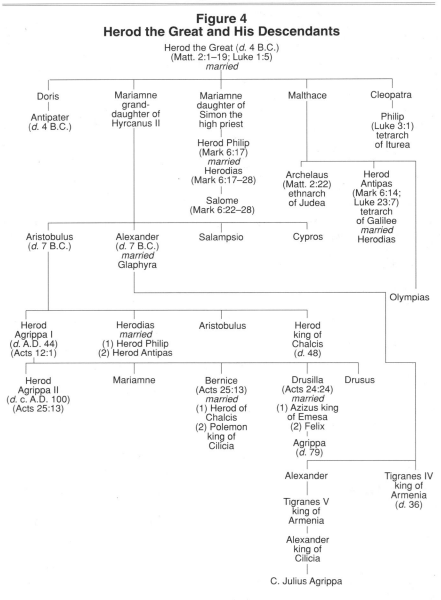

Roman Procurators (Governors)

After Archelaus was deposed, Roman civil servants were appointed to rule over Judea and later the area controlled by Philip the tetrarch. The best known of these governors is Pontius Pilate (A.D. 26–36).

Figure 5
Rulers of Palestine

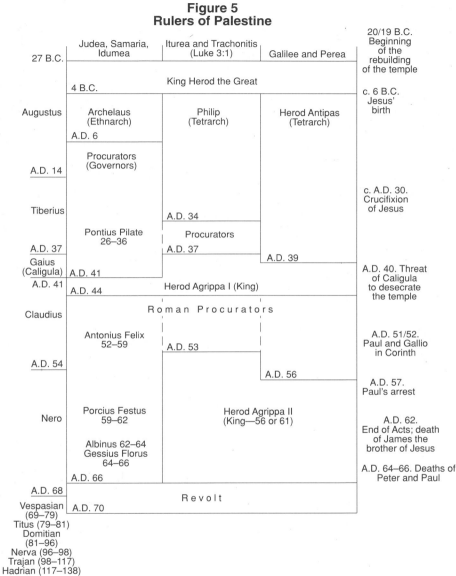

	Judea, Samaria, Idumea	Iturea and Trachonitis (Luke 3:1)	Galilee and Perea	
27 B.C.				20/19 B.C. Beginning of the rebuilding of the temple
	4 B.C. King Herod the Great			c. 6 B.C. Jesus' birth
Augustus	Archelaus (Ethnarch) A.D. 6	Philip (Tetrarch)	Herod Antipas (Tetrarch)	
A.D. 14	Procurators (Governors)			
Tiberius		A.D. 34		c. A.D. 30. Crucifixion of Jesus
A.D. 37	Pontius Pilate 26–36	Procurators A.D. 37	A.D. 39	
Gaius (Caligula) A.D. 41	A.D. 41 A.D. 44	Herod Agrippa I (King)		A.D. 40. Threat of Caligula to desecrate the temple
Claudius	R o m a n P r o c u r a t o r s			
	Antonius Felix 52–59	A.D. 53		A.D. 51/52. Paul and Gallio in Corinth
A.D. 54			A.D. 56	A.D. 57. Paul's arrest
Nero	Porcius Festus 59–62 Albinus 62–64 Gessius Florus 64–66 A.D. 66	Herod Agrippa II (King—56 or 61)		A.D. 62. End of Acts; death of James the brother of Jesus A.D. 64–66. Deaths of Peter and Paul
A.D. 68 Vespasian (69–79)	A.D. 70	R e v o l t		
Titus (79–81) Domitian (81–96) Nerva (96–98) Trajan (98–117) Hadrian (117–138)				

Herod Agrippa I

Herod Agrippa I was a grandson of Herod the Great and ruled as king over all the land of Israel until his death in 44. The early life of Agrippa, the son of Herod the Great's son Aristobulus, was far from distinguished. Financial problems brought on by extravagant

gant living, conflicts with family and officials, and administrative corruption caused difficulty and eventually led to his imprisonment in Rome. Agrippa's fortunes changed with the accession of his friend Caligula to the imperial throne in 37.

As already noted, Agrippa was made king over the territory held by Philip the tetrarch. In 39 the territory formerly held by Herod Antipas was given him as well. In 41 Agrippa happened to be in Rome when Caligula was assassinated and Claudius became emperor. The latter confirmed Agrippa in his kingship and added Judea and Samaria to his control. Thus Agrippa held the same territory and the same title as had his grandfather Herod the Great; hence in Acts 12:1 Agrippa is called "King Herod."

Agrippa sought to please the Jews. When Caligula ordered his statue erected in the Jerusalem temple, Agrippa pled the Jewish cause. Although he appears to have been an ally of the Sadducees, he even gained the goodwill of the Pharisees. Evidently, it was to secure his subjects' favor that he began the ill-fated project of extending the boundaries of Jerusalem by erecting a third wall to protect its northern limits, killed James, and imprisoned Peter (Acts 12:1–3).

After the death of Caligula, Agrippa apparently began to display considerable devotion to Judaism. He moved his capital to Jerusalem and appointed a new high priest. Josephus says, "No day passed without the prescribed sacrifices."[41] Agrippa's zeal for Judaism could have been a reason for the persecution of Christians described in Acts 12 (note esp. v. 3). Both Josephus and Acts 12:21–23 record the sudden death of Herod Agrippa I in Caesarea.[42] He left a seventeen-year-old son, Agrippa II, and three daughters, including Bernice (Acts 25:13, 23; 26:30) and Drusilla.

Roman Procurators

Because of Agrippa II's youth at his father's death in 44, the whole of the area was initially placed under the control of procurators. These proved to be poor custodians; the problems of the country multiplied. Fadus (44–46) had to deal with a messianic pretender named Theudas.[43] The renegade Jewish governor Tiberius Julius Alexander (46–48), a nephew of Philo (see p. 38), faced an uprising led by James and Simon, sons of Judas the Galilean, who himself had led and perished in a revolt at the time of the census in A.D. 6. Cumanus's reign (48–52) was characterized by constant tumults caused by Jewish resentment, Roman provocation,

41. Josephus *Antiquities* 19.7.3 (331).
42. Ibid., 19.8.2 (343–51).
43. This was probably not the Theudas of Acts 5:36.

and Galilean-Samaritan tensions. These are but a few indications of the general unrest of the time.

Two procurators, Antonius Felix (52–59) and Porcius Festus (59–62), appear in the New Testament as Paul's judges (Acts 23:23–26:32). Felix, whose third wife was Agrippa I's daughter Drusilla,[44] faced increasing insurgent activity, including the appearance of the infamous *sicarii* (dagger men or assassins). Paul was mistaken for one of them, an Egyptian who had led a group to the Mount of Olives and announced that the walls of Jerusalem would fall to permit his entrance (Acts 21:38). Paul remained in prison in Caesarea when Festus replaced Felix (Acts 24:27). Festus died in office. Before his successor arrived, Annas II, the high priest, took the opportunity to dispose of a number of his enemies in Jerusalem. One of them was James the Just, the brother of Jesus.[45]

The corruption, injustice, brutality, and high-handedness of the last two procurators of Judea and Samaria, Albinus (62–64) and Gessius Florus (64–66), accelerated the Jewish rush toward rebellion. The outbreak of the war with Rome was bathed in the history of Jewish-Roman misunderstanding and hostility begun when Pompey entered the temple in 63 B.C. Against the background of remembrance of the Maccabean revolt and the subsequent taste of independence there grew the longing for freedom intertwined with a messianic spirit which increasingly affirmed divine sanction for armed action. Josephus speaks of the Zealots and their unquenchable desire for liberty as prime movers in the revolt; but, it seems, they were but the radical fringe of a population that had long since set itself on a collision course with the imperial power.

Herod Agrippa II

In 53 the tetrarchy of Philip and later Galilee and Perea were given to Agrippa II, who ruled with the title of king; Judea and Samaria remained under procurators. This was the situation when Agrippa II and Bernice made the visit to Festus recorded in Acts 25:13–26:32.[46] When revolt broke out, Agrippa sided

44. Drusilla was first betrothed to a son of King Antiochus of Commagene, but declined to marry him when he refused to be circumcised. Later she married Azizus, king of Emesa. Felix was taken by her beauty soon after this wedding and, with the help of a magician, persuaded her to marry him.

45. Eusebius *Ecclesiastical History* 2.23; Josephus *Antiquities* 20.9.1 (199–200).

46. Like Drusilla, the wife of Felix, Agrippa II and Bernice were children of Agrippa I. After the death of her first husband, Bernice married her uncle, Herod of Chalcis. Following his death she lived with her brother Agrippa II. Rumors about an incestuous relationship between them were rampant in the ancient world (see Juvenal *Satires* 6.156–60). She deserted her next husband, Polemon king of Cilicia, and returned to her brother. It was at this time that the two of them heard the defense of Paul. Later Bernice became mistress to the emperor Titus.

with the Romans. Afterwards he was confirmed in his kingship and given additional territories to govern. He moved to Rome in 75. With his death around the year 100, the Herodian dynasty came to an end.

The Roman Period from the First through the Second Revolt

The spark which ignited the explosion came in 66, when Gessius Florus insulted Jewish religious customs. The war raged until 70, when Jerusalem, the temple, and the Jewish state were reduced to ashes. It took another three years to eliminate the last vestige of Jewish resistance at Masada. The memory of Herod's temple lies buried beneath Islamic mosques on Jerusalem's temple hill and engraved on Titus's triumphal arch, which still stands in Rome.

We have only glimpses of Jewish history during the next sixty years. The Talmud relates how Rabbi Johanan ben Zakkai was smuggled out of Jerusalem during its siege, gained the favor of Vespasian, and was given permission to establish an academy for learning at Jamnia (Jabneh or Yavneh).[47] Here he and Rabban Gamaliel II established a new center for Jewish life which continued, with adaptations and additions, the traditions of the Pharisees, and nothing but those traditions. Thus began Rabbinic Judaism. At Jamnia, Johanan and Gamaliel led legal-religious discussions which preserved and reorganized Judaism, and began the codification of tradition later inscribed in the Mishnah. In time, other cities also became centers of rabbinic discussions.

Sometime before the end of the first century, Jewish synagogue liturgy was altered to include in the Shemoneh 'Esreh (the Eighteen Benedictions [berakoth] of the daily prayer) a condemnation of Jewish Christians which effectively excluded them from synagogue worship and continuing participation in Jewish life (for the change in wording see Appendix E, pp. 366–67). There is some suggestion that the Jews may have attempted to reestablish sacrificial worship on the site of the destroyed temple, but the evidence is debated. Both in the land of Israel and abroad, Jews were subject to increased hostility and probably formal persecutions under the emperors Domitian (81–96) and Trajan (98–117).

In 132, during the emperorship of Hadrian (117–38), a second Jewish revolt broke out under the leadership of Simon Bar Kosiba, who captured Jerusalem and briefly reestablished the Jewish

47. Babylonian Talmud Gittin 56.

state.[48] A religious element in this war is confirmed by Bar Kosiba's being hailed as Messiah by some influential rabbis, including Akiba, and by his persecution of Jewish Christians who refused to acknowledge him as such. For three years there raged a savage and cruel war, the details of which are all but lost. The end came at Bethar, not far from Bethlehem, with the defeat of the Jewish forces and the death of him who had been their leader. Jerusalem was rebuilt as a Gentile city, Aelia Capitolina, and with a temple dedicated to Jupiter. Jews were forbidden to enter the city on pain of death. The Jewish state, as a political entity, was not again to emerge for over eighteen centuries.

48. Discoveries made in the Judean desert in the latter half of the twentieth century have clarified the exact name of the leader of the rebellion. Rabbi Akiba, a supporter, called him Bar Kokhba (son of the star, an allusion to the messianic prophecy of Num. 24:17); later Jewish writers refer to him as Bar Koziba (son of the lie). Christian writers refer to Kokheba or Bar Kokheba. Coins and documents from his reign, including letters by him, clarify that his name was Simon (Shimeon) Bar (Ben) Kosiba(h) (Simon the son of Kosiba).

Part 2

The Crises and Responses
of Intertestamental Judaism

6

Crises of the Sixth
and Fourth Centuries

- The Sixth-Century Crisis: The Destruction of Judah and the Babylonian Exile
- The Fourth-Century Crisis
  + Hellenism
  + Hellenistic Civilization and the Jews

Numerous events in the history we have just surveyed contributed to the unique features of the Judaism of the New Testament Era.[1] The major characteristics of any historical period or movement can hardly be traced solely to a few specific causes. The rise of the diversity which was such an important part of Intertestamental Judaism was undoubtedly affected by personality and group dynamics as well as by geographical, sociological, and economic factors. Nevertheless, there were at least two major events that brought on crises which became explosive forces in the formation of the emerging Jewish world. They were of special significance because of their implications for the people as a whole and the variety of responses they aroused from different persons and groups. Their cruciality must be recognized in any study of the background of the New Testament. The first was the destruction of the Jewish state by the Babylonians in 586 B.C. and all that that event implied. The

1. Some of the content in this chapter and those that immediately follow has appeared in J. Julius Scott, Jr., "Crisis and Reaction: Roots of Diversity in Intertestamental Judaism," *Evangelical Quarterly* 64.3 (1992): 197–212.

second was the intrusion of Hellenistic culture from the time of Alexander the Great in the fourth century B.C.

The Sixth-Century Crisis:
The Destruction of Judah and the Babylonian Exile

The fall of Judah, with the destruction of Jerusalem and the temple, was preceded by a series of ominous events. Assyria and Egypt began attacks upon Israel and Judah as early as the ninth century B.C. During the reigns of Ahab and Jehu, Israel (the northern kingdom) was virtually reduced to satellite status by Shalmaneser III (859–824) of Assyria. Later, Ahaz of Judah (the southern kingdom) accepted Assyrian domination under Tiglath-pileser III (Pul, 745–727). A series of revolts by Israel's puppet kings brought about her eventual demise in 722 at the hands of Shalmaneser V (727–722) and his successor Sargon II (722–705).

Judah lasted about 135 years after the destruction of Israel. Her end came in stages. Following the battle of Carchemish (605), at which the Babylonians defeated the Egyptians and what was left of the Assyrian Empire, they pursued the Egyptians south through the land of Israel. It seems that Jehoiakim accepted the Babylonian Nebuchadnezzar as his new master. There is no record of Judean hostages taken to Babylon at this time; some assume that such was the case, however, and that Daniel and his friends must have been included (Dan. 1:1–7 implies as much). A revolt against Babylonian sovereignty by Jehoiakim again brought Nebuchadnezzar to Judah. Jehoiakim died before the matter was settled, and his son Jehoiachin was enthroned. Jehoiachin surrendered to the Babylonians in 598. The king along with many leading citizens, including the prophet Ezekiel, was deported to Babylonia. A revolt by Zedekiah of Judah brought the final destruction of the Jewish state. Following a siege of about a year and a half, Jerusalem was taken and destroyed, the temple burned, and many of the people were killed, taken into captivity, or became refugees.

The exact number of Jews taken to Babylon is uncertain: 2 Kings 24:14 notes ten thousand for the deportation of Jehoiachin; Jeremiah 52:28–30 lists forty-six hundred in three separate deportations (this figure may include only the adult males). In either case the total was only a small part of the population; significantly, however, it seems to have included the leadership of the nation. Other Hebrews sought places of refuge in Egypt (Jer. 43:1–7) and elsewhere. It is likely that the war seriously disrupted only the immediate environs of Jerusalem, and life in surrounding areas continued somewhat as it had before.

Yet the effects of the fall of Judah were devastating and widespread. Geographically it marked the beginning of the Diaspora, the Dispersion, the scattering of Jews throughout the world. The Book of Lamentations bewails, "she lives now among the nations" (1:3). The Dispersion had wide-ranging effects upon Jewish life and psychology. Continuing proximity to other groups became a threat to Hebrew racial, ethnic, and cultural identity. So Diaspora Jews have tended to live in proximity to each other, thus forming distinct communities (later called ghettos) which were the target of anti-Semitism even before the Common Era.

Politically the fall marked loss of national identity as a recognizable self-governing entity. Although the Hebrews had previously become vassals of Assyria and Babylonia, now even the semblance of independency was gone. No longer did they live under their own native officials but under the direct control of foreigners. The Book of Esther depicts some of the typical dangers they constantly faced.

The fall of the Jewish state also precipitated a religious crisis of monstrous proportions. This fact cannot be comprehended without focusing upon three major facets of Jewish life—the land, the monarchy, and Jerusalem with her temple were religious symbols as well as national possessions and institutions. Israel's land was more than real estate. When God first offered his covenant to Abraham, he said, "Go . . . to the land that I will show you. . . . All the land . . . I will give to you and to your offspring forever" (Gen. 12:1; 13:15; 17:8). Possession of the land was an important element in and demonstration of God's special designation of Israel. To lose it meant the loss of a visible aspect of God's promise. It is possible to organize the whole of Old Testament theology around Israel's possession and loss of land.[2] Similarly in modern times, possession of a particular piece of land may have implications far beyond its monetary value; it can be vital to the self-identity and emotional well-being of individuals, especially those from a rural setting (as this writer knows all too well!).

The monarchy also held both a national and a religious significance. Although God was recognized as the only true king of Israel, rulers from the house of David were his representatives. God promised David that his descendants would rule over Israel forever (2 Sam. 7:12–16). The overthrow of that kingly line caused many in Israel to question the nation's relation to God and the dependability of his promise. Their shock is reflected in Psalm 89:38–45:

2. Walter Brueggemann, *The Land* (Philadelphia: Fortress, 1977); see also W. D. Davies, *The Gospel and the Land: Early Christianity and Jewish Territorial Doctrine* (Berkeley: University of California Press, 1974); idem, *The Territorial Dimension of Judaism* (Berkeley: University of California Press, 1982).

> But now you have spurned and rejected him; you are full of wrath
> against your anointed. You have renounced the covenant with your ser-
> vant; you have defiled his crown in the dust. You have broken through
> all his walls; you have laid his strongholds in ruins. All who pass by
> plunder him; he has become the scorn of his neighbors. You have ex-
> alted the right hand of his foes; you have made all his enemies rejoice.
> Moreover, you have turned back the edge of his sword, and you have
> not supported him in battle. You have removed the scepter from his
> hand, and hurled his throne to the ground. You have cut short the days
> of his youth; you have covered him with shame.

The city of Jerusalem and its temple were additional visible evidences of God's favor and presence among his people. Psalm 48 re-
joices in the presence of God with his people in his holy mountain;
Mount Zion (Jerusalem) is "the city of the great King" (see also
Matt. 5:35), and God its "sure defense." Now it was gone! "How
lonely sits the city that once was full of people!" (Lam. 1:1) was the
cry. The temple had been the house of God, where the God-
ordained worship was carried out, the place where God and his people could meet. It was the place where priests offered sacrifices, the
focal point of the great feasts and festivals. Could Israel come before
her God without visible symbols and means for worshiping him?

Thus the events of 586 precipitated a theological crisis as the
nation recognized that the LORD had permitted his people to be
conquered! Questions were inevitable. Was God good and loving?
Did he really care for his people? If he did, was he able to protect
them? The loss of land, monarchy, and Jerusalem with its temple
threw into doubt the continuing viability of the covenant, which
had designated the Hebrews as the distinct people of God.

Away from their land and temple, the Hebrews were thrown into
proximity with paganism. In this new situation they faced a series
of difficulties. Maintaining ceremonial cleanness was more difficult. Daily they were forced to make contact with persons and
things that brought defilement. Without the temple and the priesthood the means of eradicating this uncleanness were either not
available or far less accessible.

Syncretism, which regards all religions as equally valid or which
seeks to merge part or all of many religions into one, was another
constant threat. Some Jews succumbed and adopted various pagan
practices into the traditional worship; others actually committed
apostasy by rejecting their God for other deities. Some may have
become secular agnostics.

Another difficulty was that with the loss of the monarchy came
the loss of political support for the Hebrew religious system.
Temple-centered worship and the monarchy had been intimately

tied together. The earlier history of Judah had been marked by at least four revivals under Kings Asa, Joash, Hezekiah, and Josiah respectively. Even rulers with less zeal usually had protected the sanctity of the temple and its religious practice. Financial support for proper worship came directly from the monarchs or at their insistence.

The theological crisis also involved the Hebrew Scriptures, the Old Testament (that is, the parts then written). Their content and use were closely tied to the nation, land, political situation, history, and culture of the Hebrews. What was to be the place of Scripture after the defeat by the Babylonians? and how was it to be used and interpreted in the radically changed situation, one quite different from that presupposed by the biblical writers? As time went on, the question of translation arose. Could God's holy book be rendered in a profane language; if not, how were those Jews who did not know Hebrew to understand and conform to Scripture?[3]

It would seem that many of the surviving Hebrews believed they were faced with a prophetic silence. In times past, the prophets along with (or instead of) the priesthood had provided communication and guidance from God. Amos 3:7 says, "Surely the Lord God does nothing, without revealing his secret to his servants the prophets." The same sentiment ranges throughout the Old Testament literature associated with the divided kingdom. But several statements in both the canonical Old Testament and the Apocrypha assume the exile and postexilic period to have been times without prophets (although Haggai, Zechariah, and Malachi, all from the early part of the postexilic period, as well as select individuals later on, were recognized as authentic prophets). Note the following assumptions of prophetic silence:

> We do not see our emblems; there is no longer any prophet, and there is no one among us who knows how long. [Ps. 74:9]

> They [Judas Maccabeus and his followers] deliberated what to do about the altar of burnt offering, which had been profaned. And they thought it best to tear it down, so that it would not be a lasting shame to them that the Gentiles had defiled it. So they tore down the altar, and stored the stones in a convenient place on the temple hill until a prophet should come to tell them what to do with them. [1 Macc. 4:44–46]

> The Jews and their priests have resolved that Simon should be their leader and high priest forever, until a trustworthy prophet should arise,

---

3. Note that even to this day one of the world's great religions, Islam, does not officially recognize any translation of its holy book, the Koran.

and that he should be governor over them and that he should take charge of the sanctuary. [1 Macc. 14:41–42]

The prophetic silence could not have come at a worse time, a time when the Jews were most in need of God's message and direction. Several of the developments of the intertestamental period, such as oral law and the apocalyptic, appear to have been attempts to secure divine guidance or authoritative interpretation of the Scriptures when none seemed available.

In summary, the defeat and exile faced the surviving Hebrews with the loss of their central national and religious institutions. They were without a unifying center of influence. They were forced to rethink the nature of God, his relation to them, and the viability of Old Testament religion. They were thrown into close contact with other cultures, and their traditional way of life became difficult or impossible. They, in a new way, confronted the question of the relation between religion and culture. In every area the Hebrew race and its political and religious systems encountered a constant threat to survival.

The Fourth-Century Crisis

Hellenism

The conquests of Alexander the Great changed the world; the Jewish community was not excepted. The most sweeping part of that change was not political but cultural. Alexander deliberately set out to spread Greek culture. His army was accompanied by city planners and architects, literary figures and philosophers, biologists and botanists, musicians and actors, and other purveyors of culture. The infusion of Hellenistic culture into the broader world was his greatest legacy. Hellenistic political dominance lasted until Roman conquests absorbed the last Hellenistic kingdoms (c. 30 B.C.). Hellenistic culture was a major factor in Judaism for about 360 years, and its influence continues to this day.

What is meant by "culture"? It is the total way of thinking and lifestyle which a group of people seeks to pass on from generation to generation. External features of a culture include its form of government, city plans and architecture, styles of clothes, entertainments, and language. More subtle, and yet more important, are features of a culture which involve priorities and values, ways of thinking and problem solving, philosophical systems, religion, and norms of behavior. Relatively small changes may have a major impact on a culture (note the effect of television in modern cultures).

Alexander thought he was spreading the Greek culture of the classical period of Homer, Herodotus, Pericles, Socrates, Plato, and Aristotle, who had been Alexander's teacher. The Hellenistic culture which emerged from his conquests was different, however. Absorbing parts of other cultures which it encountered, Hellenism was simplified and adapted by people who, though it was not native to them, saw its value. An illustration is the simplification of classical Greek into Koine (common) Greek, which was widely used in the West until about A.D. 330; in fact, it is the language in which the New Testament was written.

To describe the distinctive features of any culture is difficult. Hellenism is no exception, but we must make the attempt. We will focus upon three areas: (1) government, (2) the life of the citizens, and (3) the Greek spirit.

First, a word about government. There was no uniform type of Greek or Hellenistic government. Ancient Greece was divided into city-states; this was both her strength and weakness. Each city-state (*polis*) had its king and some sort of an assembly or council (*boulē*). The relative strengths of king and council vacillated. Usually the king had absolute power. Structures for administration eventually developed, especially as the city-state gained control over wider areas or, as was the case under Alexander, developed into an empire. The officials and court personnel closest to the king were called his "friends." The leading officials outside the court were often called *stratēgoi* and may have held both civil and military responsibilities. Other civil servants were added as needed. The kings came from the royal family, which claimed distinguished ancestry, often a god. The council was made up of either all the citizens or representatives elected by them. The spread of Hellenism after Alexander's conquest brought modifications of the basic governmental system, but the essential structure remained. Some Hellenistic forms survived even under the Roman Empire, especially in the East.

Hellenism sought to provide its citizens with everything necessary for the good life; it was essentially an urban civilization, its institutions benefiting a privileged group. It is little wonder that throughout its history social and economic differences led to constant tensions and occasional revolt.

Citizens were native Greeks, including emigrés from Greece, and persons from the upper classes of non-Greek areas who embraced Hellenistic culture. Among this group were the most privileged members of society: the king, his family, and "friends." Also considered citizens were the wealthy, the chief administrators, and at least part of the merchant classes. The majority of people were noncitizens and thus excluded from the primary benefits of Hellenistic civilization. They made up the laboring classes, including craftsmen, artisans, peasant farmers, employees of the bureaucracy, day laborers, servants, slaves (whom Aristotle called human tools), and the like. The social status of women was determined by their fathers or husbands. Although some held important positions, few professions were open to the majority of women. They had only limited access to education and social life, possessed few legal rights, and occupied themselves primarily with domestic duties and home industries.

Greek cities were the focus of political, social, and economic life. They conformed to a prescribed plan. At the center was the agora (marketplace), the site of governmental, artistic, religious, and commercial activities; it was important also as the place for the exchange of ideas. Various types of buildings clustered around the agora or were in proximity to it. These included theaters, temples, gymnasiums, stadiums, and hippodromes for cultivation of the body, mind, and spirit. All exhibited Hellenist architectural styles.

The gymnasium was of special importance; indeed it was a necessity in a Hellenistic city. The gymnasium was the center of communal life, business, and learning, as well as a place for exercise and bathing. Hence the significance of building a gymnasium in Jerusalem in the days just prior to the Maccabean revolt (1 Macc. 1:14; 2 Macc. 4:12; 4 Macc. 4:9). The director or ruler of a gymnasium (*gymnasiarchos*) enjoyed great prestige.

The importance of education can hardly be overstated. Most schools were private; some were endowed by rulers or wealthy patrons. There were various levels of training in the gymnasium, both formal for the young and informal for adult male citizens. Most crucial was the training of the ephebus (an eighteen-year-old male who had just become a citizen). Some instruction was given to girls as well. The list of subjects to be mastered included "reading, writing, recitation, arithmetic, painting, playing on and singing to the lyre, comedy, tragedy, verse and song writing, and general knowledge, besides running, wrestling, boxing, and in some cases military exercises such as archery."[4]

The purpose of classical education had been to enable the citizen to function well in politics or courts of law. This goal had diminished during the Hellenistic age. By New Testament times the objective seems to have become to equip the student to make a good impression by delivering a polished speech. Rhetoric re-

4. A. H. M. Jones, *The Greek City from Alexander to Justinian* (Oxford: Clarendon, 1940), 222–23.

mained the core of the curriculum. Unfortunately, the classical dictum, "good speaking stems from good thinking," had been forgotten; and education was more concerned with the technicalities and externals of communication. The Hellenists continued the production of literature, historiography, art, science, philosophy, and the like, but, it is usually assumed, without the creativity and depth of the classical period.

The Greek spirit, which was not necessarily dependent upon the presence of a Hellenistic city, was fired by the search for principles of harmony, virtue, wisdom, courage, temperance, endurance, prudence, and justice. These principles were regarded as discoverable by the human mind within the impersonal forces in the universe. The philosophy of the Hellenistic age tended to view life as dominated by fate and sought meaning in conformity and avoidance of pain and unhappiness.

Two Hellenistic schools of philosophy are mentioned in Acts 17:18, the Epicureans and Stoics. Epicurus (c. 341–270 B.C.) assumed no supernatural being or future human existence. Consequently he sought to attain undisturbed peace of mind and soul with freedom and pleasure in the present. For Epicurus, pleasure meant friendship, mental serenity, and the absence of fear and pain; his followers defined pleasure more materially and sensually. Stoicism seems to have been the dominant philosophy of the Hellenistic world. It was founded by Zeno (c. 335–265 B.C.), a Phoenician, whose outlook has been summarized as "Live according to nature." He assumed that the natural world consists in two forms: (1) the outward and visible, and (2) the breath or spirit (*logos*) which permeates reality. Everything came into being and finds its meaning through the *logos*, which involves reason, the active universal principle. The Stoics assumed a cyclical character of the natural order. Happiness and virtue are found by living in harmony with this order, submitting to the *logos*.

The religion of the Hellenistic age was a mixture of the classical Greek worship of the Olympian deities, newer religious forms coming primarily from the East, and astrology and magic. The older classical religion was not dead and, in fact, was taken over by the conquering Romans, who gave Latin names to the Greek deities and adapted them for their own worship. Nevertheless, the traditional religion had little impact upon the populace except for ceremonial purposes. There was fear of the unseen, the fates ("the slings and arrows of outrageous fortune"), the nameless insecurities of life, and death. In addition, it appears there were a prevailing feeling of loneliness among the masses and a growing search for true companionship or intimate contact with deity and with other humans, for happiness in the present, and for security after death. Numerous cults arose, including mystery religions, claiming to offer various kinds of help, saviors, relationship with both other humans and gods. This proved a fertile environment for the growth of emperor worship in the first century.

One immediately associates temples and similar structures with religion. In the Hellenistic world, theaters, gymnasiums (including baths and a palestra for exercise and wrestling), stadiums (for footraces and other athletic contests), and hippodromes (where chariots raced) had religious functions as well. Even the games were more religion than sport. Cultivation of the mind and the body was a part of the general culture and also of religious ceremony.

Hellenistic Civilization and the Jews

It will be helpful at this point to attempt a brief comparison of Hellenism with the traditional Semitic culture of the Hebrews.[5] Linguistically, the cultural Hebrew spoke Hebrew or Aramaic, while the Hellenist used Greek. The Semitic economy and setting were essentially rural and agricultural, while the Greek was urban. The religious outlook of the Hebrews was monotheistic, ethical, and practical; that of the Hellenists was polytheistic or pantheistic, metaphysical, and speculative. Hebraic religion emphasized the worship of Yahweh and human relation to him; Hellenistic religion was pagan and secular and focused on the human and the human body. The Semitic outlook tended towards particularism and isolationism; the Hellenistic was universal and syncretistic. The Semite emphasized the community, the Hellenist the individual. Conflict between the two was inevitable.

Initial Jewish contact with Greek and Hellenistic culture was benign. After the Alexandrian conquest the Jews increasingly came in touch with Hellenism through traders and military personnel who came into their areas. When they traveled, the Jews saw Hellenistic cities, administrative procedures, and the Hellenistic way of life.

Under the successors of Alexander the Great, exposure to Hellenism grew. As part of the Ptolemaic Empire centered in Egypt, the Jews were forced to deal with a Hellenistic governmental struc-

---

5. On the general topic of Hellenism and Judaism see Martin Hengel, *Judaism and Hellenism: Studies in Their Encounter in Palestine during the Early Hellenistic Period*, trans. John Bowden, 2 vols. (Philadelphia: Fortress, 1974); Victor Tcherikover, "Prolegomena," in *Corpus Papyrorum Judaicarum*, ed. Victor Tcherikover and Alexander Fuks, 3 vols. (Cambridge, Mass.: Harvard University Press, 1957–64), 1:1–111; Victor Tcherikover, *Hellenistic Civilization and the Jews*, trans. S. Applebaum (Philadelphia: Magnes, 1961); Shemaryahu Talmon, ed., *Jewish Civilization in the Hellenistic-Roman Period* (Philadelphia: Trinity, 1991).

ture and, for at least pragmatic reasons, function within a Hellenistic framework. The Septuagint, the Greek translation of the Hebrew Scriptures, originated in this period. In the Jewish homeland most of the countryside was thoroughly hellenized. This is well attested by the Zeno Papyri. Jerusalem, the capital, was initially protected by her remote location in the hill country and by conservative, temple-centered leadership.

At first, life under the Seleucids brought about the same level of contact with Hellenism as under the Ptolemies. This, of course, changed when Antiochus IV Epiphanes (175–163) began a determined drive to thoroughly hellenize Judea. Contemporary scholars debate the reasons for Antiochus's actions.[6] They were probably a combination of political, social, and religious considerations. Furthermore, the activity of pro-Hellenist Jews already in Jerusalem must not be overlooked. In any case, the latent threats Hellenism had posed to the Jews burst forth as an open and forceful challenge to the very existence of the traditional culture of the Jews, especially their religion.

The Maccabean revolt was not directed primarily against Hellenism in general but against pagan worship. As previously noted, there were already considerable acceptance of Hellenism and many supporters among the Jews, including those in the land of Israel. The revolt broke out when Antiochus attempted to force pagan worship. His action then brought other Hellenistic institutions and practices into question. That the revolt was not aimed at Hellenism in general is also evidenced by the fact that it remained as a permanent feature in Judaism afterwards. The Hasmonean dynasty, especially the later rulers, were sympathizers or even outright supporters. Conclusive evidence of the presence of Hellenistic culture in the land of Israel is particularly strong along the coastal plain and in Galilee.[7] Hence the area is called "Galilee of the Gentiles" (Matt. 4:15). Herod the Great rebuilt Jerusalem, including the temple, after the Hellenistic model. A long-standing debate about the languages of the land of Israel at the time of Jesus is rapidly being resolved by recognition of a very strong Greek presence.[8] It is startling to learn that 40 percent of the pre–A.D. 70 burial inscriptions in Jerusalem are in Greek.[9]

6. See Lester L. Grabbe, *Judaism from Cyrus to Hadrian,* 2 vols. (Minneapolis: Augsburg Fortress, 1991–92), 1:247–56.

7. Saul Liebermann, *Hellenism in Jewish Palestine,* 2d ed. (New York: Jewish Theological Seminary of America, 1962).

8. Saul Liebermann, *Greek in Jewish Palestine* (New York: Jewish Theological Seminary of America, 1942); Joseph A. Fitzmyer, "Did Jesus Speak Greek?" *Biblical Archaeology Review* 18.5 (Sept.-Oct. 1992): 58–63.

9. Pieter W. van der Horst, "Jewish Funerary Inscriptions," *Biblical Archaeology Review* 18.5 (Sept.-Oct. 1992): 46–57.

A strong Hellenistic party was active in the land of Israel until after the second revolt (A.D. 135). Even Bar Kosiba himself wrote in Greek! Greek words continue to appear in Hebrew/Aramaic rabbinic writings of the third and fourth centuries A.D.

Explaining just why and how Hellenism in the fourth century B.C. provoked a crisis for the Jews that was every bit as serious as the earlier defeat and destruction by Babylonia in the sixth is just as challenging as is defining Hellenism precisely. It is particularly hard to clarify the exact nature of the broader threat from Hellenism because after the Maccabean revolt the threat of paganism was all but gone. Nevertheless, while a pious Jew like Philo could embrace virtually all save the religious aspects of Hellenism, other intertestamental writing, such as 1 Maccabees, Jubilees, and Sirach (Ecclesiasticus), to name a few, show strong, settled opposition.[10]

It is essential to keep in mind that there were degrees and varieties of the reaction against Hellenism, just as there were among those who embraced it. At the heart of the anti-Hellenistic reaction were strong views of Israel's election by God and her consequent relation to him and other peoples. Many exponents of the traditional Semitic-Hebraic culture adopted an outlook we may call particularism. In this setting "particularism" means the belief not only that the Jews alone were God's chosen people, but also that this status necessarily required a specific way of life. Any deviation from it was viewed as dangerous to Israel's relationship with God and to the nation and race as a whole. Deviation could lower barriers and lead to a syncretistic amalgamation of Judaism into an amorphous mass which would leave it indistinguishable from other religions.

Three points must be made to help understand the zeal of the Jewish opponents of Hellenism. (1) The Old Testament law depicted culture and conduct as the visible results of covenant relation with God. (2) The prophets from Moses onward constantly warned that national and individual well-being were dependent upon faithfulness and obedience to God. (3) Examples were aplenty of races, nations, cultures, and religions losing their identity in the great melting pots fired by the conquests of the great superpowers of the day. Unfaithfulness to God and contact with

10. Elias Bickerman, *From Ezra to the Last of the Maccabees: Foundations of Post-Biblical Judaism* (New York: Schocken, 1962), 59–64, for example, sees opposition to Hellenism in Jubilees, but a positive influence of Hellenism in the wisdom tradition of Ecclesiastes; Hengel, *Judaism and Hellenism*, 131–53, sees a strong anti-Hellenistic sentiment in another wisdom document, Sirach (Ecclesiasticus).

pagan influences were widely recognized as causes of the nation's defeat and humiliation; those who supported the traditional culture had a point!

On the other side, Jewish supporters of Hellenism could point to friendly and supportive relations between Hellenists and Jews. Rulers from Alexander until Antiochus Epiphanes had allowed Jews the free practice of their way of life. Supporters of Hellenism might have pointed as well to the benefits Judaism received as a part of the Hellenistic world. One may assume that given the advantages of participating in a new order and culture, some Jews regarded the threats from Hellenism as minimal.

Twentieth-century scholar Edwyn Bevan grasps something of the dilemma which some Jews of the Intertestamental Era faced when confronting Hellenism:

> Imagine what it must have been to a young Jew, whose mind was filled from his infancy with the solemn exhortations of the Law, the rich imagery of the prophets, the cries of Psalmists after the living God, when, for the first time, he heard read, or read himself, the utterances of Plato, quite different from anything in his own books, and yet so thrilling in its deep passion for justice and temperance, in its faith that behind the world movement there was a Power which cared for the good. Or, it may be, he would make acquaintance with some living Greek Stoic whose philosophy really governed his life—someone who made you feel by the touch of his personality, by some strange power in his eyes, that nothing except goodness and inner freedom was worth desire. Here surely the young Jew, loyal to his God, would find something akin, something which drew him by its likeness to his own ideals of righteousness, and yet something, in other respects, unlike, dissonant, Gentile. He might well be perplexed. It was impossible simply to turn your back on all that, as you had on the fantastic superstitions of Egypt or Canaan. You could hardly cast out Hellenism of that kind as evil. And yet was it safe to let it creep, with its subtle subduing power, into a mind that ought to be consecrated to the Law?[11]

Two crises, one in the sixth century, the other in the fourth. The first was primarily military and political, the latter cultural and social. Both, however, threatened the unique features and the very existence of the Hebrew identity and especially its religion. How did the Hebrews respond to these crises? The answer is, "In many different ways!" This variety of response proved a dominant influ-

---

11. Edwyn R. Bevan, "Hellenistic Judaism," in *The Legacy of Israel*, ed. Edwyn R. Bevan and Charles Singer (Oxford: Clarendon, 1927), 40–41.

ence in the shaping of Intertestamental Judaism. It determined that Intertestamental Judaism would indeed be what a modern writer has called "multiform"—a group, a community, a religion characterized by much diversity.[12] We now turn to consider some of the different ways the Jews faced and adjusted to the new situation brought on by the two crises.

12. Robert A. Kraft, "The Multiform Jewish Heritage of Early Christianity," in *Christianity, Judaism, and Other Greco-Roman Cults: Studies for Morton Smith at Sixty*, ed. Jacob Neusner (Leiden: Brill, 1975), 174–99; see also Gary G. Porton, "Diversity in Postbiblical Judaism," in *Early Judaism and Its Modern Interpreters*, ed. Robert A. Kraft and George W. E. Nickelsburg (Atlanta: Scholars, 1986), 57–80.

7

The General Response of Intertestamental Judaism to the Crises

Intertestamental Judaism was markedly changed from classical, preexilic Hebrew thought and culture. As we have said, a major feature of this difference was the variety within Intertestamental Judaism. What could have caused such modification? The dual crises of 586 and the fourth century B.C. left the Hebrew race, culture, and religion in danger of extinction. They threatened the very heart of what it meant to be Hebrew or Jewish. The diversity of responses to the postexilic situation and later to Hellenism, we suggest, was a major contributor to that variety which was so characteristic of the Judaism that emerged.

These responses were not necessarily calculated. More likely they were the gradually developed attempts of separate groups and individuals with dissimilar backgrounds and personalities to face the issues of their day. Furthermore, it is not inconceivable that a single person or group may well have responded in a variety of ways.

Our discussion of the Jewish readjustment in the face of the crises will focus on the major reactions. First, we will note some general responses of the people as a whole (ch. 7). Then we will examine some responses that seem to have been limited to separate parts of the population (chs. 8–11).

Shifts of Emphases

Monotheism, covenant, and the law constitute the essentials of the Hebrew religion. These theological pillars cannot be changed, but they may be reinterpreted and adjusted in new situations. A shift of emphasis in the way these theological essentials, especially the law, were understood and applied was a major mode of readjustment to the crises confronting Intertestamental Judaism. We can identify at least four of these shifts.

1. From Cultus to Moral Law

Israel's religious practice rested on twin foundation blocks: (1) temple and ceremonial worship, and (2) ethics and morals, the application of God's directives to daily life. During the kingdom period, temple and ceremony were primary; the law's directives for conduct and daily life, morality and ethics, were frequently relegated to a secondary role. The temple worship was supported by the institutions of the state, that is, the monarchy and priesthood, which in turn were centered and at least partly dependent on the temple. At the same time immorality, injustice, and neglect of the law were rampant in personal and corporate life.

The prophets denounced ceremony and form that were empty because there was no counterpart in ethical practice. They predicted the overthrow of the state because of violations of the moral directives of the law by both individuals and society at large. Proof of continuing acceptance of the LORD's covenant, they asserted, lay in faithful obedience and conforming all of life to his instructions in the law. Failure to follow them was symptomatic of a far more serious problem, de facto rejection of God himself. In spite of Israel's support for the formal worship, God rebuked them, "You have wearied me with your iniquities" (Isa. 43:24).

And now the nation was lost! Jerusalem had fallen! The temple was no more! The people had been led into captivity! The words of the prophets were vindicated! Now it was obvious that the LORD does indeed care more for obedience, steadfast love (*hesed*), justice, righteousness, and knowledge of and a humble walk with him than for sacrifices and burnt offerings, festivals, and solemn assemblies (Jer. 7:21–23; Hos. 6:6; Amos 5:21–24; Mic. 6:6–8).

Perhaps imperceptibly at first, there came a shift of emphasis away from the temple and ceremony to morals and ethics. After all, it had been the neglect of this part of her religion that had brought Israel to such dire straits. Since the temple stood no more, only the moral and ethical part of religious practice was still possible.

The implications of this shift are evident. The focus on participation in ritual and ceremony gave way to study of the law and its application to daily life. Whereas ceremonial observance had required a central temple, religious Jews now gathered in places designed for study, discussion, and the administration of justice (eventually synagogues). Leadership of the people moved from the professional priestly tribe to lay scholar-teachers (eventually scribes and rabbis) who knew and could apply the precepts; thus the old aristocracy of birth had to compete with one of learning.

This shift of emphasis did not mean elimination of the ceremonial foundation block of Hebrew religion. Indeed, the law had commanded the establishment of a central place of worship and had given instructions for ceremonies. So the nation yearned for the rebuilding of the temple and the reestablishment of its traditional worship. The students of the law pored over its instructions and demanded that they be followed explicitly. But the shift had been made; the religious structure now rested primarily on the moral-ethical pillar.

2. *Orthopraxy over Orthodoxy*

Whereas Christianity frequently stresses the importance of orthodoxy (right doctrine or belief), Judaism is more concerned with orthopraxy (correct and proper behavior, actions, practice). Even the discussion of whether right belief or right conduct should have priority is more Christian than Jewish. During the intertestamental period the Jewish emphasis on orthopraxy solidified.

Hebrew thought is not devoid of theology, however; far from it! Its basic assumptions about the one God, the Creator of the universe, who entered into covenant relation with Abraham, Isaac, Jacob, and their descendants, and who delivered them from slavery in Egypt, are eminently theological. The theology inherent in the three pillars—monotheism, covenant, and the law—is beyond question. Yet the Hebraic mind has always stressed orthopraxy; in the intertestamental period it did so even more. This was inevitable with the increased focus upon the meaning of the law for daily life, the first shift of emphasis.

The possibilities for variety in a communal commitment to orthopraxy are almost limitless. The general term most frequently used to describe the result is "legalism." Legalism itself is a broad category, a general way of thinking, that is popularly defined as "strict, literal conformity to a legal or religious code." A widely used New Testament survey defines it as "that concept of religion which makes religion consist in conformity to the Law, and promises God's grace only to doers of the Law."[1] Although the term is not found in the Bible, the basic concept of legalism appears to be present, and especially in the New Testament. In this setting legalism seems to be any notion of earning or contributing to salvation by human means, and in particular by observing a specific set of laws or traditions.

There is a long-standing controversy over the place of law in Jewish society and particularly over the question of whether Judaism is a religion of salvation by law keeping. The issue has been raised afresh in the latter part of the twentieth century by the writings of E. P. Sanders.[2] He insists that Judaism, especially of the Intertestamental Era, is essentially a religion of covenantal nomism, that law keeping is a response to God's gracious offer of the covenant. At this point it is sufficient for us to note that the intertestamental period saw an increasing emphasis upon and conscious awareness of the importance of orthopraxy, right conduct and actions. The result was twofold: (1) aside from general acceptance of the three theological pillars, there was room for a great variety of belief as long as one lived in accordance with some understanding of the law; and (2) there was in most segments of Intertestamental Judaism a legalistic ethos. Whether or not the majority of intertestamental Jews held that ultimately salvation was to be obtained by keeping the law, the law did in fact pervade their thinking and outlook.

3. Particularism, Exclusivism, and Superiority

Earlier we noted that in reaction to Hellenism there appeared a growth of particularism. Exclusivism and a protectionist mentality developed along with it. These were not necessarily new ideas or

---

1. Bruce M. Metzger, *The New Testament: Its Background, Growth, and Content* (New York: Abingdon, 1965), 41.

2. See especially E. P. Sanders, *Paul and Palestinian Judaism* (Philadelphia: Fortress, 1977).

attitudes; rather, there was an increased impact upon the Jews of the New Testament Era, especially those in the land of Israel.

Particularism, exclusivism, and superiority were unwarranted extensions of the Jewish conviction that God had selected Abraham and his descendants in some unique way. True, Deuteronomy 7:6 affirms that Israel is a holy people, that he "has chosen you out of all the peoples on earth to be his people, his treasured possession." Yet the passage immediately following warns that God's selection was based simply on his love, not Israel's numerical superiority.

The uniqueness of Israel's relation to the LORD is, of course, beyond question. Even Paul recognized the special advantages of Israel (Rom. 3:1–2; 9:4–5). Then, too, there were the obvious paganism of other nations and their lifestyle, which were clearly opposed to what Israel understood to be the will of God revealed in the law. The hostility of these other nations toward God's people suggested, and was often interpreted as, attacks of the evil upon the good (consider, e.g., Habakkuk's characterization of the Babylonian incursion [1:13]). The Jewish experience during the intertestamental period confirmed the notion of Israel's special position and fertilized reactionary ideas and convictions associated with it.

Israel's particular status required a specific way of life. The prophets had predicted that failure to maintain it would lead to captivity and exile. The requirements of this way of life were strict and radically different from those of other national groups; the prescriptions for ceremonial cleanliness were especially difficult to maintain while the Jew lived alongside people from other nations. It is little wonder that isolationism, as a corollary to particularism, became both a strong temptation and the actual practice of many.

Yet another development associated with this shift may be called the notion of Jewish privilege. It goes beyond particularism, exclusivism, superiority, and isolationism to include a protectionistic attitude, a determination to defend Israel's special status before Yahweh. It could manifest itself with violent reactions, even to the mere suggestion that God might show favor to a Gentile, especially if this favor came to a Gentile instead of a Hebrew. Both Jesus and Paul incurred the ire of the Jews by suggesting that indeed God had concern for Gentiles (Luke 4:24–29; Acts 22:21–22). Jesus' case was especially intolerable to his fellow townspeople because he noted that God through Elijah, while ignoring the needy in Israel, had fed a Sidonian widow and healed a Syrian leper.

This shift of emphasis clarified, asserted, and defended Israel's status and rights before her God. Resulting attitudes explain a number of features and events of intertestamental Jewish history (such as attitudes toward and treatment of Gentiles). Jewish Christians had to deal with this mentality as the gospel went beyond Jerusalem and Judea to Samaria and the ends of the earth (Acts 1:8).

4. Renewed Emphasis on Religious and Cultural Distinctives

The final shift of emphasis we will note involves a new function for old practices. Circumcision, Sabbath keeping, and observance of kosher regulations regarding clean and unclean were part of the law and life. During the readjustment period they were singled out. Emphasizing them kept the Jews distinct after their government and central institutions had been abolished and the people scattered throughout the world. Circumcision, which would be immediately evident if a Jew joined a gymnasium (the Greek word *gymnos* means "naked"), was offensive to Hellenists, who adored the natural human body. Cessation from work on the Sabbath was unknown among other cultures and appeared to many Gentiles to be slothfulness. Jewish food laws and other taboos easily identified those who observed them as different from other groups.

These religious customs, initially practiced to identify the race and protect the culture, eventually also became implements of exclusivism and segregation. They kept observant Jews at arms' length from other races. The more zealous viewed attacks upon their customs as threats against Jewish privilege. The New Testament reader can feel the tension rising as Jesus disregarded the Sabbath laws as they were then understood (Mark 2:23–3:6) and attacked the traditions about clean and unclean (Mark 7:1–23). The early church's rejection of the necessity of circumcision was well-nigh tantamount to rejecting her intertestamental Jewish heritage (Acts 15; 1 Cor. 7:19; Gal. 5:2).

Steps to Increase the Impact of the Scriptures

The crises of the sixth and fourth centuries carried implications for the Scriptures. Since they were regarded as the Word of God, they were involved in the broader questions about his existence, nature, and power. Beyond this was the primary question faced by all interpreters of literature written at a time and place other than their own: How can writings from one time, place, and culture be made understandable and relevant to another time, place, and culture? The responses by Intertestamental Judaism involved two first steps: developing interpretive methods (hermeneutical procedures) and making the Scriptures available in other languages. A third step raised the question of canon, that is, Which documents should be recognized as Holy Scripture? Each of these steps merits a major study in itself. We can here offer only brief sketches.

1. The Development of Interpretive Methods

The changes in Israel's cultural situation even before the exile had been dramatic. Organizationally the Hebrews moved from a nomadic family-tribe in Canaan to a slave people in Egypt, then a wandering nation in the wilderness, a settled confederation of tribes united only by use of a common sanctuary and blood relation, and finally a united and then divided monarchy that was a sometimes major player on the international scene. Economically the Hebrews were wandering shepherds, peasant farmers, and small manufacturers and traders. Although they were essentially a rural and small-town people, they also had their larger cities with their attendant problems. Religiously Abraham and his family were originally pagans (Josh. 24:2, 14–15). He and his descendants became monotheists who worshiped first at numerous sites, then in a portable tent, and finally in a centralized temple. They were frequently tempted to adopt some pagan practices or even full religious schemes; occasionally they succumbed to the temptation. It was in such conditions that the earlier parts of the Scriptures were written.

The postexilic period brought a very different situation. At its beginning Judea was a small temple-state within the Persian Empire. Many of her people were returned captives; the population in general struggled both to survive and to rebuild Jerusalem. Class and economic distinctions caused difficulties as did tax obligations (Neh. 5:1–13). Save for rulers and some of the aristocracy, the socioeconomic situation in general appears to have been essentially rural and agricultural and small-town, with light manufacturing and trading. On the whole, conditions were quite different from those assumed by most Old Testament writers. As a result, many intertestamental Jews, ignorant of the circumstances presupposed by the writers, found the Scriptures unintelligible and inadequate or irrelevant in their very different world. To such issues the intertestamental interpreters addressed themselves.

The intertestamental interpreters were primarily concerned to uncover the meaning of the text. In addition they sought to demonstrate how God's revelation in the law was to be applied in the changing situations of life. They also tried to persuade their followers to accept their interpretations as being the divine will for life and conduct. They produced an array of interpretive methods and procedures. Some are notoriously difficult to define; at times the lines of distinction between them are blurred. Some appear almost ludicrous to the modern Western mind; others seem the obvious approach. Because we know most about the interpretive procedures which eventually became associated with Rabbinic Judaism, we will consider them first.

Probably the oldest interpretive form is the targum (translation, interpretation), which addressed both the linguistic and the interpretive problems at the same time. Written in Aramaic, a targum is a running paraphrase-commentary on the Hebrew text. Nehemiah 8 gives an example of the situations in which targums arose and of their use. The rebuilding of the temple and the walls of Jerusalem was complete. It was now essential that the inhabitants of Judea know and apply the law to both worship and life. Although Hebrew was still the sacred language, Aramaic was the common tongue. Ezra rose to read the law of Moses in an assembly in Jerusalem. As he did so, a number of Levites stood with him and "helped the people to understand the law, while the people remained in their places. So they read from the book, from the law of God, with interpretation. They gave the sense, so that the people understood the reading" (Neh. 8:7–8). The concern was for knowledge and understanding. Presumably, Ezra read in Hebrew while his associates gave both an Aramaic translation and explanations which conveyed the meaning.

An example of a specific targum will be helpful. The Targum of Pseudo-Jonathan is a collection which dates much later than the New Testament, "but since it rests on a tradition going back to pre-Christian times it includes very early material."[3] Typical is its entry on Genesis 3:15:

> *And I will put enmity between thee and the woman, and between* the seed of your offspring and the seed of her offspring; and it shall be that when the offspring of the woman keep the commandments of the Law, they will aim right (at you) and they will smite you on the *head*; but when they abandon the commandments of the Law, you will aim right (at them), and you will wound them in the *heel*. However, for them there will be a remedy, but for you there will be none, and in the future they will make peace with [or "a cure for"] the heel in the days of the king, Messiah.[4]

3. John W. Bowker, *The Targums and Rabbinic Literature* (New York: Cambridge University Press, 1969), 26.

4. Ibid., 122.

Another category of interpretive method is found in the development of the material which was later (c. A.D. 90–200) collected, edited, and adapted in the Mishnah (commandments).[5] Its nature is reflected in Mishnah *Aboth* 1:1, which speaks of making "a hedge around the Law." This hedge (or fence), which consists of a body of laws, customs, and usages alongside the Pentateuch, developed in the postexilic and following periods and originally circulated in oral form. It constituted the so-called oral law, the tradition, which was considered just as authoritative as the written law.[6]

A particular form of tradition found in the Mishnah is called *halakah* (walking uprightly, the proper way) and deals almost exclusively with the pentateuchal laws. It often explains and interprets by citing opinions from the past. *Halakah* also includes what appear to a non-Jew to be subsidiary, additional laws which, if observed, protect against breaking the law by fencing or hedging in the written command. Such additional interpretations and laws were regarded as part of the original divine intent.

Another hedge, the *haggadah* (teaching), came later. It is associated with biblical books other than the Pentateuch. It carries further the rewriting of biblical material and includes stories, legends, and history which provide illustrations and applications of legal and ethical material.

Yet another form of interpretation is midrash (search out, seek, examine, investigate). This is biblical exposition and comes closer to what Christians recognize as exegesis or commentary than do the forms already mentioned. There are midrashim in the form of homilies or synagogue sermons; some are contained in rabbinic collections like the Mishnah. Most of the midrashim now available come from collections made well after the New Testament Era. In all likelihood, however, both the form and some midrashic material predate Christianity.

The process of interpretation was complex. It involved minute study of the text, consideration of past discussions and applications of the law, consultation among legal scholars, and more. In addition, there were clear guidelines, not all of which are now fully understood. Rabbinic literature contains at least three lists of rules for interpretation, *middot*—seven rules are ascribed to Hillel (fl. 30

5. The Mishnah is "the authorized codification of unwritten law which, on the basis of the written law contained in the Pentateuch, developed during the second temple down to the end of the second century of the common era" (Moses Mielziner, *Introduction to the Talmud*, 5th ed. [New York: Bloch, 1968], 4). The Mishnah, together with its Gemara (completion, finish), commentaries on and expansions of the Mishnah which were compiled between c. A.D. 200 and 500, constitutes the Talmud (study).

6. "The tradition is a fence around the Law," Mishnah *Aboth* 3:14.

B.C.–A.D. 10), thirteen to Rabbi Ishmael (before A.D. 132), and thirty-two to Rabbi Eliezer (the generation after the Bar Kosiba revolt). The rules were most certainly not composed by these men, but represent stages of hermeneutical development within Judaism both during and after the intertestamental period.

The seven rules of Hillel serve as a good example of the guidelines used for developing the tradition in its many forms. At least some of them were followed in the intertestamental period; some are reflected in the New Testament.

1. "Light to heavy" (*Qal wa-homer*): inferences may be made on the assumption that whatever applies in a less important situation applies all the more in a more important case.

   Jesus uses this principle in Matthew 6:26: if God cares for birds, how much more does he care for people.
2. "Verbal analogy between verses" (*Gezerah shawah*): when the same word or phrase is found in two separate passages, the same considerations apply in both cases; what is known of one may be assumed of the other.

   Exodus 22:7–8 deals with money or goods left for safekeeping but then stolen. The guardian "shall be brought before the judges" to determine whether he is the thief. We are not told how this is to be determined nor if the guardian is to make restitution. Verses 10–11 deal with animals that are delivered for safekeeping but die, are injured, or stolen. The guardian is again "brought before the judges"; if he takes an oath attesting guiltlessness before the Lord, the oath is to be accepted as proof of innocence, and no restitution is made. By analogy, the first case is also to be settled by taking an oath; it is to be accepted and no restitution required.

   Matthew 12:1–8 (Mark 2:23–28; Luke 6:1–5) reports that Jesus justified breaking the Sabbath law on the basis of analogy with David's breaking the law to meet the same human need, hunger.
3. "Constructing a family from a single text" (*Binyan ab mikathub ehad*): a word, phrase, or law found in one text pertains to all texts in the same topical family (this involves generalizing from one text to others).

   Deuteronomy 17:2–7 begins, "If there is found among you . . . a man or woman who . . . ," and continues by detailing procedure for dealing with someone who worships other gods, including the provision that the death sentence can be pronounced only on the testimony of more than one witness. Accordingly, any criminal procedure discussed in Scripture with the clause "If there is found among you . . . a man or woman who . . . ," also requires the testimony of more than one witness for conviction.

4. "Constructing a family from two texts" (*Binyan ab mi-shene kethubim*): a word, phrase, or law found in two related texts can be generalized into a principle.

Exodus 21:26 says a slave must be freed if the owner puts out his or her eye; verse 27 requires freeing a slave whose tooth is knocked out. Accordingly, if a slave loses any irreplaceable bodily part because of the owner's action, the slave must be freed.

5. "The general and the particular; the particular and the general" (*Kelal u-ferat u-ferat u-kelal*): a general principle may be limited by the particular (specific) application of it in another passage; on the other hand, a particular rule may be expanded in a general principle.

Leviticus 1:2 speaks of domestic animals in general; this statement is limited by the particular animals listed in subsequent verses. Exodus 22:10–11 speaks of "a donkey, ox, sheep, or any other animal" delivered for safekeeping. The first three are particulars; "any other animal" is general. Thus the procedure here covers the general class, any animal, not just the first three named.

In Galatians 3:28 Paul affirms that there is "no longer Jew or Greek . . . slave or free . . . male and female." He then expands these particulars into a general principle: "all of you are one in Christ Jesus."

6. "A similarity in another passage" (*Ke-yose bo be-maqom aher*): a difficulty in one passage may be solved by comparing it with another passage which has generally similar points.

7. "Something deduced from the context" (*Dabar ha-lamed me-ᶜinyano*): the meaning may be derived by understanding the context in which the text appears.

The same Hebrew word occurs in the list of unclean birds in Leviticus 11:18, where it is translated "water hen," and in the list of unclean reptiles in verse 30, where it is translated "chameleon." The exact meaning of the word is unknown to both ancient rabbis and modern scholars; however, the contexts confirm that the word must designate different creatures.

The command "Do not leave your place on the seventh day" (Exod. 16:29) could be misunderstood as requiring all Israelites to remain home on the Sabbath. However, the context makes clear that the reference is only to leaving one's place to gather manna.

The discovery of the Dead Sea Scrolls focused attention on another method of interpretation called *pesher* (interpretation), which is our first method not associated with Rabbinic Judaism. This genre makes a number of basic assumptions: (1) the biblical texts, especially those of the prophets, do not deal with the writer's time, but the end time, the final age in which God will fulfil his predictions and bring history and his work of salvation to completion—all elements in the text must be handled accordingly; (2) accurate interpretation is dependent upon a divinely appointed and inspired interpreter who will make the true meaning known to his followers (the Dead Sea community believed their own Teacher of Righteousness to be such an individual); and (3) the interpreter is living in the end time, the final age.

In *pesher* the original historical-cultural situation of the writer and often the plain meaning of the words of the text count for nothing. They are but means of conveying the mystery, the true meaning of the text. This true meaning, which is found by isolating it from the original setting, by contemporizing the historical and spiritual message, has to do only with the end time and the role of the interpreter and his followers. The Commentary (*Pesher*) on Habakkuk, for an example, transforms the prophet's message into a description of the life and faith of the Dead Sea community and their leader.

Typology and allegory are two interpretive forms that are often linked and sometimes confused. There is indeed debate about their exact nature and the relation between them. Allegory is an interpretive method which assumes that the writer is attempting to communicate something other than that which he is actually saying. Seeking to go behind the obvious to the real meaning, it treats the elements of the text as symbols. Allegory apparently originated with the Greeks, who sought to find continuing relevance in their poets (especially Homer and Hesiod) and their mythology, upon which Greek religion depended. The Jews adopted the method for a variety of purposes: (1) to bridge the historical and cultural gap between the writers of the Bible and the contemporary situation; (2) to avoid embarrassment over the anthropomorphisms found in the Old Testament; and (3) to harmonize the Old Testament with certain philosophical traditions. The best-known example of Jewish allegorical interpretation is that of Philo of Alexandria.

Typology, on the other hand, while identifying the theological or spiritual significance behind a text, at the same time accepts and appreciates the reality and significance of the historical event. Neil Fujita puts it succinctly: "A typology is an understanding of the history of salvation where persons, events, and institutions are believed to be divinely ordained in such a way that they correspond to their counterparts. For instance, Paul calls Christ the second and last Adam (Rom. 5:12–17; 1 Cor. 15:45–47), and likewise Melchizedek foreshadows Christ, according to the Letter to the Hebrews. Such a view, where the type anticipates an antitype in history, is different from allegory, which is not based on the historical process."[7]

To reiterate the distinction between the two: In allegory the historical, cultural situation is inconsequential in determining the spiritual meaning; it merely provides clues through which the spiritual import may be found. In typology the historical situation and content of the passage are significant in themselves; true, they may be played down and considered of only secondary importance at best, but they are viewed as both real and valuable.

One more method of interpretation must be noted here, the apocalyptic (see ch. 10). Apocalyptic is first and foremost a worldview and a literary form. It is also a hermeneutic, an attempt to make the Bible speak to the interpreter's own day. Hence the apocalyptist, like the writer of *pesher*, often read the biblical past in terms of his own present.

2. Translation

We have already noted that the targums sought to deal with the problem of those who understood Aramaic but not Hebrew. The fourth-century crisis, resulting from Hellenism, left many Jews, especially those outside the boundaries of the land of Israel, unable to understand either Hebrew or Aramaic. For those Jews, and ultimately for Christianity, one of the most important results of this crisis was the translation of the Old Testament into Greek. The term *Septuagint* is usually used in discussions of the Greek translation of the Hebrew Bible (including the Apocrypha). It comes from the Latin *septuaginta* (seventy); and the Roman numeral for seventy, LXX, has become a standard way of referring to the Greek Old Testament.

Our earliest sources of information about the origin of the Septuagint are fragmentary remains of the writings of an Alexandrian Jewish philosopher named Aristobulus (c. 170 B.C.) and the Letter of Aristeas (usually included among the pseudepigraphal writings), which say that the earliest translation of the Hebrew Bible into Greek took place in Egypt during the reign of Ptolemy II Philadelphus (285–246 B.C.). Additional information, much of it of doubtful

---

7. Neil S. Fujita, *A Crack in the Jar: What Ancient Jewish Documents Tell Us about the New Testament* (Mahwah, N.J.: Paulist, 1986), 135.

historical value, comes from Philo and later writers. In general they report a legend that Ptolemy desired a translation of the Jewish law for his great library. So seventy-two (or seventy) scholars were sent from Jerusalem; they accomplished the task in seventy-two days. The result was subsequently hailed as a work of high accuracy.

There are grave questions about the accuracy of this account about the seventy scholars. In addition, other considerations make the use of the term *septuagint* imprecise and misleading. It is common to use the term to refer to all ancient renderings of the Old Testament into Greek. Other possibilities exist, however. Perhaps the term should be used exclusively of the Greek Pentateuch, or the oldest known Greek translation of each biblical book, or the Greek translation of the Hebrew Bible alone, thus excluding books written originally in Greek and not included in the Hebrew canon.

There is, unfortunately, no conclusive evidence indicating precisely when the translation of the Hebrew Scriptures into Greek took place, for what reasons, and under what conditions. What is now known indicates that separate parts were translated by different persons, at different times and places, using different texts and translation methods. If indeed there was an original translation in Egypt, and there may well have been, it probably included only the Law, the five books of Moses. Translations of the other biblical books were made later. Successive copying, revisions, and additional translations introduced significant variants into the texts of the Greek Bible and resulted in an array of questions about their origin, relationships, and value. Special investigations have centered upon the grammar and vocabulary as well as the theological orientation.[8]

In any case, the Bible in Greek was widely used by Greek-speaking Jews, but evidently not highly regarded by some of the more strict Jews in the land of Israel. Most early Christians adopted the Greek Scriptures as their own. By the second century A.D., Jewish scholars produced their own editions in reaction to the Christians' use of the Greek Old Testament. These editions sought to correct apparent mistranslations used by Christians in promoting their faith and generally to conform the Greek to the Hebrew text that was most widely used in the land of Israel.

The work of Aquila (c. A.D. 128) was hyperliteralistic in its attempt to reproduce the Hebrew text as closely as possible. By the end of the second century, in reaction to Christian use of the Septu-

8. See Sidney Jellicoe, *The Septuagint and Modern Study* (Oxford: Clarendon, 1968); idem, *Studies in the Septuagint: Origins, Recensions, and Interpretations* (New York: Ktav, 1974); Emanuel Tov, "Jewish Greek Scriptures," in *Early Judaism and Its Modern Interpreters,* ed. Robert A. Kraft and George W. E. Nicklesburg (Atlanta: Scholars, 1986), 223–37.

agint, Aquila had become the official version to be read in synagogues whenever a Greek translation was appropriate. The
translation of Symmachus (late second and early third centuries
A.D.) is a mixture of precise conformity to the Hebrew and free para-
phrases attempting to convey the original meaning in an understandable and pleasing fashion. Between the two is the work of
Theodotion, a second-century scholar probably from Ephesus. Traditions differ as to whether he was a proselyte to Judaism or maybe
an Ebionite Christian. Discussion of Theodotion's version centers
on the nature of the text from which he worked, an issue upon which
recent discoveries in the Judean wilderness have shed light.

Traditional editions of the Septuagint differ from the Hebrew
Old Testament in three major ways. First, the order of books de-
parts from the threefold division in the Hebrew (Torah, Former
and Latter Prophets, and Writings). The order is essentially that
found in most English translations. Second, the content of the
books. The text of the Greek versions differs from that of the traditional Hebrew at many places. In addition, several books are divided differently; some contain more or less material than does the
Hebrew. Several of the psalms, for an example, are divided differently; there is also a Psalm 151 not found in the Hebrew. The Book
of Jeremiah is about one-eighth shorter in the Septuagint, and
some of its parts are rearranged. Finally, the number of books in
the Septuagint is larger; it contains the so-called Apocrypha,
which is absent from the Hebrew canon. Although there is a recognized core of apocryphal books, the exact number is debated.

The nature of the differences between the Septuagint and the
Hebrew is complex and has occasioned intense studies. Suffice it
to note here that at times the Septuagint is quite literal, at others
it is almost a paraphrase; sometimes it seems that a targumic or
midrashic expansion has been incorporated into the text. Rabbinic
writings recognize as legitimate various textual changes made in
the Septuagint.[9] In some cases reverence for God or accommoda-
tion to the sensitivities of the Greek world seems to have prompted
deliberate modification of the text. Other details may have been altered to protect the reputation of important persons or to remove
difficulties from the text. A few specific details, such as the number
of Jacob's family who went to Egypt and the dimensions of the tabernacle, differ from the Hebrew.

Some knowledge of the Septuagint is very important for Christian studies. Eighty percent of the Old Testament quotations in the
New Testament are taken from the Septuagint. As Christianity

9. A list is given by Bowker, *Targums and Rabbinic Literature*, 319–20.

moved out of a strictly Jewish environment, the Septuagint became the Bible of the early church. Further, it was through this channel that the Apocrypha became a part of the debates about the canon of Scripture.

The Septuagint is important to studies of Intertestamental Judaism as well. It is essential to recognize that the Greek Old Testament is a prime source of information about Hellenistic Judaism; its distinctives provide insights into the minds of its translators and so into their experiences and theology. For our purposes it is essential to recognize the Septuagint as one of the significant ways in which Jews responded to the two major crises that threatened their religion and culture.

3. Identification of the Canon

The shift of emphasis from temple and ceremony to morals and ethics made the written Scriptures even more important. They became the focal point of study, life, and worship. The Bible, especially the Law, was understood to be divinely inspired; it possessed, therefore, inherent authority.[10] This is clearly demonstrated in the account of Ezra's reading the Law (Neh. 8–10): the people gathered in solemn assembly; they stood when the book, which is specifically called the "law of God," was opened; and the people and their leaders bound themselves "to observe and do all the commandments of the LORD our Lord and his ordinances and his statutes" (Neh. 10:29). The Law was honored as God's law and accepted as normative. An example of the intertestamental attitude is found in the Book of Jubilees, where the Mosaic law is described as the "heavenly tablets" at least twenty times (e.g., Jub. 3:10, 31; 4:5, 32). The two other divisions of the Hebrew Scriptures, the Prophets and the Writings, were also recognized as divine in origin and authoritative; yet they were never regarded as holding quite the same status as has the Torah.

The importance of Scripture, especially the Law, in Judaism was hardly new. The Mosaic law was recognized as sacred from the

10. There is within modern Christianity an important difference in the understanding of the grounds of canonicity. The Greek Orthodox, Roman Catholics, and some liberal Protestants assume that official Jewish and later Christian councils gave authority to the biblical books by selecting them for the canon. The traditional Protestant view affirms that the Jewish and Christian councils simply recognized authority that was inherent by virtue of divine inspiration. The ramifications of the debate are significant. In the former view the church gives authority to Scripture (and so, in some way, sits in judgment over it), whereas in the latter view the church merely recognizes authority (and thus the Scriptures have authority over and sit in judgment on the church).

time it first appeared. It prescribed in detail how ceremonies were to be performed as well as how life was to be lived. Nevertheless, the shift in emphasis from ceremony to ethics brightened the spotlight upon the content of Scripture, and made it even more necessary to identify, protect, and obey it.

Within the traditional Hebraic culture and in the land of Israel there seems to have been little doubt about the content of the Bible. "Palestinian Jews made a sharp distinction between inspired scripture and human writings; canonization was a solemn recognition on the part of the leaders and the people that certain books were divinely revealed to prophets. Traditionally the final canonization of the whole Bible was accomplished by the men of the Great Synagogue (Assembly) in the time of Ezra and Nehemiah. Orthodox Judaism in Palestine after 400 B.C. always knew what was scripture and what was not."[11]

The first reference to the Hebraic threefold division of the Bible is in the prologue of Sirach (Ecclesiasticus), where "the Law and the Prophets and the others [i.e., other books] that followed them" are equated with "the Scriptures." The same divisions were certainly in the mind of Jesus when he spoke of "the law of Moses, the prophets, and the psalms" (Luke 24:44). Josephus speaks of twenty-two books in three divisions.[12] These twenty-two seem to be the same thirty-nine found in the modern Hebrew and Protestant Bibles.[13] Post–A.D. 70 rabbinic discussions assume that the

11. R. H. Pfeiffer, "Canon of the OT," in *Interpreter's Dictionary of the Bible,* ed. George A. Buttrick et al., 4 vols. (New York: Abingdon, 1962), 1:510.

12. "We do not possess myriads of inconsistent books, conflicting with each other. Our books, those which are justly accredited, are but two and twenty, and contain the record of all time.

"Of these, five are the books of Moses, comprising the laws and the traditional history from the birth of man down to the death of the lawgiver. This period falls only a little short of three thousand years. From the death of Moses until Artaxerxes, who succeeded Xerxes as king of Persia, the prophets subsequent to Moses wrote the history of the events of their own times in thirteen books. The remaining four books contain hymns to God and precepts for the conduct of human life.

"From Artaxerxes to our own time the complete history has been written, but has not been deemed worthy of equal credit with the earlier records, because of the failure of the exact succession of the prophets" (Josephus *Against Apion* 1.8 [38–41]).

13. Josephus's canon of twenty-two books clearly excludes the additions in the Greek version of his day. Discussions seeking to identify precisely which books he had in mind must take into consideration that some books which were counted as one in Josephus's day are divided in modern Bibles. The most dramatic example is that in the first century the Minor Prophets were considered one book, the Book of the Twelve, possibly because they all fitted on a standard-size scroll.

In a note on Josephus's statement, H. St. J. Thackeray (Josephus, *Works,* 9 vols., Loeb Classical Library [Cambridge, Mass.: Harvard University Press, 1926–65], 1:179) suggests the fol-

Old Testament canon was already well established; only the Song of Songs and Ecclesiastes were questioned.[14]

The advent of Hellenism and the subsequent appearance of the Scriptures in Greek brought a challenge to the consensus. The books in the Septuagint, other than the five of Moses, were arranged according to literary types. This undermined the threefold division and its implications for interpretation.

Further, some Greek-speaking Jews did not share the conviction that the age of prophecy had ceased and the canon thus been closed. Books with special appeal to the Greek mind began to be read along with the traditional canon, and at least some Hellenistic Jews regarded some of those books as equal in authority. Because all existing editions of the Greek Old Testament are Christian, we do not know precisely which groups of Hellenistic Jews included apocryphal books in their canon nor which ones they included. We may assume that the type of variety evident today in the lists of the Roman Catholic and Greek Orthodox churches parallels the diversity among Greek-speaking Jews during intertestamental times. For our study it is important to note that one of the responses to the sixth- and especially the fourth-century crisis was a diversity of opinion about precisely which books belonged in the Jewish Bible. Another response was concern to deal with this diversity.

---

lowing division: A. The five books of Moses; B. The Prophets: (1) Joshua, (2) Judges and Ruth, (3) Samuel, (4) Kings, (5) Chronicles, (6) Ezra and Nehemiah, (7) Esther, (8) Job, (9) Isaiah, (10) Jeremiah and Lamentations, (11) Ezekiel, (12) Minor Prophets, (13) Daniel; C. The Remaining: (1) Psalms, (2) Song of Songs, (3) Proverbs, (4) Ecclesiastes. The modern Hebrew canon assigns books to the second and third divisions somewhat differently. For fuller discussion see Emil Schürer, *The History of the Jewish People in the Age of Jesus Christ,* ed. Geza Vermes et al., 3 vols. (Edinburgh: T. and T. Clark, 1973–87), 2:317 n. 12.

14. For example, Mishnah *Yadaim* 3:5: "All the Holy Scriptures render the hands unclean. The Song of Songs and Ecclesiastes render the hands unclean. R. [Rabbi] Judah says: The Song of Songs renders the hands unclean, but about Ecclesiastes there is dissension. R. Jose says: Ecclesiastes does not render the hands unclean, and about the Song of Songs there is dissension. R. Simeon says: Ecclesiastes is one of the things about which the School of Shammai adopted the more lenient, and the School of Hillel the more stringent ruling. R. Simeon b. Azzai said: I have heard a tradition from the seventy-two elders on the day when they made R. Eleazer b. Azariah head of the college [of Sages], that the Song of Songs and Ecclesiastes both render the hands unclean. R. Akiba said: God forbid!—no man in Israel ever disputed about the Song of Songs [that he should say] that it does not render the hands unclean, for all the ages are not worth the day on which the Song of Songs was given to Israel; for all the Writings are holy, but the Song of Songs is the Holy of Holies. And if aught was in dispute the dispute was about Ecclesiastes alone. R. Johanan b. Joshua, the son of R. Akiba's father-in-law, said: According to the words of Ben Azzai so did they dispute and so did they decide." Note that the phrase "render the hands unclean" means something like "are holy, set aside for God, of divine origin"; contact with something holy required one to ceremonially wash the hands. See also Schürer, *History,* 2:320 n. 18.

Development of the Synagogue

Nothing speaks more eloquently of Jewish readjustment in the face of the intertestamental crises than does the growth of the synagogue. As study of and obedience to the law, the moral and ethical emphasis, became the primary foundation block of Jewish religion and life, the synagogue became the central institution of Jewish communities. Names for the institution vary. *Proseuchē* (place of prayer) may be the oldest name and the one most often used in the land of Israel in the first century. It occurs also in the Diaspora. In Acts 16:13 it seems to refer to a small chapel-like structure that was used for prayer because there was not a sufficient number of families for a full synagogue organization. (At least ten men were required to form a synagogue.) The most common word, *synagōgē*, means "place of assembly" or "house of worship." Josephus records a decree by Caesar Augustus which refers to a *sabbateion* (Sabbath house).[15] The Talmud frequently uses the term "the place [or house] of the assembly" or simply "the assembly." The idea of a community assembly probably most accurately conveys the nature of the institution.

The origin of the synagogue is uncertain. Some sources claim that it was present in Judaism from its inception.[16] The Talmud says there were synagogues in Babylon during the captivity. Biblical statements like "I have been a sanctuary to them for a little while in the countries where they have gone" (Ezek. 11:16) and "certain elders of Israel came to me and sat down before me" (Ezek. 14:1) are sometimes cited in support of this claim. The earliest written record comes from the time of Ptolemy III Euergetes (246–221 B.C.). The assembly of the people in Jerusalem for Scripture reading and prayer in the time of Ezra certainly reflects the type of situation from which the synagogue developed. It is worth noting that the traditions about the Great Synagogue claim it began with Ezra during the Persian period.

Most simply put, the synagogue developed as the center of Hebrew life after the loss of traditional institutions. It was not a substitute for temple worship and services as such, but a supplement to them. Concern for the temple continued, and synagogues remained after the temple was rebuilt. The New Testament assumes there were synagogues in Jerusalem at the time of Jesus, where they would have been superfluous if they were simply a replace-

---

15. Josephus *Antiquities* 16.6.2 (164).

16. Josephus *Against Apion* 2.18 (175) and Philo *Life of Moses* 2.39 (216) say the synagogue was established by Moses. This is reflected in other writings as well. See Schürer, *History,* 2:427 n. 7.

ment for the temple. The Mishnah even implies the presence of a synagogue within the precinct of the temple ("the hall of hewn stone"). Rabbinic tradition indicates there were 480 synagogues in Jerusalem, a probable exaggeration considering the size of the city.

Information is sketchy about virtually all aspects of the synagogue—organization, officers, service of worship, and buildings. There are few detailed pre–A.D. 70 accounts touching on these matters; archaeological evidence also comes primarily from later centuries. An inscription found on the Ophel hill indicates the presence of synagogues in Jerusalem and provides important information about the institution in general: "Theodotus, son of Vetenus, priest and archisynagogus, grandson of an archisynagogus, built the synagogue for the reading of the law and for the teaching of the commandments, and the guest house and rooms and supplies of water as an inn for those who are in need when coming from abroad, which synagogue his fathers and the elders and Simonides founded." The Mishnah and other rabbinic sources tell much about the synagogue, but it is often difficult to distinguish reports and descriptions of later developments from conditions and practices actually present in the intertestamental period. What evidence there is confirms the synagogue as an institution that developed over a period of time. Practices became much more standardized and prescribed after the New Testament Era; even so, there remained some opportunity for adaptation, freedom of expression, and lay participation.

The synagogue was first and foremost a place for reading of Scripture and for prayer. The most profound knowledge of the law was available only to scholars. Yet Intertestamental Judaism expected everyone to be thoroughly familiar with it as a basis for life. It was the synagogue, with its regular reading and interpretation of the Law and of the Prophets, and with its schools for the young, that wove the Scriptures into the fabric of life and experience of the people. There were no altars nor sacrifices in the synagogue; instead only the sacred books (scrolls) were absolutely necessary. Although priests who were in attendance were usually selected to be the public readers and to pronounce the blessings, their presence was not required for a synagogue service as it was for worship in the temple. The revered leaders of the synagogue were the elders of the community and those with recognizable expertise in the law.

Synagogues were organized wherever there were enough men (ten) to constitute a proper assembly, whether in the land of Israel or beyond. The older and more distinguished persons took their places in the front; others sat or stood in the rear or maybe along the sides. Although men and women were segregated by the Middle Ages, there is no evidence of the practice in the intertestamental period.[17] Non-Jews, that is, God-fearers, were allowed to attend at least some synagogue services. Services were held on the Sabbath (often more than one), and possibly on Mondays and Thursdays as well. There were also special assemblies on feast days and other important occasions of the religious and civil calendars.

The liturgy was simple but services could be several hours in length. The principal parts of the service included recitation of the *Shema*, the daily prayer (*Shemoneh 'Esreh*), and reading of the Law and the Prophets. The reading was accompanied by a translation-interpretation (a targum), and frequently a sermon-homily. All elements of the service were preceded and usually concluded with blessings. At the close of each prayer the congregation joined in saying "Amen."

The *Shema* was not a prayer, but a confession of faith. It consisted of Deuteronomy 6:4–9 ("Hear, O Israel . . ."), Deuteronomy 11:13–21 ("If you will only heed his every commandment . . ."), and Numbers 15:37–41 ("The LORD said to Moses . . ."). In the Intertestamental Era it may have included the Ten Commandments as well.

The daily prayer, the *Shemoneh 'Esreh* (Eighteen Benedictions), was an important component of both synagogue worship and private devotion. Neither the origin nor the exact intertestamental wording of the daily prayer can now be reconstructed. The text was still fairly fluid and could be adapted by the officiant. Evidently the daily prayer had ancient roots and went through many forms. Early reflections of the Eighteen Benedictions can be found in Sirach 51. The version found in the Cairo genizah, sometimes called the Palestinian version, is substantially different from the Babylonian and may be closer to the first-century text.[18] The version now used in synagogues, the Babylonian, postdates A.D. 70 and has a set form.[19]

The first three blessings praise God's power and grace, the bases for Israel's hope. The last three thank him for his goodness and request his blessing. In between are prayers for knowledge, repen-

17. Segregation by gender in the synagogue is usually assumed. Schürer, *History*, 2:447 n. 98, for example, assumes segregation. But for a summary of convincing evidence against segregation in the intertestamental period see S. Safrai, "The Synagogue," in *The Jewish People in the First Century*, ed. S. Safrai, M. Stern et al., in *Compendia Rerum Iudaicarum ad Novum Testamentum*, 7 vols. (Philadelphia: Fortress, 1974–92), 2:919–20, 939–40.

18. The text of these two versions is printed in Schürer, *History*, 2:454–63. See also the discussion by Safrai, "Synagogue," 2:916–17, 922–26.

19. "Simeon Pekoli (or: the cotton dealer) arranged the benedictions in their order in the presence of Rabban Gamaliel at Jabneh" (Babylonian Talmud *Berakoth* 28b and *Megillah* 17b, cited from Safrai, "Synagogue," 2:916).

tance, forgiveness, deliverance, health, a fruitful land, the gathering of the dispersed, restoration of the nation, rebuilding of Jerusalem, reinstitution of sacrificial worship, and the coming of Messiah. The prayer for the Messiah appears in a shorter form in the Cairo-Palestinian version.[20] It is the twelfth blessing of older versions that contains the condemnation that, as we noted earlier (p. 102), forced Jewish Christians to withdraw from synagogue worship (see Appendix E, pp. 366–67).

Scripture reading focused on the Pentateuch but included the Prophets as well. Readings of the Law were organized in a way that assured consecutive coverage of the whole of the Mosaic books in a three-year cycle. In the land of Israel several members of a congregation, usually three, five, or seven, were invited to take part in the reading, each having to read at least three verses. In Diaspora synagogues the reading was done by only one person. Both in Israel and abroad, one person alone read from the Prophets; he was free to select the passage (see Luke 4:17). The readings were accompanied by a targum, a translation-interpretation which included both a free rendering of the text into another language and a brief explanation of it. In the land of Israel the interpretation was in Aramaic, elsewhere in the vernacular, for example, Greek. The Torah was interpreted verse by verse, the Prophets in larger units.

By the latter part of the first century a sermon or homily was a frequent, though not mandatory, part of synagogue worship. An elder, rabbi, or other authority could be invited to speak, if appropriate (see Acts 13:15). The sermon was essentially a study of the Law that included interpretation and application beyond the targum. It was through this regular, systematic reading and exposition of Scripture that the mind and heart of the intertestamental Jew became saturated with its contents and requirements.

While the temple was controlled by the priests, the synagogue was basically a lay institution. Our knowledge of synagogue orga-

---

20. In the Palestinian recension, the fourteenth blessing reads as follows: "Be merciful, Lord our God, with thy great mercies, to Israel thy people and to Jerusalem thy city; and to Zion, the dwelling-place of the glory; and to thy Temple and thy habitation; and to the kingship of the house of David, thy righteous Messiah. *Blessed art thou, Lord, God of David, who buildest Jerusalem.*"

In contrast, the Babylonian version does not use the word *Messiah* but refers to the throne of David in the fourteenth blessing. The content of the Babylonian fifteenth blessing is not found in the older edition: "(14) And to Jerusalem, thy city, return with mercy and dwell in its midst as thou hast spoken; and build it soon in our days to be an everlasting building; and raise up quickly in its midst the throne of David. *Blessed art thou, Lord, who buildest Jerusalem.* (15) Cause the shoot of David to shoot forth quickly, and raise up his horn by thy salvation. For we wait on thy salvation all the day. *Blessed art thou, Lord, who causest the horn of salvation to shoot forth.*"

nization is imprecise, and the evidence demonstrates variation between synagogues. There is no evidence of government by popular assembly in either the Jewish community or the synagogue as in Greek city-states, some Christian churches (see, e.g., 1 Cor. 5), and the Dead Sea community (1QS 8:25–9:2). Actual leadership was in the hands of the elders, respected heads of families in the community. In predominantly Jewish communities in first-century Israel the town council and leadership of the synagogue probably comprised the same people; there was no separation between the religious and civic realms. In places where the majority of the population was Gentile, the elders of the synagogue would, of course, have strictly religious functions.

In Jewish areas the synagogue was the property of the town. Providing a building, necessary equipment, and supervision was the responsibility of the government. In non-Jewish areas this responsibility fell to the Jewish community as a whole. In all cases, constant contact with Gentiles and less than fully observant Jews made it necessary for the recognized leaders to be ever vigilant against intrusion of foreign elements.

Although there were some designated officers, there was no one specifically charged to conduct worship in the synagogue—to read, preach, and pray. All males, even young boys, were qualified to participate in the service. The major official was the *archisynagōgos,* the chief of the synagogue, who was in overall charge of its affairs. Evidently he was appointed by the elders and served without pay. The *hazzan* (minister or attendant) was, in Jewish areas, an executive officer for the town as well as the synagogue. He received pay from community and synagogue. The *hazzan* was in actual charge of much of the service and the activity of the synagogue. He brought out the scrolls, handed them to those selected by the chief of the synagogue to serve as readers, took back the scrolls after the readings, announced prayers and other elements of worship, and signaled for the people to say "Amen." The *hazzan* controlled the blowing of horns and trumpets to indicate the beginning and end of the Sabbath and other times of significance. He seems to have been responsible for the physical upkeep of the facilities. Even if he was not actually the supervisor and teacher, he assisted in the education of children. When punishments were prescribed in judicial cases, the *hazzan* administered them. The other regular synagogue officer was the almoner, who both received and dispensed alms.

Physical remains of intertestamental synagogues have been found only at Herodium and Masada. Both were adaptations of structures originally built for other uses. The description in the

Theodotus inscription (p. 140) provides additional pre–A.D. 70 evidence about intertestamental synagogues. The Mishnah and other rabbinic writings describe a variety, complexity, and ornamentation not likely before A.D. 70.

There was a building of some sort. The Mishnah prescribes that it was to be on the highest spot in town, near water, and facing the direction of the Jerusalem temple; many synagogues did not meet these specifications. The most important possession of the synagogue was, of course, the books; the one indispensable item of furniture was the ark, the Torah shrine, in which they were kept. This ark was sometimes set permanently in the building; in first-century synagogues some arks were placed on wheels and transported into the main room. Evidently synagogues had a raised area and stand for readers and preachers; archaeologists have found no trace of these features, but they are mentioned in written sources. A prominent seat at the front, the Moses seat (Matt. 23:2), was reserved for whoever delivered the sermon or performed some other important function. Other furniture included seats of wood or stone. Additional equipment included lamps, horns, trumpets, and possibly bells. And finally, for ceremonial purposes, ready access to water and baths for ritual cleansing (*mikvoth*) was a necessity.

Synagogues, as the word implies, were gathering places. The buildings were used for official public meetings, schools, tribunals of judgment, and social occasions. The Theodotus inscription mentions hostelry, "the guest house and rooms and supplies of water as an inn for those who are in need when coming from abroad." Archaeological remains at several sites confirm the presence of an inn in the precinct of the synagogue.

Reactions of Specific Groups

We have seen that defeat and captivity at the hands of the Babylonians and the arrival of Hellenism elicited a variety of reactions from Jews caught in the surges of traumatic changes. The synagogue, for example, arose as the nucleus of the Jewish people. A symbol of the distinctiveness of Intertestamental Judaism from the classical Old Testament period, it became the center of the whole community or of a specific group (Acts 6:9). Many intertestamental Jews, probably the majority, simply accepted and sought to adapt to the changing social order and structure. Others resisted the new society and worked for change from within, while still others sought, both from within and without, to create a totally different society modeled either on the past or on some new vision of the future. At the extreme of the social continuum were the dropouts and ascetics who withdrew completely to form their own societies and live their own way without reference to other persons and the forces driving the rest of the world.

The differing reactions to Hellenism provide a good example of the variety we have in mind. Some dissociated themselves from their Jewish heritage, became totally hellenized, adopted paganism, and were willing to work to the detriment of Jews and Judaism out of loyalty to their new commitment. Tiberius Julius Alexander, nephew of the philosopher Philo, seems to have been such an individual. He allied himself with the Greco-Roman world, held governmental positions, and even commanded a part of the Roman army in the A.D. 66–70 war against the Jews.

At the other extreme were those who, like the original Maccabees, fought against the incursion of the new, or at least some parts of it. Between the extremes were those who withstood but without violence, resorting to passive resistance or apathy toward Hellenism. Some groups and individuals seem to have emphasized, or maybe overemphasized, Hebraic distinctives against Greek influence.

Hellenistic Judaism represents the road of compromise, the attempt to be both a part of the new world order and a loyal Jew at the same time. Philo displays the better qualities of this group; for Josephus and other self-seeking members of the priestly families and aristocracy, however, commitment to the traditional national-religious concerns was but a veneer for an essentially secular orientation.[21]

That there were widely differing reactions will be nothing more than expected by observers with even a casual awareness of sociological dynamics. Our task in the following chapters will be to particularize by focusing upon some of the distinctive intertestamental Jewish trajectories which developed in reaction to the crises of the period and provided the foundation for much of the diversity within it.

There were those who attempted to reestablish the institutions of the past—monarchy, priesthood, and temple worship (ch. 8). This is the group that led the returns from exile, rebuilt Jerusalem and its temple, and sought to restore the life and worship of the past. Later representatives include the Maccabees, their supporters, and other traditionalists, the religious conservatives. However, the liberal political and social views of some persons in this group, such as the Sadducees, views which are evident in their support of

21. With regard to literary reactions to Hellenism, few would doubt the Hellenistic influence in the Letter of Aristeas, 4 Maccabees, the Sibylline Oracles, and other apocryphal and pseudepigraphal writings. Scholars are sometimes divided, however, on whether a document represents Hellenism or a polemic against it. For a few evaluations see p. 118 n. 10.

Hellenism and Roman authorities, illustrate the complexity of the subject with which we are dealing.

The scribes sought to adjust to the changed situation by developing the oral law, which they passed on to following generations through a succession of teachers (ch. 9). At least one branch of this movement became the Pharisaic and rabbinic elements of the New Testament and post–A.D. 70 eras.

Another readjustment that occurred in the intertestamental period was the apocalyptic movement, which had its own worldview, literary form, and hermeneutical methodology (ch. 10). While a few persons and groups could be classified as strict apocalyptists in outlook and commitment, the influence of apocalyptic is also evident in several other movements.

The sectarian movement included the various groups just mentioned: people seeking to restore the past, scribes who developed the oral tradition, and apocalyptists (ch. 11). Each group approached the sixth- and fourth-century crises in its own way and had its own special practices, views, emphases, and experiences. Their very existence is evidence of extraordinary diversity within Intertestamental Judaism.

In 1935 the French writer Joseph Thomas, working almost exclusively from literary evidence, postulated the existence of numerous baptismal sects in the land of Israel, especially in the Jordan Valley.[22] Thanks to discoveries in the Judean wilderness at Qumran and elsewhere, we now know more of such groups, especially the first-century group that produced the Dead Sea Scrolls. Evidence points toward including it within the Essene movement, broadly defined. We will give special attention to the Dead Sea community and literature because of its significant contributions and distinctive reaction to the cultural situation.

There is yet one other category of reactions to the crises of the sixth and fourth centuries. It is the most important, yet the most complex and difficult to assess. The *am ha-eretz* (the people of the land) were, of course, the majority of the population. To the chief priests and Pharisees they were "this crowd, which does not know the law—they are accursed" (John 7:49). Their reaction to the crises may have been an instinctive simplification of the readjustments of their leaders. Yet in the long shadow over the pages of history cast by the past, what really determined the character of Intertestamental Judaism and the future course of Jewish history was the reaction of the common people among whom Jesus lived and taught.

---

22. Joseph Thomas, *Le Mouvement baptist en Palestine et Syrie* (Gembloux: J. Duculot, 1935).

8

Intertestamental Attempts to Reconstruct Traditional (Old Testament) Institutions

- Reconstruction of the Temple and Restoration of the Priestly Worship
  + Worship in the Temple
  + Ambiguous Attitudes toward the Temple
  + Feasts and Festivals
- The Desire for Restoration of the Monarchy

It is natural for those who have sustained great loss to yearn for restoration of the past. This usually means rebuilding the past as it was. Certainly, complete restoration was at least the sentimental desire of most Jews, probably including many who did not return to the land of Israel.

The major losses in 586 B.C. were, as we have seen, of land and temple and monarchy. Attempts were made to recapture the past by returning to the land, rebuilding the temple, and reestablishing worship and life in Jerusalem. Hopes for the return of the monarchy were an important element in developing messianic expectations.

Complete reconstruction was, of course, an impossibility. The former Babylonian captives faced a radically changed situation; they could not rebuild the old on the foundation of the new political and social setting. Religiously, the shifts of emphases had already begun to take place; things would not be the same. Nevertheless, there were persistent attempts to establish exact duplications of the former institutions. This attitude contributed greatly to the character of Intertestamental Judaism. It is quite likely that most of the people did not realize that, in fact, the resulting institutions and practices were different.

Little need be said of the renewed Jewish presence in Judea. The land was but a very small portion of that over which the kings had ruled. As a matter of fact, Judea in Persian times was about thirty-two miles east to west and a little less from north to south. Yet, to the returnees, it was their land. The LORD had kept his promise. They were home!

Reconstruction of the Temple and Restoration of the Priestly Worship

Rebuilding the temple was the first objective of the initial returnees from Babylon (Ezra 3:10–13). The laying of its foundation was the occasion of both joy and weeping. Younger persons saw the beginning of the fulfilment of the dream passed on by their elders, but the elders realized that this temple would be less magnificent in size and grandeur than the former (Hag. 2:3).

Temple worship requires priests. Even before leaving Babylonia and once again upon arriving in the land of Israel, care was taken to assure that religious leaders were available, qualified, and properly certified (Ezra 2; 8:15–20; Neh. 7:39–65). Nehemiah insisted on continuing support for Levites (Neh. 13:10–14). The books of Ezra and Nehemiah are filled with evidence of concern for proper organization of temple personnel and services and for moral and ceremonial holiness among all of the people.

The books of Chronicles must be considered along with Ezra-Nehemiah as evidence of concern for city, temple, ceremony, ritual, and law-regulated life.[1] The Chronicler gives an interpretation of past history from the viewpoint of the centrality of the ceremonial worship. David, the founder of the monarchical dynasty, envisioned the temple, prepared for its building, and restructured worship. Solomon built the temple and dedicated it. Chronicles evaluates the later kings of Judah on the basis of their loyalty to the cult.

The reorganization of the priests and the Levites described in Chronicles touches on a problem. Settlement in the land of Israel at the time of Joshua had left the position of Levites uncertain; during the wilderness period their primary duty had been to transport the tabernacle and its furnishings. What was to be their function in

---

1. The near verbal agreement of 2 Chron. 36:22–23 and Ezra 1:1–3 demonstrates the close relationship between the writings.

the new situation? Eventually David and Solomon restructured the priestly and Levitical roles. The postexilic community, determined as it was to duplicate previous conditions as nearly as possible, turned to the Davidic and Solomonic restructuring. Yet there remained in Intertestamental Judaism an ambiguity about the status of the temple, priesthood, and ceremony.

Some account of the history of and attitudes toward the temple both before and during the intertestamental period is vital to any consideration of the Jewish backgrounds of the New Testament. We have already described the major physical features of the temple at the time of Jesus (pp. 50–52). Needless to say, both Old Testament and Intertestamental Judaism placed a high value on the structure and sacrificial cult. The temple was dominant on the skyline of Jerusalem and in Jewish thought. But the fact that the Hebrew religion did not disappear when the temple was destroyed in 586 B.C. and again in A.D. 70 leaves the question of its exact role and status.

The Jerusalem temple was the successor of the tabernacle, which had been constructed and used in the wilderness, set up as the central sanctuary at Shiloh after settlement in the land, and evidently destroyed during the time of Samuel following Israel's defeat at Aphek by the Philistines (1 Sam. 4:1–11; see also Jer. 7:12). David moved the ark of the covenant to a tent in Jerusalem and began plans to build a temple. Solomon carried them out. Josiah destroyed all other worship centers, thus completing the centralization of worship in Jerusalem (2 Kings 23; 2 Chron. 34).

The completion of the second temple after the captivity held both real and symbolic significance. The zeal and ferocity of the Maccabean revolt at the desecration by Antiochus Epiphanes speak volumes about the place of the temple in the hearts of the Jews. Pompey's entering the temple and the Holy of Holies as he extended Rome's domination over the Jews was an unconscionable act.

For all his faults Herod the Great's work of refurbishing (actually rebuilding) the temple was a credit to his standing among most Jews and the world at large. The importance of the temple for intertestamental Jews is further illustrated by their reaction to Caligula's threat to desecrate the temple in A.D. 40–41. The destruction of the temple in 70 was a tragedy paralleled in Jewish history only by the conflagration which had consumed its predecessor. Jewish attachment to those few Herodian stones in the retaining wall of the temple platform which stood closest to the Holy of Holies (i.e., the Wailing Wall or, as it was designated after the area came under Israeli control in the 1967 war, the Western Wall) speaks eloquently of the continuing ethnic, national, emotional, and religious significance of the temple, even in ruins.

Most intertestamental Jews, then, even those of the Diaspora, regarded the temple as a permanent structure of inestimable value and holiness. Pilgrims flocked to worship at the temple during annual festivals. Most Jews in both the land of Israel and the Diaspora voluntarily supported it by their regular payment of the temple tax (Matt. 17:24–27).

Worship in the Temple

In our discussion of Old Testament ideas and institutions, we noted the various types of sacrifices offered in the temple (pp. 67–68). We reserved a description of the sacrificial ritual for this point because the ceremony developed more fully during the intertestamental period and intertestamental sources describe it in more detail.

Probably the oldest extrabiblical description of temple worship is contained in Jesus ben Sirach's praise of the high priest Simon the Just, probably the son of Onias II. From this we can glean the basic outline of the service. The high priest

> put on his glorious robe . . . [and] went up to the holy altar. . . . He received the portions from the hands of the priests, as he stood by the hearth of the altar. . . . All the sons of Aaron in their splendor held the Lord's offerings in their hands before the whole congregation. . . . Finishing the service at the altars, and arranging the offering . . . he held out his hand for the cup and poured a drink offering . . . at the foot of the altar. . . . Then the sons of Aaron shouted; they blew their trumpets. . . . All the people together quickly fell to the ground on their faces to worship their Lord. . . . The singers praised him with their voices. . . . And the people . . . offered their prayers before the Merciful One, until the order of worship of the Lord was ended, and they completed his ritual. Then [the high priest] came down and raised his hands over the whole congregation . . . to pronounce the blessing of the Lord . . . and they bowed down in worship a second time, to receive the blessing from the Most High. [Sirach 50:11–21]

It should be noted that the high priest did not preside over each day's worship. Usually he did so only on the Sabbath and festival days. The Old Testament does not include prayers nor the priestly benediction (Num. 6:24–26) as part of the sacrificial ritual. These components, along with singing and reading of the law, were among additions made during the intertestamental period. Although Sirach omits numerous details, the essential elements of the daily ceremony are covered.

What Sirach describes is the regular daily offering, the burnt offering, the sacrifice of one lamb in the morning and another in the evening for the nation as a whole. Between these sacrifices individuals and groups presented a wide variety of offerings for themselves. These included sacrifices required for cleansing from ceremonial defilement. On Sabbaths and festival days the basic ceremony was more elaborate, so personal sacrifices were usually not offered.

In addition to Sirach, most of our information about the daily routine comes from rabbinic documents, supplemented by Josephus and other intertestamental writers. The priests were divided into twenty-four courses, each of which served in turn for a week; the rotation occurred in the middle of each Sabbath day. All priests officiating in the temple were clothed with special garments.

Each day, near dawn, the priests who had slept in the temple were summoned. An officer cast lots to determine priestly responsibilities. Those priests who had been selected for duty that day washed their hands and feet; the others were dismissed. The temple precincts were inspected to assure that the courts had not been defiled.[2] Ashes were removed from the bronze altar, and wood placed upon it. Worship began when daylight arrived. The lamps were cleaned and fresh oil put in them, ashes removed from the altar of incense, and the temple doors opened to indicate the beginning of worship. (Sacrifices offered while the temple doors were closed were not considered valid.)

A sacrificial lamb was led into the slaughter area on the north side of the bronze altar. It was given a drink of water from a golden bowl and then killed. Its blood was collected, and its bodily parts divided, arranged, and kept on a marble table until they were to be carried to the altar. Priests and worshipers recited the Ten Commandments, the *Shema,* benedictions, and other prayers. The Mishnah set the particular psalm to be sung each day of the week.[3]

The earlier casting of lots determined which priest was to offer incense in the Holy Place, the inner sanctuary. This offering was considered one of the more important parts of the ceremony. Only priests who had never made this offering were eligible. Others accompanied him into the sanctuary. After the incense was offered, the five priests who had performed the various tasks inside the

2. These inspections were necessary because sometime between A.D. 6 and 9 some Samaritans had thrown human bones into the temple (Josephus *Antiquities* 18.2.2 [30]).

3. Ps. 24 on Sunday, 48 on Monday, 82 on Tuesday, 94 on Wednesday, 81 on Thursday, 93 on Friday, and 92 on the Sabbath (Mishnah *Tamid* 7:4). Of course there is no assurance that this prescription was observed in the intertestamental period.

Holy Place (including cleaning the lamps and removing ashes from the incense altar) stood on the temple steps, the priest who had offered incense being in the middle. They then gave the benediction, which included pronouncing the divine name.[4]

At this point the priests who had been selected to offer the burnt offering threw the body parts of the sacrifice onto the altar. When the high priest officiated, the other priests handed the parts to him, and he performed the rite. The pouring out of the drink offering which followed was the signal for the Levites to begin singing, which was interspersed with the blowing of two silver trumpets. The people prostrated themselves with each trumpet blast. The end of the singing concluded the worship.

The ritual for the evening sacrifice was almost identical to that of the morning. In the evening the lamps were lit but not cleaned. The incense offering followed rather than preceded the burnt offering.

Ambiguous Attitudes toward the Temple

As previously noted, there was ambiguity toward the temple and priesthood. Of course, outward opposition to temple and sacrificial worship would hardly have been tolerated in Intertestamental Judaism. Consider as proof that threats against the temple were among the charges alleged against both Jesus and Stephen (Matt. 26:60–62; 27:40; Mark 14:56–58; 15:29–30; Acts 6:11–14). Yet from some quarters there is evidence of less than wholehearted support, even indifference, and of rivals to the dominance of the temple in Jerusalem.[5]

Even before the destruction of the first temple some of the prophets had been critical of sacrificial worship as it was practiced in their day. Israel and Judah were attempting to satisfy Yahweh's demands with formal observances; they had rejected both the inner aspects of religion and the necessary outward manifestation of it in personal and social life.[6]

---

4. This is the background for the account of the angelic appearance to Zechariah, the father of John the Baptist (Luke 1:5–23). He was present because it was the turn of his division to be in the temple (vv. 5, 8). He had been "chosen by lot" to offer the incense (v. 9). The appearance of the angel while he made the offering parallels traditions of others who had seen visions or received revelations at the altar of incense. Zechariah's inability to speak (vv. 20, 22) was all the more evident because he could not pronounce the benediction.

5. Although they did not seriously threaten the Jerusalem temple, rival temples were constructed in Samaria and in Egypt at Elephantine and Leontopolis. What some have thought to be another temple was begun, but never completed, in Araq el-Emir across the Jordan.

6. Although it is often suggested that these prophets were opposed to the temple and its sacrifices as such, a careful consideration of the texts shows that their hostility was directed against abuses of the external religious features. Note that Hosea 6:6; Amos 5:21–24; and Micah 6:6–8 insist that ceremonial worship is no substitute for godly living; similarly, other texts affirm that obedience must take priority over ceremonial worship (1 Sam. 15:22–23; Ps. 4:4–5; 40:6; 51:17–19; Isa. 1:11–20; 43:22–24; Jer. 7:21–26).

During the intertestamental period there were groups and individuals who were at least skeptical about the validity of sacrifices if not actually antisacrifice and antitemple in their outlook. For example, 1 Enoch 89:73, in words reminiscent of Malachi 1:6–14, says of worship in the second temple, "All the food which was upon [the altar was] polluted and impure." Sirach 34:18–35:12 subordinates sacrifices to ethics. The Septuagint carefully distinguishes between God's permanent dwelling in heaven and his temporary abode in the temple; this concept of a temporary home is reflected earlier in Israel's history by the Rechabites, who lived in tents rather than permanent houses (Jer. 35), and probably by the prophet Nathan, who rejected a permanent temple-house in favor of a portable tent-tabernacle (2 Sam. 7).[7]

Philo is an example of an ambivalent attitude toward temple and ceremony. He argued that God does not honor the sacrifices of a man "whose heart is the seat of lurking covetousness and wrongful cravings. . . . Though the worshipers bring nothing else, in bringing themselves they offer the best of sacrifices, the full and truly perfect oblation of noble living, as they honor with hymns and thanksgiving their Benefactor and Savior, God."[8] However, Philo honored and visited the temple,[9] and he also condemned excessive spiritualizing of it: "We shall be ignoring the sanctity of the temple and a thousand other things, if we are going to pay heed to nothing except what is shown us by the inner meaning of things."[10] Not surprisingly, then, Philo headed the delegation of Alexandrians who journeyed to Rome to attempt to dissuade Caligula from degrading the temple.[11] And yet Philo recognized that the Deity does not need a house in which to dwell,[12] because "in the truest sense the holy temple of God is . . . the whole universe."[13]

The writers of the Dead Sea Scrolls rejected the priesthood then in power. Although they sent sacrifices to the temple, they refrained from worshiping there themselves. The Temple Scroll from Qumran expects that the Jerusalem structure will be replaced with one of their own. In addition, the Dead Sea group, like Sirach and Philo, de-emphasized sacrifices in favor of a primary insistence

7. Marcel Simon, "Saint Stephen and the Jerusalem Temple," *Journal of Ecclesiastical History* 2 (1951): 128–33.

8. Philo *Special Laws* 1.270, 272; see also Philo *On Plants (Noah's Work as a Planter)* 107–9.

9. Philo *Special Laws* 1.67; Philo *On Providence* 2.64.

10. Philo *Migration of Abraham* 92.

11. Philo *Embassy to Gaius*.

12. Philo *Questions on Exodus* 2.83.

13. Philo *Special Laws* 2.66; see also Philo *Questions on Exodus* 2.85.

upon God's ethical law; other groups substituted cleansing rites for sacrifices.

Some Jews, especially those who had been hellenized, probably shared the sentiments of those Greek philosophers who polemicized against temples. Zeno the Stoic is quoted as saying, "For a temple is not of much account and is not holy, and no work of builders and mechanics is worth much."[14] Post–A.D. 70 statements show that there was within Judaism an element which truly depreciated the idea of a permanent temple.[15] It is evident that this reassessment of temple worship was but a development of an older tendency that, as we have seen, was already present in Judaism. In view of the loss of Herod's temple, the rabbis allowed various substitutes for sacrifices: (1) reading of the law, (2) fasting, (3) prayer, and (4) deeds of charity and justice.[16]

Thus we have the background for the ambiguous attitude of Jesus and the early Christians toward temple and sacrifice. Both visited and worshiped in the temple and honored the temple tax (Matt. 17:24–27). But Jesus did not accept the legitimacy of temple activities as they stood. So he cleansed the temple (Mark 11:15–19; Luke 19:45–46; John 2:13–17) and predicted its destruction (Matt. 24:1–2; Mark 13:1–2; Luke 21:5–6), affirming as well that "something greater than the temple is here" (Matt. 12:6). In addition, John 2:19–21 reports that Jesus said, "Destroy this temple, and in three days I will raise it up," but then explains that "he was speaking of the temple of his body." Jesus' words were repeated by false witnesses at his trial (Matt. 26:61; Mark 14:58) and by the crowd at the crucifixion (Matt. 27:40; Mark 15:29). It seems likely that Jesus made more negative statements about the temple than are recorded in the Gospels.

---

14. Quoted in Johannes Weiss, *Earliest Christianity*, trans. F. C. Grant (New York: Harper, 1959), 167 n. 7.

15. Reflecting the second-century A.D. situation, Justin Martyr says to Trypho the Jew, "Yet even now, in your love of contention, you assert that God does not accept the sacrifices of those who dwell in Jerusalem, and were called Israelites, but that he is pleased with the prayers of individuals of that nation then dispersed, and calls their prayers sacrifices" (*Dialogue with Trypho* 117). Likewise the Sibylline Oracles 4:6–11, 24–30: "[I am the spokesman] of the great God, whom no hands of men fashioned in the likeness of speechless idols of polished stone. For he does not have a house, a stone set up as a temple, dumb and toothless, a bane which brings many woes to men, but one which it is not possible to see from earth nor to measure with mortal eyes, since it was not fashioned by mortal hand. . . . Happy will be those of mankind on earth who will love the great God, blessing him before drinking and eating, putting their trust in piety. They will reject all temples when they see them, altars too, useless foundations of dumb stones (and stone statues and handmade images) defiled with blood of animate creatures, and sacrifices of four-footed animals."

16. Babylonian Talmud *Megillah* 31b (see also *Aboth* 4:3); *Berakoth* 17a; *Sanhedrin* 43b (=*Sotah* 5b); *Sukkah* 49b.

Stephen, in his speech to the council, clearly thought of the portable tabernacle as a more appropriate symbol and worship center for God's pilgrim people than was the permanent structure in Jerusalem. He called the temple a house "made with hands" (*cheiropoiētos*; Acts 7:48), a Greek word used in the Septuagint to refer to idols. This suggests that he saw the use made of the temple in his own day as assuming and perpetuating an idolatrous caricature of God. Although God is present everywhere in the universe, Stephen implied that his contemporaries had virtually reduced God to a tribal deity shut up in a golden box on Temple Hill in Jerusalem.

For Paul the individual Christian and the church are the temple of God (1 Cor. 3:16–17; 6:19; 2 Cor. 2:15–16; Eph. 2:21). Also noteworthy is that the Epistle to the Hebrews never mentions the temple, but depicts the tabernacle as a type of the heavenly worship center.

The significance of the temple in Intertestamental Judaism was, then, largely symbolic and sentimental. It was the visible center of religious life and the pride of the nation. Nevertheless, in fact, its role and function were in decline. Experience had demonstrated that Israel could survive without a temple; in the Diaspora, Jews were doing so every day. There was also an increasing distinction between laity and priest which could not but color the feelings of the populace toward the temple.

The truth was that a shift of emphasis had taken place within Hebrew religion. The center of Judaism had moved from temple and ceremony to morals and ethics. The piety and thought of such groups as the Pharisees were based on the law, not merely the temple and the ceremony of the law. These groups commanded the admiration of the common people. The actual center of Jewish religious life had moved to the synagogue. The temple as a spiritual center was an anachronism to both Judaism and Christianity.

Our center of attention has been primarily upon the temple as an institution. In the following chapter we will focus upon the scribes and their work as agents of adjustment to the crises. What, we should ask, was the role of the priests at this crucial time? We can do no better than summarize their role in the words of Emil Schürer:

> The internal development of Israel after the exile was essentially determined by two equally influential groups: the priests and the scribes. In the first post-exilic centuries until well into the Hellenistic period the priests were dominant. They organized the new community; it was from them that the Torah emanated; in their hands lay the leadership of the community, not only in spiritual but also in material affairs. Whereas, however, they were originally themselves the expert inter-

Table 1
The Intertestamental Calendar and Festivals

Harvest / Agriculture	Season	Month Number	Preexile	Postexile	Number of Days	Gregorian
Barley harvest; Flax harvest	Time of Latter Rains — Beginning of religious year	1	Abib	Nisan	30	April
	Dry Season — Time of Harvest	2	Ziv	Iyyar	29	May
Early figs		3		Sivan	30	June
Grape harvest		4		Tammuz	29	July
Olive harvest	Hot Season	5		Ab	30	Aug.
Date harvest; Summer-fig harvest		6		Elul	29	Sept.
	Time of Early Rains — Beginning of civil year	7	Ethanim	Tishri	30	Oct.
Winter-fig plowing	Seed-time	8	Bul	Heshvan	29	Nov.
	Winter Months	9		Chislev	30	Dec.
	Wet Season	10		Tebeth	29	Jan.
Almond blossoms		11		Shebat	30	Feb.
Citrus-fruit harvest	Springtime	12		Adar	29*	March
		13		Adar Sheni	29*	

*Adar Sheni, the thirteenth month, occurred only every third year; when it did occur, Adar was given thirty days.

Feasts prescribed in Leviticus 23:

1. Sabbath	every seventh day	Lev. 23:3; Exod. 20:8–11	
2. *Passover Unleavened Bread	fourteenth of Nisan fifteenth to twenty-first of Nisan	Lev. 23:5–8; Deut. 16:1–8	commemoration of the exodus
3. *Pentecost (Feast of Weeks)	sixth of Sivan (fifty days after Passover)	Lev. 23:9–21; Deut. 16:9–12	firstfruits of the wheat harvest
4. Trumpets	first of Tishri	Lev. 23:23–25	
5. Day of Atonement (Yom Kippur)	tenth of Tishri	Lev. 23:26–32; Lev. 16	
6. *Tabernacles (Booths)	fifteenth to twenty-first of Tishri	Lev. 23:33–43; Deut. 16:13–15	commemoration of the wilderness wanderings; the end of harvest (ingathering)

Other special observances:

1. New Moon	first of each month		
2. Feast of Purim	thirteenth to fifteenth of Adar	Esth. 9:18–32	feast of Esther
3. Feast of Lights (Dedication; Hanukkah)	twenty-fifth of Chislev	1 Macc. 4:36–59; John 10:22	commemoration of Judas Maccabeus's rededication of the temple (164 B.C.)
4. New Year for trees			
5. Sabbatical Year	every seventh year	Exod. 23:10–11	land left uncultivated
6. Year of Jubilee	every fiftieth year	Lev. 25:8–55	cancelation of all debts; freeing of Israelite slaves; return of real estate to original owner
7. New Year (?)—Rosh Hashanah			
8. Fasts commemorating the fall of Jerusalem in 586 B.C. a. Tenth month (Tebeth)—Nebuchadnezzar's attack on the city b. Fourth month (Tammuz)—Jerusalem opened to the Babylonians c. Fifth month (Ab)—Jerusalem captured d. Seventh month (Tishri)—murder of Gedaliah	Zech. 7–8		

*The three pilgrimage feasts, when all males were required to present themselves at the central sanctuary (Exod. 23:14–17; Deut. 16:16)

preters of the Torah, gradually an independent order of Torah scholars and teachers came into being alongside of them. And these were to increase in prestige and influence as zeal for the Torah cooled among the priests whilst among the people it was growing in value and significance. This was especially true following the Maccabean wars of independence. From then on, the scribes took more and more control of the nation's spiritual guidance.[17]

Feasts and Festivals

While the prestige of the temple was in decline, the intertestamental period saw the introduction of new feasts and alterations in some of the old ones. Zechariah 7:1–7 tells of an enquiry by the people of Bethel if, in the postexilic situation, they should continue mourning two events related to the end of Judah and the beginning of the exile. These had occurred on the ninth day of the fifth month (Ab = July-Aug.), when the temple was burned (2 Kings 25:8–9; Jer. 52:12–13), and the third day of the seventh month (Tishri = Sept.-Oct.), when Gedaliah was murdered (Jer. 41). The word of the LORD through the prophet was essentially negative. Nevertheless, the ninth of Ab continued as a popular ceremony. A wood offering was made in the temple, and flares or torches were lit as reminders of the torches thrown into the temple by the Babylonians to destroy it.

A better-known feast of late origin is Purim (lots). The Book of Esther provides the background and justification. According to Esther 9:26–28, Mordecai set aside two days—the fourteenth and fifteenth of Adar, the twelfth month (Feb.-March)—for remembering the deliverance from the attempted pogrom under Haman. Later, the thirteenth of Adar became a day of celebration of victory over Nicanor, a Seleucid general slain by Judas Maccabeus (1 Macc. 7:49).

First Maccabees 4:52–58 recounts the rededication of the temple on the twenty-fifth day of Chislev (Nov.-Dec.) after the Maccabees had wrested control of it from Antiochus Epiphanes. Then "Judas and his brothers and all the assembly of Israel determined that every year at that season the days of dedication of the altar should be observed with joy and gladness for eight days, beginning with the twenty-fifth day of the month Chislev" (v. 59). Second Maccabees 10:6–8 adds details:

> They celebrated it for eight days with rejoicing, in the manner of the festival of booths, remembering how not long before, during the festi-

---

17. Emil Schürer, *The History of the Jewish People in the Age of Jesus Christ*, ed. Geza Vermes et al., 3 vols. (Edinburgh: T. and T. Clark, 1973–87), 2:238–39.

val of booths, they had been wandering in the mountains and caves like wild animals. Therefore, carrying ivy-wreathed wands and beautiful branches and also fronds of palm, they offered hymns of thanksgiving to him who had given success to the purifying of his own holy place. They decreed by public edict, ratifying by vote, that the whole nation of the Jews should observe these days every year.

Second Maccabees 1:18–36 associates this feast not only with the Feast of Tabernacles, but also with the appearance of miraculous fire at the rededication of the altar in the time of Nehemiah. Rules for observing the feast included the burning of at least one lamp in each home every night of the feast. This Feast of Dedication (John 10:22), Feast of Lights, or Hanukkah is still celebrated by Jewish families.

We need not repeat our earlier brief survey of Old Testament feasts and festivals (pp. 68–70). However, noting some alterations or expansions of them is important for our purposes. Unfortunately, intertestamental sources have little to say on these matters. Later writings, however, provide elaborate descriptions of some ceremonies which are briefly mentioned in some intertestamental writings.

The Feast of Trumpets, on the first of Tishri (Sept.-Oct.), is, according to the Book of Numbers, the New Year's feast. But there are also references to the New Year's beginning in Nisan (March-April) (Exod. 12:2). According to the Mishnah, "there are four 'New Year' days: on the 1st of Nisan is the New Year for kings and feasts; on the 1st of Elul is the New Year for the Tithe of Cattle (R. Eleazer and R. Simeon say: The 1st of Tishri); on the 1st of Tishri is the New Year for [the reckoning of] the years [of foreign kings], of the Years of Release and Jubilee years, for the planting [of trees] and for vegetables; and the 1st of Shebat is the New Year for [fruit-]trees (so the School of Shammai; and the School of Hillel say: On the 15th thereof)."[18] Intertestamental Judaism seems to have observed New Year during Tishri.

As noted in our survey of Old Testament feasts, the Day of Atonement was an occasion for both national and individual repentance and cleansing from sin. Philo says it was "carefully observed not only by the zealous for piety and holiness but also by those who never act religiously in the rest of their life. . . . The high dignity of this day has two aspects, one as a festival, the other as a time of purification and escape from sins."[19] Jubilees 34:18–19

---

18. Mishnah *Rosh ha-Shanah* 1:1.

19. Philo *Special Laws* 1.186–87. In the following sections Philo finds significance in the number and types of sacrifices offered on the day.

says it was also observed as a feast of repentance for crimes against Joseph.

We would be surprised if Passover, one of the most significant feasts, did not change in some ways during the intertestamental period. Three major areas may be mentioned. First was the changing of some details.[20] Jubilees 49, for example, omits the bitter herbs and gives attention to the exact time for slaughtering the sacrifice. Second were considerable reinterpretation and development of additional meanings. Wisdom of Solomon 18 draws lessons of rewards and punishments from the experience of the Egyptians and Hebrews at the first Passover. Finally, there was an increased distinction between the Passover sacrifice and feast itself and the Feast of Unleavened Bread. This, it seems, was especially useful where one might be able to observe one but not both.[21]

The most elaborate supplements to the Old Testament instructions for any festival were those for the Feast of Tabernacles or Booths. It continued to be a commemoration of the wilderness wanderings of Israel. And Hebrew males continued to build and live in huts or booths for a week (eight days in the intertestamental period). In intertestamental times women were not required to move into the booth, but some chose to do so.

We have seen that during the intertestamental period the Feast of Tabernacles became a model for celebrating the Maccabean victory. There is some indication that the feast also came to be associated with covenant renewal and celebration of the reign of God.

In addition to general information about the Feast of Tabernacles, the Mishnah provides evidence that at least some of the supplements can be traced to the intertestamental period. The mishnaic tractate *Sukkah* begins with a discussion of what materials are acceptable for building the *sukkah* (booth or tabernacle). It proceeds to discuss collecting and binding the *lulab*, a bunch of myrtle, willow, and palm branches that were gathered in the environs of Jerusalem and to which a citron (a fruit similar to but a bit larger than a lemon) was attached. This was waved ceremonially for the duration of the festival.

Sukkah continues by describing the unique use of water in this festival.[22] On the first day of the feast a procession led by priests

---

20. On intertestamental developments of Passover see Baruch M. Bokser, "Unleavened Bread and Passover, Feasts of," in *Anchor Bible Dictionary*, ed. David Noel Freedman, 6 vols. (New York: Doubleday, 1992), 6:760–63, and the extensive bibliography on 764–65.

21. Trypho affirms that the Passover sacrifice cannot be offered away from Jerusalem (Justin Martyr *Dialogue with Trypho* 40, 46).

22. See George Foot Moore, *Judaism in the First Centuries of the Christian Era*, 3 vols. (Cambridge, Mass.: Harvard University Press, 1927–30), 2:44.

brought water to the temple from the Pool of Siloam; trumpets were blown at the city gate as the procession entered. Each day priests circled the altar while the worshipers waved their *lulabs*. The Hallel (Pss. 113–18) was recited or sung on each of the eight days. The officiating priest ascended the altar ramp and, using two silver bowls, one for water, the other for wine, poured out the libation.

Sukkah 4:9 tells us that "to the priest who performed the libation [the people] used to say, 'Lift up thine hand!'" because one year the priest "poured the libation over his feet, and all the people threw their citrons at him." Josephus identifies the culprit as Alexander Jannaeus.[23] This confirms both the water libation and *lulab* as parts of the intertestamental liturgy.

Another extrabiblical feature was the lighting of four large lampstands (menorahs); the wicks of their lamps were made from worn-out garments of the priests. These menorahs illuminated the entire temple area. The people danced as the Levites chanted the Psalms of Ascent (120–34). The celebration could last most of the night.

The climax of the festival came on the final day. The procession circled the altar seven times, and the people beat the earth with their *lulabs* instead of waving them. Later evidence suggests that there were also special readings from the law on this final day.

In John 7 Jesus arrives in Jerusalem during the latter part of the Festival of Booths. "On the last day of the festival, the great day, while Jesus was standing there, he cried out, 'Let anyone who is thirsty come to me, and let the one who believes in me drink. As the scripture has said, "Out of the believer's heart shall flow rivers of living water"'" (vv. 37–38). Given the time (the Feast of Tabernacles), the place (the temple), and the theme (water), such a declaration was bold and dramatic. Little wonder that in the following verses people debate whether Jesus might be the Messiah.[24]

During the intertestamental period Pentecost (the Feast of Weeks) seems to have grown in importance. The Old Testament presents it as essentially an agricultural event. By the intertestamental period Pentecost also celebrated the giving of the law at Si-

---

23. Josephus *Antiquities* 13.13.5 (372). The Talmud says the guilty party was a Sadducee; Jannaeus, of course, was a Sadducee.

24. In each of the accounts of the transfiguration (Matt. 17:1–9; Mark 9:2–10; Luke 9:28–36), as Peter calls for constructing three "booths," the Greek word is *skēnē* the translation of *sukkah*, the name of both the feast and the structures in which men lived during it. Luke 9:31 says the conversation between Jesus, Moses, and Elijah was "of his departure, which he was about to accomplish at Jerusalem." The Greek word translated "departure" is *exodos*, the historical event commemorated at the Feast of Booths. It should also be noted that some intertestamental Jewish groups regarded both Moses and Elijah as eschatological, if not actually messianic figures.

nai.[25] This gives added meaning to the events of Acts 2, which occurred at Pentecost.

The Desire for Restoration of the Monarchy

The role of the monarchy in Israel was somewhat problematic. The ideal was reflected by Gideon. When the Israelites wanted to establish a hereditary kingship within his family, he refused, saying, "The LORD will rule over you" (Judg. 8:23). Though the Pentateuch makes provisions for Hebrew kings, it puts restrictions upon them and insists that they know and follow God's law (Deut. 17:14–20). Samuel resisted the people's request for a king, relenting only when God said to him, "Listen to the voice of the people . . . for they have not rejected you, but they have rejected me from being king over them" (1 Sam. 8:7). Both Saul and David were selected by God and anointed by Samuel. A hereditary everlasting kingship was established in the family of David (2 Sam. 7:12–17; 1 Chron. 17:10–15). Thus kings ruled Israel with divine permission.

While God worked through the monarchy, it was anything but absolute. God is the only rightful king, human kings merely his representatives. The kings of Israel were responsible to rule in his name and carry out his will, not to establish their own laws and policies. The postexilic view is summarized in 2 Chronicles 13:8, where Judah is called "the kingdom of the LORD in the hand of the sons of David" (see also 1 Chron. 28:5).

A number of the prophets had predicted that the restoration and future blessing would include the return of rule by the house of David (Isa. 9:7; 16:5; Jer. 17:25; 23:5; 30:9; 33:15, 17, 20–22; Ezek. 34:23–24; 37:24–25; Hos. 3:5; Amos 9:11). Moreover, the promise to David and his descendants led to the expectation that the Messiah (the leader/king par excellence) would arise from that family. As would be expected, then, the immediate postexilic hopes for the reestablishment of the Hebrew kingship centered on the Davidic family.[26] Two individuals are mentioned in Ezra as political leaders: Sheshbazzar the prince and governor, and Zerubbabel the rebuilder of the tem-

25. It was assumed that fifty days was the time Israel took in traveling from Egypt to Sinai. Thus, fifty days from Passover, the day of deliverance from Egypt, the Hebrews should have been at Mount Sinai.

26. Hence the title "Son of David" (Luke 18:38–39; see also 1:32; Acts 2:25–36; Rom. 1:3) was understood as messianic; it was often thought to refer to a messianic king whose function would be primarily in the political-military realm.

ple.[27] The Book of Ezra gives no lineage for Sheshbazzar, and Zerubbabel is called simply "son of Shealtiel" (Ezra 3:2; 5:2; Neh. 12:1). First Chronicles 3:16–17 makes clear that Shealtiel was the son of King Jeconiah (Jehoiachin/Coniah) (see also Matt. 1:12; Luke 3:27). Hence Zerubbabel, who was himself later appointed governor in his own right (Hag. 2:21), was of Davidic descent.

To the silence of Ezra about Zerubbabel's royal heritage we must add Haggai's assurance that Zerubbabel and Joshua the high priest would be protected in the midst of dangerous times (2:4–5). Later the prophet delivered the LORD's word, "I will take you, O Zerubbabel my servant, . . . and make you like a signet ring; for I have chosen you" (2:23).[28] This statement is remembered in Sirach 49:11: "Zerubbabel . . . was like a signet ring on the right hand." We must also add that in the prophecy of Zechariah the LORD tells Joshua the high priest, "I am going to bring my servant the Branch" (3:8), and the "Branch . . . shall build the temple" (6:12). In Jeremiah 23:5–6 and 33:14–18 "Branch" is a title of the coming Davidic Messiah. Consider also that the LORD says to Zerubbabel regarding the restoration of the temple, "Not by might, nor by power, but by my spirit" (Zech. 4:6–9).

The silence in Ezra about Zerubbabel's Davidic descent, coupled with the LORD's reassurance to him, may indicate that some of his contemporaries viewed him as the messianic king. Other indications include the association of terms like "signet ring" and "Branch" with the Davidic rebuilder of the temple. The reason for the silence was that talk of his being a king could have placed Zerubbabel at risk in the Persian Empire.

27. For Sheshbazzar see Ezra 1:8–11; 5:14–16. The Hebrew word translated "prince" need not be taken as a reference to a person of royal descent; "governor" is also a possible meaning. The relationship between Sheshbazzar and Zerubbabel is unclear. The major theories are: (1) the two names designate the same person; Sheshbazzar is merely the court name for Zerubbabel; (2) Sheshbazzar is really Shenazzar of 1 Chron. 3:18, a brother of Shealtiel, and thus Zerubbabel's uncle; (3) the author has purposely left the relationship between the two ambiguous to cover Zerubbabel's slow response to carry out Cyrus's decree to rebuild the temple; (4) Sheshbazzar (either a Gentile or a Hebrew) was the official leader-governor, whereas Zerubbabel, a Hebrew, was the unofficial leader of the returnees; and (5) Sheshbazzar was the first and Zerubbabel the second of the several governors of Judah; though the names of these governors (including Nehemiah) have now been partially recovered, their activities were too complex to be completely understood. See Derek Kidner, "Appendix II: The Identity of Sheshbazzar," in *Ezra and Nehemiah: An Introduction and Commentary*, Tyndale Old Testament Commentaries (Downers Grove, Ill.: Inter-Varsity, 1979), 139–42; Tamara C. Eskenazi, "Sheshbazzar," in *Anchor Bible Dictionary*, 5:1207–9.

28. The wording here is particularly pointed in view of the LORD's words to Zerubbabel's grandfather Jehoiachin: "Were [you] the signet ring on my right hand, even from there I would tear you off and give you into the hands of those who seek your life" (Jer. 22:24–25).

A word needs to be said here about the priestly role in connection with the restoration of the monarchy as well as of the temple. Throughout the Book of Ezra, Joshua the high priest is present with Zerubbabel. He shares in the reassurances given Zerubbabel by Haggai and Zechariah. So he is at least as good a candidate to be the "Branch" as is Zerubbabel. Also to be noted is that within Intertestamental Judaism there was expectation of a priestly companion for the Messiah and even of a priestly Messiah.

The restoration of the monarchy did not come during the time of Ezra, Zerubbabel, Nehemiah, and their contemporaries. Nor in fact did it come through the Davidic family, but through the priestly Hasmonean line. Although Aristobulus I was the first of the Maccabees actually to claim the title of king, several of his predecessors held the office in all ways save the name. In them we see the joining of the offices of priest and king.

The association of the Davidic Zerubbabel with aspirations for the restoration of the monarchy, along with the later willingness of the Jews to accept the Maccabees as kings, shows the intense desire for the return of the office and institution. This yearning was a part of the readjustment program of many. The desire for their own king, coupled with divine promises, helped strengthen messianic expectations throughout the intertestamental period.

9

Scribes and Tradition

The Scribes

Intertestamental Judaism developed a variety of thought forms and traditions in its efforts to interpret and maintain the relevance of Scripture.[1] This, we suggest, was a part of the general readjustment in the face of the crises of the sixth and fourth centuries B.C. We come now to look at the developers of some of those forms, something of the content and transmission, and finally evidence of a multiplicity of traditions within Intertestamental Judaism.

In the previous chapter we quoted Emil Schürer's statement to the effect that Intertestamental Judaism was the result of the work of two different groups, priests and scribes. Both were interpreters of the law and leaders of their people. Scribes gradually took their

---

1. As examples, the distinctions between Semitic and Hellenistic Judaism and those between Palestinian and Diaspora Judaism immediately come to mind. Then, too, there were the differences between Jewish communities, such as those of Antioch, Alexandria, and Babylon.

place alongside the priests as an independent authoritative group. Yet many, if not most, scribes, especially in the earlier days of the intertestamental period, were themselves priests.[2] This is well illustrated in the case of Ezra, the quintessential scribe.

The descriptions of Ezra in the book bearing his name are significant. He is called priest, scribe, and scholar (7:11). As a scribe he was "skilled in the law of Moses that the LORD the God of Israel had given" (7:6). He "set his heart to study the law of the LORD, and to do it, and to teach the statutes and ordinances in Israel" (7:10). Clearly the major focus of this priest was upon the study of the law, reflecting the shift of emphasis from temple and ceremony to the law itself. Not that Ezra was unconcerned with the temple, its ceremonial worship, and religious rites in daily life— these, however, were but a part of what he learned from his study of the law and what he sought to apply in the life of the returned community.

Ezra is depicted in the Bible not only as a priest-scribe-scholar, but also as governor and reformer. Beyond Scripture, Jewish tradition affirms him as the reestablisher of the nation and religion, a second Moses.[3] Significantly, Ezra was not limited to a single office within Intertestamental Judaism.

The multifaceted role of Ezra is paralleled by that of later scribes described in Sirach 38:24–39:11. They too were sought for counsel, were eminent in the public assembly, and served as judges and rulers (38:32–33). Yet even in this important passage, the writer describes the essence of the work of the scribe as scholarly and religious:

> [He] devotes himself to the study of the law of the Most High! He seeks out the wisdom of all the ancients, and is concerned with prophecies; he preserves the sayings of the famous and penetrates the subtleties of

2. "Most of the scribes of the end of the Second Temple period whose genealogy is known were priests. . . . The rabbis said that ordinary priests were rich, so it is evident that in the days of the Second Temple scribes came almost exclusively from rich and distinguished families, most of whom were priests or levites. But with the spread of Hellenism in the land of Israel, a process of secularization and diminishing status overtook the scribal profession, and among the people many scribes arose without any connection to an official position, the priesthood or the Temple" (Mier Bar-Ilan, "Writing in Ancient Israel and Early Judaism," in *Mikra,* ed. M. J. Mulder and Harry Sysling, in *Compendia Rerum Iudaicarum ad Novum Testamentum,* 7 vols. [Philadelphia: Fortress, 1974–92], section 2, vol. 1, 22).

3. Among legends about Ezra is the claim that he was a disciple of Baruch in Babylon and had refused to return to Jerusalem as long as his master was alive. It was also believed that Ezra had a miraculous escape from death, entered paradise alive, addressed angels, and is one of the five truly pious men. See Louis Ginzberg, *The Legends of the Jews,* 7 vols. (Philadelphia: Jewish Publication Society of America, 1909–38), 4:354–59; 6:441–47.

parables; he seeks out the hidden meanings of proverbs and is at home with the obscurities of parables. He serves among the great and appears before rulers; he travels in foreign lands and learns what is good and evil in the human lot. He sets his heart to rise early to seek the Lord who made him, and to petition the Most High; he opens his mouth in prayer and asks pardon for his sins. [39:1–5]

Old Testament references to scribes other than Ezra are few; they seem to have been little more than secretaries.[4] In the ancient world scribes were primarily copyists. Virtually every court had its scribes, and they would be an essential part of the retinue of many temples. However, the scribe did not necessarily occupy an official position. Furthermore, virtually any group could and many did have scribes. Originally in Judaism as well, the scribes were copiers of the law and other sacred texts.

The dismantling of Jewish institutions at the time of the captivity left a vacuum of authorities and leaders. Simultaneously the position of scribe broadened as the result of the shift of emphasis away from temple and ceremony. We can begin to appreciate the nature of the situation only as we remember the importance and sanctity of the law in intertestamental Jewish life. The higher the elevation of the law, the more important the study and exercise of it. Needed in the new situation were those who knew and could teach and apply the law. This required professional study and exposition. In fact, however, with the shift of emphasis every Jew was expected to know and obey the law.

At the beginning of the intertestamental period the priests had filled the roles of both teachers and interpreters of law. Various sources seem to indicate that as Hellenistic culture and other secular concerns occupied more and more of their attention, they began to neglect the teaching and application of the law and of the traditions that had grown up around it. So by the second century B.C. the scribes had become an influential, respected group independent of the priests. Through copying the law, scribes had become thoroughly familiar with it. In time, because of their knowledge they became recognized as experts. They were looked to for information about what the law actually said, and later for help in understanding what it meant and required. The scribes stepped in to fill the gap left by the priests. They became the zealous guardians of the law, the real teachers and directors of spiritual life. Their concern was primarily with the legal sections of the

4. See, e.g., 1 Chron. 2:55; 24:6; 27:32; 2 Chron. 34:13; Ezra 4:8–9, 17, 23; Ps. 45:1; Jer. 8:8; Nah. 3:17. Although he is not called a scribe, Baruch performs the function as he writes at Jeremiah's dictation (Jer. 36:4, 18).

law, regarding which they began to develop traditions (*halakah*). Hence they came to be responsible for defining and perfecting the principles underlying or derived from the law, and to help administer the law as learned counselors in courts of justice. Eventually many scribes became teachers (but we must not assume that all teachers [rabbis] were scribes). Scribes were unpaid (except probably in their role as teachers of the young), supporting themselves by secular work.

The work of the scribes and the development and transmission of tradition are inseparably bound together. It is not uncommon to assume that all scribes were a part of the same group and shared the same ideology. Even more common is the assumption of a single tradition. Thus the scribes are linked with the Pharisees, whose tradition is presumed to be that which was later codified and expanded in Rabbinic Judaism. These suppositions need reevaluation.

The New Testament evidence itself is revealing. A careful study of the data indicates that scribes were associated with a variety of groups and seem, at least in some cases, to have functioned in official capacities.[5] Of even more importance is the realization that scribes were associated with a variety of traditions. To understand the work of the scribes and the variety of traditions associated with them, we will consider two intertestamental texts and a few groups with distinctive traditions.

5. The phrase "scribes and Pharisees," which leaves ambiguous the relation between them, is used six times in Matt. 23 (vv. 13, 15, 23, 25, 27, and 29). "The scribes and Pharisees" occurs in Matt. 5:20 and 12:38; "the scribes and the Pharisees" in Matt. 23:2; Mark 7:5; Luke 5:21; 6:7; 11:53; 15:2; and John 8:3; and "the Pharisees and some of the scribes" in Mark 7:1, strongly suggesting that they may have been, in a sense, at least two different groups. Mark 2:16 and Acts 23:9 clarify the situation by referring to "scribes of the Pharisees" (Luke 5:30, a parallel to Mark 2:16, reads "the Pharisees and their scribes"), indicating that only some scribes were associated with the Pharisees. The scribes are mentioned alongside Jewish officials in various contexts. They are connected with the chief priests and elders in Matt. 16:21 (=Mark 8:31; Luke 9:22); Matt. 26:57 (=Mark 14:53; Luke 22:66); Matt. 27:41; Mark 11:27; 14:43; 15:1; Luke 19:47; 20:1; and Acts 4:5–6. They appear with only the chief priests in Matt. 2:4; 20:18 (=Mark 10:33); Matt. 21:15 (=Mark 11:18); Mark 14:1; 15:31; Luke 20:19; 22:2; 23:10. The scribes are also an identifiable group by themselves in Matt. 7:29; 8:19; 9:3 (=Mark 2:6); Matt. 13:52; 17:10; Mark 1:22; 3:22; 9:11, 14; 12:28, 32, 35, 38; Luke 20:39, 46; and 1 Cor. 1:20. They are listed as both conspirators against Jesus (Mark 14:1, 43) and participants at his trial (Matt. 26:57 [=Mark 14:53; Luke 22:66]; Mark 15:1; Luke 23:10). Presumably some were members of the council (Sanhedrin). The close association of some scribes with the chief priests may indicate that some scribes were Sadducees or had Sadducean sympathies. Matt. 2:4 is particularly interesting for it refers to "the chief priests and scribes of the people." The New Testament, then, associates the scribes with a variety of groups and suggests that at least some of them functioned in official capacities.

Intertestamental Texts Testifying to Scribal Traditions

The Tractate Aboth

The first text to be considered is the mishnaic tractate *Aboth*. With the rest of the Mishnah it was compiled between A.D. 90 and 200. It contains some of the oldest teachings in the Mishnah. While its precise date is uncertain, it seems to contain material from a number of sources dating from the third century B.C. to the second century A.D. *Aboth* is a collection of sayings by a number of rabbis, some sixty-five of whom are named. Of those named, a number were active while the Jerusalem temple still stood. Thus *Aboth* gives glimpses into the minds of intertestamental Jews whose outlook and practice later gave rise to the rabbinic movement.

There is no evident method, organization, or point of view in *Aboth*; it appears that the readers are left to form their own impression. *Aboth* is, nonetheless, a classic of Jewish literature. One writer has observed, "*Aboth* speaks to the heart of the Jew in a manner and with a force seldom realized by non-Jewish readers, and attempts to expound its teachings and significance fail insofar as that fact is not understood."[6]

The purpose of the tractate is to establish the divine (Sinaitic) origin of the law, both oral and written, and the reliability of its transmission by humans. *Aboth* sets out ethical standards that should govern all Israel (teacher and student, judge and judged) in the study, administration, and fulfilment of the law. *Aboth* touches on the main themes of ethics to which probably the majority of Jews who lived at the close of the intertestamental period and the beginning of the following era were committed. Its major assumption is that to be virtuous is to do the will of God revealed in the law; the way to become virtuous is to learn what he has revealed and to take it to heart. A large portion of *Aboth*'s maxims refer, then, not only to the reading of the law, but also to the study of the divine thought revealed in it.

The tractate begins:

> Moses received the Law [Torah] from Sinai and committed it to Joshua, and Joshua to the elders, and the elders to the Prophets; and the Prophets committed it to the men of the Great Synagogue. They said three things: Be deliberate in judgment, raise up many disciples, and make a fence around the Law. Simeon the Just was of the remnants of the Great Synagogue. He used to say: By three things is the world

6. R. Travers Herford, *The Ethics of the Talmud: Sayings of the Fathers* [Pirke Aboth] (New York: Schocken, 1962), 1.

sustained: by the Law, by the [Temple-]service, and by deeds of loving-kindness. [*Aboth* 1:1–2]

The three sayings of the men of the Great Synagogue give insight into the viewpoint of *Aboth*. Deliberateness in judgment has reference to the administration of justice by judges; it may also refer to wider application of the law in a broad range of circumstances.[7] Raising up disciples has in view the teaching-learning process with its goals of both transmission of knowledge and compliance. The type of learning required is illustrated in the praise of Eliezer ben Hyrcanus, who is described as "a plastered cistern which loses not a drop" (2:8). The best type of disciple is "swift to hear and slow to lose" (5:12). Finally, building a fence around the law is clarified in *Aboth* 3:14, "The tradition is a fence around the Law."[8] To assure compliance with the law, instructions around it were multiplied; these instructions make up much of what is called oral tradition.

At the heart of the Judaism expounded in *Aboth* were at least four related steps. First was the careful study of the law by all, especially by the leader-teacher (the rabbi). Then followed the teaching of the law to students, a process that included transmitting the law along with the opinions of past and present teachers. This led to the expansion of the law by adding new laws and interpretations, and finally (although not necessarily separate from the other steps) application of the law to specific situations. The record of the discussions about law and of subsequent actions became something of a body of case law, the basis for further expansion and application.

Implicit in all this is the codification of a body of laws, opinions, and judicial activities which took its place alongside the written law. This codification, *Aboth* assumes, was the work of the Great Synagogue and set the precedent for its successors to do the same. Summarizing Jewish tradition about the Great Synagogue, Herbert Danby describes it as "a body of 120 elders, including many prophets, who came up from exile with Ezra; they saw that prophecy had come to an end and that restraint was lacking; therefore they made

---

7. Ibid., 20–21: "Deliberation in judgment originally as here, the judgment of a judge, but later 'argument,' is the key to the casuistry of the Talmud, and in the main justifies that casuistry. For deliberation expresses the desire to study a question from every point of view, and to take account of every possible even though improbable contingency."

8. George Foot Moore, *Judaism in the First Centuries of the Christian Era*, 3 vols. (Cambridge, Mass.: Harvard University Press, 1927–30), 1:33, translates the word *seyag* "barrier," and speaks of "enactments meant to guard against any possible infringement of the divine statute . . . [and] 'to keep a man far removed from transgression'" (Mishnah *Berakoth* 1:1). The barrier was intended to "protect it [Torah] by surrounding it with cautionary rules to halt a man like a danger signal before he gets within breaking distance of the divine statute itself" (1:259).

many new rules and restrictions for the better observance of the Law."[9]

In our summary of the Persian period we noted that the very existence of the Great Synagogue is questioned (p. 78). This problem of historicity cannot be finally solved. If indeed there was such a body, it is probably to be dated from Ezra (c. 444 B.C.) and the events of Nehemiah 8–10 until the time of Simon the Just. Here again we run into historical difficulties: Simon the Just has been identified with two individuals. There was a Simon who was a son of Onias I and high priest from 310 to 291 (or 300 to 270). It is to this individual that Josephus applies the title "the Just."[10] The other candidate is Simon II, high priest from about 219 to 199. He seems to be the religious and political figure described in Sirach 50. Whatever the case, the significance of the Great Synagogue is not limited by historical uncertainties. Even in legendary form it stands as the fountainhead of the reorganization of Judaism and the development of the concept of tradition, which became such an important element in Intertestamental Judaism.

At least the first two chapters of *Aboth* are as much interested in the transmission of the tradition as in the tradition itself. The tradition was passed from God (Sinai) to Moses to Joshua to the elders to the prophets to the men of the Great Synagogue, including Ezra and Simon the Just. Then followed Antigonus of Soko and the Pairs, who, according to tradition, were the presidents and vice-presidents of the Sanhedrin and transmitted the oral tradition from about 160 B.C. until Rabbi Judah the Patriarch, the compiler of the Mishnah.[11] In *Aboth* they represent those who followed Ezra in developing the religion of the law.

Observations are in order about a couple of individuals included in the Pairs. Hillel and Shammai (30 B.C.–A.D. 10) were the best known. Both were leading scholars but took different points of view, and the rabbinic writings make frequent reference to the conflict between them and between their disciples. In general (but not always) Shammai and his followers tended to be more strict in

---

9. *The Mishnah*, trans. Herbert Danby (Oxford: Oxford University Press, 1933), 446 n. 5.

10. Josephus *Antiquities* 12.2.5 (43).

11. The Pairs include (1) Jose ben Joezer of Zeredah (c. 160 B.C.) and Jose ben Johanan of Jerusalem; (2) Joshua ben Perahyah and Nittai the Arbelite (c. 120 B.C.); (3) Judah ben Tabbai and Simeon ben Shetah (c. 80 B.C.); (4) Shemaiah and Abtalion; and (5) Hillel and Shammai (c. 30 B.C.–A.D. 10). Thereafter came Rabban Gamaliel (a grandson or possibly son of Hillel); Simeon ben Gamaliel; Rabban Johanan ben Zakkai (d. A.D. 80), who "received [Torah] from Hillel and from Shammai"; the five disciples of ben Zakkai; the Rabbi (*Aboth* 2:1=Judah the Patriarch); and Rabban Gamaliel III, the son of Judah the Patriarch (see *Mishnah*, trans. Danby, 446–48).

their interpretation of law and tradition and in judicial decisions. Hillel and his school were more liberal in their handling of law, more lenient in matters of interpretation and judgment. Gamaliel was either a son or grandson of Hillel. He is probably the person (or at least a forebear of the person) mentioned in Acts 5:34–39 and 22:3 (in the former passage the milder and more cautious attitude of the Hillelites is evident).

Aboth clearly acknowledges that the tradition passed on by the Pairs included, as Danby says, "many new rules and restrictions for the better observance of the Law." These the scribes and teachers boldly set forth, claiming divine authority for them. They constitute what is called the oral law or what Jesus refers to as "the tradition of the elders."[12]

The Pharisees, of course, were a major part of the line that transmitted the oral tradition that *Aboth* has in view. Josephus confirms that they held extrabiblical teachings which had been consciously selected and passed on by earlier generations.[13] Josephus and the New Testament agree that this Pharisaic tradition included belief in fate (predestination), angels and spirits, resurrection, eternal rewards and punishments, and a virtuous lifestyle.[14] It also dealt with ceremonial and cultic matters.

At this point let us summarize the affirmations of *Aboth:* (1) In addition to the written Scriptures there is an oral tradition. (2) God originated this tradition and gave it to Moses. (3) Hence it carries divine authority. (4) The task of each generation is to apply the law judiciously, to teach it, and to protect it by adding additional laws (fences) around it. Finally, (5) the tradition has been accurately transmitted, and there is a mandate to continue passing it on to future generations. We should note here that although

---

12. Note the words and sentiments of Mark 7, where Jesus contrasts the divine commandments with human additions to them: v. 3, "the tradition (*paradosin*) of the elders"; v. 5, "the tradition (*paradosin*) of the elders"; v. 7, "teaching human precepts (*entalmata anthrōpōn*) as doctrines (*didaskalias*); v. 8, "you abandon the commandment (*entolēn*) of God and hold to human tradition (*paradosin*)"; v. 9, "the commandment (*entolēn*) of God . . . tradition (*paradosin*)"; v. 13, "making void the word (*logon*) of God through your tradition (*paradosei*)" (see also Matt. 23:23–24; John 5:39–47). In general, Jesus seems to have rejected the notion of divine authority behind the extrabiblical tradition.

13. "The Pharisees had passed on to the people certain regulations handed down by former generations and not recorded in the Laws of Moses, for which reason they are rejected by the Sadducean group, who hold that only those regulations should be considered valid which were written down (in Scripture), and that those which had been handed down by former generations need not be observed" (Josephus *Antiquities* 13.10.6 [297]). "The Pharisees . . . follow the guidance of that which their doctrine has selected and transmitted as good, attaching the chief importance to the observance of those commandments which it has seen fit to dictate to them" (*Antiquities* 18.1.3 [12]).

14. Josephus *Jewish War* 2.8.14 (162–66); *Antiquities* 18.1.3 (12–15); see also Acts 23:8–9.

it is generally assumed by modern scholars that the oral law was developed only by scribes in the tradition represented by *Aboth*, documents from other trajectories of Intertestamental Judaism strongly indicate that collections of oral material were developed by scribes in other traditions as well.[15]

Note here should also be made of an interesting reconstruction by the Jewish scholar Leah Bronner.[16] She believes that the scribes (*sopherim*) were the associates of Ezra and Nehemiah; these men of the Great Synagogue "directed, guided and supervised the religious and social life of the people competently and devotedly until the Greek invasion of Palestine. The Hellenistic onslaught disturbed and disrupted the religious life of the community."[17] Many of the upper strata of society began to follow Greek customs. Among this group were some of the scribes. Others refused and sought "to keep a safe distance from the forbidden ground."[18] Hence there came a division among the scribes, the opponents of Hellenism becoming the Early Hasidim (Pious Ones). Thus "the conquest of Alexander the Great in 333 B.C. and onwards gave rise not only to Hellenism but also to Hasidim."[19]

The Early Hasidim, Bronner believes, were the real descendants of Ezra and Nehemiah, and they were more strict in observing the law than were the other scribes. They went to extremes in observing Levitical purity. They willingly accepted martyrdom rather than compromise their understandings of the requirements of the law.

We first meet the Hasidim in 1 Maccabees where they, "mighty warriors of Israel, all who offered themselves willingly for the law" (2:42), joined the forces of Mattathias against Antiochus Epiphanes. Later they were content to live under Syrian rule after the religious battle had been won (7:13). They are usually identified with those who allowed themselves to be slaughtered rather than desecrate the Sabbath by defending themselves (1:32–38). Though the stance of nonresistance on the Sabbath is probably in keeping with

15. E. P. Sanders, "Did the Pharisees Have Oral Law?" in *Jewish Law from Jesus to the Mishnah: Five Studies* (Philadelphia: Trinity Press International, 1990), 98, summarizes different definitions for oral law, and then argues "that there are some senses in which not only the Pharisees but others must be said to have had the oral law." Moreover, he doubts that the Pharisees held to the oral law in the sense in which it is usually understood.

16. Leah Bronner, *Sects and Separatism during the Second Jewish Commonwealth* (New York: Bloch, 1967), 38–55.

17. Ibid., 39.

18. Ibid., 40; Bronner believes that this is the setting for the direction to "make a fence around Torah" (*Aboth* 1:1).

19. Ibid.; Bronner refers to this group as the *Early* Hasidim to distinguish them from the group that arose in the rabbinic period.

the convictions of the Hasidim, the text does not identify them with the martyrs.

Bronner's theory is plausible. Its weaknesses lie in the late date of the initial references to the Hasidim. She builds much of her case on rabbinic writings which may or may not be accurate reports in this case. At any rate she does make an important contribution in calling attention to divisions among the scribes during the intertestamental period.

The Secret Tradition of 2 Esdras

Second Esdras 14:19–48 is another text which throws light on intertestamental Jewish views of law, interpretation, and tradition. At the heart of this book is an apocalypse written at the end of the first century A.D. by a Jewish writer who identifies himself as the biblical Ezra and Shealtiel.[20] In a series of revelations or visions (chs. 3–14) he struggles with the nation's defeat by Rome, which he refers to as Babylon. He raises some of the same questions that his forebears had asked about God and his relation to Judah after its fall in 586 B.C. At the end the writer finds hope when it is revealed to him that the present age will soon end and the new age will see Israel's salvation and vindication. God also allows Ezra-Shealtiel to be a second Moses who makes the law once again available, this time for future generations.

The scene for the restoration of the law is set as Ezra acknowledges that the Lord has sent him to "reprove the people who are now living"; for the sake of those not yet born, however, he asks permission to write again the law which "has been burned" (2 Esdras 14:20–22). The request is granted; he writes ninety-four books in forty days and is commanded, "Make public the twenty-four books that you wrote first, and let the worthy and the unworthy read them; but keep the seventy that were written last, in order to give them to the wise among your people. For in them is the spring of understanding, the fountain of wisdom, and the river of knowledge" (vv. 45–47). We see here (1) the importance of an appointed leader, (2) the primacy of the written Scriptures, and (3) the necessity of again making the law available. These three, and especially the third, constitute an acknowledgment of the need for readjustment in the postexilic situation. But perhaps most significant is the evidence for a public and a secret tradition, both of

---

20. Chapters 3–14 seem to have been written in Aramaic or Hebrew by a Jew. Later a Christian added chapters 1–2 in order to make the writing useful for his fellow believers. Still later, chapters 15–16 were added by yet another Christian. Shealtiel is identified as the son of King Jeconiah (Jehoiachin) in 1 Chron. 3:17 and Matt. 1:12, and as the father of Zerubbabel in Ezra 3:2, 8; 5:2; Neh. 12:1; Hag. 1:1, 12, 14; 2:2, 23; Matt. 1:12; and Luke 3:27.

which come from God. Note also the implied provision for the transmission of this tradition, both open and secret.

It may be assumed that the groups represented by *Aboth* and 2 Esdras were in general agreement on the content of the written law, but what was the relationship between the content of the hedges around the law and the secret books of 2 Esdras? We do not know the subject matter of the secret tradition of 2 Esdras. Most probably it was not the same as the content of the hedges.[21]

The Variety of Scribal Traditions

The Apocalyptic Movement

Aboth and 2 Esdras, representing the Pharisaic-rabbinic tradition and the apocalyptic milieu respectively,[22] almost certainly have in view traditions different from those espoused by other intertestamental Jewish groups. The apocalyptic movement was itself a complex reaction that collected, developed, interpreted, and transmitted various traditions. Even if the roots of the apocalyptic movement predate the crises of the sixth and fourth centuries, those crises and subsequent events gave it impetus and issues to which to react, and called for new attitudes and perspectives to facilitate survival.

We will examine the apocalyptic movement in more detail in the next chapter. Here we must note only a few facts relevant to our search for evidence of the existence of multiple traditions. The Greek word *apokalypsis* itself means "revelation of that which is hidden." Thus, as we have already learned from 2 Esdras, this movement assumed a secret tradition which its writers made known. Apocalyptic claimed divine origin for this tradition, the content of which frequently dealt with the very questions and conditions brought on by the historical crises of the intertestamental period.

Two further observations about apocalypses are in order. First, apocalyptic is a means of interpreting and applying the Hebrew Scriptures just as surely as are the Pharisaic oral law and other extrabiblical traditions.[23] The apocalyptist is consciously working with the

21. Jacob M. Myers, *I and II Esdras: A New Translation with Introduction and Commentary*, Anchor Bible 42 (Garden City, N.Y.: Doubleday, 1974), 329, associates the seventy secret books with "the views of the school of apocalyptists."

22. But note W. D. Davies, "Apocalyptic and Pharisaism," in *Christian Origins and Judaism* (London: Dalton, Longman and Todd, 1962), 19–30, who, with others, sees apocalyptic influences among the Pharisees.

23. See Neil S. Fujita, *A Crack in the Jar: What Ancient Jewish Documents Tell Us about the New Testament* (Mahwah, N.J.: Paulist, 1986), 120–22; Walter Schmithals, *The Apocalyptic Movement: Introduction and Interpretation*, trans. John E. Steely (Nashville: Abingdon, 1975), 68–88.

biblical text and from it transports literary and historical structures, personal names, events, allusions, and concepts into his own context. As a hermeneutical device apocalyptic attempts both to maintain the relevance of the written Scriptures and to break through the prophetic silence. Second, we must remember that apocalyptic does not represent a united tradition. It both mirrors and contributes to the diversity of Intertestamental Judaism. For example, in apocalyptic we meet a multiplicity of eschatological schemes with many divergent details. This diversity must have contributed to the confusion of and controversies among those who, like the first Jewish Christians, viewed themselves as living in the eschatological age.

The Sadducees

It is often assumed that the Sadducees rejected oral traditions, holding to the written law alone. This is the initial impression of Josephus's statement that the Sadducees "own no observance of any sort apart from the laws,"[24] "laws" here being taken to mean written laws or the Pentateuch. However, the passage continues, "they reckon it a virtue to dispute with the teachers of the path of wisdom that they pursue." These disputes could have involved disagreements not only about the meaning of written law, but also about additional traditions associated with it.

Josephus and the New Testament emphasize that the Pharisees and Sadducees differed in doctrine and lifestyle. But Josephus also relates, "Whenever [the Sadducees] assume some office, though they submit unwillingly and perforce, yet submit they do to the formulas of the Pharisees, since otherwise the masses would not tolerate them."[25] Clearly, the difference between Sadducean preference and the formulas of the Pharisees included interpretations relating how public ceremonies and religious rituals were to be performed. Whether or not the Sadducees' preferences were spelled out in a body of traditions as well defined as that of the Pharisees, they certainly constituted part of a distinctive tradition, a Sadducean oral law. Josephus is not our only witness to this fact. For "Mishnaic and rabbinic references to the Sadducees describe them almost entirely in terms of their differences with the Pharisees on ritual, ceremonial, and judicial matters. These issues involved a wide range of questions relating to such matters as the date and observance of certain feasts, sabbath-keeping, the way sacrifices were to be offered and temple ritual performed, the con-

24. Josephus *Antiquities* 18.1.4 (16).
25. Ibid., 18.1.4 (17).

duct and penalties in criminal cases, and procedures relating to ceremonial defilement and cleanliness."[26]

Once again a disruption during an observance of the Feast of Tabernacles is relevant (see p. 161). According to Josephus, the Hasmonean priest-king Alexander Jannaeus (103–76 B.C.) was pelted with citrons while he was officiating in the temple. The worshipers disapproved of the way he carried out a part of a ritual for the feast.[27] The mishnaic tractate *Sukkah,* in describing Pharisaic-rabbinic liturgical procedures, dictates that the water libation for the festival be poured into one of two bowls placed to the right at the top of the altar ramp. However, "once a certain one poured the libation over his feet, and all the people threw their citrons at him" (4:9). The Talmud adds that the offender was "a certain Sadducee (Boethusian)."[28] Jannaeus was known to be a supporter of the Sadducees. His performance of the ritual was probably dictated by Sadducean preference. This is further confirmation of the existence of a Sadducean cultic-ceremonial tradition which differed from Pharisaic oral law.

The Dead Sea Community and Other Essenes

It is generally assumed that the Dead Sea Scrolls were produced by a community with its own scribes and represent a tradition different from those already described. The Damascus or Zadokite Document (CD) says that God "raised for [the community] a Teacher of Righteousness to guide them in the way of His heart. And he made known to the latter generations that which God had done to the latter generation, the congregation of traitors, to those who departed from the way" (col. 1). The Commentary (*Pesher*) on Habakkuk (1QpHab) condemns "those who were unfaithful together with the Liar, in that they [did] not [listen to the word received by] the Teacher of Righteousness from the mouth of God. And it concerned the unfaithful of the New [Covenant] in that they had not believed in the covenant of God [and had profaned] His holy Name" (col. 2). The document then goes on to describe the Teacher of Righteousness as the one "to whom God made known all the mysteries of the words of His servants the Prophets" (col. 7).[29] Here again is an assumption familiar from our studies of Ezra, *Aboth*, and 2 Esdras—an extrabiblical tradition coming from

26. J. Julius Scott, Jr., "Sadducees," in *New International Dictionary of New Testament Theology,* ed. Colin Brown, 4 vols. (Grand Rapids: Zondervan, 1975–78), 3:440.

27. Josephus *Antiquities* 13.13.5 (372).

28. Babylonian Talmud *Sukkah* 48b.

29. All quotations from the Dead Sea Scrolls are taken from *The Dead Sea Scrolls in English,* trans. Geza Vermes, 3d ed. (New York: Viking Penguin, 1990).

God himself through his chosen instruments is to be communicated to following generations. This tradition is described as a "mystery" (rāz), a secret, one certainly different from that of 2 Esdras.

Josephus's description of the Essenes, a group of which the Qumran community was almost certainly a part, gives a long list of their practices and ideas.[30] He clearly shows that their traditions included, among other things, unique views on ceremonial and cultic matters. For example, "they send votive offerings to the temple, but perform their sacrifices employing a different ritual of purification. For this reason they are barred from those precincts of the temple that are frequented by all the people and perform their rites by themselves."[31] These Essene traditions were to be transmitted, and transmitted accurately. Indeed, according to Josephus, the Essene inductee "swears to transmit their rules exactly as he himself received them."[32]

The list of groups with distinctive traditions is doubtless as long as the list of distinctive groups and sects. The mention of but two more, both within the land of Israel, must suffice here. The Samaritans developed their own extrabiblical tradition, cultic practices, and theological emphases, some of which they regarded as "secret tradition."[33] They too claimed divine sanction for their unique views and transmitted them to their children. Finally, the Zealots were a variant that added to Pharisaic tradition a violent religious nationalism. We note them here merely as another group with a separate transmitted tradition.

As Intertestamental Judaism readjusted in the face of the fall of Judah and the invasion of Hellenism, the scribes emerged as both ideological and practical leaders. The shift of emphasis from temple and cult to morality, ethics, and the resulting study of the law made inevitable the ascent of some such group. It was primarily the scribes who structured postexilic society.

Along with the scribes came the rise of traditions, not a single set, but several lines or bodies of traditions. These traditions dealt with the way the law was to be read, interpreted, and applied. What in the intertestamental Jewish situation precipitated the need for an authoritative oral tradition in addition to the written one? The answer, we suggest, is the perception of prophetic silence, which

30. Josephus Jewish War 2.8.2–13 (120–61); Antiquities 18.1.5 (18–22).
31. Josephus Antiquities 18.1.5 (19).
32. Josephus Jewish War 2.8.7 (142).
33. The secret tradition is reflected in the title of the English translation of one of the primary Samaritan documents, The Asatir: The Samaritan Book of the "Secrets of Moses," trans. Moses Gaster (London: Royal Asiatic Society, 1927).

accompanied the crises of the postexilic period and which appeared to have left the Jewish community without adequate divine guidance. The law and other past revelations, suitable for the wilderness or settled existence in Canaan, seemed now to give little direction for living in a ruined, defeated land or as scattered captives. The new traditions, for which divine origin was claimed, became a way of adjusting to this situation.

It appears that many factions within Intertestamental Judaism had their own scribes who guided the development of their traditions. Other scribes may have functioned in schools or associations more or less separate from any discernible group or party. The different groups of scribes and the alternative traditions they developed contributed to the multiform nature of Intertestamental Judaism.

10

Apocalyptic

- Definition and Description
  - + General Considerations
  - + A General Description of Apocalyptic
- The Origins and Contexts of Apocalyptic
- Apocalyptic as Interpretation
- Some Examples
- Apocalyptic as Readjustment

The emergence of apocalyptic is an important feature of Intertestamental Judaism. Its precise definition, origin, social and religious setting, and interpretation are subjects of both debate and continuing scholarly investigations. Disagreements extend even to the list of writings considered apocalyptic.[1] Details are available elsewhere.

---

1. Klaus Koch, *The Rediscovery of Apocalyptic,* Studies in Biblical Theology, 2d series, vol. 22 (Naperville, Ill.: Alec R. Allenson, 1972), 23, suggests that a study of apocalyptic should begin with and seek a definition from a minimal list: Daniel, 1 Enoch, 2 Baruch, 4 Ezra, the Apocalypse of Abraham, and the Book of Revelation. Other biblical literature frequently regarded as apocalyptic includes Isaiah 24–27; parts of Ezekiel, Joel, possibly Amos, Zephaniah, and Zechariah; Mark 13 (and its parallels Matt. 24–25; Luke 21); and parts of 1 and 2 Thessalonians and 2 Peter.

Volume 1 of *The Old Testament Pseudepigrapha,* ed. James H. Charlesworth (Garden City, N.Y.: Doubleday, 1983), reflects a decision that the various testaments should in some way be associated with apocalyptic literature. It also includes a number of apocalypses which come late in the Christian Era, possibly as late as the ninth century A.D. The volume divides the nonbiblical apocalypses as follows:

Our concern is with a general understanding of apocalyptic and its place in the Jewish reaction to the crises of the sixth and fourth centuries.

Definition and Description

General Considerations

"Apocalyptic" is a difficult term to define. Grammatically, the term, though often used as a noun, is more descriptive (an adjective) and designates simultaneously a general type of literature (genre), a particular way of looking at life, and a group of ideas and beliefs. Yet there are considerable differences among apocalyptic writings and apocalyptic points of view. It is worth noting the distinction between what are often called the older and the newer type of definition.

The older definitions enumerated the various features found in apocalyptic works. These included the frequent use of dreams or visions as a framework for transporting the reader into another world, extensive imagery and symbolism (animals, birds, or monsters representing nations or individuals; numbers conveying special meanings), astronomical phenomena and forces cast in unaccustomed roles (e.g., astrological). Common in the apocalyptic drama are angels and demons; natural evils such as plagues, famines, droughts; and other forms of cosmic catastrophes, including wars and political and social disruption. There are a prevailing sense of doom and predictions of woe. The writer may use false geography or recasted history, so that a place or event may actually represent some other place or event. A frequent feature is pseudonymity—the literary device that sets forth as the author someone other than the actual writer; the alleged author is usually an important person from the past. Apocalyptic is pessimistic and fatalistic in that it assumes that

---

a. *Apocalyptic Literature and Related Works*: 1 Enoch (= Ethiopic Apocalypse); 2 Enoch (= Slavonic Apocalypse); 3 Enoch (= Hebrew Apocalypse); Sibylline Oracles; Treatise of Shem; Apocryphon of Ezekiel; Apocalypse of Zephaniah; 4 Ezra; Greek Apocalypse of Ezra; Vision of Ezra; Questions of Ezra; Revelation of Ezra; Apocalypse of Sedrach; 2 Baruch (= Syriac Apocalypse); 3 Baruch (= Greek Apocalypse); Apocalypse of Abraham; Apocalypse of Adam; Apocalypse of Elijah; and Apocalypse of Daniel.

b. *Testaments (often with Apocalyptic Sections)*: Testaments of the Twelve Patriarchs; Testament of Job; Testaments of the Three Patriarchs (Abraham, Isaac, and Jacob); Testament of Moses; Testament of Solomon; and Testament of Adam.

Other writings that might be classified as Jewish or Christian apocalypses can be found among the Dead Sea Scrolls (Visions of Amram [4Q ᶜAmram], "The New Jerusalem" [5Q15], Pseudo-Daniel [4QpsDan], and parts of the Manual of Discipline [1QS] and the Damascus Document [CD]), among the apostolic fathers (Didache 16 and parts of the Shepherd of Hermas), and in some Gnostic documents. For a survey of recent studies on apocalyptic see John J. Collins, "Apocalyptic Literature," in *Early Judaism and Its Modern Interpreters*, ed. Robert A. Kraft and George W. E. Nickelsburg (Atlanta: Scholars, 1986), 345–70.

present events are beyond the control of the individual, but it is optimistic in its conviction that in the end the sovereign God will be victorious and all wrongs will be righted. There is a cosmic dualism: a heavenly, spiritual world and this material one. Although separate, these two worlds are interconnected. What happens in the spiritual realm affects the material realm. Hence the focus of apocalyptic is upon the spiritual world and future time. While a list of such features may be helpful, it does not provide an adequate description or definition of apocalyptic. No one piece of literature contains all of the features, and lists alone miss much of the essence of apocalyptic.

The so-called newer definitions seek to identify and emphasize the major universal characteristics of apocalyptic, usually dualism and eschatology, or at least a revelation of heavenly mysteries.[2] Rather than assume that all features are equally significant, these definitions accord secondary status to most of those listed in older definitions. Recent students of apocalyptic go further in seeking to distinguish between apocalyptic, apocalypticism, and apocalyptic eschatology. "Apocalyptic" designates the literary form. "Apocalypticism" denotes the social setting perceived by and worldview of the writer and his group. "Apocalyptic eschatology" refers to the description of the divine events and actions through which God will be victorious and vindicate his own when the symbolic universe of the apocalyptists' visions is transformed into a new, perfect, and glorious reality.

Another helpful distinction is between those writings which are primarily historical in character and those which describe journeys through supernatural regions.[3] The former may review history, rewrite it, or both. Journey apocalypses contain a good deal of cosmic speculation; they share some features and objectives with a broad spectrum of esoteric writings, especially the so-called *Merkabah* (chariot or chariot-throne) texts.[4] Virtually all apocalyptic writings

2. A group of scholars working on the Genres Project of the Society of Biblical Literature has proposed a helpful working definition for apocalyptic: "Apocalypse is a genre of revelatory literature with a narrative framework, in which a revelation is mediated by an other-worldly being to a human recipient, disclosing a transcendent reality which is both temporal, insofar as it envisages eschatological salvation, and spatial, insofar as it involves another, supernatural world" (*Apocalypse: The Morphology of a Genre,* ed. John J. Collins, *Semeia* 14 [Missoula, Mont.: Scholars, 1979], 9).

3. Collins, "Apocalyptic Literature," 346, classifies several apocalypses: (1) historical—Daniel, 4 Ezra, 2 Baruch; (2) otherworldly journeys—2 Enoch, 3 Baruch, the Testament of Abraham, Apocalypse of Abraham, Testament of Levi 2–5, Apocalypse of Zephaniah.

4. For a good introduction to mysticism in Jewish thought see Neil S. Fujita, *A Crack in the Jar: What Ancient Jewish Documents Tell Us about the New Testament* (Mahwah, N.J.: Paulist, 1986), 158–200. He notes the place of apocalyptic in all this. See also Michael E. Stone, *Scripture, Sects and Visions* (Philadelphia: Fortress, 1980), 31–35.

fall into one or the other category; 1 Enoch and the Apocalypse of Abraham fall into both.

A word is in order about the term *eschatology* (for a definition see p. 25) and its relation to apocalyptic. Although there may be considerable similarity between their subject matter, the two are not the same. Eschatological issues may be presented in frameworks and literary forms other than apocalyptic (Paul does so in 2 Cor. 5). Apocalyptic has a strong eschatological emphasis but other concerns as well (such as theodicy, the problem of how a just, loving, and all-powerful God can permit evil to exist). Some scholars even argue that eschatology is not a necessary part of apocalyptic.[5]

Of course, throughout history many Christians have assumed that apocalyptic form always indicates that the writer is referring to the "end time" in the restricted sense of that phrase—the very end of human history, the second coming of Christ. This can be a misleading assumption. Eschatology, as we have noted, is only a part of the apocalyptists' concern. These writers may also have in view their own day and the immediate future, as well as the more distant future. Another unwarranted approach that some Christians take in reading apocalyptic literature is to be preoccupied with questions and issues about which the writers, including New Testament writers, show little concern. We have in mind here chronological schemes and precise identification of people, events, and institutions.

A General Description of Apocalyptic

Although the apocalyptic phenomenon predates it by centuries, the first document to call itself *apokalypsis* (apocalypse) is the Book of Revelation. The Greek word means literally "revelation, disclosure, making known that which was previously hidden." The title of the book thus sets the stage for the type of writing used by the biblical author. A contemporary writer has pointed out that the first two verses of Revelation present a structure and features that are typical of apocalyptic in general: "(1) A *revelation* is given by God, (2) through a *mediator* (here Jesus Christ or an angel), (3) to a *seer* concerning (4) future events."[6]

Apocalyptic is a many-sided phenomenon in which the writers seek to understand and respond to what they perceive as evil and

5. See Christopher Rowland, *The Open Heaven* (New York: Crossroad, 1982).

6. Paul D. Hanson, *Old Testament Apocalyptic* (Nashville: Abingdon, 1987), 32; see also idem, "Apocalypse, Genre," in *Interpreter's Dictionary of the Bible,* suppl. vol., ed. Keith Crim et al. (Nashville: Abingdon, 1976), 27.

dangerous circumstances.[7] They may do so by portraying a cosmic dualism, a spiritual conflict, and ultimate divine sovereignty and victory. Apocalyptic frankly recognizes that sin, wickedness, and suffering frequently dominate the world, and that good persons are the hapless victims of evil forces. It also wrestles with the nature, will, power, and activity of a good God who permits these conditions.

In general (although this structure is not always obvious) the apocalyptists assume within the cosmic dualism a radical division between good and evil, light and darkness, God and Satan. In the spiritual spheres the power of evil is struggling with that of good, the kingdom of Satan is at war with the kingdom of God. Now the fortunes of battle ebb and flow, but God and the good will ultimately be victorious. The world, its societies and peoples, is affected by the struggle. When spiritual evil has the upper hand, its allies on earth, evil nations and people, prosper and persecute the good; when the spiritual good is winning, then there are peace and harmony on earth and good prospers. The closer history moves to its conclusion, the more furious the forces of evil become in their fight and the worse the conditions on earth. Nevertheless, the outcome is not in doubt. God will be victorious. Evil will be defeated, judged, punished, and eliminated. The good will be saved, blessed, rewarded, and share God's eternal kingdom. As a former student of mine observed, "There is no such thing as apocalyptic without a happy ending."[8]

This view of reality enables the apocalyptic writers to understand the present situation. With it they discern what God is doing. With it the apocalyptist is able to clarify the real role of human government and social institutions: largely under the control of evil forces, they are tools for achieving the goals of those forces. Good persons usually appear to be a weak minority who are abused and persecuted simply because they side with God, the enemy of Satan and evil. In reality they are the strong who are on the winning side. All humanity is really helpless to alter the situation. Humans need to understand it, to side with God, to be assured that in the end good will be vindicated.

The apocalyptists focus attention on the course of events in the heavenlies, on otherworldly places, supernatural beings and events, and especially on the war which rages in the other world.

7. Paul D. Hanson, "Apocalypses and Apocalypticism, The Genre," in *Anchor Bible Dictionary*, ed. David Noel Freedman, 6 vols. (New York: Doubleday, 1992), 1:280, defines "apocalypticism" as the "effort to establish a basis for hope transcending the ever changing experiences of this world."

8. Brian Arnold, "The Messianic Woes in Jewish and Christian Apocalyptic Literature," Wheaton College Graduate School (Dec. 2, 1985).

They look to the future and the eventual victory of God. Yet this does not mean that they are necessarily otherworldly. Rather, their "this-worldliness" is informed by their otherworldliness; they insist that only through apprehending the heavenly and spiritual are they able to understand and have hope in this world.

In attempts to explain the real meaning of what was going on, apocalyptic writings often focused on the present, providing their own interpretation of contemporary history. However, because the writers believed that they themselves, their message, and their audience would be in danger if what they were saying was understood, they used figurative language (governments and institutions are not likely to be pleased when identified as tools of the kingdom of Satan). Their symbols were readily understood by the intended readers, but seemed obscure to those outside their circle (including modern readers). Furthermore, since the apocalyptists were speaking to the feelings as much as to the intellect, they often used exaggeration, bizarre images, and other distortions of reality to create an emotive atmosphere. Their object was to portray a long, twisting passageway of danger, gloom, foreboding, and darkness which suddenly emerges into a garden of safety, security, serenity, salvation, and light.

Since true reality can be perceived only with an otherworldly perspective, the apocalyptist often purports to convey divine revelation through visions, dreams, cosmic speculations, or spiritual journeys. Usually the writer claims contact with some supernatural messenger, maybe even God himself, who conveys the message and often offers an interpretation (these interpretations are not necessarily clear to the modern reader).

The Origins and Contexts of Apocalyptic

Two facts about the origins of apocalyptic seem clear. First, it rose to prominence during the latter part of Old Testament history. Second, it came at a time when the Hebrews, both in the land of Israel and in the Diaspora, were subjected to a wide variety of influences. Precisely when apocalyptic began and under what influences remain points of debate. Part of the problem here is that differing philosophical and theological commitments among contemporary interpreters, especially their assumptions relating to the nature of the Bible, influence their evaluation of the data related to the origins of apocalyptic (see Appendix F, pp. 368–69).

The long-held assumption that the Hebrews borrowed or took over apocalyptic from Persian sources, especially Zoroastrianism, has been largely abandoned.[9] The relevant Persian documents come from the Christian Era, and it is difficult to determine to what extent they may contain pre-Christian material. Paul Hanson relates apocalyptic to exilic and postexilic Hebrew prophetic literature.[10] Others have pointed out the complexity of the situation and a variety of possible sources.[11]

For our study it is important to note here the essential difference between prophecy and apocalyptic. In prophecy God works and delivers within the structures of this world. Salvation for the individual and the community is primarily a renewal which takes place on earth, even if it is a renewed earth. In the apocalyptic drama, deliverance comes from beyond the present order; a symbolic universe becomes the new order. Apocalyptic is especially interested in such themes as resurrection of the dead, eternal judgment, and the spiritual, heavenly kingdom.

Something happened in Jewish history to change the nature of hope and expectation. No longer could the reward for righteousness be spelled out in terms of living long in an earthly Land of Promise (Deut. 4:26; 5:33; 11:9; 30:18; 31:13; 32:47). Already in the latter part of the divided kingdom the pious Hebrew had to reckon with the possibility of a violent and early death. Defeat by Babylonia, life amidst hostile peoples, the life-and-death struggle against tyrants like Antiochus Epiphanes and their ideology heightened this likelihood. The apocalyptists gave up hope for earthly deliverance and salvation. The events which really determine human fate, they believed, lie beyond this world; final vindication and retribution, real rewards, ultimate salvation come at the end, in the other world.

Whatever else may have contributed to the rise of apocalyptic, the historical, social, cultural, and religious situations in which the Hebrews found themselves must have played an important part. About these we may speak in general, but many of the particulars lie in pages of history which remain closed. We do know, however, from a careful reading of the texts, that the former assumption that all apocalyptic literature came from a more or less unified movement and the same politico-social circumstances is incorrect.

9. This was the position of the history-of-religions school. For an example see Wilhelm Bousset, *Die Religion des Judentums im späthellenistischen Zeitalter,* 3d ed., ed. Hugo Gressmann (Tübingen: Mohr, 1926).

10. Paul D. Hanson, *The Dawn of Apocalyptic* (Philadelphia: Fortress, 1975).

11. See the summaries by John J. Collins, *The Apocalyptic Imagination* (New York: Crossroad, 1984), 16–28; and idem, "Early Jewish Apocalypticism," in *Anchor Bible Dictionary,* 1:282–83.

There is no compelling evidence of an identifiable movement;[12] rather, there were separate apocalyptic writers and, probably, separate apocalyptic communities such as Qumran. The proof of this conclusion is the wide span of time, the different places and groups, and the variety of concerns represented in any collection of apocalyptic literature. While it is true that apocalyptic was most likely to be found among persons and groups who perceived themselves to be living in adverse spiritual and physical situations, their disenfranchisement resulted from a wide range of circumstances.

It is evident that Jewish apocalyptic was a widespread phenomenon with common features and points of view. The frequent designation of apocalyptic writings as tracts for bad times has a basis in fact, at least as far as the writers were concerned. Virtually all apocalyptists believed themselves and their associates to be God's remnant who were being attacked by evil as a way of assaulting God. Still, there is as much diversity among the writings as there is uniformity.

It seems better, then, to think of apocalyptic as a general point of view, a direction or trajectory within Intertestamental Judaism, rather than as a clearly defined movement or group. Its adherents evaluated their situations similarly, although those situations may have been quite different. And though literary forms, worldviews, and expectations in response to those situations were somewhat alike, they were developed and expressed differently (the various works brought together in 1 Enoch are an example).

Apocalyptic was an undeniable part of Intertestamental Judaism. Whence and why it came are complex questions impossible to answer on the basis of the information now available. Foreign influence and developments within Judaism are quite likely to have played a part in its birth and growth. It could also be explained as simply the response of certain personality types to certain types of stimuli in the environment. Apocalyptic may also have been more or less in the air at certain times and places. Whatever the cause, apocalyptic was a part of the Jewish backgrounds of Christianity which in turn became a part of Christianity itself.

Apocalyptic as Interpretation

The prophets were God's spokesmen who conveyed God's message to their contemporaries. As they did so, they interpreted

12. In spite of influential recent books such as Koch, *Rediscovery*, and Walter Schmithals, *The Apocalyptic Movement: Introduction and Interpretation*, trans. John E. Steely (Nashville: Abingdon, 1975), there is no proof of such a movement. Note that the German title of Schmithals's book, *Die Apokalyptic: Einführung und Deutung*, does not contain the word *movement*. Nevertheless, he seems to assume one (pp. 127–50).

Scripture, history, and present conditions in the light of their understanding of the person, work, and objectives of God. The prophets claimed to have knowledge of God from both the religious traditions of the past and direct special revelation.

The apocalyptic scribes were also interpreters. They drew from some of the same sources as did the prophets. But, again, there were differences. We have already noted that they exchanged hope in this world for expectation of victory and vindication in the other. They cast their interpretations in a different form (apocalyptic) and, at times, presented different evaluations and conclusions. Their interpretations of the world scene were essentially negative. Their interpretations of the reasons for earthly events were entirely spiritual. Their interpretations of the future were based on their confidence in a powerful, good, eventually victorious God. Through such interpretation they sought to adjust to their situation and to assist their readers to do the same.

A seldom observed aspect of apocalyptic is that it is itself an interpretive method, a hermeneutic. The apocalyptic scribes made copious use of the Hebrew Scriptures. Most obvious are the biblical figures, such as Adam, Shem, Enoch, Abraham, Moses, Elijah, Baruch, and Ezra, to whom they ascribed their works. Biblical accounts, from the Nephilim and Noah and the flood (in Enoch) to Jeremiah and his prediction of seventy years of captivity (in Daniel), are the framework for some narratives. Historical apocalypses retell all or parts of the biblical story. But the biblical text is more than a source for names and narratives; it is authoritative, and that is a key to the apocalyptists' use of it.

The apocalyptists, like other scribes, faced the dilemma that the authoritative writings seemed irrelevant to the needs of the day. So their visions and descriptions interpret Scripture in a way that makes it relevant. In so doing, like allegory and *pesher* apocalyptic removes the text from its original life situation and places it in another, that of the scribe himself. Apocalyptic goes beyond allegory and *pesher*, however, in introducing new imagery and focusing on a symbolic universe. The apocalyptist may be prepared for a longer span of time, a delay, between his day and the final consummation than is the writer of *pesher*.

No precise hermeneutical rules or guidelines are immediately evident for interpreting the Bible in an apocalyptic framework. The nature of the genre would probably preclude such rules. What we do know is that as the writers adjusted to their historical and cultural environment, they sought both to add authority to their own offerings and to salvage the Bible as a meaningful book for themselves and their circle. (For a few suggestions on interpreting apocalyptic see Appendix G, pp. 370–72.)

Some Examples

The texts of and commentaries on Jewish apocalyptic literature are readily available.[13] Here we offer a few examples of apocalyptic writings that illustrate some of the features we have noted.

The Book of Revelation differs from strictly Jewish apocalypses because of its Christian adaptation of the form.[14] Still, it illustrates more apocalyptic features than do most other writings in this class. Describing itself as "the revelation (*apokalypsis*) of Jesus Christ" (1:1), it assumes from the beginning that its writer sees a vision, is "in the Spirit" (1:9), and goes through an open door (4:1) into the spiritual world. A cosmic and spatial dualism is everywhere present as is war between Satan and God. The book is filled with imagery, including virtually all of the features enumerated by the older definitions of apocalyptic. The document ends with the victory of God, the establishment of his kingdom, scenes of judgment and punishments (chs. 18–20), and descriptions of the new heaven and new earth (chs. 21–22).

False geography is well illustrated by the great harlot of Revelation 17. She is identified as Babylon, who "was drunk with the blood of the saints and the blood of the witnesses to Jesus" (vv. 5–6). Babylon certainly persecuted the Hebrews, the saints, but was no longer in existence when the blood of the witnesses to Jesus was shed. Thus, in addition to the notification that the harlot's name is

13. The most complete collection of texts is *Old Testament Pseudepigrapha*, ed. Charlesworth, vol. 1. *The Apocrypha and Pseudepigrapha of the Old Testament*, ed. R. H. Charles (Oxford: Clarendon, 1913), vol. 2; and *The Apocryphal Old Testament*, ed. H. F. D. Sparks (New York: Oxford University Press, 1984), also give the texts of major apocalyptic documents, introductions to each book, and some textual notes and commentary.

Summaries of apocalyptic books can be found in Collins, *Apocalyptic Imagination*; George W. E. Nickelsburg, *Jewish Literature between the Bible and the Mishnah* (Philadelphia: Fortress, 1981); Robert H. Pfeiffer, *History of New Testament Times* (London: Adam and Charles Black, 1949); Leonhard Rost, *Judaism outside the Hebrew Canon: An Introduction to the Documents*, trans. David E. Green (Nashville: Abingdon, 1976); H. H. Rowley, *The Relevance of Apocalyptic*, 3d ed. (London: Lutterworth, 1963); Schmithals, *Apocalyptic Movement*; Emil Schürer, *The History of the Jewish People in the Age of Jesus Christ*, ed. Geza Vermes et al., 3 vols. (Edinburgh: T. and T. Clark, 1973–87), vol. 3, parts 1 and 2; *Jewish Writings of the Second Temple Period: Apocrypha, Pseudepigrapha, Qumran, Sectarian Writings, Philo, Josephus*, ed. Michael E. Stone, in *Compendia Rerum Iudaicarum ad Novum Testamentum*, 7 vols. (Philadelphia: Fortress, 1974–92), section 2, vol. 2.

14. Oscar Cullmann, *The New Testament: An Introduction for the General Reader*, trans. Dennis Pardee (Philadelphia: Westminster, 1968), 120–21, makes an important distinction between Christian and Jewish apocalypses: "Unlike Jewish apocalypses oriented towards the future only, John's revelation is characterized by the Christian notion of time according to which the centre of divine history is by anticipation already reached in Jesus Christ. Thus the present time is already the time of the end, although the end itself must still be achieved. The author shows the celestial aspect of present events, just as he describes the celestial aspect of future events. This is the key for understanding the whole book."

"a mystery" (v. 5), the reader is put on notice to look beyond the obvious for her true identity. This is resolved in verse 9, where the seven heads of the blasphemous beast upon which she is seated (v. 3) are identified as "seven mountains," an obvious reference to the seven hills upon which Rome was built. Rome, it will be remembered, persecuted both Jews and Christians.

False history is illustrated in 4 Ezra and 2 Baruch. They claim to describe the situation following the destruction of Jerusalem and Judah by the Babylonians in the sixth century. In reality they are reacting to the destruction of Jerusalem by the Romans in A.D. 70.

Of all the extrabiblical apocalypses, 1 Enoch is the most important and the most complex. It is the result of bringing together sections that were written over a period of more than two centuries. The book falls into distinct divisions:

1. The Book of the Watchers—Enoch's Visionary Journey (chs. 1–36)
2. The Similitudes or Parables (37–71)
3. The Astronomical Writings—The Book of the Movement of Heavenly Bodies (72–82)
4. The History of the World as Seen in Dream Visions (83–90)
5. Admonitions to the Righteous (91–105)
6. Conclusion (106–8)

This, however, does not represent all of the diversity in 1 Enoch. Each of the divisions contains material antedating the final compilation. Prior to the discovery of the Dead Sea Scrolls there was a general consensus regarding identification and dating of this material:

1. Apocalypse of Weeks (91:12–17; 93:1–10), early pre-Maccabean
2. Fragments of Enochic Visions (12–16), early pre-Maccabean
3. Fragments of the Book of Noah (6–11; 106–7; cf. 54:7–55:2; 60; 65:1–69:25), late pre-Maccabean
4. Independent Fragment (105), pre-Maccabean?
5. Dream Visions (83–90), c. 165–161 B.C.
6. Book of Heavenly Luminaries (72–82), c. 110 B.C.
7. Similitudes (37–71), c. 105–64 B.C.
8. Later Additions to Dream Visions (91:1–11, 18–19; 92; 94–104), c. 105–104 B.C.
9. Introductory Chapters (1–5), late pre-Christian[15]

15. This list is given by E. Isaac, "1 (Ethiopic Apocalypse of) Enoch," in *Old Testament Pseudepigrapha*, ed. Charlesworth, 1:7; he is following Charles, *Apocrypha*, 2:170–71.

The discovery of the Dead Sea Scrolls has thrown into question some of the above dates. That fragments have been found from each division except the Similitudes prompted some students to question their right to a place in this collection of Enochic literature.[16] It now seems, however, that the Similitudes come from a Jewish community and were already a part of 1 Enoch by the end of the first century A.D.[17] Aramaic fragments of the Book of the Watchers and the Astronomical Writings suggest that they may contain material at least as old as the third century B.C.

The complexity of 1 Enoch is illustrated by its inclusion of historical apocalypses (the Animal Apocalypse [85–90] and the Apocalypse of Weeks [91:11–19; 93]) and journey apocalypses (the Book of the Watchers [1–36], the Similitudes [37–71], and the Astronomical Writings [72–82]). Its concerns include the origin of evil, angels and demons, judgment and punishment, questions relating to calendars,[18] the "Son of Man" or the "Elect One" (only in the Similitudes), as well as the struggle between good and evil in history and in the heavenly spheres.

Apocalyptic as Readjustment

The apocalyptic outlook became a way both to understand and to cope with such issues as the problem of evil, the suffering of the righteous, unfulfilled promises of blessing and longevity, the defeat and humiliation of God's people, and the evident dominance and prosperity of the wicked. It became the way to understand and cope when there seemed to be no other available perspective. God, who had previously spoken through his servants the prophets, was now silent; there were no prophets. The apocalyptists sought to continue, or revive, the voice of the prophets. They too affirmed contact with God through dreams, visions, and the like. They too sought guidance for the present through an understanding of God's activities in the past.

The scribes of the Pharisees (Aboth), the Sadducees, Qumran, and other traditions sought direction in the new intertestamental situation. The Jewish apocalyptists also looked for help in identical circumstances—loss of the temple, threats from external forces

16. J. T. Milik, "Problèmes de la littérature hénochique à la lumière des fragments araméens de Qumrân," *Harvard Theological Review* 64 (1971): 333–78; and idem, *The Books of Enoch* (New York: Oxford University Press, 1976), asserts that the Similitudes were produced by Christians about A.D. 400. His views have not been accepted by the majority of scholars working in the field.

17. Isaac, "1 Enoch," 7; Adela Yarbro Collins, "The Origin of the Designation of Jesus as Son of Man," *Harvard Theological Review* 80 (1987): 404–5.

18. The Astronomical Writings argue for a 364-day year instead of the lunar calendar.

and cultures, the irrelevance of the traditional way of approaching Scripture because of historical and cultural change, and the prophetic silence. They too claimed divine origin and authority for their approach and outlook. Theirs too was ultimately a system of orthopraxy, for it sought to elicit faithfulness and obedience in the lives of its adherents.

11

Divisions, Sects, and Parties

- Samaritanism
- Sects or Parties within Judaism
  + Pharisees
  + Sadducees
  + The Herodians
  + The Fourth Philosophy
    - General Comments
    - Zealots
    - Sicarii
  + Essenes
  + The Writers of the Dead Sea Scrolls: The Men of Qumran
    - Discovery and Controversy
    - Types of Literature in the Dead Sea Scrolls
    - The History of Qumran
    - The Community and Its Organization
    - Beliefs of the Community
    - Qumran and the Essenes
    - The Relevance of the Dead Sea Scrolls to a Study of Intertestamental Judaism and the New Testament
  + Therapeutae
  + Magical Judaism

Diversity, as we have seen, was a major feature of Intertestamental Judaism. The Jewish sects, parties, or philosophies (schools of thought), as Josephus calls them (Sadducees, Pharisees, Essenes), are usually considered the most obvious mark of this diversity.[1] It is now clear that this variety had its precursors in the socioreligious

1. Palestinian sects are known, at least by name, from a variety of sources:

community of the Old Testament period, Nazarites and Rechabites being the most obvious examples.[2] The intertestamental diversity also manifested itself in the split of the Mosaic religion into two varieties (Samaritanism and Judaism), in the classifications by geographic location (the land of Israel and the Dispersion, Galilee and Judea, etc.) or by cultural orientation (Semitic and Hellenistic Judaism), and in other ways too numerous, and often too obscure, to mention. We will first center attention on the alternate variety of the Mosaic religion, Samaritanism, and then on the major sects or parties within Judaism.

Samaritanism

Two verses in the Gospel of John reveal something of the tensions between the Jews and the Samaritans. According to 4:9, "The Samaritan woman said to [Jesus], 'How is it that you, a Jew, ask a drink of me, a woman of Samaria?' (Jews do not share things in common with Samaritans)." Her statement reflects the tension and social segregation between the two groups. In 8:48 the Jews heap ultimate insults upon Jesus by asking, "Are we not right in saying that you are a Samaritan and have a demon?" Behind these sentiments lies a long history of strained relations and outward animosity between peoples who shared the hill country of the land of Israel from the Valley of Esdraelon in the north to the Negeb in the south.

Josephus	Hegesippus (cited in Eusebius *Ecclesiastical History* 4.22.7)	Justin Martyr (*Dialogue with Trypho* 80)	New Testament
Pharisees	Pharisees	Pharisees	Pharisees
Sadducees	Sadducees	Sadducees	Sadducees
Essenes	Essenes		
Fourth philosophy (=Zealots)			Zealots
Sicarii			Sicarii (Acts 21:38)
(Samaritans)	Samaritans		Samaritans
Hellenists		Hellenists	Hellenists
(Galileans)	Galileans	Galileans	Galileans
		Herodians	Herodians
		Scribes	Scribes
(Disciples of John the Baptist)			Disciples of John the Baptist
	Hemerobaptists		
	Masbotheans		
		Meristae	
		Genistae	

2. Morton Smith, *Palestinian Parties and Policies That Shaped the Old Testament* (New York: Columbia University Press, 1971).

James Purvis summarizes the problems of Samaritan origin with four questions, "Who were the Samaritans? How did the Samaritans come into being as a distinct religious community? When did the rupture between the Samaritans and the Jews occur? What was the theological *raison d'être* of the Samaritan community?"[3] A survey of historical events involving the Samaritans will prove helpful. The Solomonic grandeur had quickly crumbled with his death. His son Rehoboam presided over a schism. Israel, composed of about ten northern tribes, rebelled against the house of David. Judah, the southern two-and-a-half tribes, remained loyal to the Davidic kings, who ruled in Jerusalem. Jeroboam, the first king of Israel, took divisive action religiously as well as politically and geographically by establishing alternative worship centers, priests, and festivals (1 Kings 12:25–33). The seed for the Samaritan-Jewish division of the New Testament Era was planted.

About two hundred years later, in 722 B.C., the Assyrians defeated and destroyed the northern kingdom (2 Kings 17). The conquerors deported some Israelites and brought foreigners into the land. Intermarriage between the two groups was inevitable. Later, the Assyrian king, to ward off lions that he was told had been sent by the Hebrew God, sent a Hebrew priest to reintroduce Yahwehism (vv. 25–28). As a result, "they worshiped the LORD but also served their own gods, after the manner of the nations from among whom they had been carried away" (v. 33). There was, then, a syncretism of both race and religion. Josephus, 2 Kings, and the later rabbis say that the Samaritans came from this group.[4]

Ezra 4 tells of adversaries of Judah and Benjamin who sought to assist in the construction of the temple in the early postexilic period. Refused by Zerubbabel, they thereafter opposed the rebuilding of both temple and city. Ill will between the two groups increased.

Josephus indicates that during the Persian period Manasseh, brother of Jaddua the high priest, married the daughter of Sanballat, a Samaritan official of King Darius.[5] He and some other priests who had been rejected for service in the Jerusalem temple defected to the Samaritans. With the defeat of Darius by Alexander the

3. James D. Purvis, "The Samaritans and Judaism," in *Early Judaism and Its Modern Interpreters,* ed. Robert A. Kraft and George W. E. Nickelsburg (Atlanta: Scholars, 1986), 83.

4. Josephus calls the Samaritans "Cutheans" (*Antiquities* 9.14.3 [288–91]).

5. The name Sanballat figures prominently in the Samaritan history of this period. It appears in Neh. 2:10, 19; 4:1, 7; 6:1, 2, 5, 12, 14; 13:28. The name also occurs in the Elephantine Papyri (5th century) and those from Wadi Daliyeh (4th century). It is now assumed that these were different persons who held high positions in Samaritan society. They were probably from the same family, the name being passed from grandfather to grandson.

Great, Sanballat secured permission from the new ruler to build a temple on Mount Gerizim and made his son-in-law high priest.[6] The widespread belief that this incident marks the beginning of the Samaritan-Jewish schism is not without its difficulties, not the least of which is Josephus's claim that the break came earlier, after the defeat of Israel by the Assyrians in the eighth century B.C.[7]

When Antiochus Epiphanes was persecuting Jews who refused to accept Hellenistic ways, the Samaritans denounced the Jews before the king and dissociated themselves from them. The Samaritans claimed to be of Sidonian ancestry. To prove their acceptance of Hellenism they dedicated their temple to Zeus Hellenios. Such actions further intensified bad feelings between the two groups.[8]

Jewish irritation at the Samaritans reached a climax under the Maccabean ruler John Hyrcanus. He defeated and devastated the city of Samaria.[9] Josephus says that he had earlier destroyed the Samaritan temple (c. 108 B.C.).[10] If the final rupture between the two groups had not already occurred (and it almost certainly had), Hyrcanus's actions would undoubtedly have completed the breach.

The Samaritan Pentateuch is another factor in understanding Samaritan-Jewish relations. The Samaritans acknowledge no Scriptures save the five books of Moses, and these they hold in an edition that is significantly different from that of the Jews. Some scholars argue that the Samaritan text represents an independent tradition which may, in part, better represent the original than does the Masoretic text of the Jews. In spite of the agreement of some Dead Sea Scroll fragments with the Samaritan version, however, the best evidence seems to indicate that the Samaritans produced their Pentateuch in the second century B.C. to give legitimacy to their theological views and practices.[11]

Recent discoveries at Qumran and Wadi Daliyeh as well as archaeological excavations at Shechem and Mount Gerizim permit a fuller reconstruction of Samaritan history. It now seems that about the time of Alexander the Great the ruling families of Samaria lost control, left the city, and established a community at the site of ancient Shechem. At that time they built a temple on Mount Gerizim. Sometime later, possibly much later, this community produced the

---

6. Josephus *Antiquities* 11.7.2–8.5 (302–25).

7. See Purvis, "Samaritans," 84–85, and the literature he cites.

8. Josephus *Antiquities* 12.5.5 (257–64).

9. Ibid., 13.10.2–3 (275–81).

10. Ibid., 13.9.1 (255–56).

11. This is an involved technical issue. Bruce K. Waltke, "Samaritan Pentateuch," in *Anchor Bible Dictionary*, ed. David Noel Freedman, 6 vols. (New York: Doubleday, 1992), 5:932–40, provides an excellent survey and bibliography. Waltke seems to be in general agreement with Purvis, "Samaritans," who has also written extensively on the subject.

Samaritan Pentateuch. Their insistence that Gerizim was the divinely ordained center for religious life made permanent the split between themselves and the Jews. The Samaritans, then, are not a branch of Judaism, but a rival faith which claims to be the true religion of the Hebrews.

The Samaritan documents now available reflect developments into the medieval period and diverse influences, including Islam.[12] Information about the beliefs of modern Samaritans was augmented at the end of the seventeenth or beginning of the eighteenth century by letters from Samaritans (who thought they were writing to Samaritan brethren) to European and British scholars. Though the precise nature of the first-century beliefs and practices cannot now be determined,[13] one of the letters from the modern Samaritans states their creed, "We say: My faith is in thee YHWH; and in Moses the son of Amram thy servant; and in the holy Law; and in Mount Gerizim Beth-El; and in the Day of Vengeance and Recompense."[14] Thus in general they affirm (1) a rigid monotheism, including God's covenant with his people; (2) a position for Moses beyond what he has in Judaism—he is the mediator of the law and the last prophet; (3) the Law (in their own edition); (4) the sanctity of Mount Gerizim as the house of God, a fact made clear by the addition of the tenth commandment in the Samaritan Pentateuch;[15] and (5) an eschatology including rewards and punishments.

The Samaritan calendar and festivals differ from those of the Jews. Another important difference is the Samaritans' unique view of salvation history. Rejecting the Jewish view, they divide

12. Summaries of these documents are available in standard works on Samaritanism; e.g., John Macdonald, *The Theology of the Samaritans* (London: SCM, 1964), 40–49; Robert T. Anderson, "Samaritans," in *Anchor Bible Dictionary*, 5:945–46.

13. For a study of Samaritan thought see Macdonald, *Theology*.

14. James Alan Montgomery, *The Samaritans: The Earliest Jewish Sect* (Philadelphia: John C. Winston, 1907), 207; see also Moses Gaster, *The Samaritans: Their History, Doctrines and Literature*, Schweich Lectures (London: Oxford University Press, 1925), 180; Macdonald, *Theology*, 40–50.

15. The Samaritan Pentateuch harmonizes the different wording of the Ten Commandments in the Masoretic text of Exod. 20 and Deut. 5. It counts these commandments as nine and adds a tenth: "And it shall come to pass when the Lord thy God will bring thee into the land of the Canaanites whither thou goest to take possession of it, thou shalt erect unto thee large stones, and thou shalt cover them with lime, and thou shalt write upon the stones all the words of this Law, and it shall come to pass when ye cross the Jordan, ye shall erect these stones which I command thee upon Mount Garizim, and thou shalt build there an altar unto the Lord thy God, an altar of stones, and thou shalt not lift up upon them iron; of perfect stones shalt thou build thine altar, and thou shalt bring up upon it burnt offerings to the Lord thy God, and thou shalt sacrifice peace offerings, and thou shalt eat there and rejoice before the Lord thy God. That mountain is on the other side of the Jordan and at the end of the road towards the going down of the sun in the land of the Canaanites who dwell in the Arabah facing Gilgal close by Elon Moreh facing Sichem" (Gaster, *Samaritans*, 189).

salvation history into an age of disfavor preceding Moses and an age of grace after Moses which lasted 260 years. Samaritan eschatology looks for a repeat of the ages of disfavor and grace at the end of history. The former will be initiated by the evil priest Eli; the latter by the *Taheb* (Restorer = Messiah), the Prophet like Moses. There is also evidence that a priest is expected to accompany the Restorer.[16]

Samaria and Samaritans were a part of the New Testament world. At the beginning of this section we noted two incidents involving Samaria that are recorded in the Gospel of John. Some understanding of the hostility between Jews and Samaritans makes all the more striking the fact that a Samaritan was the hero of a parable of Jesus (Luke 10:29–37), and that, unlike the nine Jews who also had been healed from leprosy, a Samaritan returned to give thanks (Luke 17:11–19). Nor should the New Testament reader forget that Samaria was the first foreign mission field of Christianity (Acts 8:4–25).

Sects or Parties within Judaism

Some ancient sources, including the New Testament, use the word *hairesis* to describe such groups as the Pharisees, Sadducees, and Essenes. Hence they have come to be thought of as nonconforming sects whose views were wrong. In the Western world "heresy" and "sect" primarily suggest unacceptable beliefs or doctrines. But "heresy" is too strong to represent the usual meaning of the Greek *hairesis*. The word can mean "a division, opinion, or dissension" as well as "heretical group." Likewise, the English word *sect* is frequently understood to denote a heretical group, although it need not have this negative nuance.[17] A more accurate translation of the Greek word when applied to the Pharisees, Sadducees, and Essenes is "party" or "denomination."

Each party had its own distinctive traditions, including its culture, religious beliefs, ceremonies, calendar, lifestyle, and the like.

16. Moses Gaster, *Samaritan Oral Law and Ancient Traditions*, vol. 1, *Eschatology* (London: Search, 1932), 271–72, summarizes this belief: "A priest, from the descendants of Phivebar, will then appear who had been taken up to heaven by God, like Enoch of old, there to walk with the angels and to act as a priest; he will then be sent down and act as a high priest, performing all the services in the new temple." See also the Samaritan book *Yom al-Din* 67 (Gaster's edition).

17. *Webster's New Twentieth-Century Dictionary of the English Language, Unabridged*, 2d ed., s.v. "sect," gives three usages: "(1) a group of people having a common leadership, set of opinions, philosophical doctrine, etc.; a school; a following; (2) any group holding certain views, political principles, etc., in common; (3) a religious denomination, especially a small group that has broken away from an established church."

The ancient sources do not permit us to list all of the points on which the various parties differed. Of those of which we are aware, we do not know all of the reasons for them nor the exact implications they had for their respective groups. What seems strangest to modern minds is that these differences apparently concerned activities more than theology.

Judaism, it must be remembered, was essentially a religion of orthopraxy. Other than acceptance of monotheism, recognition of God's covenant with Israel, and obedience to some interpretation of the law, it was practice, one's way of life, which was the basis for acceptance or rejection by the mainstream social-religious community. The Christian writer Hippolytus says the differences between the Jewish groups arose because of "different interpretations of the declarations made by God."[18]

The presence of various religious parties is a conspicuous feature of Intertestamental Judaism as described in the New Testament, Josephus, and other sources. They seem to have constituted but a small percent of the total adherents of Judaism, both in the land of Israel and in the Diaspora. In the land of Israel, at least, their influence far exceeded their numbers.

We have previously noted the emergence of the Hasidim in the early second century B.C. (pp. 82, 83). They supported the Maccabean revolt as long as its motives were religious (1 Macc. 2:42; 2 Macc. 14:6), but withdrew when it became primarily political (1 Macc. 7:13). Unfortunately information about the Hasidim is limited. They are sometimes mentioned as precursors of later Jewish parties, particularly the Pharisees and the Essenes.

Josephus, writing primarily for the Hellenistic world, uses the phrase "schools of thought" to describe major divisions in Judaism: "Now at this time there were three schools of thought among the Jews, which held different opinions concerning human affairs; the first being that of the Pharisees, the second that of the Sadducees, and the third that of the Essenes."[19] The historian interrupts his account of the reign of Jonathan Maccabeus (160–143) to make this statement. Thus he implies that these groups originated in the second century B.C. Later on he says, "The fourth . . . school agrees in all other respects with the opinions of the Pharisees, except that they have a passion for liberty that is almost unconquerable."[20] He specifically states that this group began in the first century A.D.

18. Hippolytus *Refutation of All Heresies* 9.13.
19. Josephus *Antiquities* 13.5.9 (171); see also 18.1.2 (11) and *Jewish War* 2.8.2 (119).
20. Josephus *Antiquities* 18.1.6 (23); note that he does not mention the Zealots here.

We have already noted the relation between the schools of thought that Josephus mentions and the development of different traditions within Judaism. We now come to consider those groups in more detail. We will first deal with those parties specifically mentioned in the New Testament—Pharisees, Sadducees, Herodians, the fourth philosophy (including Zealots and Sicarii)—and then turn to the Essenes, the Dead Sea sect, and other groups that are in the background of the New Testament.[21]

Pharisees

Information about the Pharisees comes from the New Testament, Josephus, and the rabbinic writings.[22] Possible allusions in the Apocrypha, Pseudepigrapha, and the Dead Sea Scrolls are too uncertain and vague to be of assistance. There are two major parts to the debates regarding these sources. First, how accurate are they, and how are they to be interpreted? Second, what is the essential nature of the Pharisaism they depict? Theories are numerous, often influenced by the point of view of the researcher.

The root meaning of "Pharisee" is uncertain. It is probably related to the Hebrew *parash* and Aramaic *perash* (one who separates). From whom did the Pharisees separate? From those, especially priests and clerics, whose interpretation of the law was different from theirs? From the common people of the land (John 7:47–49)? From Gentiles or Jews who embraced Hellenistic cul-

---

21. See Leah Bronner, *Sects and Separatism during the Second Jewish Commonwealth* (New York: Bloch, 1967); Marcel Simon, *Jewish Sects at the Time of Jesus*, trans. James H. Farley (Philadelphia: Fortress, 1967); William W. Buehler, *The Pre-Herodian Civil War and Social Debate: Jewish Society in the Period 76–40 B.C. and the Social Factors Contributing to the Rise of the Pharisees and Sadducees* (Basel: Friedrich Reinhardt, 1974).

22. For additional information on the Pharisees see Lester L. Grabbe, *Judaism from Cyrus to Hadrian*, 2 vols. (Minneapolis: Augsburg Fortress, 1991–92), 2:467–84; Anthony J. Saldarini, "Pharisees," in *Anchor Bible Dictionary*, 5:289–303; John Kampen, *The Hasideans and the Origin of Pharisaism: A Study in 1 and 2 Maccabees* (Atlanta: Scholars, 1988); Jacob Neusner, *Formative Judaism: Torah, Pharisees, and Rabbis* (Chico, Calif.: Scholars, 1983), and *The Rabbinic Traditions about the Pharisees before 70*, 3 vols. (Leiden: E. J. Brill, 1971); Emil Schürer, *The History of the Jewish People in the Age of Jesus Christ*, ed. Geza Vermes et al., 3 vols. (Edinburgh: T. and T. Clark, 1973–87), 2:388–403; Ellis Rivkin, *A Hidden Revolution: The Pharisees' Search for the Kingdom Within* (Nashville: Abingdon, 1978); John W. Bowker, *Jesus and the Pharisees* (New York: Cambridge University Press, 1973); Louis Finkelstein, *The Pharisees: The Sociological Background of their Faith*, 3d ed., 2 vols. (Philadelphia: Jewish Publication Society of America, 1962); R. Travers Herford, *The Pharisees* (Boston: Beacon, 1962); Stephen Taylor, "Pharisees," in *Evangelical Dictionary of Theology*, ed. Walter A. Elwell (Grand Rapids: Baker, 1984), 849–51; Moisés Silva, "The Pharisees in Modern Jewish Scholarship," *Westminster Theological Journal* 42 (1979–80): 395–405; H. F. Weiss, "*Pharisaios*," in *Theological Dictionary of the New Testament*, ed. Gerhard Kittel and Gerhard Friedrich, trans. Geoffrey W. Bromiley, 10 vols. (Grand Rapids: Eerdmans, 1964–76), 9:11–48; Ralph Marcus, "The Pharisees in the Light of Modern Scholarship," *Journal of Religion* 32 (1952): 153–64.

ture? Or from certain political groups? All these would be included in the Pharisees' determination to separate themselves from the types of impurity proscribed by Levitical law or, more specifically, by their strict understanding of it. Another explanation suggests that "Pharisee" is a nickname derived from a Grecianized form of "Persian"; the Pharisees' opponents used it in accusing them of introducing foreign (especially Iranian) doctrines into Judaism.

Josephus's references are hardly neutral; he says, for example, that he governed his "life by the rules of the Pharisees."[23] His statements are selective and probably adapted to his cultured Gentile audience. Josephus's information comes in two, sometimes inconsistent, forms: (1) direct descriptions, and (2) accounts of the role the Pharisees played in history.[24]

Josephus says that the Pharisees maintained a simple lifestyle; they were affectionate and harmonious in their dealings with others, especially respectful to their elders, and quite influential throughout the land of Israel—although at the time of Herod they numbered only about six thousand.[25] Josephus mentions their belief in both fate (divine sovereignty) and the human will as well as their belief in the immortality of both good and evil persons.[26] Some Pharisees refused to take oaths.[27] Of particular importance are Josephus's statements that the Pharisees adhered to "the laws of which the Deity approves," and that they "are considered the most accurate interpreters of the laws."[28] The Pharisees "follow the guidance of that which their doctrine has selected and transmitted as good, attaching the chief importance to the observance of those commandments which it has seen fit to dictate to them."[29] In addition, they "passed on to the people certain regulations handed down by former generations and not recorded in the Laws

23. Josephus *Life* 2 (12). His more important descriptions of the Pharisees are found in *Jewish War* 2.8.14 (162–66); *Antiquities* 13.10.5–6 (288–98); 17.2.4 (41); 18.1.3 (12–15); and *Life* 2 (12); 38 (191).

24. As an example of inconsistency, the Pharisees seem to play a less significant role in his historical accounts than one would expect from his statement, "So great is their influence with the masses that even when they speak against a king or high priest, they immediately gain credence" (*Antiquities* 13.10.5 [288]). In addition, Josephus's description of the Pharisee Eleazar (he "had an evil nature and took pleasure in dissension" [*Antiquities* 13.10.5 (291)]) hardly squares with his claim that "the Pharisees are affectionate to each other and cultivate harmonious relations with the community" (*Jewish War* 2.8.14 [166]).

25. Josephus *Antiquities* 18.1.3 (12); *Jewish War* 2.8.14 (166); *Antiquities* 13.10.5 (288); 17.2.4 (41–45); 18.1.3 (15).

26. Josephus *Jewish War* 2.8.14 (162–63); *Antiquities* 18.1.3 (13–14).

27. Josephus *Antiquities* 17.2.4 (42).

28. Josephus *Antiquities* 17.2.4 (41); *Jewish War* 2.8.14 (162).

29. Josephus *Antiquities* 18.1.3 (12).

of Moses."[30] Although the term "oral law" is not used, it appears that, according to Josephus, the Pharisees affirmed a body of traditional interpretations, applications, and expansions of the Old Testament law that was communicated orally.

The way Josephus first mentions the Pharisees (in connection with the reign of Jonathan Maccabeus, but with the assumption that they had been in existence for some time) raises the much discussed question of their origin.[31] Some see the Pharisees' roots in the biblical Ezra, others in the Hasidim.[32] Recent studies suggest that the Pharisees were part of a general revolutionary spirit of the pre-Maccabean times; they emerged as a scholarly class dedicated to the teaching of both the written and oral law and stressing the internal side of Judaism. In any case, they were clearly one of the groups which sought to adapt Judaism for the postexilic situation.

John Hyrcanus was at first a disciple of the Pharisees but became their enemy.[33] The Pharisees were opponents of the Hasmonean rulers from then on. The hostility was especially great during the reign of Alexander Jannaeus (103–76), and they seem to have taken a leading part in the opposition to him; it is usually assumed that Pharisees composed either all or a large part of the eight hundred Jews he crucified.[34] The one exception to the Pharisaic opposition to the Hasmoneans was Salome Alexandra (76–67), under whom they virtually dominated the government.

Josephus's information about the Pharisees under the Romans is spotty. Under Herod (37–4 B.C.) the Pharisees were influential, but carefully controlled by the king. Some individual Pharisees did oppose Herod on occasions. Josephus gives almost no information about the Pharisees from the death of Herod until the outset of the revolt against Rome (about A.D. 66). At first, he says, they attempted to persuade the Jews against militant actions.[35] Later, Pharisees appear as part of the leadership of the people during the revolt and war against Rome.

The New Testament usually depicts the Pharisees as opponents of Jesus and the early Christians. On the other hand, they warn Jesus that his life is in danger from Herod (Luke 13:31), invite him for meals (Luke 7:36–50; 14:1), are attracted to and even believe in Jesus (John 3:1–21; 7:45–53; 9:13–16), and protect early

30. Josephus *Antiquities* 13.10.6 (297); see also 17.2.4 (41).

31. Josephus *Antiquities* 13.5.9 (171–72).

32. Ezra had been concerned for exact keeping of the law, and especially for ceremonial purity (Ezra 7:10).

33. Josephus *Antiquities* 13.10.5 (288–98).

34. Josephus *Jewish War* 1.4.6 (96–97); *Antiquities* 13.14.2 (380); see also the Nahum Commentary of the Dead Sea Scrolls (4QpNah), where "the furious young lion" is probably Alexander Jannaeus, and "the seekers after smooth things" are the Pharisees whom he crucified.

35. Josephus *Jewish War* 2.17.3 (411).

Christians (Acts 5:34–39; 23:6–9). Paul asserts he was a Pharisee before his conversion (Phil. 3:5).

The clearest New Testament statement of Pharisaic distinctives is Acts 23:8—"the Sadducees say that there is no resurrection, or angel, or spirit; but the Pharisees acknowledge all three." This would give the impression that doctrine was the basic concern of the group. However, Mark 7:3–4 says, "The Pharisees . . . do not eat unless they thoroughly wash their hands, thus observing the tradition of the elders; and they do not eat anything from the market unless they wash it; and there are also many other traditions that they observe, the washing of cups, pots, and bronze kettles." Thus we are also told of the Pharisees' concern for washing (ceremonial cleansing) and observance of the tradition of the elders, a description of the oral law. Matthew 23 calls attention to the Pharisees' position of religious authority in the community, their concern for outward recognition and honor, their enthusiasm for making converts, and their emphasis upon observing the legalistic minutiae of the law. In verse 23 Jesus condemns them, not for what they did, but for neglecting "the weightier matters of the law: justice and mercy and faith."

The portrayal of the Pharisees in rabbinic literature is particularly hard to interpret. That portrayal was, after all, compiled and written by the rabbis, who regarded themselves as the successors of the Pharisees and therefore had both historical and sociological biases. Some rabbinic statements about the Pharisees may have been propaganda to enhance or support their position against opponents. Further, the nature of this material makes it difficult to distinguish what within it represents the pre–A.D. 70 situation. Unlike Josephus and the New Testament, the rabbinic writers say virtually nothing about the beliefs of the Pharisees. Their concern is almost entirely with cultic and ceremonial matters related to purity, eating, the Sabbath, festivals, agriculture, and issues like betrothal, marriage, and divorce.

Our three sources, neither individually nor collectively, provide sufficient information for a complete understanding of the Pharisees. Each presents a different picture or has a distinct emphasis. Because of the weight given to the New Testament evidence, the Pharisees have traditionally been viewed as a legalistic and hypocritical sect, but even the New Testament portrayal of them is more complex than that.

Pharisaic zeal for the law is obvious, but what is meant by law? The sanctity of the written law was never questioned by any intertestamental Jewish group. The Pharisees' distinctive lay in their own traditions, which, we have seen, included the fences or hedges around the written law (Mishnah *Aboth* 1:1), that body of interpretations, expansions, and applications of the law which they came to regard as of divine origin. Most of these traditions, the oral law, dealt with matters of Levitical purity. Some included additions which had come into prominence in the intertestamental situation. These included belief in immortality, angels and demons, spirits, and divine sovereignty. Expansion of such doctrines led to others. For example, belief in immortality resulted in expanding messianic and eschatological views. The social and political views of the Pharisees were based on their premise that all of life must be lived under the control of God's law. They opposed the Hasmoneans who, contrary to the law, sought to combine the monarchy and priesthood. Likewise, they rejected Roman authority when it appeared to conflict with the law of God.

Modern writers' ascription of legalism and literalism to the Pharisees certainly reflects the ancient sources. At the same time the Pharisees were not as strict as some other groups, notably the Essenes.[36] On the other hand, their interpretations and manner of life were more precise than those of the common people, whom they regarded as "this crowd, which does not know the law—they are accursed" (John 7:49).

Unlike the Sadducees the Pharisees were resistant to Hellenistic culture and cooperation with foreign political powers. Apparently the Pharisees accepted a much larger body of tradition than did the Sadducees. Pharisaic tradition included not only different ceremonial and cultic regulations, but also expansions of beliefs which the Sadducees could not accept.

Sadducees

Information about the Sadducees appears in the same sources as does our information about the Pharisees: Josephus, the New Testament, and rabbinic writings.[37] Working with the name *Saddu-cee*, attempts have been made to determine the origin of this group. Suggestions include linking it with the Old Testament

---

36. The Dead Sea Scroll reference to the Pharisees as "seekers after smooth things" (4QpNah 2:11b), meaning "those who take the easy way out," is probably a derogatory description.

37. For additional information see Grabbe, *Judaism*, 2:484–87; Gary G. Porton, "Sadducees," in *Anchor Bible Dictionary*, 5:892–95; Anthony J. Saldarini, *Pharisees, Scribes and Sadducees in Palestinian Society* (Edinburgh: T. and T. Clark, 1988); Schürer, *History*, 2:403–14; Simon, *Jewish Sects*, 22–27; Rudolf Meyer, "*Saddoukaios*," in *Theological Dictionary of the New Testament*, 7:35–54; Stephen Taylor, "Sadducees," in *Evangelical Dictionary of Theology*, 965–66; E. E. Ellis, "Jesus, the Sadducees, and Qumran," *New Testament Studies* 10 (1963–64): 274–79.

priestly family of Zadok,[38] the Hebrew word for "just" or "righteous" (*ṣaddîq*), or "court officials" or "judges" (Greek, *syndikoi*). Unfortunately, there are problems with such etymologies and all other attempts to identify the origin of the Sadducees.

In the New Testament the Sadducees appear only in the Synoptic Gospels and Acts.[39] Acts 23:8 defines the Sadducees theologically, saying that they hold there "is no resurrection, or angel, or spirit." The Sadducean rejection of the resurrection is the point at issue in Mark 12:18–27 and its parallels.

Josephus describes the Sadducees as argumentative, boorish, and rude both to each other and to aliens.[40] Though few in number, they included men of the highest standing.[41] They had the confidence of the wealthy, but not the populace.[42] Accordingly, when exercising office the Sadducees were forced by public opinion to follow the formulas of the Pharisees.[43] Evidently they were more severe in administering punishments than were the Pharisees.[44]

Like the New Testament, Josephus mentions the Sadducean rejection of resurrection.[45] He notes, too, the rejection of fate (predestination) in order to dissociate God from evil and to assert the human free choice of good or evil.[46] In addition, the Pharisaic extrabiblical traditions were "rejected by the Sadducean group, who hold only those regulations should be considered valid which were written down (in Scripture)."[47] This points toward a major feature of Sadduceeism, rejection of the Pharisaic oral law or "the tradition of the elders" (Mark 7:3). We have already noted that the Sadducees had their own traditions, interpretations, and procedures instead (pp. 176–77).

In Acts 5:17 the confederates of the high priest are identified as the sect of the Sadducees. Josephus similarly depicts the Sadducees as closely associated with the priestly Hasmonean rulers. By the time of the New Testament the high-priestly family and their

---

38. Zadok is the name of a priest during David's reign (2 Sam. 15:24–36; 17:15; 19:11) who with his family gained control of the high priesthood and temple under Solomon (1 Kings 2:35; 1 Chron. 29:22). "The levitical priests, the descendants of Zadok," minister in the sanctuary in Ezekiel's vision of the reconstructed temple (44:15).

39. They appear in six different contexts: three in the Synoptics (Matt. 3:7; 16:1–12; 22:23–34 [=Mark 12:18–27; Luke 20:27–40]) and three in Acts (4:1; 5:17; 23:6–8).

40. Josephus *Antiquities* 18.1.4 (16); *Jewish War* 2.8.14 (166).

41. Josephus *Antiquities* 18.1.4 (17).

42. Josephus *Antiquities* 13.10.6 (298).

43. Josephus *Antiquities* 18.1.4 (17).

44. Josephus *Antiquities* 13.10.6 (294).

45. Josephus *Jewish War* 2.8.14 (165); *Antiquities* 18.1.4 (16).

46. Josephus *Jewish War* 2.8.14 (164–65).

47. Josephus *Antiquities* 13.10.6 (297); see also 18.1.4 (16).

Sadducean supporters appear to be the majority in the Sanhedrin. However, it must not be assumed that all Sadducees were priests nor that all priests were Sadducees.

The rabbinic references are scanty and hostile.[48] Sometimes they call the Sadducees "Samaritans" (here meaning "opponents") or "Boethusians." The latter is probably from their connection with the house of Boethus, from which came several high priests during the New Testament period. The post–A.D. 70 writings distinguish between the Sadducean and Pharisaic positions on ceremonial and judicial matters. In general it seems the Sadducees had supported those interpretations and procedures which enhanced the prestige, power, and finances of the priestly temple cult and the aristocracy. The Pharisees took the opposite position.

Religiously, the Sadducees were conservative and literalistic in handling the Old Testament law as they resisted the new ideas and traditions of the Pharisees. Politically and socially, they were open to rapprochement with Hellenistic (Greek) culture and the Roman political system. As a result of their exclusion of God (fate) from human affairs and their conviction that humans can expect nothing beyond this life, the Sadducees were essentially secularists.

Jesus and the early Christians posed a threat to the Sadducees (see, e.g., John 11:47–50). Jesus' proclamation of the reality of the spiritual realm, his denunciation of the Jewish religion as then practiced, and his wide popular support could have endangered the already precarious position of the Sadducees. Furthermore, Jesus and his followers supported some of the positions of the Pharisees. The Sadducees found particularly objectionable the Christian proclamation that in Jesus the resurrection is a present reality (Acts 4:2). Inseparably bound to the political, social, and especially the temple-centered institutions of Judaism, the Sadducees passed into the pages of history with the destruction of the Jewish state and temple in A.D. 70.

The Herodians

The Herodians appear along with the Pharisees in Mark 3:6 (after the healing of a man with a withered hand) and Matthew 22:16 (where the question of the legitimacy of paying taxes to Caesar is raised). In Mark 12:13 the Pharisees consult with them on how to

---

48. The Sadducees are mentioned in the Mishnah in *Erubin* 6:2; *Makkoth* 1:6; *Parah* 3:3; *Niddah* 4:2; and *Yadaim* 4:6–7. The postmishnaic references in the Talmud are late, confused, and generally unreliable.

entrap Jesus.[49] Their name identifies them as members of the household or court of the Herods or as supporters of the dynasty.

Josephus describes the drowning of "the partisans of Herod" in the Sea of Galilee at the hands of rebellious Galileans in the days of Herod the Great.[50] Note that the victims are not called "Herodians" but "partisans of Herod." Herod the Great would not have surrounded himself with a group of Jewish supporters. Consequently, it is likely that the so-called Herodians developed under Herod Antipas, and hence their presence in Galilee.[51]

It can be assumed that the Herodians were pro-Roman. The Herodians' teaming with the Pharisees, with whom they had no natural affinity, faced Jesus with representatives of two extreme opinions on the issue of taxation (Matt. 22:15–22; Mark 12:13–17). Similarly in Mark 3:6, the Pharisees, knowing that the Herodians had influence, sought their help, even though they had not been present at the healing of the withered hand. Finally, we should note that while the Sadducees shared the Herodians' support of the Herodian family, there is no evidence for the occasional assumption equating the Herodians and Sadducees.

The Fourth Philosophy

General Comments

Josephus is our primary source of information about the so-called fourth philosophy (the first three being the sects of the Pharisees, Sadducees, and Essenes). He says that the Jews were not acquainted with this fourth philosophy until the A.D. 6 rebellion led by Judas of Galilee when Quirinius ordered that a census be taken.[52] Josephus seems in some way to associate the Zealots with this rebellious spirit. He blames the fourth philosophy for sowing "the seed of every kind of misery," wars, murders of friends and important persons, robberies, and, in short, the general dis-

49. Some manuscripts have "Herodians" in Mark 8:15, but the reading "Herod" is better attested.

50. Josephus *Antiquities* 14.15.10 (450); *Jewish War* 1.17.2 (326).

51. Norman Hillyer, "*Hērōdianoi* (Herodians)," in *New International Dictionary of New Testament Theology*, ed. Colin Brown, 4 vols. (Grand Rapids: Zondervan, 1975–78), 3:441–43.

52. Josephus *Antiquities* 18.1.1 (1–10); 18.1.6 (23). The biblical data regarding Quirinius's census in the land of Israel pose a problem. Matthew clearly places the birth of Jesus before the death of Herod the Great (4 B.C.). Luke 2:2 places it during the time Quirinius was governor of Syria. It is usually supposed that he assumed this office only after the death of Herod. Additional problems center on the nature of the census itself. There is no completely satisfactory explanation for all the data. On this issue see the excellent summary by I. Howard Marshall, *The Gospel of Luke: A Commentary on the Greek Text*, New International Greek Testament Commentary (Grand Rapids: Eerdmans, 1978), 97–104.

orders and rebellion which eventually led to the Jewish defeat by the Romans in A.D. 70.[53]

According to Josephus, Quirinius visited Judea in order to make an assessment of the property of the Jews. This took place in A.D. 6, following the removal of Archelaus as ethnarch over Judea and Samaria. Although Quirinius's action brought widespread unrest among the populace in general, most were quieted by the high priest. But Judas of Gamala and Saddok, a Pharisee, called for rebellion, saying that

> the assessment carried with it a status amounting to downright slavery, no less, and appealed to the nation to make a bid for independence. They urged that in case of success the Jews would have laid the foundation of prosperity, while if they failed to obtain any such boon, they would win honor and renown for their lofty aim; and that Heaven would be their zealous helper to no lesser end than the furthering of their enterprise until it succeeded—all the more if with high devotion in their hearts they stood firm and did not shrink from the bloodshed that might be necessary.[54]

One may wonder why a census would cause such heated reaction. The census was preliminary to increasing taxes; that in itself could have prompted some hostilities and might also explain the cry for liberty. But why the strong religious overtones in the rhetoric of Judas and Saddok? Josephus calls Judas a "leader" (*hēgemōn*) and "sophist" (*sophistēs*).[55] Of the latter term Emil Schürer says, "This description marks out Judas as a teacher *with his own distinctive interpretation of Torah.*"[56] This means that Judas and his followers, along with numerous other intertestamental Jewish groups, held to their own set of traditions alongside the written text.

The taking of a census in Israel was no inconsequential matter. For many Jews it was an administrative measure which only God could instigate. Numbers 1 and 26 indicate God did so in the wilderness. Even David, the prototypical Hebrew ruler, incurred divine anger when he counted his people (2 Sam. 24). The assumption behind Judas's and Saddok's cries seems to be that any human who ordered a census of Israel was placing himself in a position reserved for God alone—it was a blasphemous act. If David incurred divine disfavor for so doing, how much more should the

---

53. Josephus *Antiquities* 18.1.1 (6–7).

54. Josephus *Antiquities* 18.1.1 (4–5). For a lengthy reconstruction of Judas's message see Martin Hengel, *The Zealots: Investigation into the Jewish Freedom Movement in the Period from Herod I until 70 A.D.* (Edinburgh: T. and T. Clark, 1989), 90–144.

55. Josephus *Jewish War* 2.8.1 (118).

56. Schürer, *History*, 2:600 n. 5 (emphasis added).

Hebrews rise up in righteous rebellion when a foreigner sought to number God's people! The fourth philosophy, then, was not merely a revolutionary party; its adherents sought revolution in the name of religion.[57] Josephus's comment, "They think little of submitting to death . . . if only they may avoid calling any man master," should be understood against this background.[58]

Josephus suggests that Judas's spirit and example influenced all subsequent revolutionaries. His philosophy probably became the core convictions of most of the later Jewish freedom fighters, especially those active in the 66–70 war. Indeed, Judas's family was prominent among later freedom fighters.[59]

The spirit of Judas's fourth philosophy was akin to the Maccabean patriarch who called for rebellion against the sacrilege of Antiochus Epiphanes. It is possible that the title *Zealot* may have come from Mattathias's battle cry, "Let everyone who is zealous for the law and supports the covenant come out with me!" (1 Macc. 2:27).[60] As the specter of war grew larger, some of those who adopted Judas's philosophy, as they affirmed "that Heaven would be their zealous helper," may have thought that God would protect his name by intervening (possibly by sending the Messiah) in their behalf. Such views would be in keeping with both the spirit of the movement and conditions in the land of Israel at the time.

Before considering groups possibly associated with the fourth philosophy, we must note a social situation in first-century Israel.

57. There may also have been religious financial obligations for those counted in a census. This was the case in the wilderness when the tabernacle was being built (Exod. 30:11–16; 38:26).

58. Josephus *Antiquities* 18.1.6 (23). The Greek *despotēs*, from which comes the word *despot*, may mean only the master of a house, or it may be used of an absolute ruler or even of a god (Henry G. Liddell and Robert Scott, *A Greek-English Lexicon*, revised by Henry S. Jones, 9th ed. [Oxford: Clarendon, 1968], 381). Josephus uses the term to describe the unique place of God in the fourth philosophy: "God alone is their leader and master (*hēgemona kai despotēn*)" (*Antiquities* 18.1.6 [23]). He also employs it when he describes the position of the Sicarii in Egypt, who sought to persuade their fellow Jews "to look upon the Romans as no better than themselves and to esteem God alone as their lord (*despotēn*)"; these Sicarii endured utmost torture aimed at forcing them to acknowledge "Caesar as lord (*Kaisara despotēn*)" (Josephus *Jewish War* 7.10.1 [410, 418]).

59. Schürer, *History*, 2:600–601, summarizes as follows: "His father Ezekias had opposed Herod's tyranny; his sons Simon and Jacob were crucified for anti-Roman activities under Tiberius Julius Alexander; his descendant Menahem seized Masada at the beginning of the revolt in 66, and was leader of the revolution in Jerusalem until his murder by Eleazar b. Simon's party, and Menahem's nephew Eleazar b. Jair led the last stand of the freedom fighters at Masada."

60. The concept has an even longer history. The priest Phinehas was rewarded for his zeal when he slew an immoral and idolatrous Israelite man and Moabite woman on the Plains of Moab (Num. 25:1–13). Elijah claimed to have been "zealous" for the Lord (1 Kings 19:10, 14). John 2:17 applies Ps. 69:9, "Zeal for your house will consume me," to Jesus' cleansing of the temple, thus interpreting the passage messianically.

Josephus calls the Jewish opponents of Rome "rebels" (*stasiastai*) and "revolutionaries" (*neōterizontes*). It is also significant that both Josephus and the Greek New Testament make a distinction between (1) *kakourgos*, an evildoer and common criminal (Luke 23:32–33, 39; 2 Tim. 2:9), and (2) *lēstēs*, which can denote a robber, highwayman, and bandit (Matt. 27:38; Mark 11:17; 15:27; Luke 10:30, 36; John 10:1, 8; 2 Cor. 11:26), or a revolutionary and insurrectionist (Matt. 26:55; Mark 14:48; Luke 22:52). Luke describes those who were crucified with Jesus as "criminals" (*kakourgoi*), but Matthew, probably preserving more of the exact flavor, designates them as bandits or revolutionaries (*lēstai*).

Josephus indicates that the groups to which we have been referring could be found throughout Galilee and Judea. The rural areas were especially overrun with "bandits," to whom he ascribes the same type of activities as he ascribes to the followers of the fourth philosophy. Now banditry is a multisided phenomenon. "Bandit" (*lēstēs*) can designate one who was forced to steal to support himself and his family, or who stole from the rich to give to the poor (à la Robin Hood). In such a situation the ruling authorities, the upper classes, and the wealthy would view bandits as thieves and thugs, whereas the common people might hail them as heroes and saviors. One person's terrorist is another's freedom fighter!

Zealots

Josephus does not mention the Zealots as a distinct group until his account of the outbreak of the A.D. 66–70 war, where he portrays them as one of several revolutionary factions.[61] He names the Sicarii, John of Gischala and his followers, Simon son of Giora and his followers, and the Idumeans as other revolutionary groups. Other sources indicate that the *Barjone* and Galileans were among those involved in the struggle against Rome.[62] Some modern scholars even include the bandits (*lēstai*) among the groups within the freedom movement.[63] But these groups fought each other as much as or more than they did the Romans.

Who precisely were the Zealots?[64] Josephus says John of Gischala rallied various bandit and militant groups in Jerusalem about

61. Josephus *Jewish War* 4.3.9 (161).
62. See Hengel, *Zealots*, 53–59, who draws from rabbinic as well as first-century sources.
63. Richard A. Horsley with John S. Hanson, *Bandits, Prophets, and Messiahs: Popular Movements at the Time of Jesus* (New York: Harper and Row, 1985); Hengel, *Zealots*, 24–46.
64. For additional information see Hengel, *Zealots*; David Rhoads, "Zealots," in *Anchor Bible Dictionary*, 6:1043–54; Morton Smith, "Zealots and Sicarii: Their Origins and Relation," *Harvard Theological Review* 64 (1971): 1–19; Richard Horsley, "The Zealots," *Novum Testamentum* 27 (1986): 159–92; William R. Farmer, *Maccabees, Zealots, and Josephus* (New York: Columbia University Press, 1956).

A.D. 66. This action caused a split among those who had previously followed Eleazar son of Simon.[65] At that time John's followers, the more extreme group, were, for the first time, called Zealots.[66] However, as we have seen, Josephus also associates the term specifically with the insurrection led by Judas the Galilean sixty years earlier. The issue is made more difficult because Luke 6:15 and Acts 1:13 identify Simon, one of Jesus' apostles, as the Zealot,[67] an anachronistic use if "Zealot" here refers to a group that surfaced more than thirty years after Jesus had concluded his ministry.

Recent studies seek to distinguish between several possible referents for the term *Zealot*: (1) individuals with fervent devotion to God's law (Sirach 45:23–24; 48:1–2; Jubilees 30:18–20; 1 Macc. 2:27); (2) a general attitude and movement illustrated by Judas of Gamala and Saddok, who, promising "that Heaven would be their zealous helper," led an abortive revolt against a Roman census in A.D. 6 (it is this violent, religious, revolutionary movement that Josephus calls the fourth philosophy); and (3) the Jewish revolutionary factions which emerged during the 66–70 war under John of Gischala (Josephus calls them a coalition of bandits and miscreants). Contemporary scholarship differs on the relation, if any, both between these groups and with the Sicarii.

Discussions on the specific meaning of the term *Zealot* and the date of its first use may be reading into Josephus a precision he did not intend. He says that Judas and Saddok "started" the fourth philosophy among the Jews and inspired zeal in the younger element.[68] Thus he appears to describe an orientation, a spirit, which gave birth to and nurtured the type of thinking and actions which eventually led to war with Rome. Hence a popular writer like Luke might well use "Zealot" to refer to one who embraced the spirit of Judas and Saddok well before the outbreak of hostilities; more technically, "Zealot" refers to a member of one of the revolutionary factions during the war.

From our point of view, it is important to note carefully that Josephus describes the Zealot movement as being in agreement with the Pharisees (at least with their general orientation). The Zealots added a violent, revolutionary nationalism to a firm religious context. From them we can learn something about the Pharisees (among whom there also seems to have been a quietistic, semipacifist element), the prewar revolutionaries, and the Jewish military groups who fought the Romans.

65. Josephus *Jewish War* 2.20.3 (564).
66. Josephus *Jewish War* 4.3.9 (160).
67. In Matt. 10:4 and Mark 3:18 he is called a Cananaean.
68. Josephus *Antiquities* 18.1.1 (9–10).

Sicarii

The Sicarii was the terrorist group with which Paul was mistakenly identified (Acts 21:38).[69] Josephus says that they arose during the procuratorship of Felix (52–59), but also equates them with the much earlier disturbances in the time of Quirinius.[70] They were certainly active in and around Jerusalem from the time of Felix through the procuratorship of Albinus (62–64) and were later present in the fortress of Masada (72–73).

During the procuratorship of Felix, the Sicarii conducted a campaign of terror—kidnaping, extortion, robbery, and murder. Josephus distinguishes them from other bandits: "A new species of banditti was springing up in Jerusalem, the so-called *sicarii*, who committed murders in broad daylight in the heart of the city. The festivals were their special seasons, when they would mingle with the crowd, carrying short daggers concealed under their clothing, with which they stabbed their enemies. Then, when they fell, the murderers joined in the cries of indignation, and, through this plausible behavior, were never discovered."[71] The favorite weapon of these urban terrorists or guerrillas was a curved dagger to dispatch opponents, usually Jewish supporters of the Romans.

During their latter period of prominence, at Masada, the Sicarii participated in the futile stand against the Romans. The suicide of the defenders of Masada brought the end of organized Jewish resistance to the Romans in the land of Israel in the first century. Josephus also tells of the seditious activities of some Sicarii who fled to Egypt after the fall of Jerusalem.[72]

The Sicarii leader at Masada, Eleazer son of Jairus, was a relative of Judas the Galilean, as was Menahem, a revolutionary leader who had set himself up as virtually a king in Jerusalem, but was attacked and killed by other insurgent Jews led by Eleazer son of Simon.[73] The exact relation of Menahem to the Sicarii is unclear. Although Josephus blames the Sicarii for beginning the disturbance in which Menahem asserted himself and was killed,[74] he refrains from identifying Menahem with the Sicarii. Eleazer son of Jairus and his followers may have been both supporters of Mena-

---

69. The Greek term *sikarioi* comes from the Latin *sicarius* (murderer, assassin), which in turn comes from *sica* (curved dagger). English translations render *sikarioi* "murderers" (KJV), "assassins" (NASB, RSV, NRSV), and "terrorists" (NIV).

70. Josephus *Jewish War* 2.13.2–3 (252–54); 7.8.1 (253–54); Schürer, *History*, 2:602, suggests that they were organized at the earlier time.

71. Josephus *Jewish War* 2.13.3 (254–55).

72. Josephus *Jewish War* 7.10.1 (409–19); 7.11.1–2 (437–46).

73. Josephus *Jewish War* 2.17.8–9 (433–48).

74. Josephus *Jewish War* 2.17.6 (425).

hem and also Sicarii, or the followers of Menahem may have joined the Sicarii at Masada after his death. In any case, the connection between Judas the Galilean, the fourth philosophy, and the Sicarii is well established.

A more difficult question is the relation between the Zealots and Sicarii. Recent scholarly opinions differ on the point.[75] Menahem's bodyguard is described as "armed zealots," but "zealot" here need not be a technical, party name.[76] The Zealots and Sicarii may have been completely separate groups. It is also possible that prior to the stand at Masada the Sicarii operated only as an undercover force. Accordingly, when Josephus describes their role in open battle, he designates them as Zealots or as members of some other revolutionary group. This could explain why there is no reference to the Sicarii actually engaging the Romans in battle in Jerusalem. It is also possible that following the death of Menahem they withdrew from the city and were simply not present in Jerusalem during her final agony.

Essenes

The Essenes are not mentioned in the New Testament. The major descriptions of and comments about them come from Jewish writers Josephus and Philo and the Gentile Pliny the Elder.[77] Almost a dozen Christian writers, including Hegesippus, Hippolytus, Eusebius, Epiphanius, and Jerome, mention the Essenes; of these only Hippolytus adds noteworthy information.[78]

The Essenes remain an enigma of Jewish history; even the meaning of their name is uncertain.[79] Furthermore, "the sect as a whole exerted no marked influence on Judaism."[80] Their relevance for our study lies in their (1) example of another of the divisions within Intertestamental Judaism, (2) reaction (withdrawal from society) to

75. Gary G. Porton, "Diversity in Postbiblical Judaism," in *Early Judaism,* ed. Kraft and Nickelsburg, 72–73.

76. Josephus *Jewish War* 2.17.9 (444).

77. Josephus *Antiquities* 18.1.5 (18–22); *Jewish War* 2.8.2–13 (119–61); Philo *Every Good Man Is Free* 75–91; *Hypothetica: Apology for the Jews* 11.1–18; Pliny the Elder *Natural History* 5.73.

78. Hippolytus *Refutation of All Heresies* 9.13–22; at one point Hippolytus confuses the Essenes with the Sicarii and Zealots. A compilation of all ancient texts (in Greek and Latin) dealing with the Essenes is available in Alfred Adam, *Antike Berichte über die Essener,* Kleine Texte 182 (Berlin: Walter De Gruyter, 1961).

79. Attempts to relate the term to various Greek and Hebrew words and to find clues in the descriptions of the community have produced a number of proposed meanings of the name *Essene:* "Holy," "Doers of the Law," "Silent," "Worshipers," and "Healers" have all been suggested. The best guess, and it is only that, is "Pious."

80. Bronner, *Sects,* 103; see also Schürer, *History,* 2:558.

the crises which molded the distinctive character of the period, and (3) probable relevance to the Dead Sea Scrolls. The fascination they held for early Christian writers demonstrates that they had some special significance for some branches of Christendom.

There is no information about the origin of the Essenes. Josephus's first reference to the Essenes comes with his story of the prophet Judas, who was active during the reign of Aristobulus I (104–103 B.C.).[81] They may have come from a branch of the Hasidim after the withdrawal of support from Judas Maccabeus.

In general the Essenes represent a monastic, ascetic, puritanical strain within Intertestamental Judaism. Some lived in towns and cities, while others withdrew into their own communities in the wilderness. All lived a communal life in which all property, goods, money, and wages were placed in a central treasury for the use of all. They took their meals of simple food together. Most were engaged in agricultural work but some in trades.

The Essene life was open to adult males; the sources differ on whether they were entirely celibate or could be married, and whether women were permitted any association with the group. They adopted children and reared them in their own traditions. There were no slaves among them.

The organization of the Essenes was hierarchal, led by priests and officers elected by a show of hands. Applicants for membership underwent preliminary probation for a year and then another two years of probation while they were examined and taught. Only then were they administered the oath required of all in the fellowship (otherwise Essenes took no oaths). From that point on they were part of the community and permitted to eat with the rest. Still there were ranks between members. For example, senior members bathed if even touched by a junior member.

Essenes devoted themselves to study of the Scriptures and other ancient writings. Their concern was for morals and ethics rather than speculative philosophy. They revered the lawgiver Moses next to God and stressed the observance of the law. Their interpretation and practice of the law were more strict than any other known Jewish group. Their Sabbath practice even prohibited building a fire or emptying their bowels. The Essenes placed strong emphasis on maintaining Levitical purity. They frequently bathed with cold water, rejected anointing with oil, wore only simple white clothing, and practiced an extremely modest style of life.

In beliefs the Essenes were fundamentally Jewish, although they differed from other Jewish groups in a number of areas. They re-

---

81. Josephus *Jewish War* 1.3.5 (78–80); *Antiquities* 13.11.2 (311–13).

jected the traditions of others, especially the Pharisees. They were completely deterministic (fatalistic), believing that God is in absolute control of all. They believed that the body will be destroyed but that the soul is immortal. They rejected the legitimacy of those controlling the Jerusalem temple; instead they believed only the family of Zadok should have that prerogative. They sent offerings to the temple, but did not sacrifice there themselves, apparently having their own ceremonies and liturgy. They lived by their own calendar.

The ancient writers who describe the Essenes mention their rejection of war, except possibly for self-defense. However, Josephus lists John the Essene among the officers in the war against Rome.[82] As noted above, at least one Essene was recognized as a prophet; others, because of their intense study of the Bible, were also believed to have the prophetic gift. Both Philo and Josephus mention their practice of medical arts.

The Writers of the Dead Sea Scrolls: The Men of Qumran

There is significance in our discussing the Dead Sea sect in conjunction with the Essenes yet marking a division between them. Although the identification of the men of Qumran as Essenes is extremely likely, there are unexplained differences between the lifestyle and beliefs of the two groups. We must also raise the question of the relation of this obscure, out-of-the-way group to the New Testament and Christianity. Here, too, modern students differ on the answer.

A few points need to be made at the outset. The scrolls from the caves along the western shore of the Dead Sea, which are assumed to have been produced by the inhabitants of the settlement at Qumran, are not all of the same type; they touch on a number of fields of study. They were written by and reflect the life and mind of one group of Intertestamental Judaism, a group which had separated itself from the mainstream both in physical location and in thought. Some of the writings are limited to the life and thought of this one group; others touch on the general history and thought of the intertestamental period. Although the scrolls provide abundant new information for a study of Judaism, there are still many gaps in our knowledge of the scroll writers and the intertestamental period. The scrolls do not answer all of our questions; in fact, they often raise new ones.

82. Josephus *Jewish War* 2.20.4 (567).

Discovery and Controversy

How the Dead Sea Scrolls were discovered is fairly well known.[83] They came to light in early 1947, when a Bedouin shepherd boy sought to catch a goat that had fled into a cave. Initially the importance of the documents was not recognized. Collecting them was made difficult and hazardous because of the 1948 Arab-Israeli war. Some portions of the story rank well with any cloak-and-dagger mystery; some aspects of it are still not fully known.

Eventually a committee of scholars was assembled to examine and publish the newly found documents. Publication began in the early 1950s; the longer and what were seen to be the more important scrolls were published fairly quickly. Other parts of the material remained unpublished (primarily fragments from Cave 4) in the keeping of the official committee. Other scholars were prohibited from working on them. Over the years scholarly and public pressure mounted against the seclusion of the unpublished material by the committee. Finally, in the fall of 1991, the rest of the Dead Sea Scrolls were made public, first unofficially, then by proper authorities.

There are almost no issues related to the Dead Sea Scrolls that are not embroiled in controversy. Who wrote them and when? What is their meaning and significance? To whom should they now rightly belong? Are modern translations and reconstructions correct? Why has it taken so long to make them available to the scholarly world and the general public? These are but a few of the questions and debates about the scrolls. (For a brief discussion of some legitimate reasons for delay between discovery and publication see Appendix H, pp. 373–74.)

Types of Literature in the Dead Sea Scrolls

The Dead Sea material includes (1) copies of or fragments from all of the Old Testament books except Esther; (2) parts of the Apocrypha and Pseudepigrapha; (3) writings of the Qumran community; and, depending on how widely one defines the phrase "Dead Sea Scrolls," (4) letters, reports, and biblical, religious,

---

83. Helpful general surveys of the Dead Sea Scrolls and related issues include F. F. Bruce, *Second Thoughts on the Dead Sea Scrolls,* 2d ed. (Grand Rapids: Eerdmans, 1961); Millar Burrows, *Burrows on the Dead Sea Scrolls* (Grand Rapids: Baker, 1978); Frank Moore Cross, *The Ancient Library of Qumran,* 2d ed. (London: Duckworth, 1961); Lawrence H. Schiffman, ed., *Archaeology and History in the Dead Sea Scrolls: The New York University Conference in Memory of Yigael Yadin* (Sheffield, Eng.: Sheffield Academic Press, 1990); André Dupont-Sommer, *The Essene Writings from Qumran,* trans. Geza Vermes (Cleveland: World, 1962); idem, *The Jewish Sect of Qumran and the Essenes,* trans. R. D. Barnett (London: Valentine, Mitchell, 1953); Geza Vermes, *The Dead Sea Scrolls: Qumran in Perspective* (Cleveland: Collins and World, 1978); Yigael Yadin, *The Message of the Scrolls* (New York: Grosset and Dunlap, 1962).

military, commercial, and contractual material written by persons or groups not a part of the Qumran community.

The most extensive, and for our purposes most important, documents are those which reflect the life, thought, and expectations of the Qumran group. Additional information about them comes from archaeological discoveries at the site of their headquarters. The sect's writings deal with (1) the organization and operation of the community; (2) biblical exposition; (3) worship—hymns, prayers, blessings, meditations—and (4) expectations of the future—the sect's part in the final battle, the Messiah, the new temple, and the like. It is from these documents that the history, thought, and practices of the group must be pieced together.

The History of Qumran

Qumran is located on a small, barren plateau overlooking the northwest end of the Dead Sea. The pattern of the settlement's walls, cisterns, and water courses was largely visible even before formal archaeological work began. Excavations revealed pools for ritual bathing, a kitchen, an assembly and dining hall, a pottery workshop, a stable, coins, and more.[84] Some artifacts for writing, including pens and inkwells, and a room assumed to be a scriptorium were found. The earliest remains found at the site come from a Judean city or military fortress of the eighth or seventh century B.C.

Sometime during the period 134–105 B.C., a monastery was built around the old fortress.[85] It was small, and could accommodate only about fifty monks. Between 105 and 31 B.C. the monastery was enlarged and an extensive water system was added. Evidence indicates an increase both in the size of the community and in the number of vocations it supported. In the latter part of the first century B.C., the settlement was damaged and abandoned. The exact cause is uncertain. The monks might have been attacked by their Jewish enemies or invading Parthians (40 B.C.); more probably, the buildings were damaged by the earthquake that struck the area in 31 B.C. Earthquake damage is still evident in the remains of a cracked pool and building foundations. The Qumran site was abandoned from about 31 until the last part of the reign of Herod the Great (just before 4 B.C.), who is known to have been favorable to Essenes. The final stage of occupation came when the site was reactivated toward the end of Herod's life. The buildings

84. J. van der Ploeg, *The Excavations at Qumran: A Survey of the Judean Brotherhood and Its Ideas,* trans. Kevin Smyth (New York: Longmans, Green, 1958).

85. In addition to information in the general studies listed in n. 83, see Phillip R. Callaway, *The History of the Qumran Community* (Sheffield, Eng.: Sheffield Academic Press, 1988).

were destroyed in A.D. 68 and the site occupied by the tenth Roman legion. Whether the occupants of Qumran were slaughtered by the Romans, after either armed or passive resistance, or fled before their coming is unknown. Obviously they hid their precious scrolls in caves, hoping to reclaim them later.

Additional information about the history of the sect can be gleaned from the writings themselves. Most historical data are cryptic, their meaning often debated. Among the more important sources are the Damascus Covenant (CD), the Manual of Discipline (1QS), and the *peshers* (commentaries) on Nahum (4QpNah or 4Q169) and Habakkuk (1QpHab).

The Damascus Document refers to the beginning of the group three hundred and ninety years after the conquest of Nebuchadnezzar (c. 196 B.C.) and then to the appearance of the Teacher of Righteousness twenty years later (c. 176 B.C.).[86] The same writing tells of "the converts of Israel [priests] who depart from the Land of Judah and (the Levites are) those who join them" (CD 4). This seems to refer to a voluntary withdrawal from society. The Manual of Discipline says that the group withdrew into the wilderness to separate from the ungodly, to prepare the way for God through the study of the law.[87]

The *Pesher* on Habakkuk tells of the Wicked Priest who invaded the place of retreat and caused confusion during the community's Day of Atonement.[88] Other documents include similar references

86. CD 1:5–12: "For when they were unfaithful and forsook Him, He hid His face from Israel and His Sanctuary and delivered them up to the sword. But remembering the Covenant of the forefathers, He left a remnant to Israel and did not deliver it up to be destroyed. And in the age of wrath, three hundred and ninety years after He had given them into the hand of king Nebuchadnezzar of Babylon, He visited them, and He caused a plant root to spring from Israel and Aaron to inherit His Land and to prosper on the good things of His earth. And they perceived their iniquity and recognized that they were guilty men, yet for twenty years they were like blind men groping for the way.

"And God observed their deed, that they sought Him with a whole heart, and He raised for them a Teacher of Righteousness to guide them in the way of His heart. And He made known to the latter generations that which God had done to the latter generation, the congregation of traitors, to those who departed from the way."

87. 1QS 8:14: "And when these become members of the Community in Israel according to all these rules, they shall separate from the habitation of ungodly men and shall go into the wilderness to prepare the way of Him; as it is written, *Prepare in the wilderness the way of . . . make straight in the desert a path for God* (Isa. 40:3). This (path) is the study of the Law which He commanded by the hand of Moses, that they may do according to all that has been revealed from age to age, and as the Prophets have revealed by His Holy Spirit."

88. 1QpHab 11: "*Woe to him who causes his neighbors to drink; who pours out his venom to make them drunk that he may gaze on their feasts!* Interpreted, this concerns the Wicked Priest who pursued the Teacher of Righteousness to the house of his exile that he might confuse him with his venomous fury. And at the time appointed for rest, the Day of Atonement, he appeared before them to confuse them, and to cause them to stumble on the Day of Fasting, their Sab-

to the Scoffer, the Liar, and the Spouter of Lies. It is unclear if the referents are to be identified with each other and with the Wicked Priest.[89] The contexts, particularly in the Damascus Document, the Psalm Scroll (1QH), and probably "Some of the Precepts of Torah" (4QMMT), do make clear that there was a faction which broke with the Teacher of Righteousness and remained in opposition to him.

The *Pesher* of Nahum refers to the Seleucid kings Demetrius III Eukairos and Antiochus Epiphanes by name, and to the opposition of the "seekers after smooth things" to the "young lion" who for vengeance "hangs men alive."[90] As we have already seen, this is usually assumed to refer to what happened after some Jews had invited the Seleucid king Demetrius to attack Alexander Jannaeus— Jannaeus was victorious and in retaliation crucified eight hundred of his enemies (Pharisees?) in Jerusalem.[91]

Although the people associated with the community cannot be conclusively identified, the time of its existence is quite clear. It flourished from the second century B.C. into the latter third of the first century of the Common Era. It represents one of the numerous groups which reacted in different ways to the intensification of the Hellenistic presence, various pressures within the land of Israel, and political, social, and religious developments associated with the Maccabean rulers. Like the Essenes the Qumran community represents a monastic, ascetic, puritanical strain within Intertestamental Judaism. But before we can consider the exact nature of their relation with the Essenes, we must understand a bit about the community's life and beliefs.

---

bath of repose." Note that as a result of their use of a 12-month, 364- (or 365-)day solar calendar instead of a lunar calendar, the Qumran community probably observed the Day of Atonement on a different day than did the majority of their contemporaries.

89. Jerome Murphy-O'Connor, "The Judean Desert," in *Early Judaism*, ed. Kraft and Nickelsburg, 139–41.

90. 4QpNah 2:11b–12: *"Whither the lion goes, there is the lion's cub, [with none to disturb it.* Interpreted, this concerns Deme]trius king of Greece who sought, on the counsel of those who seek smooth things, to enter Jerusalem. [But God did not permit the city to be delivered] into the hands of the kings of Greece, from the time of Antiochus until the coming of the rulers of the Kittim. But then she shall be trampled under their feet. . . .

"The lion tears enough for its cubs and it chokes prey for its lionesses. [Interpreted, this] concerns the furious young lion who strikes by means of his great men, and by means of the men of his council.

"[And chokes prey for its lionesses; and it fills] its caves [with prey] and its dens with victims. Interpreted, this concerns the furious young lion [who executes revenge] on those who seek smooth things and hangs men alive, . . . formerly in Israel. Because of a man hanged alive on [the] tree, He proclaims, *'Behold I am against [you, says the Lord of Hosts].'"*

91. Josephus *Jewish War* 1.4.6 (96–97); *Antiquities* 13.14.2 (380).

The Community and Its Organization

Information about the nature and organization of the community comes from a number of documents, the most important of which are the Manual of Discipline (1QS), the Covenant of the Damascus Community (CD), and the Messianic Rule (1QSa); additional data are scattered through other documents, of which the War Scroll (1QM) and the Temple Scroll (11QTemp) deserve special mention.[92]

The objectives of the community are best expressed in their own words:

> The Master shall teach the saints to live [according to] the Book of the Community Rule, that they may seek God with a whole heart and soul, and do what is good and right before Him as He commanded by the hand of Moses and all His servants the Prophets; that they may love all that He has chosen and hate all that He has rejected; that they may abstain from all evil and hold fast to all good. . . . [The Master] shall admit into the Covenant of Grace all those who have freely devoted themselves to the observance of God's precepts . . . that they may love all the sons of light, each according to his lot in God's design, and hate all the sons of darkness . . . that they may purify their knowledge in the truth of God's precepts. . . . All those who embrace the Community Rule shall enter into the Covenant before God to obey all His commandments so that they may not abandon Him during the dominion of Satan because of fear or terror of affliction. [1QS 1]

> They shall separate from the congregation of the men of falsehood and shall unite, with respect to the Law and possessions, under the authority of the sons of Zadok, the Priests who keep the Covenant, and of the multitude of the men of the Community who hold fast to the Covenant. Every decision concerning doctrine, property, and justice shall be determined by them. [1QS 5]

In these statements we see the outline of a community under the authority of a Master or Guardian who is charged to administer the Rule. Each person functions in the community "according to his lot in God's design." The priests, the sons of Zadok, have a special role. The community sees society, including Israel, marked by a clear dichotomy between the good and the bad. Their purpose is to separate themselves, the sons of light, from evil, to practice truth and righteousness, and to hold fast to all good. Toward this end they seek to know God's law and to live in purity. Although legal

92. Some question whether the Temple Scroll should be classified as a sectarian document in the same sense as the Damascus Document and the Manual of Discipline are; see the summary by Murphy-O'Connor, "Judean Desert," 136–37.

requirements have an important place, there is no pure legalism; the objective is to "seek God with a whole heart and soul."

The documents mention two different lifestyles for members of the "new covenant" (the name they chose for themselves). Some lived in towns and others in camps. The former seem to have lived alongside yet apart from their neighbors. They engaged in normal urban activities. They observed carefully the rules of the community, primarily ritual purity, "that they may distinguish between unclean and clean, and discriminate between the holy and the profane" (CD 12). Little else is known of the urban members.

Residents of the camps, presumably wilderness monasteries like Qumran, lived a very different life. For example, they took their meals in common, where the seating was by rank. Some of those meals were solemn assemblies at which a priest presided and gave his blessing. Seeing themselves as the true Israel, the camp members modeled their organization after Exodus 18:25: "Those who follow these statutes in the age of wickedness until the coming of the Messiah of Aaron and Israel shall form groups of at least ten men, by Thousands, Hundreds, Fifties, and Tens. And where ten are, there shall never be lacking a Priest learned in the Book of Meditations; they shall be ruled by him" (CD 12–13). This was undoubtedly an idealistic goal; the community never numbered thousands, only a few hundred at most.

The major officers, the Guardian and Bursar, both probably priests, were responsible for oversight of all affairs. The Manual of Discipline (1QS 8) refers to the Council of the Community, which was composed of twelve laymen and three priests. This body is not mentioned elsewhere, so it is uncertain whether the term refers to an executive committee of the community or to the community as a whole, the numbers here being the minimum for a quorum.

The phrase "according to his lot" frequently appears in the Qumran documents and refers to a hierarchal order. One passage mentions a division into priests, Levites, Israelites, and proselytes (CD 14). Further divisions distinguish between the older and younger, and between those of lesser and greater rank.

Full membership required a probation period of graded instruction, trial, and examination lasting at least two years, maybe three. If approved by the Guardian and the body, the candidate took an oath.[93] His property was then merged with that of the community,

---

93. The candidate swore "to return with all his heart and soul to every commandment of the Law of Moses in accordance with all that has been revealed of it to the sons of Zadok, the Keepers of the Covenant and Seekers of His will, and to the multitude of the men of their Covenant who together have freely pledged themselves to His truth and to walking in the way of His delight" (1QS 5).

and he was admitted to the life of the group. That life centered on learning and putting into practice the law and the traditions of the community. Among the many regulations was a requirement that all members of the community annually attend a general meeting at Pentecost, which they called the Feast of the Renewal of the Covenant. A court of inquiry exacted strict penalties for failure to observe all of the biblical laws and the regulations of the community.

Community members who lived in towns were expected to marry. The question of women at Qumran is debated. Celibacy would accord well with the ascetic lifestyle. Yet nothing is said on the subject. The bones of a few women and children were discovered in excavations of the outer limits of the Qumran cemetery. Archaeological evidence also indicates the Qumranites supported themselves with a variety of occupations. However, as we have seen, their primary concerns were to maintain purity, engage in frequent ritual washings, study law, and pray.[94]

Beliefs of the Community

The Qumranites believed themselves to be the true Israel, a "new covenant."[95] By joining the group one became a part of God's elect and received the gifts of salvation, true knowledge, and the ability to accept the truth and to live justly. This led the member to a life of purity and holiness and to visions of the heavenly throne.[96]

Distinctive features of Qumran belief include the community's relation to the Jerusalem temple. Because they regarded non-Zadokite priests as illegitimate, the monks did not, or were prohibited from, worship in Jerusalem. They sent offerings, but seem to have had their own sacrificial liturgy. Another distinctive feature is an ethical dualism with a spiritual foundation. The major source here is what modern scholars call the "Two Spirits Essay" (1QS 3–4).

According to the Manual of Discipline (1QS 8), the men of Qumran also saw themselves as preparing "in the desert a highway for our God" (Isa. 40:3). Even more they believed themselves to be immediately involved in Israel's salvation:

94. "Where the ten are, there shall never lack a man among them who shall study the Law continually, day and night, concerning the right conduct of a man with his companion. And the Congregation shall watch in community for a third of every night of the year, to read the Book and to study Law and to pray together" (1QS 6).

95. For "new covenant" see CD 8 and 1QpHab 2 (on 1:5).

96. Several fragments suggest this theme, especially "The Songs of the Sabbath Sacrifice," which is also called the Angelic Liturgy (4QSirShabb). Visions of *merkabah* (the chariot-throne of God in the Book of Ezekiel) are an important part of Jewish apocalyptic and mystical thought. See Neil S. Fujita, *A Crack in the Jar: What Ancient Jewish Documents Tell Us about the New Testament* (Mahwah, N.J.: Paulist, 1986), 158–66.

> They shall preserve the faith in the Land with steadfastness and meek-
> ness and shall atone for sin by the practice of justice and by suffering
> the sorrows of affliction. . . . When these are in Israel, the Council of
> the Community shall be established in truth. It shall be an Everlasting
> Plantation, a House of Holiness for Israel, an Assembly of Supreme
> Holiness for Aaron. They shall be witnesses to the truth at the Judge-
> ment, and shall be the elect of Goodwill who shall atone for the Land
> and pay the wicked their reward.

Thus the men of Qumran seem to view themselves as in the tradition of righteous sufferers who bear affliction vicariously for the
nation of Israel.

The fall of 1994 saw the official publication of the fifth volume of
materials from Qumran Cave 4.[97] It contains a number of fragments
which, when viewed together, constitute a single document, the long-
awaited *Miqsat Ma'ase ha-Torah* ("Some of the Precepts of Torah")
(4QMMT).[98] Following the partial remains of a 364-day calendar, this
document gives more than twenty laws accompanied by comments
and instructions on how to observe them. It appears that a specific
type of observance of these laws, most from the Old Testament, may
have separated the group that produced this document from all others. It may in fact have separated them not only from other Jews in
general, but also from members of another faction within the community. For it states specifically, "[And you know that] we have separated
ourselves from the multitude of the people [and from all their im-
purity]."[99] What we do know is that the document stresses the importance the group placed upon ceremonial parts of the Torah and
their own distinctive interpretation and application thereof. In addition, linguistic similarities may make the document a helpful background for understanding some New Testament passages.[100]

97. Elisha Qimron and John Strugnell, *Discoveries in the Judaean Desert,* vol. 10, *Qumran Cave 4* (New York: Oxford University Press, 1994).

98. Martin Abegg, "Paul, 'Works of the Law' and MMT," *Biblical Archaeology Review* 20.6 (Nov.–Dec. 1994): 54, prefers to render the title "Pertinent Works of the Law."

99. The manuscript at this point is fragmentary. The word translated "people" could also be rendered "council" or "congregation." Either of the alternate readings would indicate that the group represented by the writer may have separated from others within the Dead Sea community. See Abegg, "Paul," 54.

100. E.g., Abegg, "Paul," notes that *ma'ase ha-Torah* ("precepts of Torah") is the equivalent of the Greek *erga nomou* in the Septuagint. The Hebrew phrase never occurs in rabbinic writings. The Greek, however, does occur in the New Testament, but only in Rom. 3:20, 28, and Gal. 2:16; 3:2, 5, 10, where it literally means "works of the law" (so the RSV, the NASB, and in Gal. the NRSV; but "observing the law" in the NIV, and "deeds [works] prescribed by the law" in Rom. in the NRSV). Abegg suggests that Paul may be using the phrase to counter a kind of thinking akin to what is found in 4QMMT, i.e., a kind of thinking that sought to separate those groups, possibly even Christians (and, I would suggest, Jewish Christians), that looked for justification through some special works of the law rather than through Jesus Christ (note Gal. 2:16).

The Damascus Document reveals the Qumran community's view of history: "This is the Rule for the assembly of the camps during all [the age of wickedness, and whoever does not hold fast to] these (statutes) shall not be fit to dwell in the Land [when the Messiah of Aaron and Israel shall come at the end of days]" (CD 13). This division of time into the age of wickedness and another age which shall come afterward and be marked by a messianic presence is expressed, in one way or another, throughout the scrolls. The men of Qumran view themselves as the community of the last days. It is through their organization that Messiah will come.

The phrase "Messiah of Aaron and Israel" occurs in a number of documents. Two passages are of particular importance and raise an interesting question:

> The men of holiness . . . shall be ruled by the primitive precepts in which the men of the Community were first instructed until there shall come the Prophet and the Messiahs of Aaron and Israel. [1QS 9:10–11]

and

> He shall come [at] the head of the whole congregation of Israel with all [his brethren, the sons] of Aaron the Priest, [those called] to the assembly, the men of renown; and they shall sit [before him, each man] in the order of his dignity. And then [the Mess]iah of Israel shall [come]. . . .
> When the common table shall be set for eating and the new wine [poured] for drinking, let no man extend his hand over the first-fruits of bread and wine before the Priest; for [it is he] who shall bless the first-fruits of bread and wine, and shall be the first [to extend] his hand over the bread. Thereafter, the Messiah of Israel shall extend his hand over the bread, [and] all the Congregation of the Community [shall utter a] blessing, [each man in the order] of his dignity. [1QSa 2]

Did the Qumran monks expect a number of messianic figures? The first quotation uses the plural, designating a Messiah of Aaron (a priestly Messiah) and a Messiah of Israel (probably a royal, political Messiah); the Prophet (like Moses) may be a third such figure. The latter quotation does not actually refer to the Priest with the title *Messiah,* but does give him precedence over the Messiah of Israel. In fact, if the High Priest of the War Scroll (1QM) is to be identified with the priestly Messiah, it is the priestly Messiah who leads to victory in the final battle.

The Qumran community believed not only that they were the vehicle through which the messianic age would come, but also that the end time was imminent. The War Scroll lays the plans for the final battle. The Temple Scroll (11QTemp), at least in part, looks to the new order to be established when the age of wickedness has passed. The Qumran *peshers* assume that the prophetical books are speaking of the day when one age will pass into the new; that day, the commentators believed, was their own! The time of salvation, the Qumran covenanters believed, was at hand.

Qumran and the Essenes

Almost from the beginning of the study of the scrolls many assumed that they were written by a group of Essenes. Nevertheless, there have also been those scholars who doubt this identification.[101] Among the more intriguing counterproposals is that the scrolls were written by a Sadducean group; "Some of the Precepts of Torah" (4QMMT) and the Temple Scroll (11QTemp) seem to lend support to this possibility.[102] Additional evidence and study will be needed to convince most researchers to abandon their conviction that we must look to the Essenes for the origin of the scrolls.

It seems to me that even the brief surveys given above are sufficient to make obvious many similarities between the Essenes and the Qumran group. These similarities, along with the fact that Pliny the Elder locates the Essenes on the west coast of the Dead Sea, present a powerful case for identifying Qumran as an Essene community. Although a detailed comparison of the scrolls with the ancient descriptions of the Essenes reveals discrepancies, we should keep in mind that these are generally the same types of discrepancies which we find between the various ancient accounts of the Essenes as well as between some of the individual Dead Sea Scrolls. Further, the scrolls present a far more in-depth depiction of the Qumran group than the ancient summaries do of the Essenes.

The most significant difference lies in the points of view from which the subjects are addressed. Josephus and Philo seek to place the Essenes within the framework of the Greek philosophical world. The scrolls, by contrast, are written from a Jewish perspective and are far more interested in Levitical purity, proper conduct, and eschatology than in Greek speculative thought. This gives to the scrolls an entirely different ethos.

In conclusion, there is no substantial reason against assuming that the Qumran group was a branch of Essenes. At the same time,

---

101. For a summary see James C. VanderKam, *The Dead Sea Scrolls Today* (Grand Rapids: Eerdmans, 1994), 87–98; Edward M. Cook, *Solving the Mysteries of the Dead Sea Scrolls: New Light on the Bible* (Grand Rapids: Zondervan, 1994), 104–26.

102. For a summary of the case for Sadducean origins see VanderKam, *Scrolls Today,* 93–95; Cook, *Solving the Mysteries,* 111–16. Qimron and Strugnell, *Qumran Cave 4,* make frequent reference to the possibility of the Sadducean theory.

lest we define "Essene" too precisely, the words of Matthew Black raise a healthy note of caution: "The Qumran sect was identical with the people known to the ancient historians as 'Essenes.' But it is well to recall that the name . . . is a Greek formulation, possibly a popular description, and in that case might well be descriptive of a general sectarian type, and embrace within it different, but closely affiliated groups."[103]

The Relevance of the Dead Sea Scrolls to a Study of Intertestamental Judaism and the New Testament

It would be hard to overestimate the relevance of the Dead Sea Scrolls for a study of the text of the Old Testament. They provide copies of portions of the Old Testament that are almost a millennium older than any previously known Hebrew manuscript. Although in general they support the traditional Masoretic text, this is not always the case. Old Testament textual critics have more than enough to keep themselves occupied for the foreseeable future, and beyond. The scrolls also give significant insights into the history of the Old Testament languages.

Another major contribution of the scrolls is the enriched view they provide of Intertestamental Judaism, especially at the end of its history. The information they give about the life and thought of Qumran is far more extensive than what was previously known about any group of the period. In addition, they finally put to rest any notion of a normative, united Judaism in the intertestamental period.

For the student of the Jewish background of the New Testament and early Christianity the Qumran discoveries are of more importance than was first imagined. There are still attempts to identify Jesus or John the Baptist as the Teacher of Righteousness or at least as a member of the Qumran community. Such endeavors have been thoroughly discredited by a wide range of scholars. What the scrolls do attest is "another Jewish community which, like the early Christians, lived in the belief that the end of days was at hand and that its struggle was with principalities and powers, and which reinterpreted the Scriptures in that context."[104]

Perhaps the single most important contribution of the scrolls is one that is often overlooked. They provide new information and also a different perspective from which to view previously available data. We are now able to see more clearly in Josephus, the Apocrypha and Pseudepigrapha, and other ancient writings ideas

---

103. Matthew Black, *The Essene Problem* (London: Dr. Williams's Trust, 1961), 27.
104. John J. Collins, "Dead Sea Scrolls," in *Anchor Bible Dictionary*, 2:100.

which were previously perceived only dimly. One example will suffice. Having been alerted to the two-age theology by the scrolls, we now see it more clearly in various other ancient writings. Awareness of this theology provides a powerful key to understanding many passages in the New Testament.[105]

Therapeutae

Philo's *Contemplative Life* contains a description of a group called the Therapeutae. They were located near Alexandria and are especially interesting because they represent the only known example of a clear-cut sect or party within Diaspora Judaism.[106]

Philo introduces his account with reference to his earlier descriptions of the Essenes. He clearly intends to include the Therapeutae within this movement. The Therapeutae manifest many similarities with the Essenes of Josephus and the Qumran group. However, differences from the Essenes and Qumranites have raised the question as to whether the Therapeutae were really Essenes.[107] The major difference is the contemplative lifestyle of the Therapeutae and the more active life of the Essenes. The Therapeutae abstained from meat and wine, the Essenes did not. They ate only one meal a day, while the Essenes ate two. There were clearly women living in the settlements of the Therapeutae, but this is far from clear of Essene groups. Nor is there record of all property being held in common among the Therapeutae.

We should keep in mind that our information about the Therapeutae is much less than what we know of the Essenes; in fact, it comes from but a single source. The Therapeutae appear generally to apply Essene customs rather than diverge from them. Certainly, at least in the broad sense of the term *Essene* suggested by Black, it seems safe to concur with Philo's implied classification. The importance of the Therapeutae for the present study is that they provide further illustration of two features noted earlier: (1) the monastic, ascetic tendency within Judaism, and (2) the diversity which existed even within Diaspora Judaism.

---

105. For additional information see the general studies listed in n. 83; Matthew Black, *The Scrolls and Christian Origins* (New York: Thomas Nelson, 1961); Krister Stendahl, ed., *The Scrolls and the New Testament* (New York: Harper and Row, 1957); Fujita, *Crack in the Jar*.

106. Eusebius *Ecclesiastical History* 2.17 suggests that the *Contemplative Life* describes a Christian monastery and is not a genuine product of Philo. This position had its defenders in the mid-nineteenth century. However, E. R. Goodenough, *An Introduction to Philo Judaeus*, 2d ed. (New York: Barnes and Noble, 1963), 32, says that this "controversy has now been long settled, and no one for years has questioned that Philo wrote it."

107. See the excellent discussion in Schürer, *History*, 2:591–97.

Magical Judaism

Superstition, astrology, and magical arts, especially for curative purposes, were quite popular in the ancient world.[108] And the Jewish people were often regarded as possessing special magical skills. On the strength of 1 Kings 5:12 ("The LORD gave Solomon wisdom"), Solomon was usually given credit for originating the art in Israel. Josephus says, "And God granted [Solomon] knowledge of the art used against demons for the benefit and healing of men. He also composed incantations by which illnesses are relieved, and left behind forms of exorcisms with which those possessed by demons drive them out, never to return. And this kind of cure is of very great power among us to this day."[109] Certain intertestamental writings, including 1 Enoch and the Wisdom of Solomon, contain similar reports. A later Greek document, the Testament of Solomon, says that Solomon used his magical powers to subdue demons and force them to assist in the construction of the temple. The same legend is found in rabbinic literature and is reflected in at least one fragment from Qumran.

Among the Jewish parties we have mentioned, the Essenes and Therapeutae were especially noted for their healing arts.[110] These skills were frequently associated with magic. In addition, there appear to have been groups on the fringes of Judaism who were serious practitioners of magical arts in the name of religion.[111] This was certainly the case in Ephesus, as the incident reported in Acts 19:13–16 shows. The Talmud and other sources also give the impression that superstition played an important part in the everyday life of many average Jews.[112]

Magical Judaism, probably more than most occult groups, seems to have maintained a lively interest in written materials. Most certainly this was an extension of the legends related to Solomon and his activity. The literary element is evident in Acts 19:19, where certain individuals are reported to have burned their books as evidence of their determination to distance themselves

---

108. See G. H. C. MacGregor and A. C. Purdy, *Jew and Greek: Tutors unto Christ*, rev. ed. (Edinburgh: Saint Andrew, 1959), 291–301.

109. Josephus *Antiquities* 8.2.5 (45).

110. Josephus *Jewish War* 2.8.6 (136); Philo *Contemplative Life* 1 (2).

111. On magical Judaism see Marcel Simon, *Verus Israel: A Study of the Relations between Christians and Jews in the Roman Empire* (A.D. 135–425), trans. H. McKeating (New York: Oxford University Press, 1986), 339–68, 498–506, and the literature he cites; Michael E. Stone, *Scripture, Sects and Visions* (Philadelphia: Fortress, 1980), 82–86.

112. See Henri Daniel-Rops, *Daily Life in the Time of Jesus,* trans. Patrick O'Brian (New York: Hawthorn, 1962), 306–7.

from their past association with magic.[113] While one might expect that the magical element in Judaism could be closely related to esoteric writings like the so-called *Merkabah*, the evidence for such an association in the intertestamental period is slight at best. Rather, it was in later centuries that magic took its place within such mystical movements as the Cabala.[114]

As might be expected, most of the magical activities in Jewish communities took place in the Diaspora. The Jews of Phrygia appear to have been particularly deeply involved in the practice of magic and were notorious for their religious laxity. Some scholars have suggested that involvement in the occult was an important element in virtually all Hellenistic Judaism (and later in Gnosticism).[115] It was, however, not restricted to the Diaspora. Acts 8:9–24 places Simon the magician in Samaria. Because the Old Testament is strong in its condemnation of the use of magic (see, e.g., Deut. 13), the presence of magic in Intertestamental Judaism must be regarded, at least to a limited extent, as evidence of Judaism's being syncretized with pagan religions.[116] The magical element is also one more evidence of the wide variety within Intertestamental Judaism.

Our survey by no means completes the list of first-century Jewish parties. It appears that there were many other minor groups in Intertestamental Judaism. Several, like the Qumran covenanters, placed special value on cleansing rituals and immersion, even to the extent of substituting such rites for temple sacrifices.[117] Eschatological and messianic speculation also played a prominent part. For some the complicated disputes over the calendar were of extreme importance. A few groups which adopted a mystical approach seem to have operated within the mainstream of Judaism,

---

113. See Emil Schürer, *The History of the Jewish People in the Time of Jesus Christ*, 5 vols., trans. J. MacPherson et al. (Edinburgh: T. and T. Clark, 1897–98), 5:151–54; Wilfred L. Knox, *St. Paul and the Church of the Gentiles* (New York: Cambridge University Press, 1939), frequently mentions both the Jewish element evident in some pagan Greek magical papyri and forms of magical influence in Judaism; see his "Note II: Jewish Influence on Magical Literature," 208–11.

114. See Gershom G. Scholem, *Major Trends in Jewish Mysticism*, 3d ed. (New York: Schocken, 1961); and idem, *Jewish Gnosticism, Merkabah Mysticism and Talmudic Traditions* (New York: Jewish Theological Seminary, 1965).

115. E.g., E. R. Goodenough, *By Light, Light: The Mystic Gospel of Hellenistic Judaism* (New Haven: Yale University Press, 1935).

116. Charles Guignebert, *The Jewish World in the Time of Jesus*, trans. S. H. Hooke (London: Kegan Paul, Trench, Trubner, 1939), 240.

117. More than a decade before the discovery of the Dead Sea Scrolls, Joseph Thomas, *Le Mouvement baptiste en Palestine et Syrie* (Gembloux: J. Duculot, 1935), used written sources to postulate the existence of many virtually unknown groups, including Qumran-type sects.

but were closely related to syncretistic tendencies. These may have been precursors to Gnosticism. And there were certainly some groups, in addition to the men of Qumran, that were formed in protest against existing Jewish religious practices, leaders, and institutions. Others were probably preoccupied with political or social aims. Although our knowledge of these parties is scant, their existence proves that the Judaism of the land of Israel, and perhaps beyond, included many practices and beliefs different from those of the Pharisees and Sadducees. These groups further demonstrate the eclectic and conglomerate nature of the Jewish environment of the New Testament.

12

Common Life in First-Century Israel

The vast majority of Jesus' contemporaries in the land of Israel were common people whose chief concern was basic survival. They were caught in a society more complex than appears on the surface. Our task here is not to describe that society in detail, but to seek to understand some of the major features affecting the daily lives of the common people. Historians seldom describe this group;

they are the faceless ones, yet far more influential than they themselves or later writers realized. What can be said of the common people in Israel in the first century?[1]

Average Jews: The "Am ha-Eretz"

The religious and political parties consisted largely of the sophisticated intellectual minority. In addition there were a few rich and powerful Jews and Gentiles in the land of Israel. But the vast majority of the population belonged to no specific group. They were, of course, the masses from whom the others distinguished themselves. The term *am ha-eretz* (the people of the land) is often used of the common people of first-century Israel. Use of the term may, however, cause misunderstanding since the later rabbis employed it as a technical term for those whom, in contrast to themselves and their associates, they considered "ignorant and careless boors."[2] Although it is certain that the pre–A.D. 70 Pharisees looked down on the common people,[3] it is a mistake to assume that their opinions were as clearly drawn as those found in the Mishnah and later writings. For our purposes, in spite of difficulties inherent in the word *average,* we will refer to the nonsectarian, nonelite inhabitants of first-century Israel as average Jews.

We have noted that the leaders described the average Palestinian Jews as "this crowd, which does not know the law—they are accursed" (John 7:49). Nevertheless, we must not assume they were an irreligious mass. They were largely, with varying degrees of intensity, devoted to the tenets of their religion. Some were the

---

1. Two very important works dealing in detail with important features of Jewish life are Joachim Jeremias, *Jerusalem in the Time of Jesus,* trans. F. H. and C. H. Cave (London: SCM, 1973); and Sean Freyne, *Galilee from Alexander the Great to Hadrian, 323 B.C.E. to 135 C.E.* (Wilmington, Del.: Michael Glazier, 1980). Details of everyday life and society are found elsewhere: Madeline S. and J. Lane Miller, *Harper's Encyclopedia of Bible Life,* revised by Boyce M. Bennett, Jr., and David H. Scott (San Francisco: Harper and Row, 1978); Henri Daniel-Rops, *Daily Life in the Time of Jesus,* trans. Patrick O'Brian (New York: Hawthorn, 1962); at the more technical level see *The Jewish People in the First Century,* ed. S. Safrai, M. Stern et al., in *Compendia Rerum Iudaicarum ad Novum Testamentum* (Philadelphia: Fortress, 1974–92), vol. 2. In addition, the growing interest in sociological studies of ancient peoples and of religion has produced a wealth of information. For two examples of works of special interest to students of the New Testament see Bruce J. Malina, *The New Testament World: Insights from Cultural Anthropology* (Atlanta: John Knox, 1981); and Jacob Neusner et al., eds., *The Social World of Formative Christianity and Judaism* (Philadelphia: Fortress, 1988).

2. Kaufmann Kohler, "The Pharisees," in *Jewish Encyclopedia,* 12 vols. (New York: Funk and Wagnalls, 1925), 9:661.

3. George F. Moore, "The Am Ha-Areṣ (the People of the Land) and the Ḥaberīm (Associates)," in *The Beginnings of Christianity,* ed. F. J. Foakes Jackson and Kirsopp Lake, 5 vols. (Grand Rapids: Baker, 1979), 1:439–45.

humble, devoted folk from whose numbers came Jesus and many of his followers. There were, however, others who, even if circumcised, were Jews in name only, for they had given up all pretense of adherence to any form of the distinctive Jewish life.

It is useless to seek to identify a general consensus of opinion or normative position of average first-century Jews.[4] Yet it may be possible to detect the prevailing tenor of their thought and feeling. The average Jew's commitments to religion and nationalism were so intertwined that they could be distinguished only with greatest difficulty. Inner yearnings were controlled by desire for politico-religious deliverance from foreign domination. This deliverance most Jews expected to come with the appearance of the Anointed (= Messiah) of the LORD and of the kingdom of God. T. W. Manson says that this is the spirit behind Mary's Magnificat (Luke 1:46–55), the Benedictus of Simeon (Luke 2:29–32), and the pseudepigraphal Psalms of Solomon.[5] Certainly the combination of political and religious deliverance is evident in the prayer of Zechariah, the father of John the Baptist: "Grant us that we, being rescued from the hands of our enemies, might serve him without fear, in holiness and righteousness before him all our days" (Luke 1:73–75).

Strict adherence to the law commanded the admiration of average Jews, if not their imitation; they respected the Pharisees. The average Jews were faithful in attendance at synagogue and the temple services, in observance of festivals, and in payment of the temple tax. Apocalyptic and mystical speculations seem to have been popular among them. Even at the cost of their lives many zealously threw themselves behind one or another messianic pretender or nationalistic leader in revolts against Rome. Political hopes combined with religious commitment to give the average Palestinian Jew's faith an air of expectation and a flavor of hope. It was, however, an unsophisticated and undeveloped hope which incorporated many diverse elements and was subject to varied interpretations. The average first-century Jews in the land of Israel had zeal without full knowledge, hope without understanding, religious practice without clear theology. In short, they were not different from the lower socioeconomic group of any civilization. They could be easily led into mob action. They were followers with deeply ingrained and often irrational prejudices and attitudes.

4. T. W. Manson, *The Servant-Messiah* (New York: Cambridge University Press, 1953), 11, suggests that average Jews made up some 92 percent of the population.

5. Ibid., 4, 24.

Divisions within Society

No attempt to understand the average Jew would be complete without discussing the divisions within society. We have already observed that Intertestamental Judaism was incredibly diverse. For example, there was the cultural division between those who held to the traditional Semitic culture and those who embraced Hellenism. Geographic divisions were equally significant, for example, between Jews resident in the land of Israel and those of the Diaspora. Often overlooked is the difference between the three predominantly Jewish areas in the land of Israel—Judea, Galilee, and Perea. In Mark 14:70 and Luke 22:59 Peter is recognized as a Galilean; Matthew 26:73 explains that his accent betrayed him. The differences between the regions went deeper than pronunciation patterns, however; at times the three regions "were regarded as being in certain respects different lands."[6]

Political differences could also be profound. Those who were pro-Roman were set against the nationalists. Loyalties to a particular ruling family, such as the Herodians or the priestly family of Annas, could be intense. The Pharisees and Sadducees had their supporters; Josephus identifies several different militant groups just before and during the 66–70 war.

Sirach (Ecclesiasticus) provides a valuable glimpse of intertestamental Jewish society. The author, Jesus ben Sirach, was a sage, a teacher of the young, possibly a priest, who viewed himself as from neither the rich and powerful nor the poor and despised. He wrote in about 200–180 B.C., before the most bitter part of the struggle with Hellenism, an influence which he opposed. Writing before the Maccabean revolt, he pictured a society with divisions which, although very real, had not hardened and become as malevolent as those of a century and a half later.[7]

Jesus ben Sirach mentions a number of social groupings and vocations and testifies to animosities between them. He separates himself from the farmer, artisan, smith, and potter, who, although necessary to society ("Without them no city can be inhabited. . . .

6. Emil Schürer, *The History of the Jewish People in the Age of Jesus Christ*, ed. Geza Vermes et al., 3 vols. (Edinburgh: T. and T. Clark, 1973–87), 2:14; there were differences in "marriage laws; different customs in the relations between betrothed couples; different weights in Judaea and Galilee. There is even reference to a different observance of Passover: in Judaea, the people worked on 14 Nisan until noon, in Galilee not at all."

7. On Jesus ben Sirach's depiction of his environment see Edwyn R. Bevan, *Jerusalem under the High-Priests* (London: Edward Arnold, 1918), 49–68; Victor Tcherikover, *Hellenistic Civilization and the Jews*, trans. S. Applebaum (Philadelphia: Magnes, 1961), 143–51; and Martin Hengel, *Judaism and Hellenism: Studies in Their Encounter in Palestine during the Early Hellenistic Period*, trans. John Bowden, 2 vols. (Philadelphia: Fortress, 1974), 1:131–53.

They maintain the fabric of the world" [Sirach 38:32, 34]), have no place or voice among the influential and no opportunity to seek wisdom (38:24–34). Yet he has special words of praise for the farmer (7:15) and the physician (38:1–8).

Contemporary writers, recognizing that first-century Israel was more complex than most societies, seek to understand its makeup. Shaye J. D. Cohen speaks of two fundamentally different grids, one religious and the other economic (see table 2).[8] The situation, he observes, is made even more complicated by the fact that the relationship between them is unclear. The economic grid was typical of society in the Roman Empire as a whole. The religious structure was unique to the Jews.

Table 2
Major Divisions in First-Century Israel

Economic	Religious

I. The rich
  A. The city rich
  B. The country rich (owners of large estates)
	I. Jews
	  A. The religious establishment
	    1. High priest, priests, and Levites
	    2. The patriarch and his court (post-70)
	    3. Scribes, elders, rabbis, sages, members of the Sanhedrin

II. The middle class
  A. Artisans, merchants (city)
  B. Owners of moderate estates (country)
	B. The sects and unofficial authority figures
	    1. Hasidim, Pharisees, Sadducees, Boethusians, Essenes, Qumran sect, fourth philosophy, Judeo-Christians, Samaritans (?), *Haberim* (?), rabbis (?)

III. The lower class
  A. The city poor
  B. The country poor
    1. Peasant farmers
    2. Landless peasants
	2. Holy men, magic men, charismatics, healers, exorcists, messiahs, etc.

IV. Non-persons
  A. Women and children
  B. Slaves
	C. Other Jews
	    1. The *am ha-eretz* and other non-sectarian Jews
	    2. Hellenistic Jews
	    3. Proselytes

	II. Non-Jews
	  A. The Romans and the Roman army
	  B. Greeks, hellenized pagans, not-so-hellenized pagans
	  C. Samaritans (?)

8. Shaye J. D. Cohen, "The Political and Social History of the Jews in Greco-Roman Antiquity: The State of the Question," in *Early Judaism and Its Modern Interpreters*, ed. Robert A. Kraft and George W. E. Nickelsburg (Atlanta: Scholars, 1986), 46–48.

Even if we do not accept all of the details of Cohen's proposed reconstruction of the social structure, we must recognize its two major elements and seek to understand their makeup, relationship, and implications for the New Testament reader. Clearly, the New Testament writers assume something like what Cohen suggests—a society built on two distinct hierarchies, one religious and the other economic.

A reading of Josephus and the New Testament indicates considerable interrelationship between the economic rich and the religious establishment. As might be expected, they either held or were closely aligned with the political power. Their actions were frequently designed to protect their wealth and privileged status (see, e.g., John 11:49–50). Thus the gap between the upper and lower classes was perhaps greater than might be concluded from a casual glance at Cohen's grid. The animosity between the groups could be great—as suggested by Josephus's note that on one occasion lower-class rebels drowned the principal men of Galilee in that sea.[9]

As is usually the case, the lower levels of society were more aware of their economic disadvantage than of any other. In the land of Israel the usual causes of economic hardship—low wages, high prices, taxes, and debt—were compounded by religious demands. The Old Testament tithe (10 percent) was but the beginning of the contributions required by the religious establishment. Sacrifices, offerings, gifts for special occasions such as cleansing ceremonies and the like added to the religious economic demands. In addition each Jew was expected to pay annually the half-shekel or didrachma tax to the temple. The total levy for religious duties could come close to 50 percent of the income of a working person.

The priestly aristocracy was itself oppressive, not only toward the common people but also toward other priests. Describing the period preceding the revolt, Josephus says that during the high priesthood of Ishmael (58–60) "there now was enkindled mutual enmity and class warfare between the high priests, on the one hand, and the priests and the leaders of the populace of Jerusalem on the other." He goes on to indicate the greed and self-seeking of the high priests: "They actually were so brazen as to send slaves to the threshing floors to receive the tithes that were due to the priests, with the result that the poorer priests starved to death."[10] The Talmud preserves a lament of Abba Joseph ben Hanan, who

---

9. Josephus *Jewish War* 1.17.2 (326); *Antiquities* 14.15.10 (450).
10. Josephus *Antiquities* 20.8.8 (180–81).

lived during the era of Herod's temple; he conveys the plight of the common person under the high-priestly families:

> Woe is me because of the house of Boethus, woe is me because of their staves.
> Woe is me because of the house of Hanan, woe is me because of their whisperings.
> Woe is me because of the house of Kathros, woe is me because of their pens.
> Woe is me because of the house of Ishmael ben Phiabi, woe is me because of their fists.
> For they are high priests and their sons are treasurers and their sons-in-law are trustees and their servants beat the people with staves.[11]

Villages and Cities

Towns and cities are usually assumed to be a measure of civilization.[12] Hellenistic civilization was unapologetically urban-centered. Yet cities must have a complex substructure to sustain them; few can be self-supporting. In general it can be said that a city is supported by a combination of four enterprises: agriculture, manufacturing, trade and commerce, and service. Agriculture provides the basic food and goods for survival, and manufacturing turns raw materials into usable and desirable commodities. Trade and commerce involve the distribution of goods and services. The most obvious and largest component of service is government, but religion, education, and entertainment can also play significant roles. A city offers protection and services, but depends heavily upon its ability to exact taxes, fees, and tariffs.

Ancient cities were dependent upon their geographical environment. An adequate supply of water, defensible location, favorable climate, and proximity to trade routes were necessities for an urban center to flourish. Sufficient arable soil in the vicinity was equally essential. S. Applebaum puts it succinctly: "With few exceptions, ancient cities were based on agriculture, with whose proceeds they covered most of their tax-obligations, imports and amenities. If the cultivators of their territories were forced to contribute more than was needed to maintain a minimal standard of

11. Babylonian Talmud *Pesahim* 57a; Tosephta *Menahoth* 13:21 (cited by Menahem Stern, "Aspects of Jewish Society: The Priesthood and Other Classes," in *Jewish People*, ed. Safrai and Stern, 2:602–3).

12. On ancient cities see A. H. M. Jones, *The Greek City from Alexander to Justinian* (Oxford: Clarendon, 1940); John E. Stambaugh, *The Ancient Roman City* (Baltimore: Johns Hopkins University Press, 1988); John McRay, *Archaeology and the New Testament* (Grand Rapids: Baker, 1991), 37–88.

living, they ceased to use the services which the city had to offer, and decline set in, to be further accelerated by excessive taxation. Thus ultimately only those cities continued to flourish which were entrepôts of commerce."[13]

The distinction between a town or village and a city is difficult to determine; this difficulty is reflected in the New Testament.[14] Size and importance were the marks of a city; it is frequently assumed that a city was bounded by a wall. Towns located around cities and, in times of danger, the inhabitants of the towns fled to the city for the protection of its walls. Cities also provided a wide range of services such as a central water supply, police protection, public toilet facilities, and sewage disposal. But even large cities were small by modern standards.

Ancient Hebrew settlements grew up haphazardly. The gate was the center of government and commerce. Hellenistic cities, in contrast, were marked by careful planning: the physical center and focal point of activity was the agora (marketplace). Public buildings ranging from gymnasiums and theaters to palaces and stoas were usually in proximity to the agora. In smaller cities such luxuries were limited or nonexistent. Roman cities resembled, with modifications, those of the Greeks, though their walls tended to be more regularly rectangular. Roman street patterns were organized around two major thoroughfares oriented toward the points of the compass—the north-south *cardo* and the east-west *decumanus* crossed near the city center. Both written and archaeological sources indicate that streets were very narrow, typically from 6 1/2 to 13 feet wide, though major streets could be up to 26 feet or more. Public alleys led from the streets to courtyards surrounded by several residences. Shops might be located in these alleys as well as along major arteries.

13. S. Applebaum, "Economic Life in Palestine," in *Jewish People,* ed. Safrai and Stern, 2:667.

14. *Polis* is used for both a major city like Jerusalem and smaller locations as well; translations use both "city" and "town" for this word. *Kōmē* is usually translated "village," but sometimes as "town." Bethsaida is called *kōmē* in Mark 8:23, 26, and *polis* in Matt. 11:20–21; Bethlehem is *kōmē* in John 7:42 and *polis* in Luke 2:4, 11. Hermann Strathmann, *"Polis,"* in *Theological Dictionary of the New Testament,* ed. Gerhard Kittel and Gerhard Friedrich, trans. Geoffrey W. Bromiley, 10 vols. (Grand Rapids: Eerdmans, 1964–76), 6:530, states that in the New Testament the word *polis* is "non-political. [It] means an 'enclosed place of human habitation' as distinct from uninhabited areas, pastures, villages and single houses. . . . In general walled towns are *poleis* while open places of habitation are *kōmai.*" Mark 1:38 uses the term *kōmopolis,* meaning something like "population center" or "market town." *Agros* usually means "field" or "country," but in the plural it may mean "farm(s)" or "hamlet(s)" (Walter Bauer, *Greek-English Lexicon of the New Testament,* trans. William F. Arndt and F. Wilbur Gingrich, 2d ed. [Chicago: University of Chicago Press, 1979], 14).

That there were few cities in first-century Israel speaks volumes about the social sphere.[15] History and religion played a part in painting the essentially rural and agricultural face of intertestamental Israel. The reforms under Nehemiah had revamped the financial structure and secured the land for the small farmers, who were in danger of being swallowed up by the greed of the nobles and officials (Neh. 5:1–13). His policies reinstituted both the Mosaic laws against exacting interest from fellow Israelites (Exod. 22:25–27; Lev. 25:35–38; note also the provision for the remission of debts in the Sabbatical Year [Deut. 15:1–11]) and a recognition of the solidarity of the people of God (Neh. 5:7–9). Later the Maccabean revolt "freed the Jewish peasants from the oppressive taxation associated with [the Seleucid] regime, and distributed newly acquired lands among them in return for the obligation to military service."[16] Thus the foundations were laid for an essentially agrarian society in which the small farmer could survive.

By the first century, however, the safeguards for small landholders had been severely weakened if not actually overthrown. The threat of losing their land was a constant reality, and many were in fact displaced. Accordingly, most of the common people in first-century Israel lived in settlements outside the cities. Many Hebrew towns and villages, however, were free-standing, that is, not immediately associated with a city. From these the people went out to their fields or fishing boats to earn a livelihood. Trade, commerce, and manufacturing took place in the towns, each of which had at least one synagogue.

Even at best, life in villages, towns, and cities was spartan by modern standards and, for all but the wealthy, difficult. Most settlements were crowded, noisy, and potentially dangerous. There were no street lights, so "when night fell everyone stayed home behind locked doors and shuttered windows."[17] Homes were cramped, with poor ventilation and limited heating facilities for cold seasons. There is also evidence of antagonism between city dwellers and those who lived in small towns or rural areas.[18] Such conditions should be kept in mind when we envision the house churches and the life of the early urban Christians.

---

15. Of Jewish settlements only Jerusalem could claim true city status. Both Tiberias and Sepphoris in Galilee might also be included. Along the coast Caesarea, Ashkelon, and Gaza were important centers but essentially Gentile; only the port of Joppa may have had a substantial Jewish presence.

16. Applebaum, "Economic Life in Palestine," 635.

17. McRay, *Archaeology*, 86. After noting the illegal practice of emptying chamber pots from upper-story windows at night, he adds, "Problems of comfort and hygiene were especially difficult to deal with at night because the streets of Rome and other ancient cities were totally dark."

18. Applebaum, "Economic Life in Palestine," 663.

The Economy

An Agricultural Society

By the first century the land of Israel was intertwined with the Greco-Roman economy.[19] Yet it had its own distinctives. Its craftsmen were probably ahead of their Gentile counterparts, and "slavery was strongly tinged with moral reservations."[20] Manual labor was valued and drew participants from intellectual classes, especially the rabbis. But the salient fact is that the area was less urban than most. "The Jews were preponderantly a people of the hinterland, preoccupied with agriculture."[21] Statements by the ancients confirm this conclusion:

> Bend your back in farming,
> perform the tasks of the soil in every kind of agriculture,
> offering gifts gratefully to the Lord.
>
> Thus the Lord will bless you with the first fruits, as he has blessed all the saints from Abel until the present. For to you is given no other portion than the fertility of the earth, from which comes produce through toil.[22]

Likewise Josephus, in a well-known statement, confirms the intertestamental Jewish focus on agriculture, both because of location and by choice: "Well, ours is not a maritime country; neither commerce nor the intercourse which it promotes with the outside world has any attraction for us. Our cities are built inland, remote from the sea; and we devote ourselves to the cultivation of the productive country with which we are blessed."[23]

The variety in soil, topography, climate, and access to water dictates the locations and types of farming in the land of Israel.[24] The interior, the central hills, presented formidable challenges to the ancient farmer. Enhancement of natural terracing to conserve soil and water, construction of cisterns and other water transport and storage facilities, preservation of forests and fruit trees, and careful

---

19. For studies of the economy in specific parts of Israel see Jeremias, *Jerusalem*, 3–57; Freyne, *Galilee*, 155–300.

20. Applebaum, "Economic Life in Palestine," 631.

21. Ibid., 632.

22. Testament of Issachar 5:3–5; note also 6:2, which speaks of one of the sins of the last times: "Giving up agriculture, they pursue their own evil schemes."

23. Josephus *Against Apion* 1.12 (60). For the role of commerce and trade see Applebaum, "Economic Life in Palestine," 667–92.

24. Applebaum, "Economic Life in Palestine," 638–41, gives an excellent overview of geographical features as they relate to agriculture.

crop selection were necessary. The relatively flat area just north of Jerusalem, the central Benjamin Plateau, offered especially favorable conditions in the interior for both farming and cattle raising. Other areas of the country had their own assets. Galilee was generally better suited to agriculture than was the hill country, and it also had the advantage of the fishing industries around the Sea of Galilee.[25] The coastal plain and Valley of Esdraelon did, and do, offer the best situations for farming. The Negeb, the far south, is a desert in the dry months, but with careful utilization of water during the wet seasons can be a productive agricultural area.

Israelite farmers produced a wide variety of crops. They also engaged in raising sheep and goats and other livestock.[26] In spite of the hardships imposed by natural phenomena it appears that the first-century farmer could have made an adequate, even at times a good living. Unfortunately, however, other factors, especially political and social, stacked the deck against him. In addition to raising enough to feed his family, the farmer had to buy necessities he could not produce, save enough seed for the next year's planting, and meet other obligations. These other obligations proved to be the ruin of many in the first century. Included were taxes required by both Jewish and Roman authorities, tariffs for both importing and exporting, fees to owners of large estates, special religious charges, and interest on loans (scribes provided means of avoiding the Old Testament prohibition on charging interest to another Hebrew). These obligations remained constant in spite of negative factors that periodically threatened the farmer—social disruptions such as war or changes in the administrative or economic structure, governmental inefficiency as well as corruption, shifts in population patterns, to say nothing of losses because of climatological factors, natural disasters, agricultural pests.

Taxes could rise at an unpredictable rate. Conditions at the time of Herod the Great are a notorious example. The king so lived beyond his means that he was forced to raise taxes although he realized the adverse reaction it would bring from his subjects.[27] And

25. Freyne, *Galilee*, 1–19, 155–200.
26. Applebaum, "Economic Life in Palestine," 646–56.
27. "For Herod loved honors and, being powerfully dominated by this passion, he was led to display generosity whenever there was reason to hope for future remembrance or present reputation, but since he was involved in expenses greater than his means, he was compelled to be harsh toward his subjects, for the great number of things on which he spent money as gifts to some caused him to be the source of harm to those from whom he took this money. And though he was aware of being hated because of the wrongs that he had done to his subjects, he decided that it would not be easy to mend his evil ways—that would have been unprofitable in respect of revenue—, and, instead, he countered their opposition by seizing upon their ill-will as an opportunity for satisfying his wants" (Josephus *Antiquities* 16.5.4 [153–55]).

Tacitus, no friend of the Jews, notes that during the reign of Tiberius "the provinces of Syria and Judea, exhausted by their burdens, implored a reduction of tribute."[28]

Under such burdens the farmer had to struggle not only to feed his family, but also to keep his land. Many failed. This situation gave rise to unemployment and hostility of the lower classes against the aristocracy and government officials. Other consequences included a new bandit class, and eventually rebellion and revolution against Rome and those who supported her.

The Bandit Underclass

Banditry is a socioeconomic, prerevolutionary phenomenon.[29] It usually arises in essentially rural societies in the face of social disruption, economic and judicial vulnerability of the poor. It is frequently the last resort of people who have been forced from their land or otherwise deprived of their livelihood without recourse. City dwellers and the aristocracy, who are generally the focus of bandits' wrath and attacks, regard them as criminals. The common people frequently share the bandits' plight and sense of justice; they may support and protect the bandits. Bandits, like Robin Hood, may give aid to those in distress.

Josephus says that bandits were prevalent throughout the countryside and took a leading part in the war against Rome. But Rome was not the only object of the bandits' wrath. In one uprising, insurgents burned the public records of debts; on an earlier occasion, which we have mentioned, they drowned some members of the aristocracy.[30] From such data the picture of the desperate situation faced daily by many of the underclasses in Jesus' world begins to emerge.

We have already noted the difficulties faced by a farmer. Old Testament legislation had instituted the Year of Jubilee to maintain an equitable division of land (Lev. 25:8–54; 27:17–24). Evidently this law was not observed in Intertestamental Judaism. More and more

28. Tacitus *Annals* 2.42.

29. In the following discussion I have drawn heavily upon Richard A. Horsley with John S. Hanson, *Bandits, Prophets, and Messiahs: Popular Movements at the Time of Jesus* (New York: Harper and Row, 1985); Applebaum, "Economic Life in Palestine," 656–64, 691–92; Sean Freyne, "Bandits in Galilee: A Contribution to the Study of Social Conditions in First-Century Palestine," in Neusner et al., eds., *Social World*, 50–65. See also Martin Goodman, *Ruling Classes of Judaea: The Origins of the Jewish Revolt against Rome, A.D. 66–70* (New York: Cambridge University Press, 1987).

30. The Sicarii "burst in and set fire . . . to the public archives, eager to destroy the money-lenders' bonds and to prevent the recovery of debts, in order to win over a host of grateful debtors and to cause a rising of the poor against the rich, sure of impunity" (Josephus *Jewish War* 2.17.6 [427]); *Jewish War* 1.17.2 (326); *Antiquities* 14.15.10 (450).

of the best land was progressively incorporated into royal estates or large aristocratic holdings. Consequently, less and less was available for the common person. When agricultural reversals and rising taxes forced the small farmer to borrow, interest could be quite high; lenders and tax collectors could be merciless in demanding payment. A growing number of peasants were driven from their land by forces beyond their control. These displaced peasants probably made up a significant portion of the hired hands depicted in Jesus' parable of the laborers in the vineyard, some of whom were so desperate that they searched for work all day (Matt. 20:1–16).

The Gospels contain other hints of the desperate plight of some of the common people of the day. Jesus' admonition not to worry about food and clothing (Matt. 6:25–34; Luke 12:22–34) is especially relevant to persons in a survival economy. His condemnation of the Pharisees for not being concerned about justice and mercy (Matt. 23:23) would have rung true to those who felt themselves deprived of justice and mercy. Could Mary's song in Luke 1 have in mind the average Jew's suffering at the hands of the rich and powerful, and provide a self-portrait of herself and her associates as lowly and hungry (vv. 52–53)? 貴族

As a member of the aristocracy, Josephus minimizes the wretched conditions that existed in the land of Israel in the middle of the first century. Yet these conditions were the seedbed for the birth and growth of the rampant banditry he portrays. The frustration of the peasants against the aristocracy is clearly shown in the historian's report that "Simon, son of Gioras, mustering a large band of revolutionaries, devoted himself to rapine; not content with ransacking the houses of the wealthy, he further maltreated their persons."[31]

The evidence indicates that although banditry was a force during the time of Jesus, it grew in intensity as the Jews moved closer to rebellion and war with Rome. It was largely an economic banditry. Its rise suggests that the haughty, oppressive wealthy class was in constant conflict with an increasingly desperate, vulnerable lower class, especially the peasant farmers within it. They felt themselves exploited and deprived of justice through regular channels. Banditry and revolution appeared as their only option.

Money

The discussion of money in the ancient world presents special problems. It was not the only medium of exchange; barter was also common. Further, a number of monetary systems could be in use

31. Josephus *Jewish War* 2.22.2 (652).

in the same area. Understanding the worth of monetary units is particularly perplexing because of frequent changes in valuation—both of ancient and of modern money. Also, monetary units could designate a standard weight as well as a coin. One way to determine equivalent monetary worth is to compare the amount paid a laborer as a day's wage in the ancient and modern cultures. However, this too can be deceiving because of the changing purchasing power of a day's wage.

In the New Testament Era, there were at least three different types of money in circulation in the land of Israel: Jewish, Greek, and Roman (the Gentile coins were not acceptable for paying religious dues; hence the need for moneychangers in the temple courts). Jewish coins included the shekel, half shekel, quarter shekel, and the lepton. The latter is the copper coin, the widow's mite of Mark 12:42 and Luke 21:2; it represents the smallest imaginable amount of money.[32] The Greek drachma was a day's wage for a laborer. The pound or mina (Luke 19:11–27) was the equivalent of a hundred drachmas. The didrachma held the value of two drachmas while the stater was worth four drachmas.[33] The talent (Matt. 18:24; 25:14–30) was not actually a coin but a unit of laboring. It represented a very large sum. The ten thousand talents of Matthew 18:24 is an almost incomprehensible amount of debt, especially for a common person. In Roman currency the denarius (Matt. 20:9) represented a day's wage and was thus equal in value to the Greek drachma. One hundred denarii equaled a Greek mina.

House and Home

Dwellings

The wealthy lived in mansions or palatial structures.[34] We may assume that the middle class had homes less luxurious and smaller than those of the wealthy. The typical dwelling in the land of Israel was, of course, that of the lower classes. It was made of stone, mud, or mud brick with hard-packed dirt floors. An open courtyard

32. One lepton was worth about one-half of the Roman quadrans (penny) or one-eighth of the assarion.

33. The didrachma was equivalent to the half shekel, the amount of the annual temple tax paid by all Jews (Matt. 17:24). The stater is probably in view when Matt. 26:14 speaks of the thirty pieces of silver paid to Judas Iscariot to betray Jesus. Although the exact value is uncertain, Judas was probably paid in the neighborhood of 120 days' wages.

34. For archaeological evidence of dwellings see McRay, *Archaeology,* 76–88. Most of his discussion is about dwellings outside the land of Israel.

in most cases serviced several families. The courtyard was surrounded by a number of individual houses and rooms. Also in the
court were storage sheds for various commodities, shelters for animals, cisterns, a garbage collector, and toilet facilities (when available). A family house could consist of only a single room, but most
had more. The rooms, which were divided by curtains or mats,
were quite small, so people tended to spend as much time as possible outdoors. Windows were usually small and left open during
warm months; when the weather turned cold, they were covered
with glass or some translucent material. At night, lamps, lanterns,
and torches were the only sources of light. Each home was
equipped with a door, bolt, and lock. Frequently the house consisted of more than one story; access to upper floors was by exterior
ladder or steps. Most roofs were flat, so families often went there
to eat, to sit in the cool parts of the day, and possibly to sleep.

The furniture, most of which could be moved or stored when not
in use, included beds which, except in the poorest of homes, were
raised from the floor, a stove and an oven, a table for meals,
couches on which to recline during meals, chairs and benches
(only mourners or those under some sort of a ban sat on the floor),
and a variety of chests, baskets, and other containers for storage.
Water, oil, and wine were used in quantity; whatever was to be consumed had, according to laws regulating ritual purity, to be stored
in covered pots. There were separate vessels for storing, for cooking, and for serving. Of various shapes and sizes these vessels were
made of clay, stone, or glass; wealthy homes also used containers
of bronze, copper, silver, or gold. Cooking and serving utensils such
as spoons, knives, and mixing bowls were of similar materials.
Stone was not susceptible to ceremonial uncleanness and thus was
often favored for eating surfaces, vessels, and other household implements. Household equipment made of wood was not common
until after the New Testament period. The economic status of a
home was reflected in the materials, quality, and quantity of its
household equipment.

In warm, dry months cooking was frequently done in the courtyard; in other seasons the stove and oven were moved inside and
placed near a window. Weekly baking of bread frequently involved
the whole family: "the children gather wood, the fathers kindle fire,
and the women knead dough" (Jer. 7:18). Diners would recline on
couches around the table and eat from a common dish. A chip of
wood or possibly a small knife might be used in eating; spoons and
other knives were employed in food preparation only.

The Home and Family Life

Rabbinic writings are filled with information and requirements relating to the family as a unit and as an institution of society. Also covered are individual responsibilities and functions within the family. Most of our information comes from the post–New Testament period, but a substantial part of it probably reflects the pre–A.D. 70 situation. Modern archaeology has enhanced and supplemented data from written materials. A detailed accounting of the customs in vogue during Intertestamental Judaism would require an extremely lengthy discussion. We will, then, merely summarize some of the more important aspects.[35]

Early marriage was the norm. Family was seen as an institution established by God, and the procreation of children his command. The family was highly valued as the basis of social life. Intertestamental Jewish marriages were usually monogamous, but polygamy was known among the aristocratic classes.[36] The birth of children was greatly desired; if a man had no children after ten years of marriage, he was required to divorce his wife and marry another.

The husband led the household and was expected to provide food and clothing. The rabbis affirmed that a wife from a home more well-to-do than her husband's had to be supported at the level to which she was accustomed; if she came from a poorer home, she was supported at a level commensurate with her husband's standing. The husband led in family religious ceremonies and had responsibilities for the education of the children. It was the husband who usually purchased necessary goods at the market. He had special duties to his wife, ranging from taking care of her personal expenses to sexual relations. Respect for her was a part of his family duty; they could not have sexual relations without her consent. Rabbinic writings also include the husband's obligation to eat with his wife at least on the evening of every Sabbath.

"From a legal point of view . . . the wife's status was inferior to that of her husband. There is no doubt, however, that socially the woman's position in the house was highly esteemed."[37] She had certain rights regarding where the couple lived and did not need her husband's permission to visit her parents. She also had duties prescribed by custom. The wife ground flour, cooked and baked, washed clothes, made the beds, and spun wool. She nursed the

35. What follows draws heavily from S. Safrai, "Home and Family," in *Jewish People*, ed. Safrai and Stern, 2:748–91.

36. Safrai, "Home and Family," 749–50, makes the telling comment, "Among all the stories about married life of the Tannaim and Amoraim [rabbinic schools] . . . there is not a single case of bigamy."

37. Safrai, "Home and Family," 763.

children (for as long as eighteen months to three years). She was not required to assist with the husband's work, though many wives seem to have done so. She bore primary responsibility for extending hospitality and preparing the children for school. She could engage in crafts and other work at home; some women seem to have kept the money earned as their own. A wife was expected to dress and adorn herself so as not to lose her charms in her husband's eyes.

Pregnancy and childbirth were considered a blessing. Both men and women occasionally practiced birth control. Abortion was regarded as murder. The numbers of miscarriages and of women dying at childbirth were high. Midwives assisted in births; any work that involved preparing for the birth of a child and caring for the mother was exempt from the restrictions of Sabbath laws. The birth of the child was an occasion for rejoicing, more so for a son than a daughter.

Following a birth, mother and child went through prescribed rites for cleansing and dedication. The circumcision of a boy on his eighth day was performed by a professional physician. It was a time for celebration. But because of the increasing expense of the required sacrifices, even of the doves which Leviticus 12:8 had prescribed only for the poor, measures were taken during the rabbinic period to hold down the cost.

All members of the family, including older children, assisted in caring for and raising the child. Children were taught to honor and respect their parents. (By extension, adults were expected to care for their aging parents.) Discipline could be administered by either parent; written sources frequently enjoin Proverbs 13:24, which connects parental discipline with love. Children participated in all ceremonies in the home, community, and synagogue.

The passage from childhood to adolescence was physical, social, legal, and religious. By tradition it was associated with a girl's twelfth year and a boy's thirteenth, but these are only approximate figures. Even persons not physically mature were considered so legally at the age of eighteen by the followers of Shammai, or at twenty by the followers of Hillel.

The age of puberty approximately coincided with most boys' leaving school to begin learning a craft and assuming the responsibility of regular work. Girls too began to assume more responsibility. Girls and young women were not so secluded in Intertestamental Judaism as they were in some other cultures. When old enough they could draw water at the common well or stream, frequent shops, and even seek employment.

Betrothal and marriage involved a lengthy process of steps and customs. A candidate for marriage had to have both family lineage and ceremonial status agreeable to the family of the prospective mate. Men were considered ready for marriage at about eighteen to twenty, girls at a much younger age. Young people could meet prospective marriage partners on their own. More often marriages were arranged by parents or through marriage brokers.

訂婚 Betrothal involved both financial and legal implications and could be the subject of extended negotiations. Formal betrothal took place in the home of the bride's father, where the groom gave the bride money or something of value as a token of his intention. He also presented a written marriage contract listing his responsibilities and the amount of money she would receive at his death or in case of divorce.[38] The legal aspects of the betrothal required the presence of formal witnesses. The ceremony included a time of joyous celebration and the giving of gifts. Afterwards the bride remained in her father's home. Sources as early as the Mishnah do not exclude the possibility of sexual contact between betrothal and marriage.[39]

Marriage took place when both bride and groom felt themselves ready. There were prescribed stages for the wedding celebration: "(1) preparation of the bride, (2) transfer of the bride from her father's home to that of the groom, (3) the bride's introduction into the home of the groom, and (4) blessings and festivities within the husband's home."[40] The celebration included many guests, both invited and otherwise. Witnesses were required for the reciting of blessings throughout the week of the wedding. There were feasting and a general atmosphere of merriment and rejoicing. Even after the wedding week there were additional customs to be observed.

Death was another event marked by well-established custom. Mourning began as soon as death occurred or when it was announced to a relative. Burial was required as soon as possible, preferably on the day of death. Preparations for burial included washing the body, making sure that it remained straight, and wrapping it in a shroud. Spices and other ointments could be used. A coffin was also usually required.

Burial often took place in a natural cave or one hollowed out for the purpose. Sometimes the dead were buried in fields, in which

38. Philo *Special Laws* 3.67 (311) mentions this arrangement, confirming existence of the practice in the intertestamental period.

39. Hence the significance of the statements in Matt. 1:18 ("before they came together," which is more literal and exact than the NRSV's "before they lived together") and 1:25 ("he was not knowing her" or "had no marital relations with her," NRSV). The claim of Mary's virginity in Luke 1:27, 34 (see also 35–38), is strengthened by Joseph's contemplation of putting her away (Matt. 1:19), which indicates he knew he was not the father of Mary's child.

40. Safrai, "Home and Family," 757.

case steps were taken to mark the grave in order to avoid ritual defilement (Luke 11:44) and to preserve the memory of the dead. The body was carried on the shoulders of pallbearers, who might be changed en route. Pipers, professional mourners (keeners), and family members lamented the deceased at the home, on the way to the burial site, at the grave, and afterwards. Eulogies were offered on the way to the burial and at the grave. Even strangers might join the funeral procession. A large but movable stone was used to block the entrance of the cave. It was customary to visit the grave within three days to assure the person was really dead; mistakes were possible because of the speed with which the dead were buried.

Mourning continued for a week, but could be prolonged. Signs of grief included lowering all beds in the house ("overturning the bed" in rabbinic phraseology), rending the garments, covering the head, sitting shoeless on the ground, and refraining from work, from washing, and from sexual intercourse. The bereaved family was visited by friends and consolers (John 11:19), who frequently brought food and drink. At least in the rabbinic period, special blessings of consolation were pronounced when a quorum of ten men was present.

Toward the end of the intertestamental period it became customary to revisit the grave after the flesh had rotted away, that is, a year or so after death. The more affluent families collected the bones into ossuaries, specially prepared boxes or chests, and reinterred them, frequently in niches within the tomb structure.

Personal and Family Religion

Public religious observances were centered at the temple. Sacrifices and associated ceremony were, with some adaptations, like the Old Testament services. The synagogue was the focal point for local religious practice. The third avenue for religious expression was the home.

A distinctive mark of Intertestamental Judaism was that the law, Torah, was the center of daily life. It regulated the living of each day, not just special occasions. At the most basic level, no food was eaten without the pronunciation of a blessing. The *Shema* and other prayers were recited before the household started the affairs of the day and at other times. There were several different tithes: of produce, of land, of dough or bread, and of money. Tassels worn on the fringes of cloaks, Scripture portions affixed to the right-hand doorpost of homes and buildings (mezuzahs), phylacteries (or tefillin) that bound the words of the law to head and arm all served as constant reminders of God, his law, and the obligation to obey. The Letter of Aristeas (157–60) speaks of these symbols:

> So he exhorts us to remember how . . . blessings are maintained and preserved by divine power under his providence, for he has ordained every time and place for a continual reminder of the supreme God and upholder (of all). Accordingly in the matter of meats and drinks he commands men to offer first fruits and to consume them there and then straightaway. Furthermore in our clothes he has given us a distinguishing mark as a reminder, and similarly on our gates and doors he has commanded us to set up the "Words," so as to be a reminder of God. He also strictly commands that the sign shall be worn on our hands, clearly indicating that it is our duty to fulfill every activity with justice, having in mind our own condition, and above all the fear of God. He also commands that "on going to bed and rising" men should meditate on the ordinances of God, observing not only in word but in understanding the movement and impression which they have when they go to sleep, and waking too, what a divine change there is between them—quite beyond understanding.

We will focus our attention on three other family observances: the Sabbath, purity laws, and the special seasons.

Sabbath

Observance of the Sabbath was a fundamental mark of a Jewish community and individual. The fourth commandment enjoins rest on the seventh day (Exod. 20:8–11; Deut. 5:12–15).[41] Exodus 31:13 states, "You shall keep my sabbaths, for this is a sign between me and you throughout your generations, given in order that you may know that I, the LORD, sanctify you." Thus the intent of the command is that the Sabbath be observed as a sign of the covenant and of God's having set Israel apart for himself.[42] This idea is reiterated by the intertestamental writer of Jubilees 2:17–22.

The degree of specificity of Sabbath instructions in the Bible was not sufficient for Intertestamental Judaism. So the traditions and oral laws of the various groups provided more detailed instructions. For example, Jubilees 2:29–30 makes it clear that the children of Israel "should not prepare [on the Sabbath] anything which will be eaten or drunk, which they have not prepared for themselves on the sixth day. . . . [Nor is it lawful] to draw water or

---

41. For other biblical statements of the Sabbath command see Exod. 16:23–30; 23:12; 31:12–17; 34:21; 35:1–3; Lev. 23:3; Num. 15:32–36; cf. Neh. 10:31; 13:15–22; Isa. 58:13; Jer. 17:21–24; Ezek. 22:8; Amos 8:5 (this list has been adapted from Schürer, *History*, 2:468).

42. Note also Isa. 56:6: "Foreigners who join themselves to the LORD . . . all who keep the sabbath, and do not profane it, and hold fast my covenant. . . ."

to bring in or to take out any work within their dwellings which is carried in their gates. And they shall not bring in or take out from house to house on that day." Chapter 50:6–13 similarly prohibits marital relations, discussion of any business dealings, drawing or carrying water "which was not prepared . . . on the sixth day," going on a journey, plowing, building a fire, riding on an animal, killing an animal or fowl, fasting, or making war. The Damascus Rule (CD 10–12) contains a similar but expanded list of these prohibitions. Both documents limit the sacrifices that can be offered in the temple on the Sabbath to those prescribed for the day.

The Mishnah, and later the Talmud, devote a whole tractate, *Shabbath*, to instructions for the Sabbath. Another tractate, *Erubin* (the fusion of Sabbath limits), deals with many limits that pertain to the Sabbath.[43] Mishnah *Shabbath* 7:2 lists the classes of work from which a person is to refrain on the Sabbath:

> The main classes of work are forty save one: sowing, ploughing, reaping, binding sheaves, threshing, winnowing, cleansing crops, grinding, sifting, kneading, baking, shearing wool, washing or beating or dyeing it, spinning, weaving, making two loops, weaving two threads, separating two threads, tying [a knot], loosening [a knot], sewing two stitches, tearing in order to sew two stitches, hunting a gazelle, slaughtering or flaying or salting it or curing its skin, scraping it or cutting it up, writing two letters, erasing in order to write two letters, building, pulling down, putting out a fire, lighting a fire, striking with a hammer and taking out aught from one domain to another.

Other rabbinic writings both elucidate and expand this list.

From all this it is evident that the Sabbath command had a profound effect not only on religious experts and leaders, but also in the humblest home. The Sabbath was to be a day of abstention from any form of work except what was necessary to preserve life. Alongside the prohibitions were Sabbath obligations to attend synagogue services and to partake of common meals as a family or in an expanded group. The Sabbath meal, usually on Friday evening, was a special occasion for the family and its guests; of course the meal had been prepared before the actual arrival of the Sabbath. Both Josephus and Philo note that the Sabbath was occupied with the study of the law.[44]

43. From the Talmud tractate comes the practice known as *erub:* "the technical casuistic device whereby adjacent properties were amalgamated as one on the eve of the Sabbath or Holy Days in order to mitigate the severity of the restrictions for the observance of these days" (Salo W. Baron and Joseph L. Blau, *Judaism: Postbiblical and Talmudic Period* [New York: Liberal Arts, 1954], 242).

44. Josephus *Against Apion* 2.18 (175); Philo *Life of Moses* 2.39 (211–12); *Every Good Man Is Free* 81.

There are various evidences that trumpets were blown on the Sabbath in intertestamental times. For instance, the Old Testament prescribes the blowing of trumpets for religious purposes (Lev. 23:24; 25:9; Num. 10:8–10; 29:1). The Talmud indicates that trumpets sounded the arrival and conclusion of the Sabbath. A stone from the southern wall of Herod's temple bears the inscription "corner of blowing to announce," confirmation that the sounding of trumpets for religious purposes was practiced during the intertestamental period. Although the inscription does not indicate the exact purposes for blowing trumpets, it is probable that one purpose was to announce the Sabbath.

Ceremonial Purity

Priests were told to abstain from strong drink because they were "to distinguish between the holy and the common, and between the unclean and the clean" (Lev. 10:10). The concept of making "a distinction between the unclean and the clean" occurs again in Leviticus 11:47. This statement, in turn, immediately follows the declaration "I am the LORD your God; sanctify yourselves therefore, and be holy, for I am holy. You shall not defile yourselves. . . . For I am the LORD who brought you up from the land of Egypt, to be your God; you shall be holy, for I am holy" (vv. 44–45). Also of note is Leviticus 20:24–26: "I am the LORD your God; I have separated you from the peoples. You shall therefore make a distinction between the clean animal and the unclean, . . . which I have set apart for you to hold unclean. You shall be holy to me; for I the LORD am holy, and I have separated you from the other peoples to be mine." The principles of making a distinction between unclean and clean and of Israel's being holy, a reflection of the nature of the God with whom they are in covenant relationship, are assumed to be the bases for laws of both ritual purity and moral behavior.[45]

The Bible contains numerous laws relating to unclean persons, foods, and objects and to the requisite cleansing rituals (see especially Lev. 11–22; Num. 5:1–4; 19). These matters were developed at length in the first century A.D. and afterwards; a whole division of the Mishnah—*Tohoroth* (Cleannesses)—as well as many other parts addresses the issue of clean and unclean. Little else had more impact on daily life than did these regulations. The Gospel writer hardly scratches the surface with the well-known statement of Mark 7:3–4: "For the Pharisees, and all the Jews, do not eat unless they thoroughly wash their hands, thus observing the tradition of the elders; and they do not eat anything from the market unless

45. Note Lev. 19, where part of the statement "You shall be holy, for I the LORD your God am holy" is frequently repeated as the justification or standard for the preceding injunctions.

they wash it; and there are also many other traditions that they observe, the washing of cups, pots, and bronze kettles" (see also Matt. 23:25–26; Luke 11:38–41). Rabbinic discussion notes that the material and shape of these vessels could affect the nature of uncleanness and the type of cleansing required.

The various groups had their own approaches to the ceremonial regulations. "Some tried to restrict their ambit, but others enlarged it, aiming at raising all Israel to the same level of holiness as the priests. The Sadducees maintained that purity was only for the latter, while some at least of the Pharisees held that it should be preserved by all who were willing to accept the obligation, though not necessarily incumbent on all Israel. The Essenes insisted on the full rigour of the law for all their groups, and ritual purity was one of their priorities."[46]

The best-known regulation, at least from the Gentile point of view, was the distinction between kosher and unclean foods. But it was those items that dealt with personal uncleanness that required the most conscious effort by the average Jews. The biblical list of situations entailing impurity included (1) sexual intercourse; (2) touching the carcass of an animal (except one killed for food); (3) a flux from the body of male or female, including menstruation and childbirth; (4) contact with leprosy; and (5) contact with a dead body. The oral law added contact with a Gentile individual or residence, with land outside Israel, and with idolatry.[47]

Rituals for purification depended upon the source of uncleanness. Washing hands before eating and prayer is attested during the intertestamental period. Bathing the whole body was a frequent requirement; the remains of ritual baths, *mikvoth* (sing. *mikveh*), are common at archaeological sites in Israel.[48] While the temple stood, sacrifices and other rituals, including the sacrifice of the red heifer (Num. 19:1–10), were required.

Special Seasons

There is no need to repeat here what was said about feasts, festivals, and special seasons in our discussions of Old Testament institutions and the reestablishment of traditional institutions after the exile. However, since they were such an important part of intertestamental Jewish life, both in general and in the home, some comments are in order.

Although the observance of most of the feasts required elaborate ceremonies in the temple, most also called for special notice in the

46. S. Safrai, "Religion in Everyday Life," in *Jewish People,* ed. Safrai and Stern, 2:828.
47. Ibid., 829.
48. McRay, *Archaeology,* 48–50.

home. Fasting or feasting was associated with festivals, and special prayers were usually offered in the home. Each festival had its own requirements for the adult members of the community. Festivals also provided opportunities for both direct and indirect instruction of the young in the law of God and the traditions of the people.

During the three pilgrimage feasts all or a part of the family might travel to Jerusalem. These feasts also involved observances and rituals in the home. For example, careful preparations were made for Passover. All leaven was removed from the home. Work ceased. A special meal was eaten commemorating the deliverance from Egypt. Children were encouraged to ask questions about the feast.[49] The beginnings of the nation were thus remembered and taught.

The Feast of Tabernacles, in addition to featuring special ceremonies in Jerusalem and the temple, could be celebrated in a booth (sukkah) built near the family residence, although it might be far removed from Jerusalem. And it was primarily in the home that Purim lamps were burned. Even the most solemn occasions could have their lighter moments with ramifications for family life: "Rabban Simeon b. Gamaliel said: There were no happier days for Israel than the 15th of Ab and the Day of Atonement, for on them the daughters of Jerusalem used to go forth in white raiments . . . to dance in the vineyards. And what did they say? 'Young man, lift up thine eyes and see what thou wouldest choose for thyself.'"[50]

Education

The truth of the matter is that we know very little about education in Intertestamental Judaism. Some attempts to describe it assume that what we know of Jewish education in the early rabbinic period was true in the age of Herod's temple as well. Another assumption is that Jewish education was an adaptation of that in the Greco-Roman world. It would seem reasonable to conjecture that intertestamental Jewish education also contained features distinct from rabbinic and Greco-Roman forms, but our information is limited. Three things do seem certain: the centrality of the law in the curriculum, the duty of the home in providing education, and the involvement of community and synagogue.

Again we begin our consideration of a subject with data from Josephus. He speaks of both the importance and content of education: "Above all we pride ourselves on the education of our

49. As a part of the modern liturgy, a child asks, "Why is this night different from all others?" This occasions a recounting of the first Passover.
50. Mishnah Taanith 4:8.

children, and regard as the most essential task in life the observance of our laws and of the pious practices, based thereupon,
which we have inherited."[51] To this we may add the testimony of
Philo: "For all men guard their own customs, but this is especially
true of the Jewish nation. Holding that the laws are oracles vouch-
safed by God and having been trained in this doctrine from their
earliest years they carry the likenesses of the commandments en-
shrined in their souls."[52]

Education, then, focused upon the study of the law. It was
clearly understood that to live in accordance with the law required
knowing the law. To know the law one had to be able to read it.
Hence the basic curriculum involved reading, studying, and, we
may assume, applying the law to daily life.[53]

Depending primarily upon those rabbinic sources which have a
fair claim to represent the pre–A.D. 70 situation, we may outline
the educational process.[54] From at least the time of Ezra's reading
of the law (Neh. 8), education was a public process; study of the
law was the focus of Jewish society as a whole. It was a lifelong
commitment for all men. It began with the very young. The Mishnah requires that children be taught "therein one year or two years
before [they are of age], that they may become versed in the commandments."[55] Other sources set different ages for beginning formal studies, some as early as five years.

Fathers held a special responsibility for educating their children.
Domestic religious ceremonies like the Passover seder usually included the children and were a vehicle for teaching by word and
example. The mother's religious observance was evident as she lit
the Sabbath and other ceremonial candles.

Communities provided schools. The situation differed from one
place to another. There is evidence that during the high priesthood
of Joshua ben Gamala (Jesus son of Gamaliel, A.D. 63–65) "great

51. Josephus *Against Apion* 1.12 (60).
52. Philo *Embassy to Gaius* 31 (210).
53. Note Schürer, *History*, 2:464: "The whole purpose of education in family, school and
synagogue was to transform the Jewish people into 'disciples of the Lord.' The ordinary man
was to know, and do, what the Torah asked of him. His whole life was to conform to the precepts
and commandments of the 'Instruction' or 'Enlightenment.' Obedience to these rules, which
were firmly believed to have been laid down by God himself, was seen by Torah scholars, Pharisees and rabbis alike as the only way to put into practice the heavenly command, 'You shall be
for me a kingdom of priests and a holy nation' (Exod. 19:6)."
54. This summary is heavily dependent upon S. Safrai, "Education and the Study of the Torah," in *Jewish People*, ed. Safrai and Stern, 2:945–69. See also Schürer, *History*, 2:417–21;
James L. Crenshaw, "Education in Ancient Israel," *Journal of Biblical Literature* 104.4 (Dec.
1985): 601–15.
55. Mishnah *Yoma* 8:4.

progress was made in the establishment of a network of schools in every town."[56] Schools frequently met in the synagogue precincts; the synagogue service itself required males to be able to read and was arranged to provide instruction and continuing education. In addition, synagogue officials sometimes participated in the teaching of children.

The Talmud distinguishes between the *bet ha-sefer* (house of the book), where the child was taught to read the law, and *bet ha-talmud* (house of learning), where traditions (the oral law of the Mishnah) was the subject. Reading required learning the alphabet and proper pronunciation of the words of the sacred text. Vowels were not added to the text until about A.D. 500, so "reading could only be learned by repeating the reading of the teacher and auditive memory."[57] This meant that pronunciation had to be learned with exactness in order to assure accurate transmission of the law. At least during rabbinic times, reading began with Leviticus 1–8 and the early chapters of Genesis, probably because these were the only passages permitted to be written on small scrolls apart from the rest of the books in which they appear. Later the pupil was taught to read all of the Torah and the Prophets as well as certain liturgical texts. Instruction in reading the sacred text did not necessarily proceed to teaching the skill of writing. Although evidence suggests that many could write, that ability was not as widespread as facility in reading.

From learning reading skills and the content of the text, the student then moved to the *bet ha-talmud* and the study of oral tradition. This entailed memorization, unison reading, questions and answers, and group study. The objective was to equip the student to understand the law and to apply it to life situations.

Formal education was usually concluded at the age of twelve or thirteen. At that point many young men began learning a craft or trade. Students who showed exceptional ability and desire might continue studies with a teacher or sage. The highest level of instruction was probably available only in Jerusalem.[58] The end of formal education did not mean the end of study. Many men continued either personal or group study throughout life.

Finally, were girls and women educated in Intertestamental Judaism? The evidence is too slight and inconsistent to give a clear answer. Both intertestamental and rabbinic literature agree that the obligation to educate boys was not extended to girls. Religious duties expected of the woman in the home did, however, assume some basic knowledge

56. Safrai, "Education," 948.
57. Ibid., 950.
58. Schürer, *History*, 2:322–80, focuses attention upon the training and work of experts in the law.

which had to be communicated in some way. Apparently at least some girls did have some sort of formal education which may have even included learning to read. It is unlikely that girls attended schools. Most were probably taught in the home; some families may have provided tutors for their daughters. Attending synagogue services provided additional instruction. A few women were sufficiently educated to be recognized as Torah scholars in the rabbinic period.

Measurements and Time

Measurements

The modern reader of the New Testament seldom feels the strangeness of its world more than when confronting such a mundane matter as its system of measurements.[59] Not only are they different from modern ones, but they were subject to change. We will consider two of them. The length of a cubit, the linear measure most commonly mentioned in the Bible, cannot be precisely determined; originally it had to do with the length of the forearm. That there was a change in the standard length of a cubit is noted in 2 Chronicles 3:3 (Ezekiel 40:5; 43:13). A general approximation sets the Old Testament "cubit" at about 17.5 inches (44.5 centimeters). The "new cubit," that of the Roman Empire, including New Testament Palestine, was about 20.6 inches (52.5 centimeters).

"A Sabbath day's journey" (Acts 1:12) was not an exact measurement at all, but one of the fences around Torah. It prescribes the distance one could travel from one's place of residence without breaking the fourth commandment. According to the Talmud, a Sabbath day's journey was only about 2,000 cubits (or about 1,150 yards),[60] but it could be expanded, almost limitlessly, by using the practice of *erub* (extending limits by establishing temporary residences or amalgamating adjacent properties).

Calendar

The calendar was of immense importance in the ancient world. Since the calendar was a measurement of the regular cycle of sea-

59. For ready explanations of biblical weights and measures see *The NIV Study Bible*, ed. Kenneth Barker et al. (Grand Rapids: Zondervan, 1985), 1952; *The New Oxford Annotated Bible with the Apocryphal/Deuterocanonical Books* (NRSV), ed. Bruce M. Metzger and Roland E. Murphy (New York: Oxford University Press, 1992), 424–25 (New Testament); *Interpreter's Dictionary of the Bible*, ed. George A. Buttrick et al., 4 vols. (New York: Abingdon, 1962), 4:828–38; *New Bible Dictionary*, ed. J. D. Douglas, 2d ed. (Downers Grove, Ill.: Inter-Varsity, 1982), 1245–49; *Harper's Bible Dictionary*, ed. Paul J. Achtemeier et al. (San Francisco: Harper and Row, 1985), 1126–31; *Anchor Bible Dictionary*, ed. David Noel Freedman et al., 6 vols. (Garden City, N.Y.: Doubleday, 1992), 6:897–908.

60. Babylonian Talmud *Erubin* 51a.

sons, it was assumed to have special relation to nature and to the God (or gods) who made and controlled the natural order. We have already noted that some Jewish parties held to a particular calendar as one of their distinctives. Here we can make only a few general observations to clarify the major difference between groups of calendars and to alert the reader to this important subject.[61]

Old Testament Israel and, it seems, most first-century Jews followed some version of the lunar calendar. Lunar calendars have a built-in problem. A system in which months last 29.5 days does not easily correlate with the solar year. Without adjustments any given lunar month will wander through the year, coming now during the spring planting season, later at autumn harvest, or in summer or winter.[62] This is intolerable in a society in which religious feasts and festivals also commemorate agricultural events. Consequently, in some societies adjustments were made by adding days or even extra months when needed. Table 1 (pp. 156–57) proposes a reconstruction of the Old Testament postexilic calendar along this line. Something similar seems to have been operative in the mainstream of Intertestamental Judaism.

Other groups used solar calendars. Instruments were not available to measure the precise length of the solar year, so determinations had to be made by observation. Although some ancient calculations were close to the astronomical year, adjustments had to be made from time to time.

Hours of the Day

The ancients' calculation of time differed from that of the modern world in two ways. First, any part of a unit of time (year, month, or day) was counted as a whole. Hence the final year of a king's reign was also the first of his successor's. Similarly, the period between Jesus' being placed in the tomb on Friday evening and rising on Sunday morning was counted as three days. Second, the new day began at sunset.[63] In some cultures this was deter-

61. For detailed discussions of this immensely complicated issue see M. D. Herr, "The Calendar," in *Jewish People*, ed. Safrai and Stern, 2:834–62, and the literature he cites, 862–64; Daniel-Rops, *Daily Life*, 179–85; J. Van Goudoever, *Biblical Calendars*, 2d ed. (Leiden: E. J. Brill, 1961); James C. Vanderkam, "Calendars: Ancient Israelite and Early Jewish," in *Anchor Bible Dictionary*, 1:814–20; Roger T. Beckwith, *Calendar and Chronology, Jewish and Christian* (Leiden: E. J. Brill, 1996).

62. This situation occurs in Islamic societies. The fast when followers of the Prophet abstain from all food and drink during daylight hours is observed during the ninth month, the holy month of Ramadan. The requirements are difficult enough in cooler periods of the year. They pose special hardships during those years when Ramadan falls in summer.

63. Thus in Mark 1:32 the crowds seeking healing from Jesus gathered at sunset when the Sabbath was over.

mined by noting the moment at which a white thread could no longer be distinguished from a colored one.

Calculations of the hours of the day were divided into two: the hours of daylight and of night. The times could not be calculated exactly and varied, of course, with the seasons. Daytime was divided into twelve generally equal sections between sunrise and sundown; the first hour was the first of the daylight period, and the twelfth was the last. As a general rule of thumb, the third hour was approximately 9:00 A.M., the sixth hour noon, the ninth hour about 3:00 P.M., and the twelfth hour 6:00 P.M.[64]

The night was divided into a series of watches, a watch being the period of time a group of soldiers stood guard before being relieved. It appears that during Old Testament times the Jews used a system of three watches per night. This is the implication of the reference to "the middle watch" in Judges 7:19. During the Roman period, the New Testament Era, there were four watches. The first watch (*opse*, late) ran roughly from 6:00 to 9:00 P.M.; the second (*mesonyktion*, midnight) from 9:00 to midnight; the third (*alektorophōnia*, cock crowing) from midnight until 3:00 A.M.; and the fourth watch (*prōi*, early) from 3:00 to 6:00 A.M. All four of the night watches are mentioned in Mark 13:35.

64. Note the use of ancient time references in Matt. 20:1–9 and in the accounts of the crucifixion of Jesus.

Part 3

The Religious Thought of Intertestamental Judaism: A Background for Christian Customs and Controversies

13

Religious Thought of Intertestamental Judaism

- The Existence and Nature of God
- Worldview
- The Law and Legalistic Practices
- Particularistic, Elitist Attitudes
- Immortality and Resurrection

The term *theology*, in the sense employed by Christians, especially Protestants, is inappropriate in a discussion of Intertestamental Judaism.[1] For the Jews of that period were concerned first for right practice, orthopraxy, rather than right thought or doctrine. "Religious thought," then, is a better description of the content of the faith of Intertestamental Judaism than is any term that connotes a logically organized, coherent whole.

Intertestamental Jewish thought retained all the essential features of the Old Testament faith and most of its other parts and structures. The effort to reinstate the traditional institutions of the nation is testimony to the conscious desire to maintain continuity. Whatever additions and adaptations were made were responses to

---

1. A systematization of intertestamental Jewish thought is attempted by Joseph Bonsirven, *Palestinian Judaism in the Time of Jesus Christ,* trans. William Wolf (New York: Holt, Rinehart and Winston, 1964), but he is not always successful in keeping clear the distinction between the intertestamental period and rabbinic sources. A more modest effort, but one which deals more carefully with the sources, is F. F. Bruce, "Inter-testamental Literature," in *What Theologians Do,* ed. F. G. Healey (Grand Rapids: Eerdmans, 1970), 85–102.

challenges and circumstances different from those of the Old Testament world. As we have noted, there were a variety of responses, and this miscellany was focused upon religious thought and practice. The religious thought of the post–A.D. 70 period continued the traditions of at least one branch of the intertestamental period (the Pharisees), but it too had to respond to a changed situation. Our concern is to look at some key elements of religious thought which made Intertestamental Judaism distinct from its predecessor.

The three major pillars of Old Testament religion—monotheism, covenant, and law—retained their place of primacy. It was the way in which they were interpreted and applied to practice that constituted much of the uniqueness of Intertestamental Judaism.

The Existence and Nature of God

The *Shema,* "Hear, O Israel: the LORD is our God, the LORD alone" (Deut. 6:4), is, as Joseph Bonsirven notes, both a daily prayer and a confession of faith.[2] It is an affirmation of the Existent One, the Being whose reality need not be proved. The Old Testament emphasis on monotheism remained strong, if it in fact did not grow even stronger, in intertestamental thought. God continued to be recognized as Creator and the Being who by his providence sustains the created order. Of course, Israel's God was the covenant-making God who had chosen and redeemed her for himself.

Intertestamental Jews, except some involved in Hellenistic culture, saw no need to prove the existence of their God. Josephus, himself a Hellenistic Jew, reflected the practice of demonstrating God's existence primarily from his works rather than by argument:

> [Abraham] was thus the first boldly to declare that God, the creator of the universe, is one. . . . This he inferred from the changes to which land and sea are subject, from the course of sun and moon, and from all the celestial phenomena; for, he argued, were these bodies endowed with power, they would have provided for their own regularity, but since they lacked this last, it was manifest that even those services in which they cooperate for our greater benefit they render not in virtue of their own authority, but through the might of their commanding sovereign, to whom alone it is right to render homage and thanksgiving.[3]

How deeply faith in the centrality of the one God affected intertestamental life and thought is illustrated in the Letter of Aristeas. After questioning Jewish scholars who had come to translate their

---

2. Bonsirven, *Palestinian Judaism,* 3.
3. Josephus *Antiquities* 1.7.1 (155–56).

Scripture into Greek (the Septuagint), the Egyptian king observed, "When asked questions . . . unexpectedly they give appropriate answers, all making God the basis of their argument" (v. 200).

Of the numerous influences to which intertestamental Jews were subjected, there were at least three that had major effects on the way they thought about and acted toward God. The first was the fall of Jerusalem in 586 B.C., the captivity, and then the subsequent restoration. We have already noted the theological crisis precipitated by the overthrow of the Hebrew state and the destruction of the temple. The questions those disasters had raised about God were, of course, reassessed in view of the return from captivity and reconstruction of the Jewish state.

The precise effects that the experiences of 586 and the aftermath had on Intertestamental Judaism's corporate view of and attitude toward God are difficult to assess. Written records reflect views similar to those found in the Old Testament. Nevertheless, there must have been at least a subconscious emotional impact. The prophetic predictions of judgment were now viewed as accomplished facts. The recognition that God had allowed his people to be conquered was a sobering reality. It provided a powerful reminder that God's person, will, and requirements are not to be taken lightly. The consequences of doing so are considerable. The joy of the new exodus, the return from captivity, gave new insights into the LORD's faithfulness, mercy, and power. Intertestamental writings emphasize the tenderness of God, his fatherhood to the nation;[4] there is even a tendency to personify his lovingkindness as God himself.[5] Alongside this development was increased discussion of the concept of divine providence: rejected by the Sadducees, it was firmly held by the Essenes and Qumran sectarians, with the Pharisaic view falling somewhere between.

One concrete effect of captivity and restoration was that shift of emphasis which took study of and obedience to the law more seriously. God's revealed will and instructions were not to be trifled with. There were increased efforts to please God by careful observance of prescribed forms, ceremonies, and behavior, and to remember his roles as lawgiver and judge.

It should also be noted that the Jews who returned from living in pagan cultures had an increased abhorrence of idolatry and all

4. E.g., "And the Lord will rejoice in his children; he will be well pleased by his beloved ones forever" (Testament of Levi 18:13).

5. The Hebrew word ḥesed is usually translated "lovingkindness" or "mercy." Bonsirven says the word is "sometimes presented as a divine name" (Palestinian Judaism, 18). It actually connotes the outreaching of God's love and mercy because of both his nature and his covenant with his people.

associated with it. Although some later individuals and probably groups were attracted to various pagan religions and practices, it seems that these never again threatened to become national policy, as had been the case during the monarchy. The intertestamental heroine Judith said, "Never in our generation, nor in these present days, has there been any tribe or family or people or town of ours that worships gods made with hands, as was done in days gone by. That was why our ancestors were handed over to the sword and to pillage, so they suffered a great catastrophe before our enemies. But we know no other god but him" (Judith 8:18–20). Still, modern scholars frequently mention that there was also a greater distance between God and his people in intertestamental thought: "There is an increasing emphasis on God as transcendent and 'wholly other.'"[6] This had major effects on all aspects of intertestamental Jewish life.

The second influence to which intertestamental Jews were subjected was Hellenism's introduction of an entirely new way of thinking. This included speculative approaches in discussions about deity. Hellenistic Judaism adapted some of these approaches. Parts of the works of Philo are but one example. A more influential one is the way passages relating to God are handled in the Septuagint. The translation tended to make accommodations in the face of the sensitivities of the Greek world, for example, to the Greek view of deity. Most obvious is the softening or eliminating anthropomorphic language about God.[7]

Third was an avoidance of the word *God*. Intertestamental writers employ circumlocutions, roundabout ways of referring to him. Such phrases as "the God of heaven," "the heavens," "the power," and "the Blessed One" are common in the writings of the period. Use of the most sacred personal name was particularly shunned. Substitutes were increasingly sought for YHWH (the tetragrammaton [the four letters] = Yahweh). *Adonai* (Lord) began to replace the sacred name in public readings of Scripture. Priests mumbled or swallowed it in temple prayers and benedictions. The Aramaic targums replaced it with *Memra* (Word). The Septuagint translated it with *kyrios* (Lord), the form in which it occurs in New Testament quotations of the Old. The Talmud and other rabbinic sources indicate that by the time of the death of Simon the Just (c. 200 B.C.) the divine name (YHWH) was no longer pronounced, except by the

---

6. Bruce, "Inter-testamental Literature," 88–89.

7. Examples are numerous: the Masoretic text of Gen. 5:22, 24 (NRSV) reads, "Enoch walked with God"; the Septuagint, "Enoch was well-pleasing to God"; the Hebrew of Judg. 18:6, "Go in peace. The mission you are on is under the eye of the LORD"; the Septuagint, "Go in peace; your way in which you go is before the Lord."

high priest on Yom Kippur. This was almost certainly the culmination of a long process during which use of the name had become progressively restricted.

There were probably two concerns behind this development. First, the fences around the third commandment restricted use of the name—a protection against misuse of it was to avoid all use of it. Second, increased contact with Hellenism and other forms of paganism probably made the use of the personal name of God seem too materialistic, too much like dragging him to the level of the supposed deities of other religions. Whatever the reason, the result was to increase mentally the distance between Israel and her God. For, as a general rule, calling someone only by a generic term or title tends toward a subconscious depersonalization of that individual.

Worldview

A corollary to the Hebrew belief in the existence of God is his presence and activity within history and in the material world as well as beyond it. From this comes a general understanding of how God relates to the universe and how it should operate. Here we have what is called a worldview, a way of looking at and explaining reality, how and why things happen. Although the biblical writers assume a distinct worldview, it is nowhere stated explicitly. Yet it controls their religious thought and writing. From what the writers imply, we can reconstruct the general contours of a four-phase worldview.

Phase I: Creation. The world came into being by the will, action, and power of God. Biblical writers focus on the fact, not on the method of creation, save to record that God spoke and it was done. This means that for the biblical writer the universe is not eternal; it is separate (distinct) from God but not independent of him.

The Bible also affirms that God created the world "good." We do not know the full implications of this word. Certainly it means that the universe was made in a morally perfect condition, for a worthwhile purpose, and with inherent harmony and orderliness (according to a plan). The created order was made to function under the control of God, its king. God, the writers assume, continues to be intimately involved in directing the universe he has made. Hence, the notion of God's kingdom, his sovereign control over all things, is an inseparable part of the biblical understanding of creation.

Phase II: The Fall. Human beings rebelled against God's rule by disobeying his command; this spiritual treason is called sin. Both humanity and God were affected; God's moral nature was offended, human nature and the human status were changed. In some manner not explained by the biblical writers, human sin opened the way for an invasion and takeover of the world by an evil power that is hostile to God and sometimes called the kingdom of Satan or evil.

Sin resulted in a break in all relationships. Because of it human beings are separated and alienated from God, each other, society, and even themselves. The universe became apparently evil, purposeless, and disharmonious.[8] The moral structure of human beings was changed: a person not only sins, that is, commits sinful acts, but also *is* a sinner, that is, has a sinful nature or being. The results and consequences of sin are far-reaching. Humans live in a universe that has become morally polluted, and they share that pollution. Humanity is both guilty before God and liable to punishment. The ultimate punishment is "death," a term with moral, spiritual, and eternal as well as physical and temporal implications. Sin, the writers of the Bible assume, renders humankind helpless to alter their situation and condition; they are unable to regain the position and nature that they lost, or even to do anything to contribute to their own restoration or salvation.

Phase III: Regeneration (Reconciliation, Redemption, or Restoration). God has taken action to reclaim and restore his rebellious and spoiled creation, to reverse the present conditions brought about by sin. This period, which is the chief concern of the biblical writers, corresponds approximately with human history. In his redemptive, restorative work God is intimately involved in doing what human helplessness cannot; he is making salvation available. It is important to note that the biblical view assumes that God has both taken the initiative and done what was necessary to effect reconciliation.

The worldview of the Hebrews, then, includes the conviction that God's activities are not restricted to the spiritual sphere, but are present here on this earth as well. The phase of restoration entails a series of sometimes apparently unrelated events and themes that actually constitute a drama that is being played out both in and beyond history. The biblical writers are also convinced that God is working within a special history within world history. This idea is evident in the prophecy of Micah; he tells Israel to remember the events of Old Testament history "that you may know the saving acts of the LORD" (Mic. 6:5b; see also Exod. 33:13; 34:10; 1 Sam. 12:6–

---

8. The word *apparently* is crucial here. Rom. 8:20 insists that the world *became* "futile," with all that that entails. Hence the present sad state of the universe is a result of sin, not a part of its inherent nature.

7). He has in mind those earthly events through which God acts to reveal himself and his will, provide salvation, call persons to himself, and live in relationship with them. Contemporary scholars have termed this history within history "salvation history," the "history of salvation," "saving history," "redemptive history," and the like (all are attempts to capture the meaning of the German *Heilsgeschichte*).

The intertestamental worldview also held the belief that there are two distinct ages within the period of redemption.[9] While the intertestamental documents present numerous views of this dichotomy, one of the clearest statements is that of 2 Esdras 6:6–7, where God is depicted as saying, "The end shall come through me and not through another." Ezra then responds, "What will be the dividing of the times? Or when will be the end of the first age and the beginning of the age that follows?"[10] It is assumed that these ages will occur within the period of redemption (see figure 6).

The former age, which began after the fall, was a time of preparation for and prediction of something expected in the future. Dur-

9. Oscar Cullmann, *Christ and Time: The Primitive Christian Conception of Time and History*, rev. ed. (Philadelphia: Westminster, 1964), 37–60, argues that the Hebraic world seems to view time as linear, as progressing from a beginning to an end point. It assumes that God is at work to bring time to its appointed purpose and conclusion. Thus, salvation involves deliverance both in time and in the world. This, he says, is in contrast to the understanding held by the Greek world, which seems to have viewed time as cyclical; consequently, salvation involved deliverance out of time and the world.

Both Cullmann's view of time and his assumption that salvation takes place in the material world have been hotly debated; see James Barr, *Biblical Words for Time* (Naperville, Ill.: Allenson, 1962); and Rudolf Bultmann, "The New Testament and Mythology," in *The New Testament and Mythology and Other Basic Writings*, trans. Schubert M. Ogden (Philadelphia: Fortress, 1984), 1–43. See also Bultmann's "History of Salvation and History," in *Existence and Faith*, trans. Schubert M. Ogden (New York: Meridian, 1960), 226–40.

10. See also 7:3–44, 113; 8:1. We previously noted that this concept of two ages appears in the thought of the writers of the Dead Sea Scrolls (p. 226). Other examples include 1 Enoch 16:1, "From the days of the slaughter and destruction, and the death of the giants and the spiritual beings of the spirit, and the flesh, from which they have proceeded forth, which will corrupt without incurring judgment, they will corrupt until the day of the great conclusion, until the great age is consummated, until everything is concluded (upon) the Watchers and the wicked ones" (note also the reference to "the world that is to become" in 71:15); 2 Baruch 15:7, "With regard to the righteous ones, those whom you said the world has come on their account, yes, also that which is coming is on their account" (see also 14:13–19); Mishnah *Aboth* 4:1, "Happy shalt thou be—in this world; and it shall be well with thee—in the world to come" (see also 6:4, 7). See the discussion in Gustaf H. Dalman, *The Words of Jesus* (Edinburgh: T. and T. Clark, 1902), 147–56.

The concept of two ages is often assumed in the New Testament; e.g., Matt. 12:32; Mark 1:14–15; 10:30; Rom. 8:18. In the Epistle to the Hebrews note the tension between that which is here now (in contrast to the Old Testament)—1:2; 3:18–4:11; 6:4–5; 8:10; 9:11, 24–26; 11:39–40—and that which is coming, that is, is still in the future for the writer—2:8; 9:27–28; 10:12–13, 25.

ing this age God's work was primarily through indirect means and symbols. His saving activity focused upon the nation Israel and took place mainly within her history.

The former age was expected to come to an end with a special direct intervention by God within history. Some thought the passage from one age to another would come as God himself entered history; others expected the appearance of God's agent (one or more messianic figures) through whom he would accomplish his divine will. In any case this decisive moment, this crisis point, would result in a radical change in salvation history and the way God carries on his redeeming activities.

The latter age was looked to as the final period and the culmination of God's struggle against hostile forces. God would defeat Satan and the power of evil; he would reassert his right to rule (his sovereignty) over his universe. Through these actions salvation would be made available as God dealt directly and conclusively with the fact and consequences of sin. Thus God would express love, mercy, and forgiveness as well as vindicate his person and satisfy his divine justice. (For more on the latter age see ch. 14.)

Phase IV: Consummation. The age to come is the final period of the biblical worldview. The conditions caused by the fall will be completely reversed. In the consummation, fellowship and harmony will be restored between those elements alienated by the fall. The goal of God's saving work, forgiveness and reconciliation, will indeed be achieved. The original and ultimate goal of history will be realized as the rule (kingdom) of God is reestablished in its fullest and most far-reaching form.

Figure 6
The Phases of World History

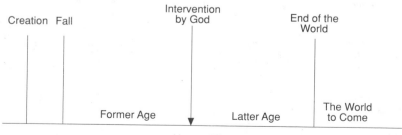

The Law and Legalistic Practices

At the heart of Judaism is the conviction that Israel is the people of God by election. This was expressed through God's covenant with Abraham in which he made his loving, free choice of Israel. The Abrahamic covenant ("I will . . . be God to you and to your offspring"—Gen. 17:7) was reaffirmed through Moses at the time of the exodus[11] and then echoed throughout the Old Testament. Torah is inseparably bound to this covenant. Through the requirements of the law Israel was constantly reminded of her inclusion in the covenant. By keeping the law Israel accepted God's gracious offer made in the covenant.

We have already seen that law occupied a significant place in the life and experience of Intertestamental Judaism. But what exactly was the relation between law and religion? What was the relation between law and salvation—a favorable standing before God? Again we must beware of assuming there was a single view. But perhaps it is fair to assume there was a general, although possibly vague, idea held by the populace at large.

At this point we must ask about Intertestamental Judaism's understanding of salvation. George Foot Moore's comment about Rabbinic Judaism's understanding is in general applicable to the earlier period as well: "'A lot in the World to Come,' which is the nearest approximation in rabbinical Judaism to the Pauline and Christian idea of salvation, or eternal life, is ultimately assured to every Israelite on the ground of the original election of the people by the free grace of God, prompted not by its merits, collective or individual, but solely by God's love, a love that began with the Fathers. . . . 'A lot in the World to Come' is not wages earned by works, but is bestowed by God in pure goodness upon the members of his chosen people."[12] This does not mean that an individual could not remove himself from this corporate salvation; indeed, the Old Testament and succeeding thought assumed that some individuals did. Nevertheless, salvation was, as Moore says, believed to be the possession of all true Israelites. It involved this life as well as the hereafter.

Moore's statement emphasizing grace as the heart of Judaism is not the traditional understanding of intertestamental thought. On the contrary, it is usually supposed that both Intertestamental and

11. Exod. 20:2: "I am the LORD your God, who brought you out of the land of Egypt, out of the house of slavery." Note both God's identification of himself with Israel and his provision of redemption.

12. George Foot Moore, *Judaism in the First Centuries of the Christian Era*, 3 vols. (Cambridge, Mass.: Harvard University Press, 1927–30), 2:94–95; see also idem, "Christian Writers on Judaism," *Harvard Theological Review* 14.3 (July 1921): 199–254.

Rabbinic Judaism were legalistic in nature, that they sought to earn or merit salvation by meticulous observance of the law. In the wake of a number of earlier writers on Judaism who, as illustrated by Moore, challenged this traditional assessment, E. P. Sanders has led a group of late-twentieth-century scholars who propose a new perspective on Paul which is actually a new perspective on Intertestamental Judaism as well.[13]

Sanders argues that it is wrong to assume a legalistic framework for Judaism. Rather, he argues, "the pattern [of the religion of Judaism] is based on election and atonement for transgressions, it being understood that God gave commandments in connection with the election and that obedience to them, or atonement and repentance for transgression, was expected as the condition for remaining in the covenant community. The best title for this sort of religion is 'covenant nomism,'. . . the covenant by God's grace and Torah obedience as man's proper response within the covenant."[14] Or, to put it another way, Judaism is a religion based on God's grace expressed through the covenant; the law "has to do with 'staying in' rather than 'getting in.'"[15]

Sanders supports his case by a careful, magisterial study of the targums, tannaitic literature, the Dead Sea Scrolls, the Apocrypha, and Pseudepigrapha. An adequate response to him would entail an equally thorough investigation and analysis of these sources. There are, however, some general reasons to question his conclusion. First, the conglomerate nature of Intertestamental Judaism causes us to raise our eyebrows at any claim that one view encompassed all. There was no normative position in this period. Second, as Moore points out, the rabbinic writings give evidence of a merit motive as well as of higher motives for law keeping. There was also belief in laying up treasure for the future by present good deeds: "Judaism had no hesitation about recognizing the merit of good works or in exhorting men to acquire it and to accumulate a store of merit laid up for the hereafter."[16] These evidences that fear of punishment and hope of reward motivated law keeping did not emerge in the post–A.D. 70 period out of nothing. They had earlier

13. E. P. Sanders, *Paul and Palestinian Judaism* (Philadelphia: Fortress, 1977); idem, *Paul, the Law, and the Jewish People* (Philadelphia: Fortress, 1983). For an excellent survey and bibliography of this movement see Donald A. Hagner, "Paul and Judaism—The Jewish Matrix of Early Christianity: Issues in the Current Debate," *Bulletin for Biblical Research* 3 (1993): 111–30.

14. Sanders, *Palestinian Judaism*, 236, 420.

15. Hagner, "Paul and Judaism," 118.

16. Moore, *Judaism*, 2:90. See also pp. 89–111 and Emil Schürer, *The History of the Jewish People in the Age of Jesus Christ*, ed. Geza Vermes et al., 3 vols. (Edinburgh: T. and T. Clark, 1973–87), 2:464–67.

roots.[17] Third, there may well have been a difference between the theory and practice of some groups, as expressed in their written statements and the convictions which actually informed their lifestyle. The Qumran writings, for an example, have a positive commitment to covenantal grace. Yet the community's daily manner of life and attitude toward those outside their group leave open the possibility that theirs was in fact a religion which sought salvation by human efforts. Fourth, this kind of legalistic thought is found in some intertestamental writings, 2 Esdras, 2 Baruch, and probably "Some of the Precepts of Torah" (4QMMT) being the clearest examples.[18]

Finally, those who would deny the presence of a legalistic view of religion in at least some intertestamental Jewish quarters tend to discount the one source which has the best claim to reflect the views of the average Jews, the New Testament. We immediately think of Paul and his constant fight against the concept of salvation earned by keeping the law. The proponents of the new perspective on Paul argue that, recognizing Judaism as a religion of grace, he did not condemn the law as such, but the barrier the law had erected between Jewish and Gentile believers and all attempts to impose it upon Gentile Christians. Yet, we must point out, Paul himself says that Israel "did not strive for [righteousness] on the basis of faith, but as if it were based on works" (Rom. 9:32). He also insists that we are not justified "by doing the works of the law, because no one will be justified by the works of the law" (Gal. 2:16). Evidences of such sentiments in Paul could be multiplied. Obviously he was convinced that some Jews were seeking justification through works.

There is also evidence in the Gospels that at least some in Israel held to a "wage-price" theory of righteousness, the view that eternal life is granted on the basis of faithfulness in keeping the law. This is an issue which Jesus, no less than Paul, had to face. Note the question of the young ruler in Mark 10:17, "Good Teacher, what must I do to inherit eternal life?" Similarly, when Jesus spoke of working for "the food that endures for eternal life," the crowd asked, "What must we do to perform the works of God?" (John

17. E.g., Tobit 4:8–11: "Give according to the little you have. So you will be laying up a good treasure for yourself against the day of necessity. For almsgiving delivers from death. . . . It is an excellent offering in the presence of the Most High"; and Testament of Levi 13:5: "Therefore, my sons, do righteousness on earth in order that you might find it in heaven."

18. Even Sanders, *Palestinian Judaism*, 409–18, seems to recognize this. The second column of 4QMMT reads in part: ". . . You may rejoice at the end of time, finding that some of our practices are correct. And this will be counted as a virtuous deed of yours, since you will be doing what is righteous and good in His eyes, for your own welfare and for the welfare of Israel."

6:27–28). In the parable of the prodigal son the older brother, who may represent the Pharisaic way of looking at things, expects acceptance on the grounds that "all these years I have been working like a slave for you, and I have never disobeyed your command" (Luke 15:29). And the parable of the publican and the Pharisee was directed toward those "who trusted in themselves that they were righteous and regarded others with contempt" (Luke 18:9). These examples are evidence of at least a legalistic ethos. Such is probably inevitable in any religion whose primary concern is orthopraxy. Nevertheless, it seems likely that even more is involved here.

It is beyond question that in its theoretical formative statement in the Old Testament the Hebrew religion was essentially one of grace, and that Torah keeping was intended as the response to God's gracious offer through the covenant. This understanding was certainly a part of intertestamental Jewish religious thought.[19] But it is also true that Intertestamental Judaism was characterized by an increasing focus upon doing the law, and that reading, learning, and discussing it were becoming ever larger parts of the religious duties of average Jews. In such a situation it became difficult to keep a proper perspective on the relationship between God's grace in the covenant and observance of the law. The relationship between the two could easily be inverted and law looked upon as prior, the means of obtaining as well as maintaining covenant grace. In all likelihood this is precisely the situation Paul addresses in Galatians 3:17: "The law, which came four hundred thirty years later, does not annul a covenant previously ratified by God, so as to nullify the promise."

When we take cognizance of both the religious views which the New Testament writers took pains to oppose and various statements in intertestamental and rabbinic writings, we see a picture very different from that proposed by Sanders. An additional consideration is the probable difference between the beliefs of the common people on the one hand, and those of the theologians, rabbis, and scribes on the other, which are more likely to be reflected in the surviving sources. In short, although in the Old Testament and in the ideal of Intertestamental Judaism the law stands as the response to covenant grace, law keeping became the essence of Hebrew religion for many, especially the average Jews. A mis-

19. Note the statement in Psalms of Solomon 9:8–11: "And now, you are God and we are the people whom you have loved; look and be compassionate, O God of Israel, for we are yours, and do not take away your mercy from us, lest they set upon us. For you chose the descendants of Abraham above all the nations, and you put your name upon us, Lord, and it will not cease forever. You made a covenant with our ancestors concerning us, and we hope in you when we turn our souls toward you. May the mercy of the Lord be upon the house of Israel forevermore."

guided zeal led some to trust in external observances alone for salvation. Others probably looked to such practices as the means of acquiring merit without a clear understanding of its purpose.[20] As the history of Christianity eloquently attests, Judaism would not be the only religion in which the relation between law and grace was misunderstood by a substantial portion of the laity and some of the leaders.[21]

Particularistic, Elitist Attitudes

Growing attitudes of particularism, exclusivism, and superiority were one of the shifts of emphasis we found among the readjustments during the intertestamental period (pp. 124–26). Here we need point out only that there was but a small step from the concept of Israel as the LORD's chosen, his special treasure (Gen. 12:1–3; Exod. 19:5; Deut. 7:6; 14:2), to the notion that Israel was his exclusive concern. This feature of intertestamental religious thought was more characteristic of Semitic than Hellenistic Judaism. For those committed to it, either consciously or otherwise, the result was an increasing separation and isolation from other groups, notions of superiority, and zeal to protect Jewish privilege.

Among the more obvious consequences was the attitude toward Gentiles. Israel's experience with Gentiles throughout this period certainly heightened negative feelings toward foreigners. Three general observations are pertinent here: (1) An elitist, particularistic attitude was a significant part of the religious thought of some intertestamental groups; religion and nationalism were usually united. (2) Each Jewish group had its own unique stance toward Gentiles and Jewish relations with them. In some cases, the attitude depended on the particular class of Gentiles that was in view. (3) Especially in the land of Israel, these matters could become vehemently emotional issues, leading even to violence (see ch. 18 for more detail).

20. It is gratifying to find essentially the same reconstruction proposed more eloquently by my respected friend Don Hagner, "Paul and Judaism," 117:

"In the post-exilic period, beginning with the proto-typical scribe Ezra, there was understandably a turning to the law with a new intensity of commitment. In this new development, which constitutes the beginning of Judaism, it is hardly surprising that the law assumed a central importance. Judaism is of course in continuity with the OT and grace was not necessarily occluded by the heightened emphasis on the law. But that it was overshadowed by the emphasis of the law seems probable to me.

"It is a good question to what extent the rabbis or proto-rabbis of the first century assumed and articulated the grace that is foundational to the religion of their OT forebears."

21. The call to accept grace, which requires acknowledging that the human is helpless to contribute to salvation, goes against the grain of the "can do" outlook of many, particularly in the Western world. It is a humbling experience to have to accept grace.

Immortality and Resurrection

Once again we turn to the precise meaning of "salvation" in Intertestamental Judaism. The term could have reference to either a this-worldly or an other-worldly framework. It often centered on the hope for a racial and national deliverance from oppression by enemies. This occasionally combined with a hope for increased religious fervor, as is seen in the prayer of Zechariah, the father of John the Baptist (Luke 1:73–75). Salvation might also mean deliverance from danger, sickness, or death.

The other-worldly, futuristic side of salvation was the anticipation of acceptance into the presence of God. A common phrase here was, as Moore noted, "a lot in the World to Come." The Testament of Benjamin 10:6–9 looks for that time when "we shall prostrate ourselves before the heavenly king." Vindication, rewards for the good, and punishments for evil were parts of the expectation of salvation. Of particular interest was the inclusion of the righteous in the kingdom of God. While "kingdom" carried the connotation of the reign of God which is present now, it also pointed to his dominion beyond history. Many expected that, at least in this latter phase, the nation Israel would play a prominent role and would receive honor and glory as the people of the King. In the intertestamental period, then, many understood salvation to include immortality and resurrection.

The concept of immortality is present in the Old Testament, but there is no Hebrew word for it. For example, Proverbs 12:28 reads, "In the way of righteousness is life, and in its pathway there is no death" (NASB); the phrase "no death" ('al-māwet) means "immortality" (and is so translated in the NIV). Deuteronomy similarly enjoins righteousness, so "that you may live long in the land" (Deut. 5:33; 11:9; 30:20; 32:47). The term *Sheol,* which occurs sixty-five times throughout the Old Testament, refers to an obscure, shadowy, gloomy place of existence and forgetfulness after death. However, some writers express hope for deliverance from Sheol (Ps. 16:10; 49:15; 86:13).[22] Job 10:20–22 anticipates only a Sheol-like state after death, but 19:25–26 seems to look for something more. While Isaiah's prophecy may end with a vague expectation of continued existence for good and evil (Isa. 66:22–24; cf. Ps. 23:6), there are much clearer expressions in Isaiah 26:19 ("Your dead shall live, their corpses shall rise. O dwellers in the dust, awake and sing for joy! . . . The earth will give birth to those long dead") and Daniel 12:2 ("Many of those who sleep in the dust of the earth

---

22. See J. A. Balchin, "Life after Death in the Psalms," *Theological Students Fellowship Bulletin* 29 (Spring 1961): 1–4.

shall awake, some to everlasting life, and some to shame and everlasting contempt").[23]

Within Intertestamental Judaism the situation is quite different. Numerous pseudepigraphal texts directly state or imply belief in immortality or resurrection from the dead.[24] Both Josephus and the New Testament attest that the Pharisees believed in resurrection, and that it was one of the points of contention between them and the Sadducees. Josephus seems to imply that the Pharisees believed both in immortality and in bodily resurrection.[25] He himself in his speech before his troops at Jotapata espouses a belief in the afterlife.[26] He also records that, although the desire for liberty and honorable death were stronger, an expectation of immortality was part of Eleazar's appeal urging his comrades at Masada to commit suicide rather than fall into the hands of the Romans.[27]

Intertestamental Judaism had a number of diverse views regarding what the afterlife actually entailed:[28] (1) posterity's remembrance of a good person's virtues;[29] (2) the survival of the soul, especially of the souls of the righteous, which are in the hands of God so that no evil may befall them;[30] (3) the resurrection of the body one possessed while on earth (any members mutilated by martyrdom will be restored);[31] (4) the supremacy of right reason

23. Note also that Jesus quotes Exod. 3:6 in support of a continuing existence after death (Matt. 22:31–32; Mark 12:26–27; Luke 20:37–38).

24. E.g., 1 Enoch 51:1–2, "In those days, Sheol will return all the deposits which she had received and hell will give back all that which it owes. And he shall choose the righteous and the holy ones from among (the risen dead), for the day when they shall be selected and saved has arrived"; Psalms of Solomon 3:12, "Those who fear the Lord shall rise up to eternal life, and their life shall be in the Lord's light, and it shall never end"; Psalms of Solomon 14:1–3, "The Lord is faithful . . . to those who live in the righteousness of his commandments, in the Law, which he has commanded for our life. The Lord's devout shall live by it forever"; 2 Esdras 7:32, "The earth shall give up those who are asleep in it, and the dust those who rest there in silence; and the chambers shall give up the souls that have been committed to them"; Testament of Judah 25:4, "And those who died in sorrow shall be raised in joy; and those who died . . . on account of the Lord shall be wakened to life"; Testament of Benjamin 10:6–9, "And then you will see Enoch and Seth and Abraham and Isaac and Jacob being raised up at the right hand in great joy. Then shall we also be raised, each of us over our tribe, and we shall prostrate ourselves before the heavenly king. Then all shall be changed, some destined for glory, others for dishonor, for the Lord first judges Israel for the wrong she has committed and then he shall do the same for all nations"; in addition, 2 Baruch 50:1–51:6 records a detailed discourse on the resurrection of the body.

25. Josephus *Antiquities* 18.1.3 (14); *Jewish War* 2.8.14 (163).

26. Josephus *Jewish War* 3.8.5 (374).

27. Josephus *Jewish War* 7.8.6 (323–88).

28. The following is a summary of F. F. Bruce, "Paul on Immortality," *Scottish Journal of Theology* 24.4 (Nov. 1971): 458–61; see also idem, "Inter-testamental Literature," 97–98.

29. Sirach 44–50.

30. Wisdom of Solomon 3:1–9.

31. 2 Maccabees 7:10–11.

over physical pain and death (to use the language of Stoicism);[32] (5) the fire of Gehenna not merely to punish the ungodly, but also to purge them so they might eventually enter paradise (this view seems to have been popular in first-century Israel);[33] (6) preservation of the souls of the dead in storehouses or treasuries between death and resurrection;[34] and (7) eternal life for the righteous and annihilation for the wicked.[35] Note that only views (3) and (5) require some sort of bodily resurrection. Not only a resurrection but an unchanged body is expected by 2 Baruch 50:2–3: "The earth will surely give back the dead at that time; it receives them now in order to keep them, not changing anything in their form. But as it has received them so it will give them back. And as I have delivered them to it so it will raise them. For then it will be necessary to show those who live that the dead are living again, and that those who went away have come back." Other descriptions emphasize that the resurrected body of the righteous will be radiant and glorified in the future kingdom.[36]

There were probably several reasons for Intertestamental Judaism's rising consciousness of and interest in the afterlife. Most commonly mentioned is that in times of persecution, especially from the persecution under Antiochus Epiphanes and onward, a long life could not be expected as a reward for righteousness; the pious might well experience an early and violent martyrdom. Under such circumstances none wanted to contemplate gloomy existence in a vague Sheol; therefore, the hope of resurrection came more sharply into focus. The clearest evidence is found in 2 Maccabees 7, where seven martyr-brothers and their mother steadfastly affirm belief in the resurrection (vv. 9, 11, 14, 23, 29, 36). Later, Judas Maccabeus took a collection for a sin offering for dead soldiers on whose bodies

32. 4 Maccabees 5:14–38.

33. Babylonian Talmud *Rosh ha-Shanah* 16b.

34. 2 Esdras 7:32, 75–101; 2 Baruch 21:23; 30:2.

35. The Qumran sect's Psalm Scroll (1QH 11), "Thou [art] . . . directing my steps into the paths of righteousness that I may walk before Thee in the land [of the living], into paths of glory and [infinite] peace which shall [never] end," and Manual of Discipline (1QS 4), "all who walk in this spirit . . . [shall have] everlasting blessing and eternal joy in life without end, a crown of glory and a garment of majesty in unending light." See *The Dead Sea Scrolls in English*, trans. Geza Vermes, 3d ed. (New York: Viking Penguin, 1990), 55–56; Millar Burrows, *Burrows on the Dead Sea Scrolls* (Grand Rapids: Baker, 1978), part 2, 344–47; George W. E. Nickelsburg, *Resurrection, Immortality, and Eternal Life in Intertestamental Judaism* (Cambridge, Mass.: Harvard University Press, 1972), 144–59, 165–67.

36. E.g., Psalms of Solomon 3:12, "Those who fear the Lord shall rise up to eternal life, and their life shall be in the Lord's light, and it shall never end"; and 14:3–5, "The Lord's devout shall live by [the Law] forever; the Lord's paradise, the trees of life, are his devout ones. Their planting is firmly rooted forever; they shall not be uprooted as long as the heavens shall last, for Israel is the portion and inheritance of God." See also 2 Esdras 7:97.

pagan fetishes had been found. He did so "taking account of the resurrection. For if he were not expecting that those who had fallen would rise again, it would have been superfluous and foolish to pray for the dead" (2 Macc. 12:43–44).

But the reason for the development of beliefs about life after death was more complicated than simply a reaction to persecution of Jews by outsiders. A variety of situations prompted apocalyptic writers to focus on the afterlife.[37] In *Resurrection, Immortality, and Eternal Life in Intertestamental Judaism* George Nickelsburg carefully studies relevant texts and concludes that beliefs about the afterlife are primarily conveyed in three frameworks: "the story of the Righteous Man," "the judgment scene," and "two-ways theology." Within these frameworks prominent themes such as vindication of the just and punishment for the unjust provide assurance for the righteous and promote moral behavior.

By the time of the New Testament, belief in immortality and some form of resurrection seems to have been accepted by most Jewish groups (except the Sadducees) and the average Jews. It was generally believed that all Israelites would in some way participate in the kingdom of God. Thus the second petition of the daily prayer (the Eighteen Benedictions) ends, "Blessed are you, O Lord, who bring the dead to life." Clearly, immortality and resurrection were among the components of intertestamental religious thought.

37. D. S. Russell, *The Method and Message of Jewish Apocalyptic* (Philadelphia: Westminster, 1964), 357–90.

14

The Final Age

The following chapters deal with five key topics of intertestamental Jewish religious thought: the final age, the kingdom of God, the messianic hope, covenant and law in the final age, and Gentiles. We will see that behind these and all other aspects of intertestamental Jewish thought lie the assumptions of the worldview we described in the previous chapter. These topics are concerned with the final acts of the drama of God's dealing with his creation.

Our chapter "The Final Age" looks more carefully at what Intertestamental Judaism believed to be the last phase of both human and salvation history. It was expected that this age would arrive with the coming of the kingdom of God (ch. 15) or the Messiah (ch. 16). In addition, we must consider the effect that the arrival of the final age was expected to have upon covenant and law (ch. 17), which, with monotheism, were the pillars of Judaism. Our final chapter seeks to bring together the main elements of intertestamental Jewish attitudes toward non-Jews; included are expectations about the fate of the Gentiles in the final age and the consummation.

The five topics were chosen because they are parts of Jewish eschatology that are of unique importance to the New Testament reader. Acceptance of Jesus as the Messiah meant that the New Testament writers believed the religious situation to be different from the way their contemporaries saw it. The Christ event altered the way the early Jewish Christians looked at virtually every part of their Jewish heritage. They believed the eschatological age had begun. Not surprisingly, then, the five topics discussed in the remainder of this book encompass most of the issues the early Christians had to face.

A Word on Eschatology

In our introduction we sought to clarify the word *eschatology*. There we noted that it may have meanings other than beliefs regarding the events expected at the return of Christ, the end of history and of the world. "Eschatology" may involve "a recurring pattern in which divine judgment and redemption interact until this pattern attains its definitive manifestation. Eschatology may therefore denote the consummation of God's purpose whether it coincides with the end of the world (or of history) or not, whether the consummation is totally final or marks a stage in the unfolding pattern of his purpose."[1] When we use the term, we will have reference to the final age and beyond, to the end of God's work of redemption. Hence the phrase "intertestamental Jewish eschatology" will refer to what was believed about such topics as the final age, the consummation, and eternity; "eschatological age" will refer to the final age or the consummation. "Eschatological figure" denotes someone who appears in the eschatological age and has a specific function in it.

It is particularly difficult to give an accurate comprehensive view of intertestamental Jewish eschatology. The ancient sources do not offer systematic descriptions of the writers' views, which took a variety of forms. For example, the nationalistic model of eschatology centered on the deliverance and glorification of the nation. Other models focused on religious, sociological, economic, apocalyptic, or legalistic factors that were expected to be radically affected in the final age.

The writers tend to discuss individual events or only limited parts of the final drama. Thus the chronological sequence between events is frequently not clear, and different writings present different chronological arrangements. Some of the ancient books combine material from several writers, dates, and locations. Consequently, the

---

1. F. F. Bruce, "Eschatology," in *Evangelical Dictionary of Theology*, ed. Walter A. Elwell (Grand Rapids: Baker, 1984), 362.

same book may reflect differing, even contradictory, eschatological perspectives. Such is the case in 1 Enoch.

Some contemporary writers who seek to describe the eschatological views of the time of Jesus consciously set forth the thought of Rabbinic Judaism.[2] As a result, some distinctive rabbinic thoughts or emphases may be mistaken for accurate portrayals of the pre–A.D. 70 situation.[3] Yet, under proper constraints, rabbinic material merits a place in a study of Intertestamental Judaism. Modern studies which seek a distinctively intertestamental Jewish eschatology have been able to identify a common core, major patterns, and some details. These are helpful insights. However, they must not be allowed to obscure the variety within the intertestamental views of the final age.

It seems that as the intertestamental period moved toward its close, its eschatological thought may have begun to assume a bit more structure and agreement. The eschatology of 2 Baruch, 2 Esdras, and possibly the Dead Sea Scrolls, all of which come from just before or just after the end of the period, seems to indicate as much. Additional supporting evidence is the views of the subsequent historical period, Rabbinic Judaism, which are more clearly defined. Emil Schürer provides a good overview of the major topics included in intertestamental eschatology:

1. The final ordeal and confusion
2. Elijah as precursor
3. The coming of the Messiah
4. The last assault of the hostile powers
5. Destruction of hostile powers
6. The renewal of Jerusalem
7. The gathering of the dispersed
8. The kingdom of glory in the Holy Land
9. The renewal of the world
10. A general resurrection
11. The last judgment, eternal bliss, and damnation[4]

2. E.g., George Foot Moore, *Judaism in the First Centuries of the Christian Era,* 3 vols. (Cambridge, Mass.: Harvard University Press, 1927–30), 2:279–395; Joseph Klausner, *The Messianic Idea in Israel,* trans. W. F. Stinespring (New York: Macmillan, 1955), 388–517. Note that the first and second parts of Klausner's work deal with the biblical material and that of the Apocrypha and Pseudepigrapha separately.

3. This occasionally occurs, I fear, in Joseph Bonsirven, *Palestinian Judaism in the Time of Jesus Christ,* trans. William Wolf (New York: Holt, Rinehart and Winston, 1964), 163–251. Yet his work remains a helpful starting point for our investigation.

4. Emil Schürer, *History of the Jewish People in the Age of Jesus Christ,* ed. Geza Vermes et al., 3 vols. (Edinburgh: T. and T. Clark, 1973–87), 2:514–47.

What follows utilizes material from modern as well as ancient writers.[5] Only a general survey, more or less dependent upon the pattern which seems to be behind 2 Baruch and 2 Esdras, is offered here. A more accurate procedure, but with fragmented results, would have been to describe the eschatology of each individual writing.[6] No attempt has been made to limit our sources to a narrow time frame or particular groups. Consequently, exceptions to the general pattern will meet us at almost every point of this overview. Yet a composite sketch can assist the modern reader to grasp the drift of the eschatological thought of the several groups within mainstream Intertestamental Judaism.

The Final Age: A General Overview

In the preceding chapter we introduced the general concept of two ages within human history. Our concern here is to look in more detail at the second of these two ages. This second age was expected to arrive by means of some form of divine intervention as God would break into human history in a unique way. He would thus introduce a new phase in his dealings with humankind and bring about radical changes in the manner in which he works upon earth.

The expectation of a future final age is more often assumed than stated explicitly.[7] At times it is unclear whether a writer distinguished between the coming age as a period of human history and as eternal life. The phrase "the world to come" could be taken either way or possibly reflects some confusion of the matter within the author's mind.[8]

5. The moderns include Schürer, *History*; D. S. Russell, *The Method and Message of Jewish Apocalyptic* (Philadelphia: Westminster, 1964), 205–390; Sigmund O. P. Mowinckel, *He That Cometh*, trans. G. W. Anderson (New York: Abingdon, 1956), 261–450; Klausner, *Messianic Idea*; and Bonsirven, *Palestinian Judaism*, 172–225.

6. See Schürer, *History*, 2:497–513; Klausner, *Messianic Idea*, 246–386.

7. Gustaf H. Dalman, *The Words of Jesus* (Edinburgh: T. and T. Clark, 1902), 148–54, provides a survey of the intertestamental background. The New Testament abounds with evidence that the concept of two ages had been in some form assumed: "the end of the age" (Matt. 28:20; Heb. 9:26); "when the fullness of time had come" (Gal. 4:4); and "the last days" (Acts 2:17). Of particular significance is Mark 1:14–15: "Jesus came to Galilee, proclaiming the good news of God, and saying, 'The time is fulfilled, and the kingdom of God has come near; repent, and believe in the good news.'" The phrase "good news" (gospel) refers to the report of a coming time of peace, salvation, and the reign of God as a result of an intervention of God (cf. Isa. 52:7). The Greek word used here for "time" is *kairos*, a specific important moment, a crisis point. It refers to the arrival of an expected crisis in salvation history, the day of salvation. The phrase "has come near" is especially important. The verb is in the perfect tense, which views the action as having arrived at a point of completion while the results continue. The Greek word itself means "to approach or be in process of drawing near." Hence the sense here is "has just arrived." With the beginning of Jesus' ministry the crisis point in human history has been reached!

8. 1 Enoch 71:15; 2 Baruch 15:7; Mishnah *Aboth* 4:1; 6:4, 7.

Intertestamental writers use a number of terms to refer to the whole or a part of that age which was expected to follow God's breaking into human history.[9] Perhaps the simplest procedure is to call it the final age, with the understanding that it is a part of the salvation history within human history.[10]

The final age is also the age of the kingdom of God. Of course, the biblical writers do assume that God is and always has been the sovereign ruler of the universe, the king. At the same time they understand that his kingdom is contested by the kingdom of evil (of Satan) which is present in the universe. With the dawning of the final age, God will reassert his rightful authority and rule in a more positive and forceful way on the earth. The final age was thus looked on as the time at which the kingdom of God would arrive in this special sense. Because of the unique relationship between Israel and God, the presence of the kingdom was expected to bring favorable results (politically, spiritually, economically, etc.) for Israel.

In addition, the final age was looked on as the age of the Messiah. Both the precise nature and the work of the Messiah were debated. Diverse views abounded among the various groups and individuals. Some looked for the Messiah to be a specific person or group of persons. Some thought the Messiah might be a spirit or maybe only an idealized concept. Some intertestamental Jews expected the Messiah to be a human being, others a supernatural or divine person. Moreover, there was little consensus regarding what the Messiah was to accomplish. Whatever the expectation, there seems to have been general agreement that the arrival of the final age would indicate either the presence or imminent appearance of the kingdom and the Messiah. Likewise, the arrival of the kingdom or the Messiah was to be a sure sign of the final age.

Preliminary Events

Some intertestamental groups expected the final age to be preceded by a special period of affliction and trouble, the woes or the birth pangs of the Messiah.[11] According to the War Scroll (1QM 1),

9. Some of the more common are "the day," "the day of the Lord," "in that (those) day(s)," "the last days," "the final age," "the messianic age," "the days of Messiah," "the kingdom (of God)," "the coming age," "the world to come," "the hour," and "the time."

10. Modern writers frequently employ the word *eschaton* (a transliteration of the Greek adjective meaning "last") to refer to this final period of history.

11. Babylonian Talmud *Sanhedrin* 97a; Sibylline Oracles 3:635–61; 2 Baruch 25. The term *birth pangs* (*ōdines*) is used in Matt. 24:8 and Mark 13:8 to describe the preliminary period of distress. The concept, used often in an eschatological setting to describe God's judgment, is rooted in the Old Testament (Isa. 13:8; 26:17; 66:7–9; Jer. 4:31; 6:24; 13:21; 22:23; 49:22; 50:43; Hos. 13:13; Mic. 4:9–10). It became a technical term in rabbinic literature.

"this shall be a time of salvation for the people of God . . . the battle of destructions for the sons of darkness. And it shall be a time of [great] tribulation for the people which God shall redeem; of all its afflictions none shall be as this, from its sudden beginning until its end in eternal redemption."[12] The times will change, and there will be threatening signs in the cosmic order, between nations, between individuals, and in the spiritual realm. Sin and wickedness will run rampant and rule the earth. Relationships between individuals and nations will be disrupted, animosities and hostilities will increase.[13]

The coming of the Messiah and the final age will be announced by a prophetic forerunner, frequently identified as Elijah.[14] His task will be to prepare the way for the LORD by restoring all things, making peace on earth, and in general substituting order for disorder.[15] This he will accomplish by issuing a call to Israel to repent.

The Nature of the Final Age

What the final age was expected to be like was not always clear. The national glorification of Israel was certainly a fundamental feature of most expectations. The final resurrection, last judgment, and the renovation of nature and the social order were also important components of the final age.

Although anticipated as a future event, the final age was frequently described with terms alluding to the past. Three moments of biblical history which provided frameworks for thinking about the final age are worth noting. The final age could be described as Paradise returned, the Garden of Eden restored. It would be marked by a return of peace, rest, and prosperity among people and within nature. In such a setting the Messiah might be described as

12. See also 1 Enoch 1:3–8, "The God of the universe, the Holy Great One, will come forth from his dwelling. And from there he will march upon Mount Sinai and appear in his camp emerging from heaven with a mighty power. And everyone shall be afraid, and Watchers shall quiver. And great fear and trembling shall seize them unto the ends of the earth. Mountains and high places will fall down and be frightened. And high hills shall be made low; and they shall melt like a honeycomb before the flame. And earth shall be rent asunder, and all that is upon the earth shall perish. And there shall be a judgment upon all, (including) the righteous. And to all the righteous he will grant peace. He will preserve the elect, and kindness shall be upon them. They shall all belong to God and they shall prosper and be blessed; and the light of God shall shine unto them." All this is prelude to the announcement of the coming of the Lord: "Behold, he will arrive with ten million of the holy ones in order to execute judgment upon all" (v. 9, quoted in Jude 14–15).

13. Sibylline Oracles 3:796–808; 2 Baruch 26–29; 48:38–41; 2 Esdras 4:52–5:13; 6:20–24; 9:1–6; 13:29–32; Testament of Moses 10.

14. Mal. 4:5; Sirach 48:10; cf. Matt. 17:10–12; Mark 9:11–13.

15. Isa. 40:1–5; Mal. 3:1–4 (cf. Matt. 11:10); Mal. 4:5–6; Sirach 48:10; Mishnah *Eduyoth* 8:7.

the second Adam. The classic expression of the Edenic model is Isaiah 11:6–9:

> The wolf shall live with the lamb, the leopard shall lie down with the kid, the calf and the lion and the fatling together, and a little child shall lead them. The cow and the bear shall graze, their young shall lie down together; and the lion shall eat straw like the ox. The nursing child shall play over the hole of the asp, and the weaned child shall put its hand on the adder's den. They will not hurt or destroy on all my holy mountain; for the earth will be full of the knowledge of the LORD as the waters cover the sea.[16]

The final age might also be likened to a new exodus (Isa. 51:9–11; 52:12). Deliverance from Egypt brought freedom, covenant renewal, divine provision, nationhood, and new revelations of God. The final age–new exodus would be marked by similar blessings, but at a higher, a spiritual as well as material, level. The Messiah would be a Prophet like Moses (Deut. 18:15, 18).

Of course, the most widespread image likened the final age to a renewed Davidic kingdom, the golden age of Hebrew history. This image looked to the return of the conditions which existed during the era of David and Solomon, when Israel was the superpower of the day.[17] The final age, it was hoped, would restore the nation to the political, military, geographical, and spiritual grandeur it had reached during that time. The Messiah as the Son of David and Davidic king would fulfil the promises of an eternal kingship and dominion.

Whatever the dominant model, most Jews expected the final age to contain features which were common to all of them. It was looked to as a time of unparalleled joy and gladness.[18] There would be peace among individuals and nations;[19] the wild beasts would lose their ferocity.[20] The life span of human beings would increase, sickness and pain (including that of childbearing) would be eliminated.[21] Labor and work would lose their tiresome characteristics.[22] Second Baruch 73 summarizes:

16. See also Isa. 4:2; 55:13; 65:25; Amos 9:13–15; Testament of Levi 18:10–14; Testament of Dan 5:12; 2 Baruch 4; 2 Enoch 8; 2 Esdras 7:36–44, 123.

17. See 2 Sam. 7:13, 16; the Royal Psalms (e.g., 2; 19; 20; 21; 72; 89:19–37; 101; 110; 132:11; 144:1–11); Isa. 9:6–7; 11:1; Jer. 23:5–6; 30:8–9; 33:14–22; Amos 9:11; Zech. 12:7–9; Psalms of Solomon 17:4–10, 21; 2 Esdras 12:31–32.

18. 1 Enoch 45:4–5; 62:15; Sibylline Oracles 3:371–80.

19. 1 Enoch 10:17; Jubilees 23:29; Sibylline Oracles 3:751–80; 2 Baruch 73:1.

20. Isa. 11:6–9; 65:25; 2 Baruch 73:6; Philo On Rewards and Punishments 15 (85–90).

21. Jubilees 23:27–28, 30; 2 Baruch 73:2–5, 7; cf. Isa. 65:20.

22. 1 Enoch 10:18–19.

And it will happen that after he has brought down everything which is in the world, and has sat down in eternal peace on the throne of the kingdom, then joy will be revealed and rest will appear. And then health will descend in dew, and illness will vanish, and fear and tribulation and lamentation will pass away from among men, and joy will encompass the earth. And nobody will again die untimely, nor will any adversity take place suddenly. Judgment, condemnations, contentions, revenges, blood, passions, zeal, hate, and all such things will go into condemnation since they will be uprooted. For these are the things that have filled this earth with evils, and because of them life of men came in yet greater confusion. And the wild beasts will come from the wood and serve men, and the asps and dragons will come out of their holes to subject themselves to a child. And women will no longer have pain when they bear, nor will they be tormented when they yield the fruit of their womb.

Above all, the messianic age would be a time when the earth shall be cleansed from all defilement and from sin.[23] Israel, delivered from her enemies, will lead all nations to "serve [the Lord] without fear, in holiness and righteousness" (Luke 1:74–75). All nations will flock to the Jerusalem temple to worship. The rule of the Messiah will be universal and characterized by righteousness, for the dominating mark of the messianic age will be universal obedience to the law.[24]

The Events of the Final Age

There was no unanimity on the precise sequence of events leading up to and resulting from the restoration of Israel. Details differ from source to source. A general scenario seems to have been commonly held among the populace, however. At some point after the beginning of the final age the heathen powers would assemble under an unidentified leader (the Antichrist), attack, but be defeated by the forces of the LORD.[25]

There was disagreement whether God himself or the Messiah was to lead in battle.[26] Some believed that it would be won by God

---

23. 1 Enoch 10:20–22; Psalms of Solomon 17:26–46; 18:9; Sibylline Oracles 3:377–80.

24. Sibylline Oracles 3:767–95; Jubilees 23:26.

25. The New Testament calls the unidentified leader Antichrist (1 John 2:18, 22; 4:3; 2 John 7; cf. 2 Thess. 2; Rev. 13); less specific is 2 Baruch 40:1–2: "The last ruler who is left alive at that time will be bound, whereas the entire host will be destroyed. And . . . my Anointed One . . . will kill him and protect the rest of my people." In the Dead Sea Scrolls the enemy is usually called the Evil King or Satan; in the Melchizedek Scroll (11QMelch) he is the antitype of Melchizedek. See Wilhelm Bousset, *The Antichrist Legend*, trans. A. H. Keane (London: Hutchinson, 1896). On the battle see 1 Enoch 90:13–19; Sibylline Oracles 3:663–68; Jubilees 23:22–24; 2 Esdras 13:31–35; 2 Baruch 39–40; War Scroll (1QM) 15–19.

26. 2 Baruch 30:1 indicates that the Messiah will appear after the woes.

himself[27] and that the Messiah would appear only after the conquest.[28] There is also evidence of a belief that the Messiah would remain in concealment because of the sins of the people.[29] But the prevailing opinion seems to have been that the Messiah, empowered by the Lord, would defeat the enemy.[30]

Judgment follows the victory over the forces of evil. Again opinions differ, this time as to the identity of the judge. In 1 Enoch 90:20–27 God, "the Lord of the sheep," sits upon the throne and condemns both fallen angels and blind sheep (apostate Israelites). However, in most of 1 Enoch and elsewhere,[31] the Messiah is the sovereign judge; nothing is hidden from him as he sits on the throne of glory to judge human beings and angels.[32] The evil, especially the oppressors of Israel, will then be punished.[33]

After victory and judgment the messianic kingdom will be set up in the land of Israel and have dominion over the whole world.[34] The Messiah will be king, but God will be the supreme ruler as his sovereignty is reestablished.[35] The city of Jerusalem and the temple will be purified from defilement and made more beautiful.[36] In some views earthly Jerusalem will be replaced by a celestial city already existing in heaven;[37] it will appear on earth in place of the old, and be superior in magnificence and beauty.[38]

The Jewish daily prayer voices the ancient hope for the gathering of dispersed Israelites to the native homeland: "Raise a banner to

27. Joel 3:1–12; 1 Enoch 90:15–19; Testament of Moses 10:7; Midrash on Ps. 7:1; War Scroll (1QM).

28. 1 Enoch 90:37–39; 2 Esdras 7:26–28.

29. John 7:27; Justin Martyr *Dialogue with Trypho*; Targum on Mic. 4:8.

30. Psalms of Solomon 17:21–25, 28, 39–40; 18:6–7; Sibylline Oracles 3:652–56; Philo *On Rewards and Punishments* 16 (95); 2 Baruch 39:7–40:2; 70:2–6; 2 Esdras 12:32–33; 13:26–38; Targum on Isa. 10:27, "The nations shall be destroyed from before the Anointed One (Messiah)"; Targum (Neofiti recension) on Gen. 49:11, "How beautiful is King Messiah who shall arise from the house of Judah, He girds his loins and goes forth to battle against them that hate him, and he slays kings and rulers" (quoted from Schürer, *History*, 2:528).

31. E.g., 2 Esdras 13:37–38.

32. 1 Enoch 45:3; 49:3–4; 53:2; 55:4; 61:8–10; and especially chs. 62 and 69.

33. 1 Enoch 54; Testament of Moses 10:7; Sibylline Oracles 3:669–701, 761.

34. Jubilees 1:28–29; 32:19; Sibylline Oracles 3:767–95; 2 Esdras 9:8.

35. Sibylline Oracles 3:705–6, 716–17, 757–61; Psalms of Solomon 17:1, 38; War Scroll (1QM); *Shemoneh 'Esreh* 11 ("Reign over us, thou Lord alone, in grace and mercy; and justify us in judgment"); cf. Josephus *Jewish War* 2.8.1 (118).

36. Testament of Dan 5:12–13; Psalms of Solomon 17:30; 2 Baruch 32:2; 2 Esdras 10:44; Isa. 54:11–12; 60; Ezek. 40–48; Hag. 2:7–9; Zech. 2:6–12; Gal. 4:26; Heb. 12:22; Rev. 3:12; 21–22.

37. This was a common assumption at Qumran. According to 2 Baruch 4, the heavenly Jerusalem originally stood in Paradise; but after Adam sinned, it was taken to and preserved in heaven. It was shown to Abraham in a vision and to Moses on Mount Sinai. According to 2 Esdras 10:44–59, Ezra also had a vision of the heavenly city.

38. 1 Enoch 53:6; 90:28–29; 2 Esdras 7:26; 2 Baruch 32:2–4.

gather our dispersed, and gather us from the four ends of the earth."[39] Among the older intertestamental writings Jesus ben Sirach cries, "Gather all the tribes of Jacob, and give them their inheritance, as at the beginning."[40] This hope and expectation that dispersed Israel will share in the joys of the coming age is among the more consistent elements of intertestamental Jewish eschatology. Assembling and settling the dispersed in their own land are messianic tasks.[41] Several writers describe the return from all parts of the earth;[42] some held that deceased Israelites would at this time be raised from the dead.[43]

The Chronology of the Final Age

Some intertestamental writers believed that with the divine intervention into history the final age (whether it was viewed as the messianic age or the kingdom of God) would begin immediately and be eternal.[44] Others supposed that after a period of time there would be another crisis event which would introduce the final period of redemptive history, the phase of consummation ("the age [world] to come" or eternity).[45] For instance, while 2 Baruch 73:1 speaks of Messiah's sitting down "in eternal peace on the throne of the kingdom," 40:3 says that "his dominion will last forever until the world of corruption has ended," thus anticipating something more. There is also diversity of opinion about the length of the final age—messianic kingdom. While 2 Baruch is vague, saying simply "until the world of corruption has ended," 2 Esdras 7:28 gives four

39. *Shemoneh 'Esreh* 10.

40. Sirach 36:13–14; the Hebrew of chapter 51 adds, "Give thanks to him who gathers the dispersed of Israel." See also Isa. 49:22; 60:4; 66:20.

41. Psalms of Solomon 17:28: "He will distribute them upon the land according to their tribes; the alien and the foreigner will no longer live near them" (cf. Targum of Jonathan for Jer. 33:13).

42. 1 (Greek) Baruch 5:5–9, "Arise, O Jerusalem, stand upon the height; look toward the east, and see your children gathered from west and east at the word of the Holy One, rejoicing that God has remembered them. For they went out from you on foot, led away by their enemies; but God will bring them back to you, carried in glory, as on a royal throne. For God has ordered that every high mountain and the everlasting hills be made low and the valleys filled up, to make level ground, so that Israel may walk safely in the glory of God. The woods and every fragrant tree have shaded Israel at God's command. For God will lead Israel with joy, in the light of his glory, with the mercy and righteousness that come from him." See also 4:36–37; 2 Esdras 13:39–47; Psalms of Solomon 11; Philo *On Rewards and Punishments* 28–29 (164–65).

43. Dan. 12:2–3; 1 Enoch 51; Psalms of Solomon 3.

44. 1 Enoch 62:13–14; Sibylline Oracles 3:49–50, 767–68; Psalms of Solomon 17:4; cf. John 12:34. The same expectation appears to be reflected in the promise of permanence for the throne of David (Jer. 33:17, 20–22; Ezek. 37:25; cf. Dan. 7:27).

45. One of the rabbinic writings, the tannaitic midrash *Sifre* on Deut. 11:21, distinguishes between "the days of the Messiah" and "the world to come."

hundred years as the length of the messianic period.[46] Jubilees 23:27 mentions, but in a rather ambiguous context, a period of one thousand years (cf. Rev. 20:1–7). The Talmud tractate *Sanhedrin* 97a sets a period of two thousand years.

Those who anticipated the inauguration of the final age and the consummation to occur simultaneously expected the new world to appear immediately.[47] Others looked for it only at the conclusion of the interim messianic period.[48] The latter group, who expected another age to follow the final age, believed the world would undergo further changes as the age to come was inaugurated.[49] Intertestamental Jewish thought expected that whenever the consummation occurred, perishable and corruptible elements would be consumed in a purifying fire and the world would be made new.[50] The kingdom would undergo changes. Then too there would be the resurrection of the dead, or the final resurrection from the perspective of those who expected one earlier.

Again, ideas differed on the number of judgments; would there be a single judgment or a series? It was generally agreed that in his function as judge God will seal the fate of all, both the people of Israel and the whole of humankind.[51] Some seem to have expected the final judgment to precede the arrival of the messianic kingdom and the righteous to be raised to share in it forever.[52] In other writings, such as 1 Enoch 91–104, the judgment comes at the close of the kingdom; the righteous are not raised to share it, but later enjoy a blessed immortality. Second Baruch 50:4 also seems to allude to a judgment after the conclusion of the kingdom, and 2 Esdras speaks of it in even more detail.[53] The righteous will be accepted into paradise to occupy the high places and to behold the majesty of God.[54] The wicked will be cast into Gehenna, which is characterized by fire and intense

46. See also Babylonian Talmud *Sanhedrin* 99a.

47. 1 Enoch 45:4–6; cf. 91:16; Isa. 65:17; 66:22; Matt. 19:28; 2 Peter 3:13; Rev. 21:1–5.

48. E.g., the Qumran Commentary on Habakkuk (1QpHab 2:3b): ". . . when the final age is prolonged. For all the ages of God reach their appointed end as He determines for them in the mysteries of His wisdom." This is also clearly the situation in 2 Esdras 7:28–33; 12:32–34.

49. 2 Baruch 44:15; 2 Esdras 7:13–16—note that the terms *messianic age* and *age to come* were frequently confused or used interchangeably; both were future from the point of view of pre-Christian and non-Christian Jewish writers.

50. 2 Esdras 7:31–44; 8:1; cf. 2 Peter 3:7–13.

51. 2 Esdras 7:33, 37; 2 Baruch 50:4–51:6.

52. 1 Enoch 83–90 ("The Dream Visions"); Testament of Judah 25; Testament of Zebulun 10; and Testament of Benjamin 10:4–10—but some of these may be Christian alterations or additions to Jewish books!

53. 2 Esdras 6:17–28; 7:33–44.

54. 2 Esdras 7:38–42, 88–99; 2 Baruch 51:3, 7–14; Testament of Moses 10:9–10.

suffering.[55] It is usually assumed that one's assignment to heaven or Gehenna will be permanent. However, in 2 Esdras a description of the dichotomy between paradise and hell is followed with the puzzling statement, "It will last as though for a week of years" (7:43). Later rabbis suggested that the torment of the wicked might be for only a limited time.

The Final Age in Christian Thought

Although there were a variety of views about the effects of the arrival of the final age, there was general agreement that its arrival would result in significant change in all areas of life. We must stress again that these were expected to be radical changes in the environment, human experience, and the spiritual sphere. Of course there was no unanimity of opinion as to the nature, degree, and results of these changes. Yet it seems many intertestamental Jews anticipated that the final age would place them in a situation much different from that to which they were accustomed.

Jesus' original announcement of himself and his ministry equated his arrival with that of the final age (Mark 1:14–15). Yet his view of that age did not correspond exactly with any of the intertestamental Jewish views of which we are now aware. National renewal, as expected by the majority of the populace, was not a part of his immediate agenda. Rather, his call was to individuals for personal repentance and acceptance of him. His program did not involve taking up the sword against Caesar, but "the things which make for peace" (Luke 19:42). Even so, because that peace required acceptance of his person, he would also be the cause of conflict and division, even within families (Luke 12:49–53). He rejected the notion of a dramatic entrance of an apocalyptic kingdom or a materialistic one. Rather, he spoke of a kingdom which "is not coming with things that can be observed. . . . For, in fact, the kingdom of God is among you" (Luke 17:20–21). Although not oblivious to the sins and oppression of the Gentiles, it was with the sins of God's people that he was most concerned. His call was for Israel to "give . . . to God the things that are God's" (Mark 12:17). Hence the ministry of Jesus involved not only implementing, but also redefining the final age. This, we shall see, was true of the kingdom of God and messiahship as well.

55. 2 Esdras 7:33–42, 79–87; 2 Baruch 44:15; 51:4–6, 15–16. Gehenna (or Gehinnom) pictures the Hinnom Valley, the southern boundary of Jerusalem. It represented the place of exclusion, of refuse (which was constantly being burned), of execution, the place for the unclean, the unburied.

Finally, that Intertestamental Judaism expected major changes also has important implications for understanding the attitudes, deeds, and conflicts of the disciples of Jesus and the early Jewish Christians. They understood that they were actually living in the final age. For them the future was now!

15

The Kingdom of God

Background Elements

Both John the Baptist and Jesus began their preaching with the announcement of the imminence of the kingdom (Matt. 3:2; 4:17; Mark 1:14–15). In the Synoptic Gospels the announcement, clarification, and implementation of the kingdom of God constitute the major theme of Jesus' ministry. Without some awareness of the connotations which the term had in Jewish society the modern reader will miss much of the significance of Jesus' deeds and teachings.

We need to note first that in the Hebrew, Aramaic, and Greek languages the words for "kingdom" are all abstract. In the ancient world, "kingdom" referred to lordship, rule, reign, or sovereignty, not primarily to a geographical area. Hence "sovereignty (or rule) of God" would be a better translation than "kingdom of God." Such a translation designates God's sphere of influence or control and includes any person or group who, regardless of their location, acknowledge his sovereignty. Furthermore, the phrases "kingdom of God" and "kingdom of heaven" are interchangeable in Jewish sources, the latter being a circumlocution to avoid using the word *God*; it also stands as a reminder that God's sovereign rule extends beyond the time and space limits of the material order.

A few words need also be said about the general nature of the kingdom as presupposed by the New Testament writers. Although it was envisioned as an eschatological fact to be established in the Holy Land, it was more than that. It was both material and spiritual, both present and yet future. At times Jesus accepted some of the kingdom notions of his contemporaries; more often he challenged and undertook to correct them. Jesus certainly accepted the broad concept of the kingdom of God, especially as it arose from the Old Testament. But he rejected or sought to redefine numerous descriptive details that were current in his day.

The essential background elements may be summarized concisely. The Old Testament doctrine of God included belief that he is sovereign.[1] The affirmation that he created the universe had as a corollary the expectation that it would function under the direct rule of God. Human sin was a rejection of God's rule, spiritual sedition. Even in the face of human rejection and rebellion, however, God continues to assert his kingship and kingdom. Israel was the particular vehicle for the kingdom; indeed, the Old Testament shows a special relationship between the reign of God and the Davidic kingship in Israel. Eschatologically, the Old Testament holds that while God's sovereignty is not now universally acknowledged, it will be some day.

In intertestamental literature explicit occurrences of the phrase "kingdom of God" are rare, although the concept is assumed. For example, references to "his" or "your" kingdom suppose divine sovereignty.[2] In the Wisdom of Solomon 10:9–10 Jacob's vision of heaven is equated with "the kingdom of God" ("Wisdom rescued from troubles those who served her. When a righteous man fled from his brother's wrath, she guided him on straight paths; she showed him the kingdom of God, and gave him knowledge of holy

---

1. E.g., Exod. 15:18, "the LORD will reign forever and ever"; 1 Sam. 12:12, "the LORD your God was your king"; 1 Chron. 29:11, "Yours, O LORD, are the greatness, the power, the glory, the victory, and the majesty; for all that is in the heavens and on the earth is yours; yours is the kingdom, O LORD, and you are exalted as head above all."

The psalmists affirm, "Dominion belongs to the LORD, and he rules over the nations" (22:28); "the LORD is king" (93:1; 97:1; 99:1); and "They shall speak of the glory of your kingdom, and tell of your power, to make known to all people your mighty deeds, and the glorious splendor of your kingdom. Your kingdom is an everlasting kingdom, and your dominion endures throughout all generations" (145:11–13).

In the Book of Daniel, King Nebuchadnezzar says, "His sovereignty is an everlasting sovereignty, and his kingdom endures from generation to generation" (4:34). Daniel himself speaks of the kingdom as future: "In the days of those kings the God of heaven will set up a kingdom that shall never be destroyed, nor shall this kingdom be left to another people" (2:44; see also 7:14, 27; 1 Chron. 17:14; 28:7; Isa. 45:23; Zech. 14:9).

2. Wisdom of Solomon 6:4; Song of the Three 33; see also Psalms of Solomon 5:18; 17:3, 30–34.

things; she prospered him in his labors, and increased the fruit of his toils"). In Tobit 13:1 "kingdom" appears in a context referring to the rule of God in general.

In the pseudepigraphal Testament of Moses the kingdom is an apocalyptic manifestation. The poetic tenth chapter summarizes the writer's view of the kingdom:

> Then his kingdom will appear throughout his whole creation.
> Then the devil will have an end.
> Yea, sorrow will be led away with him.
> Then will be filled the hands of the messenger,
>   who is in the highest place appointed.
> Yea, he will at once avenge them of their enemies.
> For the Heavenly One will arise from his kingly throne.
> Yea, he will go forth from his holy habitation
>   with indignation and wrath on behalf of his sons.
> And the earth will tremble, even to its ends shall it be shaken.
> And the high mountains will be made low.
> Yea, they will be shaken, as enclosed valleys will they fall.
> The sun will not give light.
> And in darkness the horns of the moon will flee.
> Yea, they will be broken in pieces.
> It will be turned wholly into blood.
> Yea, even the circle of the stars will be thrown into disarray.
> And the sea all the way to the abyss will retire,
>   to the sources of waters which fail.
> Yea, the rivers will vanish away.
> For God Most High will surge forth,
>   the Eternal One alone.
> In full view will he come to work vengeance on the nations.
> Yea, all their idols will he destroy.
> Then you will be happy, O Israel!
> And you will mount up above the neck and the wings of an
>   eagle.
> Yea, all things will be fulfilled.
> And God will raise you to the heights.
> Yea, he will fix you firmly in the heaven of the stars,
>   in the place of their habitations.
> And you will behold from on high.
> Yea, you will see your enemies on the earth.
> And recognizing them, you will rejoice.
> And you will give thanks.
> Yea, you will confess your creator.[3]

Psalms of Solomon 5:18 affirms, "Those who fear the Lord are happy with good things. In your kingdom your goodness (is) upon

3. Cf. the targums on Isa. 31:4; 40:9; 52:7.

Israel"; and 17:3, "The kingdom of our God is forever over the nations in judgment" (see also vv. 29–46).

The targums also contain references to the kingdom,[4] as do the Dead Sea Scrolls. The War Scroll says (1QM 6:5–6): "The first battalion being armed with lance and shield and the second with shield and sword to slay through the judgement of God and to vanquish the line of the enemy by God's might, to exact retribution for their wickedness upon all nations of vanity, and the kingdom shall be of the God of Israel, and He shall do valiant deeds through the saints of His people." In the Kaddish the pious Jew prays, "May he let his kingdom rule . . . speedily and soon."

There is, at times, confusion between the final age, the messianic kingdom, and the kingdom of God. The latter two were expected during the final age and in this sense were often regarded as synonymous with it. The relation between the kingdom of God and the messianic kingdom is more complicated. Some sources seem to keep them distinct; more often they seem to be linked with the same phenomena. Although, as already noted, direct references to the kingdom of God are limited, references to the messianic kingdom, both implicit and explicit, are relatively numerous.

Some Basic First-Century Assumptions

First-century Jewish notions about the kingdom of God were often confused and contradictory. There were, however, some generally accepted ideas. First, God is the king, and he alone has the absolute right to rule all things in heaven and earth. He has this right to rule because of his nature. As the Supreme Being, he alone has the qualities necessary to govern the universe perfectly. These qualities include (but are not restricted to) God's perfect knowledge, wisdom, strength, justice (fairness), and goodness (including love). God also has the right to rule because as Creator of the universe (the one who brought it into being) he owns it. The universe owes God obedience and respect.

Furthermore, the universe functions properly, and life within the universe is happy and harmonious, only when God is in absolute control. For the universe is an intricate thing. Each person and part must function in precise relation to others. The maintenance of this balance is not automatic; it requires overall intelligent supervision. Only God is able to keep all persons, forces, and components of nature functioning in their proper relation to each other.

4. E.g., the targums on Ezek. 7:7, 10; 11:24; see also n. 3.

Human beings were made with the ability to make moral choices. In exercising this freedom, humankind as a whole and as individuals rebelled against God's rule. This has brought disharmony into the universe. The rejection of God's right to rule and violation of God's kingly commands constitute spiritual mutiny. When one part of the universe, that is, human beings, refuses to function within God's overall plan, the other parts of the universe are also thrown into disarray.

Even before the creation of the material universe God's kingly authority was contested by a spiritual force (being) called Satan (adversary). So in rebelling against God, humanity did not gain spiritual autonomy. Humanity passed from God's control (God's sphere of influence = the kingdom of God) to rule by Satan (Satan's sphere of influence = the kingdom of Satan). Thus Satan's kingdom is both real and present. It is not confined to some other world, but is present in this world and world order. Through human rebellion against God the influence of Satan has invaded the souls, bodies, and environment of human beings. Consequently, the kingdom of Satan is operating in the very territory in which the kingdom of God should operate—in the material world and especially in the life and experience of humans.

As God reasserts his rightful authority over the universe, especially as he seeks to reclaim the allegiance of humanity, a collision between the kingdom of God and the kingdom of Satan is inevitable. Before God can again extend the influence of his kingdom to the material world and to humanity, he must first subdue the occupying force, the kingdom of Satan. The conflict between God and Satan involves the right to rule, the right of complete sovereignty, in the world. It is a struggle for the hearts, lives, souls, society, and environment of human beings. This struggle is presumed to be in the background of all the events recorded in the Bible.

The biblical writers assume that the present world order—especially pagan rulers, political systems, and religions—are under the control of Satan. God's people are those individuals, groups, nations, and races who have accepted the rule of God and are his representatives and agents in the struggle. The coming of the kingdom of God refers generally to God's reassertion of his right to rule over the universe. It includes his bringing humankind under his control. Sometimes the coming of the kingdom refers to the initial thrust of God's decisive invasion into the territory occupied by the kingdom of Satan. At other times it refers to the final victory and restoration of complete control by God.

The Kingdom of God and the Nation of Israel

Israel believed that through God's covenant with Abraham (Gen. 12–17) she enjoyed a unique, special relationship with the LORD. However, Israel, as the people of God, was forced to live in a hostile environment dominated by the kingdom of Satan. Political, military, and social forces which oppressed Israel were usually regarded as representatives of the kingdom of Satan. (However, without their knowing it, pagan powers were sometimes used by God to accomplish his purposes, especially in punishing Israel.) The coming of God's kingdom would bring an end to control of the material world by Satan. This would produce favorable results for God's people.

In the Hebrew Scriptures, although human kingship in Israel is portrayed as a divine concession,[5] the Hebrew kings are looked upon as representatives and legates of God, the Great King. Consequently the kingdom of God is often described in metaphors drawn from the Hebrew kingship and is frequently expected to come into being through the Davidic line. The promises made to David of an everlasting kingdom are the basis of this expectation (2 Sam. 7). The Chronicler, reflecting the views of Intertestamental Judaism, quotes David as saying, "The LORD. . .has chosen my son Solomon to sit upon the throne of the kingdom of the LORD over Israel. He said to me, . . . 'I will establish his kingdom forever'" (1 Chron. 28:5–7). Later, the Chronicler depicts King Abijah of Judah rebuking King Jeroboam of Israel for thinking "that you can withstand the kingdom of the LORD in the hand of the sons of David" (2 Chron. 13:8). In addition, both the psalmists and the prophets frequently speak of the coming agent of God as the Son of David (Ps. 2; Isa. 9:6–7; Jer. 23:5–6).

During the intertestamental period there evolved the expectation that the kingdom would become a reality when, at the outset of the final age, God's intervention would deliver his people (the Hebrew nation) from oppression by satanic power. Exactly what would happen when the kingdom of God arrived was debated. It was expected to bring wide-sweeping change, but there was no agreement as to which area would receive the primary attention from the King. The majority of the people in Jesus' day expected the kingdom of God to deal with the political situation.

5. Gideon expressed the Old Testament ideal, "The LORD will rule over you," when he rejected the offer of a hereditary kingship for his family (Judg. 8:22–23). Israel's request for a king was initially rejected by Samuel. He acquiesced only at the instructions of God (1 Sam. 8:4–9), who saw the request as a diminution of his own authority ("they have rejected me from being king over them" [v. 7]). Samuel then warned the people of the negatives of the kingship they requested (vv. 10–18; cf. Deut. 17:14–20).

National deliverance would bring freedom from Rome and the restoration of the political power and prestige of the Hebrew nation. Many felt that the kingdom of God would also bring a change in the world of nature. As a result of cosmic renewal, natural evils, agricultural pests, and physical disease would be eliminated. The world of nature would function harmoniously as intended by God. Natural (agricultural) productivity would be greatly increased. Further, the social order was expected to be changed when the kingdom of God arrived. Prosperity would greatly increase. Peace would be established between people; justice would prevail; God's purposes in history would be realized. Finally, the spiritual disposition of humanity and nations would be so reordered that all would properly serve, obey, and worship God. The revelation of God's will would be either reinterpreted or reissued in such a form that people would have little difficulty in conforming to it. Apocalyptic writers stressed all of these features of the coming kingdom: political, cosmic, social, and spiritual.

Predictions of the Kingdom of God

Isaiah proclaimed, "How beautiful upon the mountains are the feet of the messenger who announces peace, who brings good news, who announces salvation, who says to Zion, 'Your God reigns'" (52:7). In this verse the phrase "good news" (Hebrew, *basśēr*) is the announcement of a period of time which is coming in the future. That future time will be characterized by peace, salvation, and the reign (kingdom) of God. In short, the arrival of the kingdom of God will result in peace and salvation. The prediction of this coming time, the affirmation that the kingdom of God will arrive, is, to use the Greek word, the *euangelion*, that is, the good news, the gospel. In the Old Testament the gospel is the announcement that the kingdom is coming and with it salvation and peace.

The nature and features of the coming kingdom of God are similar to, if not identical with, those of the final age described in chapter 14. The Old Testament stresses the reestablishment and reign of the Davidic throne (Isa. 9:1–7; Jer. 23:5; 33:15; Zech. 3:8). Isaiah 11 predicts the restoration of the Davidic throne, and a vision of a renewed natural order (vv. 6–9) is placed in the midst of this oracle. Ezekiel's vision of dry bones made alive (ch. 37) predicts the restoration of the nation Israel. Joel 2:28–32 describes the coming kingdom age in apocalyptic terms.

Other passages in both the Old Testament and noncanonical writings could be added to this survey. Of particular interest are references to the kingdom in Psalms of Solomon 17. The psalm provides a good illustration of how the concept of the kingdom of God is more implied than overtly described. It also shows how the concepts of the final age and the Messiah are used in intertestamental writings.

The psalm both begins and ends with an affirmation of the rule of God: "Lord, you are our king forevermore" (v. 1); "The Lord Himself is our king forevermore" (v. 46). Reaffirming the eternal nature of the kingdom of God ("The kingdom of our God is forever over the nations in judgment" [v. 3]), the writer sees no incompatibility with God's establishment of a human kingship in the family of David ("Lord, you chose David to be king over Israel, and swore to him about his descendants forever, that his kingdom should not fail before you" [v. 4]).

A historical review then describes the sad plight of God's people (vv. 5–20), which has come "(because of) our sins" (v. 5). Hope for deliverance is expressed in verse 21: "See, Lord, and raise up for them their king, the son of David, to rule over your servant Israel in the time known to you, O God." The divine King will bring deliverance through a Davidic king. The time known to God is probably a reference to the final age.

The writer then describes the future restoration in a poetic apocalyptic form (vv. 26–31). This passage anticipates the freedom, gathering, and purification of God's people and the judgment of the wicked. The renewed society will be under the rule of God through his Messiah: "And he will be a righteous king over them, taught by God. There will be no unrighteousness among them in his days, for all shall be holy, and their king shall be the Lord Messiah. (For) he will not rely on horse and rider and bow, nor will he collect gold and silver for war. Nor will he build up hope in a multitude for a day of war. The Lord himself is his king, the hope of the one who has a strong hope in God" (vv. 32–34).

The final, eschatological, messianic age will be idyllic in character. The reign of God will be "compassionate to all the nations" (v. 34). The people of God will be blessed "with wisdom and happiness" (v. 35). Free from sin and "powerful in the holy spirit" (v. 37), the king will be "faithfully and righteously shepherding the Lord's flock" (v. 40). The "beauty of the king of Israel" will be the holiness, justice, and sanctity of the people (vv. 41–43).

The Hebrew concept of the kingdom of God is encapsulated at the end of the song of Moses, "The LORD will reign forever and ever" (Exod. 15:18). From the Christian context, the Book of Revelation concurs. Concerning the material universe "loud voices in heaven" say,

> The kingdom of the world has
>   become the kingdom of our Lord
>   and of his Messiah,
> and he will reign forever and ever. [Rev. 11:15]

Concerning the heavenly sphere the great multitude cries,

> Hallelujah!
> For the Lord our God
>   the Almighty reigns. [Rev. 19:6]

16

The Messianic Hope

The Messianic Hope and the Messiah

The title "Messianic Hope" is better for this chapter than one which might imply a unified view or a particular kind of Messiah. Messianic expectations were as diverse as any other part of intertestamental Jewish thought, if not more so. These matters were "the center of a vast mass of confused, involved and even contradictory notions, from which there arose few certainties that were acknowledged by all."[1] A contributing factor was the plethora of divisions within intertestamental Jewish thought itself, yet the diver-

---

1. Henri Daniel-Rops, *Daily Life in the Time of Jesus,* trans. Patrick O'Brian (New York: Hawthorn, 1962), 409.

sity of thought about the Messiah may even be present within parts of the Old Testament.[2]

Modern scholarship has yielded far from unanimous conclusions about pre-Christian views regarding the Messiah.[3] Debate centers on whether the messianic idea was an importation into Jewish thought or an article of genuine revelation to the Hebrews.[4] Most of the Old Testament messianic material is in the writings of the prophets. They maintained staunch opposition to pagan influence, especially religious ideas and practices. So it is difficult to see how they would have imported the messianic idea. Accepting the prophetic writings as inspired Scripture strengthens the case for regarding the messianic hope as Hebrew in origin. That the intertestamental Jewish expectation may sometimes be expressed in language and figures that reflect Gentile sources does not destroy its essentially Hebrew character.

It is helpful to distinguish between the older and newer forms of messianic views within Judaism. In the former the restoration and glorification of the nation Israel received primary consideration. There was little or no attention to the person of a Messiah. Later, when the hope became universalized and individualized and included the person of a Messiah, the establishment of the true spiritual Israel as first among the nations remained the central point. This nationalistic orientation provided an important link between the hopes of biblical Israel and later forms of Judaism.

Titles and Names

Many of the ideas and concepts associated with the messianic hope were expressed and passed on through various names and ti-

2. Joachim Becker, *Messianic Expectation in the Old Testament,* trans. David E. Green (Philadelphia: Fortress, 1980); Joseph Klausner, *The Messianic Idea in Israel,* trans. W. F. Stinespring (New York: Macmillan, 1955), 241.

3. James H. Charlesworth, ed., *The Messiah: Developments in Earliest Judaism and Christianity* (Minneapolis: Augsburg Fortress, 1992); Jacob Neusner et al., eds., *Judaisms and Their Messiahs at the Turn of the Christian Era* (New York: Cambridge University Press, 1987); Emil Schürer, *History of the Jewish People in the Age of Jesus Christ,* ed. Geza Vermes et al., 3 vols. (Edinburgh: T. and T. Clark, 1973–87), 2:488–554; George A. Riggan, *Messianic Theology and Christian Faith* (Philadelphia: Westminster, 1967); Joseph Bonsirven, *Palestinian Judaism in the Time of Jesus Christ,* trans. William Wolf (New York: Holt, Rinehart and Winston, 1964), 172–225; Sigmund O. P. Mowinckel, *He That Cometh,* trans. G. W. Anderson (New York: Abingdon, 1956); David Daube, *The New Testament and Rabbinic Judaism* (New York: Arno, 1973), 3–51; Klausner, *Messianic Idea.*

4. Some scholars argue that messianism entered Hebrew thought from Assyrian, Egyptian, Babylonian, or Persian sources (the literature is cited by Klausner, *Messianic Idea,* 13 n. 1). Others suggest it was basically a Hebrew idea, but differ as to whether it represents a postexilic development (e.g., Mowinckel, *He That Cometh*) or has Old Testament roots.

tles which also revealed the functions of Messiah. Most of the titles came from the Old Testament but were adapted by intertestamental writers. Some were actual Old Testament messianic titles; in other cases Old Testament persons or images became entailed with the messianic hope. It is usually supposed that the titles were merely alternative designations for the Messiah or the eschatological figure. On the other hand, some groups may have believed that each title represented a separate figure expected to appear in the final age.

Some groups did indeed look for several Messiahs or messianic figures. Moses and Elijah were among those whose names were included in speculations about the final age. Their appearance alongside Jesus the Messiah at the transfiguration would, for those who expected a number of eschatological figures, have confirmed the arrival of the final age. The Qumran community expected a Messiah of Levi, a Messiah of Israel, and possibly a Prophet like Moses. The Fourth Gospel records that Pharisees and Levites (who were part of the mainstream of Jewish life) asked John the Baptist if he were the Messiah, Elijah, or the Prophet (John 1:19–23). The disciples seem to have had no difficulty in acknowledging Jesus' messiahship, nor with Jesus' expanding the concept by equating it with the Son of man. What they found difficult was his insistence that the Messiah–Son of man would endure the suffering of the Servant of the LORD (Mark 8:29–33).

Messiah

The term *Messiah* (literally, the Anointed) could be applied to any person who held office by the gift, grace, and anointing of God. Thus, technically it could be applied to all leaders of Israel, especially the anointed kings. In Isaiah the Persian king Cyrus is foretold to be the divine agent for the reconstruction of Jerusalem; accordingly, he is called the Lord's "anointed" (Isa. 45:1). God says, "He is my shepherd. . . . I have aroused Cyrus in righteousness . . . he shall build my city and set my exiles free" (44:28; 45:13). Although the idea is implicitly widespread throughout the Old Testament, the term *Messiah* to designate the leader par excellence occurs only rarely (e.g., Dan. 9:25–26).

Some of the earlier intertestamental sources ascribed to the Coming One characteristics which might be ascribed to a preexistent angelic or divine being. The coming king of Psalms of Solomon 17 is described as "a righteous king . . . the Lord Messiah" (v. 32), "free from sin" (v. 36), "powerful in the holy spirit and wise in the counsel of understanding, with strength and righteousness"

(v. 37). Later Judaism, possibly in reaction against Christianity, emphasized the humanity of the Messiah.

The messianic hope of each specific group within Intertestamental Judaism probably had its own distinctive features. It is usually believed that some groups (e.g., the Sadducees) completely rejected the concept.[5] In contrast, Qumran expected more than one Messiah or eschatological figure and produced lengthy descriptions of the final war as well as of the messianic blessings and banquet.[6] By the time of Jesus the majority of the common people thought of the coming Messiah primarily as a political, military king who would deal with the external crises faced by the nation.

The underlying theme of the popular concept was that the Messiah would be king. For this coming figure most looked to the tribe of Judah and the Davidic dynasty, the family so designated by divine promise (2 Sam. 7:4–16). Originally the messianic hope may have expected simply the reestablishment of the Davidic kingship; by the time of Jesus the people looked for a single individual to be the Messiah, the Son of David. The degree to which average Jews adhered to the messianic expectation is attested in the Gospels by their willingness to follow various claimants to the office, and their later readiness to engage in holy wars against Rome in A.D. 66–70 and 132–35. Although the anticipation of the common people may have been more intense and militant, if less carefully worked out than that of the learned, it seems to have been in general accord with the messianic hope of the Pharisees.

In summary, although the term *Messiah* could refer to any divinely appointed leader, it came to be used primarily in eschatological contexts. Most frequently it referred to the coming Davidic king. It could convey other ideas as well. In fact, at times it seems to have been used as a generic term to designate any agent of God—individual, idealized concept, or corporate entity—expected to appear in the final age.

5. But G. H. C. MacGregor and A. C. Purdy, *Jew and Greek: Tutors unto Christ*, rev. ed. (Edinburgh: Saint Andrew, 1959), 99, note, "On the other hand, the Messianic hope in the wider sense, as the coming and manifestation of the rule of God in the whole earth, must have been held by the Sadducees because of its Scriptural basis."

6. 1QS 9:11; 1QSa 2; CD 12:13; 14:19; 19:10; 21; cf. Testament of Reuben 6:7–8; Testament of Levi 8:14; Testament of Judah 21:1–5; Testament of Dan 5:10; Testament of Joseph 19:5–11. See Geza Vermes, *The Dead Sea Scrolls: Qumran in Perspective* (Cleveland: Collins and World, 1978), 52–57; Schürer, *History*, 2:550–54; Karl Kuhn, "The Two Messiahs of Aaron and Israel," in Krister Stendahl, ed., *The Scrolls and the New Testament* (New York: Harper and Row, 1957), 54–64.

Levitic Messiah

During the intertestamental period the expectation of a Davidic kingly Messiah was rivaled by the hope, in certain circles, for a Messiah of the tribe of Levi.[7] First Maccabees reflects this longing for a Levitic kingly Messiah. This idea probably grew among supporters of the Hasmonean dynasty. There was also the expectation that the Levitic Messiah would be a priest. The promise of an eternal priesthood for Phinehas because of his zeal for God (Num. 25:10–13) is couched in language similar to the promise to David on which the expectation of a Davidic Messiah is at least partly based (2 Sam. 7; see also Sirach 45:23–26). Psalm 110:4, "The LORD has sworn and will not change his mind, 'You are a priest forever according to the order of Melchizedek,'" gives grounds for expecting a coming agent of God who, like Melchizedek, would be both priest and king. Several passages in the Testaments of the Twelve Patriarchs point toward the expectation of a priest-leader from the tribe of Levi.[8] In the Dead Sea Scrolls the priestly Levitic Messiah is expected to take precedence over the political Davidic one.[9]

Son of Man

In a vision the author of 2 Esdras 13 sees "something like the figure of a man come up out of the heart of the sea . . . this man flew with the clouds of heaven" (v. 3). He defeats the hostile cosmic powers and delivers captives through a series of actions which precede the confirmation of his reign. Linguistic and conceptual affinities between the man of 2 Esdras and the Son of man who appears in Daniel 7:13–14 and in the Similitudes or Parables of 1 Enoch (37–71) lead many to equate them.[10]

In Daniel 7 the prophet sees "one like a son of man[11] coming with the clouds of heaven. And he came to the Ancient One and

7. Becker, *Messianic Expectation*, 83–86.

8. E.g., Testament of Reuben 6:7–8; Testament of Judah 21:1–5; Testament of Dan 5:10–11; and Testament of Joseph 19:5–11.

9. In Samaritan thought the *Taheb* (messianic deliverer) was to be accompanied by a priest. Similarly, Simon Bar Kosiba, the pseudo-Messiah who set himself up as king during the second revolt (132–35), had a priestly companion.

10. The Aramaic *bar ʾĕnāš* (Greek, *ho huios tou anthrōpou*) probably means "man" or "the man." See H. E. Tödt, *The Son of Man in the Synoptic Tradition*, trans. Dorothea M. Barton (Philadelphia: Westminster, 1965).

11. The NRSV, in keeping with its policy of avoiding sexist language, translates the Aramaic *bar ʾĕnāš* "human being." This is an unfortunate rendering. It might be justified in most cases in Ezekiel, where the phrase "son of man" is the standard form of address with which God calls the prophet to ministry (although even here the phrase is addressed to a male person who is singled out for a special role and responsibilities). In Daniel the context requires that "the Son of man" be recognized as at least a transcendent figure. The NRSV translators made an interpre-

was presented before him. To him was given dominion and glory and kingship, that all peoples, nations, and languages should serve him. His dominion is an everlasting dominion that shall not pass away, and his kingship is one that shall never be destroyed." Here the reference is somewhat uncertain; the "one like a son of man" may be equated with "the holy ones of the Most High" (v. 18), possibly the nation of Israel as a corporate Messiah that rules after the judgment.

In 1 Enoch the Son of man, once again a heavenly figure, is personalized and associated with "the traits of sovereignty grouped around the traditional Last Judgment and its execution."[12] We shall let the major references to the Son of man that appear in the second and third parables speak for themselves:

> At that place, I saw the One to whom belongs the time before time [literally, Head of days]. And his head was white like wool, and there was with him another individual, whose face was like that of a human being. His countenance was full of grace like that of one among the holy angels. And I asked the one—from among the angels—who was going with me, and who had revealed to me all the secrets regarding the One who was born of human beings [the Son of Man], "Who is this, and from whence is he who is going as the prototype of the Before-Time [Head of days]?" And he answered me and said to me, "This is the Son of Man, to whom belongs righteousness, and with whom righteousness dwells. And he will open all the hidden storerooms . . . he is destined to be victorious before the Lord of the Spirits in eternal uprightness. This Son of Man . . . is the One who would remove the kings. . . . He shall loosen the reins of the strong and crush the teeth of the sinners. He shall depose the kings. . . . For they do not extol and glorify him, the source of their kingship." [46:1–5]

> That Son of Man was given a name, in the presence of the Lord of the Spirits, the Before-Time [Head of days], even before the creation. . . . He will become a staff for the righteous ones. . . . He is the light of the gentiles and he will become the hope of those who are sick in their hearts. All those who dwell upon the earth shall fall and worship before him. . . . For this purpose he became the Chosen One; he was concealed in the presence of (the Lord of the Spirits) prior to the creation of the world, and for eternity. And he has revealed the wisdom of the Lord of the Spirits to the righteous and the holy ones, for he has preserved the portion of the righteous . . . they will be saved in his name and it is his good pleasure that they have life. [48:2–7]

---

tive judgment which removes even the possibility of a connection between Daniel's "son of man" and Jesus' frequent employing the title (especially in the Synoptic Gospels) as his favorite self-designation.

12. Tödt, Son of Man, 29.

On the day of judgment, all the kings, the governors, the high officials, and the landlords . . . shall be terrified and dejected; and pain shall seize them when they see that Son of Man sitting on the throne of his glory. . . . For the Son of Man was concealed from the beginning, and the Most High One preserved him . . . then he revealed him to the holy and the elect ones. . . . Those who rule the earth shall fall down before him on their faces, and worship and raise their hopes in that Son of Man; they shall beg and plead for mercy at his feet. [62:3–9]

The righteous and elect ones shall be saved on that day. . . . The Lord of the Spirits will abide over them; they shall eat and rest and rise with that Son of Man forever and ever. [62:13–14]

[In the day of judgment the rulers of the world will plead for mercy before the Lord of the Spirits.] After that, their faces shall be filled with shame before that Son of Man; and from before his face they shall be driven out. [63:11]

They blessed, glorified, and extolled (the Lord) on account of the fact that the name of that (Son of) Man was revealed to them. He shall never pass away or perish from before the face of the earth. But those who have led the world astray shall be bound with chains. . . . Thenceforth nothing that is corruptible shall be found; for that Son of Man has appeared and has seated himself upon the throne of his glory; and all evil shall disappear from before his face; he shall go and tell to that Son of Man, and he shall be strong before the Lord of the Spirits. . . . And it happened after this that his living name was raised up before that Son of Man and to the Lord from among those who dwell upon the earth. [69:27–70:1]

There shall be length of days with that Son of Man, and peace to the righteous ones; his path is upright for the righteous, in the name of the Lord of the Spirits forever and ever. [71:17]

It is evident that the Enochic Son of man is preexistent, heavenly, and majestic. He possesses dominion and will judge all humankind and angels.

Considerable scholarly debate centers on a number of issues related to the title *Son of man*. For example, it is an open question whether the Son of man and the Messiah were usually equated or considered separate figures before the time of Jesus.[13] Whatever answer be given, at least some Jewish groups expected a remarkable figure to appear in the final age. This is "the Chosen One, the

13. In the Synoptic Gospels "Son of man" is Jesus' favorite self-designation. "Messiah" and "Son of man" are equated in John 12:34, as are "Son," "Son of God," and "Son of man" in John 5:22–27.

Son of Man, a transcendental being, pre-existent, close to God. He is invested with divine gifts, shares God's throne and exercises the divine function of judgment; the support of men, he is the object of their adoration and reigns with God for all eternity." With regard to this expected Messiah–Son of man, Joseph Bonsirven concludes, "It seems that certain Jewish schools thought of the Messiah as a divine being";[14] he may well be pushing the data in existing sources too far. Emil Schürer is probably closer to the truth when he says that "the Messiah was thought of as a human king and ruler, but one endowed by God with special gifts and powers. . . . The whole view of His person is . . . one essentially supernatural."[15]

The Servant of the LORD

Another Old Testament figure of importance is the Servant of the LORD (ʿebed YHWH). References to the Servant are found in a number of places in Isaiah. Four passages, the Servant Songs (Isa. 42:1–4; 49:1–7; 50:4–11; and 52:13–53:12), are of special importance. Interpreters debate the nature and identity of the Servant. Is he a real person or an idealized concept? Is the Servant a contemporary individual, such as the prophet himself, or some future person who would come to fulfil God's purpose? Do these passages speak of a collective figure, such as the Israelites as a whole or the righteous remnant of the nation? Actually, there may be vacillation between several of these alternatives, even within Isaiah; this is more evident if our study includes all the references to the Servant, not just the four Servant Songs.

The divine and human perspectives on the Servant are quite different. From God's perspective the Servant is his chosen one, his delight, the one with whom he is well pleased. God will anoint him with the Spirit and will eventually raise up and vindicate his Servant. But by human beings the Servant is rejected. At their hands he is mocked, tortured (suffers), and killed. In Isaiah 53 the task of the Servant of the LORD is to suffer for the sins of others, to take the place of the many who should have suffered. By this vicarious

---

14. Bonsirven, *Palestinian Judaism*, 189. Not all agree that the Jewish sources portray the Son of man as a preexistent figure; see T. W. Manson, "The Son of Man in Daniel, Enoch and the Gospels," in *Studies in the Gospels and Epistles* (Philadelphia: Westminster, 1962), 123–45.

15. Emil Schürer, *A History of the Jewish People in the Time of Jesus Christ*, trans. J. MacPherson et al., 5 vols. (Edinburgh: T. and T. Clark, 1897–98), 2:1, 160–61. The new edition (1973–87) says, "Pre-Christian Judaism—in so far as its messianic expectations can be conclusively documented—regarded the Messiah as a fully human individual, a royal figure descended from the house of David . . . but as one endowed by God with special gifts and powers. . . . In 4 Ezra and the Parables of Enoch, his appearance is raised to the level of the supernatural and he is credited with pre-existence" (2:518–19).

suffering he makes them righteous before God. Through his Servant, God reestablishes his covenant between himself and his chosen people.[16]

In Intertestamental Judaism the interpretation of the Servant moved between the collective and individual understandings of the term. The Septuagint (with three exceptions) translates ʿebed YHWH as pais theou.[17] Pais can mean either "child" or "servant." In Hellenistic Judaism most interpreters seem to have understood the term as "son" and interpreted it as a collective representing Israel as a whole.[18]

However, there was another tradition, probably also within Hellenistic Judaism, "which used the 'Servant Hymns' and certain other prophecies to characterize the history and personage of an exceptional man."[19] A classic example is Wisdom of Solomon 1–5, which uses Servant motifs in describing the persecution and suffering of the just man.[20] In the land of Israel the Servant passages were variously understood as referring to Israel (Isa. 44:1–2, 21; 45:4; 48:20; 49:3), to a specific group in Israel (this appears to be the position of the Qumran community), to the prophet himself (49:5; 50:10), and to the Messiah.[21]

What is the relationship between the Servant and the expected Messiah or messianic figure? The occasional identification of the

16. Oscar Cullmann, *The Christology of the New Testament,* trans. Shirley C. Guthrie and Charles A. M. Hall (Philadelphia: Westminster, 1959), 55, summarizes, "The most essential characteristic . . . is that his vicarious representation is accomplished through suffering. The *ebed* [servant] is the *suffering* Servant of God. Through suffering he takes the place of the many who should suffer instead of him. A second essential characteristic of the *ebed Yahweh* is that his representative work *re-establishes the covenant* which God has made with his people."

17. Hence the use of the phrase in Christian writings: Matt. 12:18; Acts 3:13, 26; 4:27, 30; Didache 9:2; 10:2; 1 Clement 59:2–4.

18. Joachim Jeremias in Walther Zimmerli and Joachim Jeremias, *The Servant of God,* trans. Harold Knight (Naperville, Ill.: Allenson, 1957), 51. This is a translation of *"Pais theou,"* in *Theologisches Wörterbuch zum Neuen Testament,* ed. Gerhard Friedrich, vol. 5 (Stuttgart: Kohlhammer, 1954).

19. Pierre Prigent, *Les Testimonia dans le christianisme primitif: L'Epitre de Barnabé I–XVI et ses sources* (Paris: Lecoffre, 1961), 215–16, as quoted in a review by R. A. Kraft, *Journal of Theological Studies,* n.s., 13 (1962): 403.

20. E.g., 2:10, "Let us oppress the righteous poor man; let us not spare the widow or regard the gray hairs of the aged."

21. Isa. 42:1–4 and 53:13–15 were consistently interpreted messianically in the pre-Christian centuries, as were, on occasion, 43:10 and 49:1–7. Ezek. 34:23–24 and 37:24–25 refer messianically to "my servant David," as does Zech. 3:8 to "my servant the Branch." See also the targums for Isa. 42:1; 43:10; Ezek. 34:23–24; 37:24–25; and Zech. 3:8. In 1 Enoch 37–71 the Son of man and Servant of God are combined (on this see Jeremias, *Servant,* 58–60); 2 Baruch 70:9 refers to "my Servant, the Anointed One"; 2 Esdras 7:28–29; 13:32, 37; and 14:9 speak of "my son the Messiah" and "my Son," which Jeremias (*Servant,* 49) interprets as a reference to the Servant (*pais*).

Servant of Isaiah with the Messiah raises the question whether some Jews may have expected a suffering Messiah. It is almost commonplace for scholars to deny the possibility of such a belief in pre-Christian times.[22] The evidence, however, is not so definitive. The suffering of just or righteous persons for the benefit of others is well established in the Old Testament and beyond. It is not by chance that in Isaiah 53:11 the righteous (just) one and the Servant are equated: "The righteous one, my servant, shall make many righteous, and he shall bear their iniquities." In the targums and rabbinic literature there is a definite messianic interpretation of this passage.[23] The Targum of Jonathan to Isaiah dates from the fourth or fifth century of the Common Era. Here usually "the Messiah is a figure intimately associated with the restoration."[24] Yet in the very period of time in which one would expect Jewish sources to put distance between the Servant and the Messiah the targum on 52:13 equates the Servant and the Messiah.[25] Similarly, in the second century A.D., Justin Martyr, in discussion with Trypho the Jew, assumes a pre-Christian Jewish belief in a suffering Messiah. Trypho does not deny this assumption, objecting only to the idea of a crucified Messiah,[26] which would be an impossibility to the Jewish mind because of the curse in Deuteronomy 21:23—"anyone hung on a tree is under God's curse." How could the Messiah, who by definition is blessed, be crucified and therefore be cursed because of the method of his death?[27]

The editors of the new edition of Emil Schürer's *History of the Jewish People in the Age of Jesus Christ* note that the essential issue

22. Examples include Paul Volz, *Jüdische Eschatologie von Daniel bis Akiba* (Tübingen: 1903), 237, as quoted by W. D. Davies, *Paul and Rabbinic Judaism,* 2d ed. (London: SPCK, 1955), 275; Charles Guignebert, *The Jewish World in the Time of Jesus,* trans. S. H. Hooke (London: Kegan Paul, Trench, Trubner, 1939), 145–50; and George Foot Moore, *Judaism in the First Centuries of the Christian Era,* 3 vols. (Cambridge, Mass.: Harvard University Press, 1927–30), 1:551–52; 2:370.

23. Samson H. Levey, *The Messiah: An Aramaic Interpretation; The Messianic Exegesis of the Targum* (Cincinnati: Hebrew Union College–Jewish Institute of Religion, 1974), 65–67; Bruce D. Chilton, *The Glory of Israel: The Theology and Provenience of the Isaiah Targum* (Sheffield: JSOT, 1982), 86–96. Yet in discussing rabbinic views about the Messiah, Jacob Neusner, *Messiah in Context* (Philadelphia: Fortress, 1984), does not even mention a possible relationship between the Servant and the Messiah.

24. Chilton, *Glory of Israel,* 87.

25. Targum for Isa. 52:13, "Behold, my servant, the Anointed One (or, *the Messiah*), shall prosper"; similarly, 53:10, in the general context of the work of the Servant, "they shall look upon the kingdom of their Anointed One (or, *Messiah*)" (*The Targum of Isaiah,* trans. J. F. Stenning [Oxford: Clarendon, 1949], 178, 180). On the other hand, the targum on chapter 53 generally makes the nation Israel the Suffering Servant.

26. Justin Martyr *Dialogue with Trypho* 89–90.

27. It is with this problem that Paul seems to wrestle in Gal. 3:1–14.

is not whether there was any idea of a suffering Messiah. Rather, the question is whether there was any idea of a suffering Messiah "whose sufferings and death could have atoning value." The Schürer editors do acknowledge that Rabbinic Judaism may have entertained the notions that a "perfectly just man . . . [can] atone . . . through suffering for past sins, and that the excessive suffering of the just is for the benefit of others." But they cite "the behaviour of both the disciples and the opponents of Jesus (Mt. 16:22; Lk. 18:34; 24:21; Jn. 12:34)" as evidence that the notion of a Messiah who suffers for sin was, if existent, not common in first-century Judaism.[28]

On the other hand, various New Testament references claim an Old Testament basis for the contention that the Messiah must suffer (Luke 24:25–26, 44–46; Acts 3:18; 17:3; 26:22–23). Where, one asks, do we find this idea outside the Servant passages? We might point first to the experience of suffering by the nation, especially if the Messiah were understood to be corporate Israel. Certain of the psalms (e.g., 22) speak of mysterious sufferers. The shepherd of Zechariah was betrayed (11:12–13) and smitten of God (13:7). Both within the Old Testament and beyond is the tradition of the suffering righteous one (Isa. 53:11; the Septuagint of Isa. 3:10;[29] and Wisdom of Solomon 2:10).

Assistance in understanding the New Testament references to the suffering Messiah comes from studies by C. H. Dodd.[30] He not only studied the individual Old Testament references in the New, but also noted that many of them come from the same general Old Testament contexts, where what he calls a similar "plot" can be discerned.[31] In this scheme an innocent individual or group is rejected, tortured, and sometimes killed; then through a dramatic reversal of fortune, the sufferer is vindicated, honored, and glorified. Dodd goes on to suggest that when the New Testament writer quotes from the Old Testament, he intends to call attention to the entire context, including the plot, as well as to the actual words. It is, he believes, from the plot of unjust suffering followed by a dra-

28. Schürer, *History* (1973–87), 2:547–49.

29. Contrast the Greek in the Septuagint, "Let us bind the righteous one, for he is burdensome to us," with the Hebrew (NRSV), "Tell the innocent how fortunate they are, for they shall eat the fruit of their labors."

30. C. H. Dodd, *The Old Testament in the New* (Philadelphia: Fortress, 1963); idem, *According to the Scriptures: The Sub-Structure of New Testament Theology* (New York: Scribner, 1952).

31. In addition to the Servant Songs of Isaiah, the Old Testament plot texts include Ps. 69; Ps. 80 (the vine); Isa. 6:1–9:7; Joel 2–3; Zech. 9–14; the Son of man passages (Ps. 8; Dan. 7:13–14); and the Stone passages (e.g., Ps. 118:22; Isa. 8:14; Dan. 2:34–45; cf. Matt. 21:42; [=Mark 12:10–11; Luke 20:17–18]; Acts 4:11; Eph. 2:20; 1 Peter 2:4–8).

matic reversal and honor that the New Testament writers understand the Old Testament to proclaim the necessity of the death of the Messiah.

It seems, then, that there is among certain groups a faint trace of a Jewish expectation of a suffering Messiah or at least of some suffering eschatological figure.[32] This expectation began to grow in intensity and acceptance in some circles during the second century before the Christian Era.[33] However, the evidence does not support the idea that at the time of Jesus there was a widespread expectation of messianic suffering. Such an expectation may have been limited to the more learned circles or to the periphery of Judaism.[34]

The Prophet like Moses

Yet another title with messianic importance is the Prophet or the Prophet like Moses.[35] Deuteronomy 18:9–22 warns Israel against engaging in idolatrous practices and using magical, occult means of seeking divine revelation and guidance (see also Deut. 12:29–13:18). It promises that God will raise up a Prophet like Moses to communicate with Israel. This passage is the basis for the prophetic office in Israel. However, some Jewish groups came to interpret Deuteronomy 18 to mean that one particular prophet, another Moses, would come.[36] A messianic Prophet like Moses could be expected to lead a new exodus from bondage, reestablish the covenant, bring a better revelation of God (a new law or better interpretation of the law), and, in short, serve as a new national founder.

Elijah

The name of the prophet Elijah also figured in some intertestamental Jewish expectations. There were, however, a number of ideas about the role Elijah would play in the final age. On the basis

32. After a careful survey of the data Davies, *Paul*, 283, concludes that it "is at least possible that the conception of a Suffering Messiah was not unfamiliar to pre-Christian Judaism."

33. Schürer, *History* (1897–98), 2:2, 186.

34. Cullmann, *Christology*, 56–57.

35. See Cullmann, *Christology*, 13–50; Howard M. Teeple, *The Mosaic Eschatological Prophet* (Philadelphia: Society of Biblical Literature, 1957).

36. 1 Maccabees 14:41; Testament of Levi 8:14–15; Philo *Special Laws* 1.11 (64–65); 4QTest; 1QS 9:11. It has also been suggested that the idea of a new Moses lies behind at least some of the servant ideology of Isaiah; see Aage Bentzen, *King and Messiah* (London: Lutterworth, 1955), 65–67.

The Samaritans had a doctrine of a *Taheb* (Restorer) which was based on Deut. 18:15 coupled with Deut. 34:10–12 (where the Samaritan Pentateuch reads "No prophet shall arise like Moses" instead of "Never since has there arisen a prophet in Israel like Moses"). They believed that Moses did not really die but was hidden away until the appointed time. He would then reappear as Messiah.

of Malachi 4:5–6, some expected Elijah (or an Elijah-like figure) to be the forerunner who would prepare the way for the Messiah. Others seem to have expected Elijah to come back to life to be the Messiah.[37] Justin Martyr preserves a tradition that the Elijah-forerunner would actually anoint the Messiah.[38]

Other Terms and Titles

In addition to the terms we have been discussing, the Old Testament and apocalyptic sources use other titles for an expected eschatological figure.[39] The concept of a present or coming Savior,[40] Judge, or Deliverer is prominent in the Old Testament, intertestamental writings, and Hellenism.[41] It may, at times, reflect the position and work of the Old Testament judges,[42] as well as the broader concept of a rescuer from distressing or dangerous situations, sickness, death, or rejection by God. In Ezekiel 34:11–16 "shepherd" is an image describing God's gathering his scattered people; it also seems to be a messianic term in the context of Zechariah 9–14 (especially 11:4–17; 13:7).[43] "Word" (*logos*) is clearly a messianic-christological title in John 1:1–18; Wisdom may at times be virtually identical with it.[44] Both titles are usually assumed to have come from a Hellenistic environment, but they may have Hebrew roots as well.[45] Other designations include the Righteous or

37. See Sirach 48:1–11, esp. 10–11.

38. Justin Martyr *Dialogue with Trypho* 49.

39. Note the apocalyptic background in the messianic discussion of Luke 17:20–21.

40. The proper Hebrew name Joshua translates into Greek as *Iēsous* or Jesus, which means "Yahweh saves." The verbal connection raises the possibility that some Hebrews may have looked for a messianic figure who would be a leader-savior like Joshua, just as some looked for a Prophet like Moses. Heb. 4:1–11 may reflect some such idea. A textual variant in Jude 5 has "Jesus/Joshua" where the NRSV has "the Lord"; hence, "I desire to remind you, though you are fully informed, that *Joshua* [or *Jesus*], who once for all saved a people out of the land of Egypt, afterward destroyed those who did not believe."

41. Werner Foerster, *"sōtēr,"* in *Theological Dictionary of the New Testament,* ed. Gerhard Kittel and Gerhard Friedrich, trans. Geoffrey W. Bromiley, 10 vols. (Grand Rapids: Eerdmans, 1964–76), 7:1003–14; Cullmann, *Christology,* 236–40.

42. A related concept may lie behind the use of *archēgos* (pioneer, founder, victor, leader, ruler, hero) in Acts 3:15; 5:31; Heb. 2:10; 12:2. The word is also used in one of the Greek texts of Judg. 11:6, 11 to describe the position of Jephthah. See also Isa. 9:6.

43. Ancient shepherds presented a mixed image. Hence Jesus carefully identifies himself as the *good* shepherd who cares and provides for his flock (John 10:11–16).

44. Prov. 8–9; Sirach 4:11–19; 14:20–27; 24:1–34; 51:13–30; Wisdom of Solomon, esp. 6:12–11:1; see Ulrich Wilckens, *"Sophia,"* in *Theological Dictionary of the New Testament,* 7:498–505.

45. On "Wisdom" see n. 44. "Word" has well-known roots in Greek philosophy, especially Stoicism. It is also the usual translation for the Hebrew *dābār,* the creative word of God and the oracle through which he reveals himself and his message. The Aramaic *memra* can be a translation for *logos* and also for the divine name. See Cullmann, *Christology,* 254–58.

Just One,[46] the Branch,[47] the Elect or Chosen One,[48] the Son of God or of David,[49] the Stone,[50] and the Coming One.[51]

Signs and Proofs of Messiahship

There was messianic ferment in the land of Israel in the first century. The conduct if not the claims of messianic pretenders before as well as after Jesus must have raised the question, "Is this the Messiah?" (John 1:19–22; 4:29). Jesus predicted that many would present themselves as such (Mark 13:6); ancient writings confirm the accuracy of his statement.[52] Thus the question, "On what grounds were the Jews to accept or reject a messianic candidate?" There was no formally prescribed procedure. There are, however, hints in the New Testament and other writings which permit us to say something on this subject.

The evaluation of a messianic claim was both an individual and an official matter. Those who committed themselves to Jesus did so on the basis of their own assessment of him (John 1:38–45; 4:42). The same could be said for the followers of Theudas,[53] of the Egyptian,[54] and of other supposed eschatological figures. Decision by officials needed more solid bases.

46. 2 Sam. 23:3; the Septuagint of Isa. 3:10; Isa. 32:1; 53:11 (cf. Isa. 42:6, where Yahweh says to his servant, "I have called you in righteousness"); 1 Enoch 38:2; 45:6; 53:6; Psalms of Solomon 17:26; Wisdom of Solomon 2:10–20. In the Dead Sea Scrolls the concept of righteousness often appears; it is ascribed to God (e.g., 1QS 10:12), the Righteous Teacher (e.g., 1QpHab 5:10), and the "Righteous Messiah" (4QPBless 1:3); see Frank Moore Cross, *The Ancient Library of Qumran*, 2d ed. (London: Duckworth, 1961), 80ff. The community itself is called the Righteous Ones (1QH 1:36; 1QS 3:20, 22; 9:14; CD 11); however, *qĕdōšîm* (saints) is usually used in this connection in preference to *ṣadîqim*.

47. The Branch or Shoot (= offspring) of David—Isa. 11:1; Jer. 23:5; 33:15; Zech. 3:8; 6:12.

48. Isa. 42:1; 43:10; 44:1 (= Israel); 1 Enoch 45:3–5; 49:2; 51:3–4; 52:6, 9; 53:6; 55:4; 61:8; 62:1.

49. Isa. 9:6–7; 1 Enoch 105:2; 2 Esdras 7:28–29; 13:32, 37, 52; 14:9; 4QFlor 1:10–12; see also Cullmann, *Christology*, 272–75.

50. Ps. 118:22; Isa. 8:14; 28:16; Dan. 2:35, 44–45; see also Gen. 28:18.

51. Apparently this term does not appear directly in the Old Testament or intertestamental writings. Two of the three New Testament usages of the construction—definite article and participle (*ho opisō mou erchomenos*, literally, "the behind-me Coming One")—occur in the preaching of John the Baptist (Matt. 3:11 [but not in the Lucan parallel] and John 1:27) and thus may be a peculiarity of his preaching. The term may also reflect a common means of referring to the expected eschatological figure. Heb. 10:37 seems to strengthen this possibility.

52. For a list and description of messianic movements in the first century see Richard A. Horsley with John S. Hanson, *Bandits, Prophets, and Messiahs: Popular Movements at the Time of Jesus* (New York: Harper and Row, 1985), 110–31.

53. Acts 5:36; Josephus *Antiquities* 20.5.1 (97–98); on whether or not Josephus and Acts refer to the same individual see F. F. Bruce, *The Book of the Acts*, rev. ed. (Grand Rapids: Eerdmans, 1988), 116 n. 57.

54. Acts 21:38; Josephus *Jewish War* 2.13.5 (261–63); idem, *Antiquities* 20.8.6 (169–72).

In Matthew 15:1; Mark 3:22; and 7:1 we read of individuals who came from Jerusalem to hear Jesus. They are identified as scribes or Pharisees. Were they some sort of an official board of enquiry? Earlier a group of "Jews sent priests and Levites from Jerusalem to ask [John the Baptist], 'Who are you?'" (John 1:20). It is reasonable to assume that the authorities would seek to gather information about any charismatic person and that some of those from Jerusalem who joined the crowds around Jesus were sent for that purpose. In the case of John the Baptist they asked the pointed questions, "Are you the Messiah? Elijah? the Prophet?"—all messianic titles. At least once, when Jesus was in the temple, "the Jews . . . said to him, If you are the Messiah, tell us plainly" (John 10:24).

John 7:30 tells of an attempt to arrest Jesus. The purpose was probably to examine him personally in view of the popular excitement he had aroused. This may represent another step in an official investigation. We read in the following verse that the crowds were asking, "When the Messiah comes, will he do more signs than this man has done?" (v. 31). Hence we must assume that signs were expected as indications of the Messiah's presence. Jesus himself says, "The works that the Father has given me to complete, the very works that I am doing, testify on my behalf that the Father has sent me" (John 5:36; see also 10:24–26; 14:11). Peter says that Jesus was attested by "deeds of power, wonders, and signs that God did through him" (Acts 2:22). John 12:37 complains that the crowds had not believed in Jesus "although he had performed so many signs in their presence."

What kind of signs was the Messiah expected to perform? Miracles were generally expected in first-century Palestine. The issue was not so much whether a miracle was genuine as in whose name it had been performed,[55] which was the test for true prophecy. Deuteronomy 13:1–5 calls for the death of any prophet who seeks to turn Israel after other gods. We might also assume that the characteristics that Deuteronomy 18 expects of a prophet would be expected of the Prophet as well. A prophet was to be a Hebrew called by Israel's covenant God, to speak in his name, have an awareness of history, display social and ethical concerns, and be able to combine proclamation and prediction.

An indication of the miracles that might be expected of the Messiah comes from the New Testament. When John the Baptist sent

55. The apostles declared before the council, "Let it be known to all of you, and to all the people of Israel, that this man is standing before you in good health by the name of Jesus Christ of Nazareth, whom you crucified, whom God raised from the dead" (Acts 4:10; see also Matt. 7:22; Mark 9:38–39; John 10:25; Acts 3:6, 16; 4:7, 30; 16:18; 19:13).

to enquire of Jesus, "Are you the one who is to come, or are we to wait for another?" Jesus called attention to his miracles: "the blind receive their sight, the lame walk, the lepers are cleansed, the deaf hear, the dead are raised, and the poor have good news brought to them" (Matt. 11:2–5; see also Luke 7:21–22). These are essentially the miracles predicted by Isaiah.[56] Jesus asserts that they, his works, are his attestation. Such miracles, we might note, are not incompatible with the conditions expected in the final or messianic age.[57]

We should also note that what otherwise appears to have been outrageous behavior by the Sanhedrin at Jesus' trial may in fact have been another test for Messiahship. Following his acknowledgment that he was the Messiah, they blindfolded and struck him, and demanded that he identify who had struck him (Mark 14:61–65). These actions appear to be based on "an old interpretation of Isa. 11:2–4, according to which the Messiah could judge by smell without the need of sight."[58] Identifying who had struck him while he was blindfolded would presumably prove Messiahship.

Jesus also offered the sign of Jonah: "just as Jonah was three days and three nights in the belly of the sea monster, so for three days and three nights the Son of Man will be in the heart of the earth" (Matt. 12:39–40; see also 16:4; Luke 11:29–30). This his contemporaries could not, or would not, understand. The sign for which the vast majority awaited was national deliverance, independence from Rome. They looked for the Messiah to enter Jerusalem as "the one who comes in the name of the Lord! Blessed is the coming kingdom of our ancestor David!" (Mark 11:9–10). And they reserved the right to define precisely what those words meant. Clearly there was a wide diversity of opinion as to what signs would indicate the presence of Messiah.

---

56. Isa. 29:18–19, "the deaf shall hear . . . the eyes of the blind shall see. The meek shall obtain fresh joy in the LORD, and the neediest people shall exult"; 35:5–6, "the eyes of the blind shall be opened, and the ears of the deaf unstopped . . . the lame shall leap . . . the tongue of the speechless sing"; 61:1, "he has sent me to bring good news to the oppressed."

57. For a description of the signs by which the Messiah was expected by the rabbinic writings to produce the idyllic conditions of the messianic age, see Klausner, *Messianic Idea*, 502–17.

58. William L. Lane, *The Gospel According to Mark*, New International Commentary on the New Testament (Grand Rapids: Eerdmans, 1974), 539–40. As Lane explains (n. 148), the Babylonian Talmud *Sanhedrin* 93b renders Isa. 11:3–4, "He smells [a man] and judges, as it is written, 'and he shall not judge after the sight of his eyes, neither reprove after the hearing of his ears, yet with righteousness shall he judge the poor.'" The rabbis thus assumed that 11:3 says, "His smell is through the fear of the LORD"—the Hebrew word usually translated "his delight" they read as "smell." The talmudic passage immediately following speaks of the pseudo-Messiah Bar Kosiba: "Bar Koziba reigned two and a half years, and then said to the rabbis, 'I am the Messiah.' They answered, 'Of Messiah it is written that he smells and judges: let us see whether he can do so.' When they saw that he was unable to judge by scent, they slew him."

The Work of the Messiah

The nature of the messianic task was another subject on which Intertestamental Judaism had diverse opinions. The Messiah was expected to be at the center of the great eschatological drama of the final age which we outlined in chapter 14. He was to be the inaugurator of that age, the one to bring it into existence. He was looked to as the founder of the kingdom of God and the supreme ruler in it. Above all he would "restore the kingdom to Israel" (Acts 1:6). Each of the Old Testament models of the final age (Eden, the exodus, and the Davidic-Solomonic era) had its corresponding messianic work. Each eschatological term or title likewise carried with it an implied unique messianic task.

The Messiah's anticipated role as Savior may have been vague, but the New Testament affirmation that Jesus "will save his people from their sins" (Matt. 1:21) was certainly within the contours of the intertestamental Jewish messianic hope.[59] Such sentiments were compatible with the expectation of the final age and the consummation, when God would complete his work to reverse the effects of the fall.

---

59. The Son of man seems to have been looked for more as a spiritual, cosmic ruler. So Jesus' teaching that "the Son of Man came not to be served but to serve, and to give his life a ransom for many" (Mark 10:45) and "to seek out and to save the lost" (Luke 19:10) would have been difficult for his disciples to understand.

17

Covenant and Law in the Final Age

- Covenant in the Final Age
- Law in the Final Age

Covenant in the Final Age

Monotheism, covenant, and law are the foundational pillars of the Hebrew faith. The psalmist expresses confidence in God's unchangeable nature as he cries, "Long ago you laid the foundation of the earth, and the heavens are the work of your hands. They will perish, but you endure; they will all wear out . . . but you are the same, and your years have no end" (Ps. 102:25–27). But what of the other two? Could the arrival of the final age, which was expected to bring radical change, affect covenant and law?

In the Old Testament, Jeremiah speaks most explicitly of a new, or at least a renewed, covenant:

> The days are surely coming, says the LORD, when I will make a new covenant with the house of Israel and the house of Judah. It will not be like the covenant that I made with their ancestors when I took them by the hand to bring them out of the land of Egypt—a covenant that they broke, though I was their husband, says the LORD. But this is the covenant that I will make with the house of Israel after those days, says the LORD: I will put my law within them, and I will write it on their hearts; and I will be their God, and they shall be my people. No longer shall they teach one another, or say to each other, "Know the LORD," for they

shall all know me, from the least of them to the greatest, says the LORD; for I will forgive their iniquity, and remember their sin no more. [Jer. 31:31–34; see also Ezek. 36:22–36]

The concept is found elsewhere. In Ezekiel 37, for an example, the vision of the resuscitation of dry bones and the joining of the two sticks (Judah and Joseph) concludes with the promise, "I will make a covenant of peace with them . . . an everlasting covenant" (v. 26).

The vast majority of references to "covenant" in intertestamental writings affirm its eternal nature or confess Israel's sin in breaking it. References to a new covenant are sparse and usually ambiguous. In speaking of the restoration of Israel to her land, Baruch 2:35 says, "I will make an everlasting covenant with them to be their God and they shall be my people; and I will never again remove my people Israel from the land that I have given them."

The Book of Jubilees assumes the permanent validity of the law and implies that the future age is in some sense already present.[1] Within this context, although the word *covenant* is not used, a statement like Jubilees 1:22–25 is significant:

And the LORD said to Moses, "I know their contrariness and their thoughts and their stubbornness. And they will not obey until they acknowledge their sin and the sins of their fathers. But after this they will return to me in all uprightness and with all of (their) heart and soul. And I shall cut off the foreskin of their heart and the foreskin of the heart of their descendants. And I shall create for them a holy spirit, and I shall purify them so that they will not turn away from following me from that day and forever. And their souls will cleave to me and to all my commandments. And they will do my commandments. And I shall be a father to them, and they will be sons to me. And they will all be called 'sons of the living God.' And every angel and spirit will know and acknowledge that they are my sons and I am their father in uprightness and righteousness. And I shall love them."

This statement is similar to the Jeremiah passage in both word and concept. It clearly points to a new relationship between God and his people sometime in the future.

Our earlier discussion of the Dead Sea community noted that it regarded itself as the Israel of the last days (pp. 224–27). Covenantal terminology and concepts are prominent in the scrolls, even use

---

1. Jubilees 2:33, "This law and testimony was given to the children of Israel as an eternal law for their generations"; see also 6:14; 13:25–26; 15:25, 28–29; 16:29–30; 30:10; 49:8. Jubilees several times asserts that the law is "written in the heavenly tablets" (3:31; 6:17; 15:25; 16:29; 49:8). With regard to the presence of the future age see *The Apocrypha and Pseudepigrapha of the Old Testament*, ed. R. H. Charles, 2 vols. (Oxford: Clarendon, 1913), 2:9.

of the phrase "new covenant." The group believed it was living under such a covenant; this conviction held it together and dominated its life.

In the New Testament the Last Supper is a ceremony renewing the covenant. Jesus pronounces, "This is my blood of the covenant" (Matt. 26:28; Mark 14:24; Luke 22:20; 1 Cor. 11:25). Some manuscripts of Matthew and Mark join Luke and 1 Corinthians in including the word "new" to modify "covenant."

The Epistle to the Hebrews clearly affirms that because the final age ("these last days," 1:2) is present,[2] the new covenant has made the former "obsolete. And what is obsolete and growing old will soon disappear" (8:13). Twice the author cites the "new covenant" passage in Jeremiah 31 (Heb. 8:8–12; 10:16–17); he also asserts that Jesus is "the mediator of a better covenant" (Heb. 8:6; see also 7:22; 9:15; 12:24). All this because Jesus has appeared "at the end of the age" (Heb. 9:26).

Although there is some obscurity as to exactly what is meant by "a new covenant," both the Old Testament and the intertestamental writers believe that something will happen to the covenant at the dawn of the final age. Nevertheless, when Jeremiah speaks of "a new covenant," he summarizes its content with the same words that state the essence of the old covenant, "I will be their God, and they shall be my people." Hence it is clear that the essential nature of the new covenant is the same as that of the old. The real newness of the new covenant seems to be in the way it is to be administered, and particularly in the way the law relates to it.

Law in the Final Age

The close relation between covenant and law could lead to the supposition that what was to happen with one would also happen with the other; if there was to be a new covenant, there would be a new law as well. This expectation is not, however, explicitly stated in the Jewish writings from before and during the period of Herod's temple.

Before continuing we must ask what sort of evidence would point to belief in a change in law in the final age. We must understand clearly that the intertestamental Jew viewed the law as a whole. If one part were affected, all would be affected; if part of the law were set aside, the whole would in some sense be abrogated. This Jewish view is clearly summarized in James 2:10: "For

2. For the underlying structure see J. Julius Scott, Jr., "*Archēgos* in the Salvation History of the Epistle to the Hebrews," *Journal of the Evangelical Theological Society* 29.1 (March 1986): 47–54.

whoever keeps the whole law but fails in one point has become accountable for all of it" (see also Gal. 3:10). Thus any evidence of expectation of an alteration, replacement, or setting aside of any commandment or legal institution during the final age would point to a belief that the law as a whole would change.

Careful studies of the place of law in the final age have been few. Most important is a small book by W. D. Davies, *Torah in the Messianic Age and/or the Age to Come*.[3] The major lines of his argument have served to shape the remainder of this chapter.

In the intertestamental period it was assumed that the law would remain the standard for righteousness and judgment in the final age. Hence those intertestamental passages which speak of the righteous or judgment presuppose continuing validity of the law.

In Sirach, 1 Enoch, and Wisdom of Solomon, Davies notes, there is a close connection between Wisdom and law; this is significant, he says, "because from early times wisdom had been associated with Torah as in Deuteronomy 4:6."[4] In 1 Enoch 42:1–2 Wisdom finds no earthly home and returns to heaven. When this passage is placed beside several others "where it is claimed that Wisdom in its fullness is the mark of the Messianic existence," we have the implication that law will cease to be present on the earth until the dawn of the final age.[5] Hence the arrival of the final age does indeed have some effect upon law.

Ezra 2:63 looks for a future priest to use the Urim and Thummim to solve the dilemma of those priests whose genealogies are missing. Similarly, 1 Maccabees 4:46 and 14:41 anticipate a time when a coming prophet will solve problems not clearly addressed by the law. Presumably, both this priest and prophet were expected to arrive in the eschatological age. Although Psalms of Solomon 17 says nothing to suggest that the Messiah will bring a new law, it does imply that the final age will be marked by conditions not now

3. W. D. Davies, *Torah in the Messianic Age and/or the Age to Come* (Philadelphia: Society of Biblical Literature, 1952); see also idem, "The Role of Torah in the Messianic Age," appendix 6 in *The Setting of the Sermon on the Mount* (New York: Cambridge University Press, 1964), 447–50; idem, *Paul and Rabbinic Judaism*, 2d ed. (London: SPCK, 1955), 60–61. The subject has also been addressed by H. L. Strack and Paul Billerbeck, *Kommentar zum Neuen Testament aus Talmud und Midrasch*, 6 vols. in 7 (Munich: C. H. Beck, 1922–61), 1:244 and Excursus 29 ("Diese Welt, die Tage des Messias und die zukünftige Welt," 4.2:799–976); Alfred Edersheim, "The Law in Messianic Times," appendix 14 in *The Life and Times of Jesus the Messiah*, 8th ed., 2 vols. (New York: Longmans, Green, 1907), 2:762–66; and Joseph Klausner, *The Messianic Idea in Israel*, trans. W. F. Stinespring (New York: Macmillan, 1955), 408–19; the latter three depend almost exclusively on rabbinic sources.

4. Davies, *Torah*, 42.

5. Ibid., 43; Davies lists 1 Enoch 5:8; 48:1; 49:1–3; 91:10; and 2 Baruch 44:14, and notes that R. H. Charles interprets 1 Enoch 42:1–2 to mean that Wisdom will return in messianic times.

present. These conditions will enable people to live righteously, in accordance with the law. The Dead Sea Scrolls say the community cannot know more of the law until the arrival of the Messiah, who will reveal new things.[6] From these scattered references Davies concludes that although the intertestamental writers believed in the continuing validity of the law, they anticipated that "there would be at least a better understanding [of it] in the future than in the present."[7] More specifically, they expected that (1) the law would be interpreted more satisfactorily and gloriously, and that (2) Gentiles would be included under its sway (see ch. 18).

As he turns to the rabbinic sources, Davies points out that in this period the law had become the cornerstone of Jewish life. This was evident in the fact that loyalty to it was the crucial factor governing both religious and political affairs; it was also evident in the way in which the law was glorified in Jewish thought. Law was believed to be preexistent, instrumental in the creation of the world, and immutable. However, he continues, rabbinic literature represents "only one current within . . . one stream [of Judaism]. . . . The possibility is always to be reckoned with that many emphases or tendencies in Judaism in the first century are not represented in our sources; . . . it may be that much material in the tradition about the nature and role of Torah in the Messianic Age has been either ignored or deliberately suppressed or modified."[8]

To the question whether there is any evidence of another view, Davies replies that some quarters were aware that various modifications of law would be necessary in the future age. He calls attention to writings which suggest that in the messianic age certain festivals would no longer be celebrated, laws concerning clean and unclean might be changed, and some sacrifices discontinued. There is also the suggestion that Gentiles would come to share in the blessings of the law in the messianic age. Common was the anticipation of new interpretations and clarifications of the law. This includes the expectation that difficulties or incomprehensibilities would be adequately explained and understood. For example, the

6. Davies, *Torah*, 46, quotes the so-called Damascus or Zadokite Document (CD 6): "The well is the Law, and they who digged it are the penitents of Israel who went forth out of the land of Judah and sojourned in the land of Damascus, all of whom God called princes. For they sought Him and His glory was not turned back in the mouth of one (of them). And the Law giver is he who studies the Law in regard to whom Isaiah said, 'He bringeth forth an instrument for his work.' And the nobles of the people are those who came to dig the well by the precepts in which the Law giver ordained that they should walk throughout the full period of the wickedness. And save them they shall get nothing until there arises the Teacher of Righteousness in the end of the days."

7. Davies, *Torah*, 44.

8. Ibid., 53.

messianic age was expected to be a time when God would explain to his people the reasons for commandments for which there now seem to be none.

Some passages coming from a period well after the Intertestamental Era claim that the law will be changed or completely abrogated in the messianic age or that a new law will come. The *Sifre* on Deuteronomy 17:18 says, "Mishnah Torah . . . was destined to be changed."[9] Since "teaching" is a possible translation for *Torah*, the targum on Isaiah 12:3 is relevant here: "And you shall receive a new teaching with joy from the chosen of righteousness." Furthermore, although the exact meaning is debated, Davies believes that Babylonian Talmud *Shabbath* 151b implies "that Torah no longer holds in the Messianic Age."[10] The text in question reads: "R. Simeon b. Eleazer (165–200 A.D.) said: . . . *and the years draw nigh, when thou shalt say, I have no pleasure in them* (Ecclesiastes 12:1) this refers to the Messianic era, wherein there is neither merit nor guilt. Now, he disagrees with Samuel, who said: The only difference between this world and the Messianic era is in respect of servitude to (foreign) powers, for it is said, For the poor shall never cease out of the land." The point is that there is no reward or punishment in the messianic age because there is no law.

Davies concludes that although the Old Testament, Apocrypha, Pseudepigrapha, and rabbinic sources generally expect that "Torah in its existing form would persist into the Messianic Age . . . there were also occasional expressions of expectations that Torah would suffer modification in the Messianic Age. . . . [However,] all changes envisaged were deemed to occur within the context of the existing Torah. . . . [The] yoke [of Torah], in some passages, was expected to become even heavier in that age."[11] With regard to the scarcity of evidence for the doctrine of a changed or new law in the final age, Davies suggests that it may have been suppressed by Jews in reaction to Christianity.[12] He argues that the polemic against the doctrine does, in fact, indicate its existence.[13]

One of the talmudic passages to which Davies refers, *Sanhedrin* 97a–b, is also important to Leo Baeck's understanding of Paul's view of the law: "The Tanna debe Eliyyahu [the school of Elijah]

9. Tosephta *Sanhedrin* 4:7 similarly says, "The Torah is destined to be changed."
10. Davies, *Torah,* 65.
11. Ibid., 84, 66.
12. Ibid., 86–89.
13. Ibid., 87, where Davies cites *Deuteronomy Rabbah* 8: "It is written, 'For this commandment is not in heaven' (Deut. XXX. 11, 12). Moses said to the Israelites, Lest you should say, Another Moses is to arise, and to bring us another Law from heaven, therefore I make it known to you now that it is not in heaven: nothing of it is left in heaven." Davies also notes Justin Martyr's "claim that he has read 'that there shall be a final law (and an eternal one).'"

teaches: The world is to exist six thousand years. In the first two thousand there was a desolation [literally, no Torah]; two thousand years the Torah flourished; and the next two thousand years is the Messianic era, but through our many iniquities all these have been lost."[14] Here is the clear belief that the period of the law would come to an end and be replaced by the messianic age. Baeck contends that among at least some Jewish groups there was a pre-Christian belief in the supersession of law during the final age and that the background of Paul is a case in point. Furthermore, he suggests, to properly understand Paul's doctrine of the law we must assume that Paul took this conviction with him in his move from Judaism to Christianity. Seen from this perspective, Baeck argues, the apostle "fought, not against 'law,' but against the 'present' validity of the law."[15] This issue was important to Paul because "not the 'law' as such but the Messiah, his presence, his actuality were at stake. . . . Whoever maintained the law was still abiding was an unbeliever; he did not believe in the presence of Christ."[16] Whatever may be said of Baeck's view of Paul, he does show that the place of law in the final age is a potentially significant issue in any study of Christian thought.

Earlier we noted the unified nature of the law. If one part is set aside, the whole is affected; the breaking of one law makes the offender guilty of breaking all. With this in mind we must look at the New Testament. Jesus challenged the Sabbath command, at least in the way it was interpreted in his day (Matt. 12:1–14 [=Mark 2:23–3:6; Luke 6:1–11]; Luke 13:10–17; 14:1–6; John 5:2–18; 7:19–24; 9 [esp. vv. 14, 16]). His authority for so doing was, "The Son of Man is lord even of the sabbath" (Mark 2:28)—the presence of an eschatological figure was sufficient authority for changing past interpretations and practices. So too with his challenge of the validity of the traditions of the elders (Mark 7:2–23). The statement "Thus he declared all foods clean" (v. 19) speaks for itself. He then went on to argue that legality is dependent upon what comes "from within, from the human heart" (v. 21). One can hardly miss the parallel with Jeremiah's prediction that "after those days . . . I will put my law within them, and I will write it on their hearts" (Jer. 31:33). Jesus affirmed that the law is permanent only "until all is accomplished"—"Not one let-

14. See Davies, *Torah*, 78–83; Leo Baeck, "The Faith of Paul," *Journal of Jewish Studies* 3 (1952): 105–6.

15. Baeck, "Faith of Paul," 106–7; see also idem, *The Pharisees* (New York: Schocken, 1947), 72–74.

16. Baeck, "Faith of Paul," 107.

ter, not one stroke of a letter, will pass from the law until all is accomplished" (Matt. 5:18).[17]

We could go further, to the words of Paul: "Christ is the end of the law so that there may be righteousness for everyone who believes" (Rom. 10:4), and "Christ redeemed us from the curse of the law" (Gal. 3:13). Remembering the principle that one part of the law stands for the whole, consider also the implication of Galatians 5:2: "If you let yourselves be circumcised, Christ will be of no benefit to you." Perhaps we could paraphrase this statement, "If you submit to ordinances of the law (for salvation), then you are acting as if the Messiah, who brings in the final age, has not come; the life and ministry of Jesus have no significance or benefit for you." The Epistle to the Hebrews is even stronger. It argues that in Christ the old revelation—the leadership of Moses, the Levitical priesthood, sacrifices—has already given way to the new.

Davies concludes that the evidence of a pre-Christian belief in an altered or new law in the final age is not sufficiently definite and unambiguous in the Jewish sources to afford certainty. The strongest evidence of such a belief is "that the early Christians, who were conscious that they were living in the Messianic Age, did in fact find room in their interpretation of the Christian Dispensation for such a concept."[18] For the early Jewish Christians, Davies believes, the new law of the final age was a reality; it was not a code but the person of Jesus Christ himself.[19]

Although we embrace the generalities of this conclusion, we recognize that numerous questions and issues remain about law in the final age. To say that the coming age will bring changes to the law fails to specify what kind of changes. Implications in Jewish

17. The word translated "is accomplished" is the Greek *genētai*, which means something like "comes to pass" or "happens." It must be considered along with "to fulfill" (*plērōsai*) in the previous verse ("I have come not to abolish but to fulfill"). The same word is used in Mark 1:15 to announce the crisis point which introduces the new age ("the time is fulfilled [*peplērōtai*]"). So the statement "until all is accomplished" in Matt. 5:18 may, I suspect, be a veiled reference to the arrival of the final age.

18. Davies, *Torah*, 90.

19. Ibid., 93–94: "Although Paul regards the words of Jesus as the basis of a kind of Christian halakah, it is Christ Himself in His person, not only or chiefly in His words, who constitutes the New Torah: and so too in the Fourth Gospel the New Torah is not only epitomized in the commandment of *agapē* which finds its norm in the love of Christ for His own and in the love of God for Christ, but is realized also in the Person of Jesus, who is the Way, the Truth and the Life, i.e., the personalized Torah who is set over against Moses. This personification of Torah in Christ goes beyond anything which we have found in the Jewish sources: there is no premonition of a Messiah becoming in Himself the Torah. . . . Then we must assert that those in the Early Church who saw their Torah in Jesus Himself, as well as in His words, found not only that any possible expectations of a New Torah that Judaism may have cherished were fulfilled in Him, but that they were also transcended."

sources give rise to several options: (1) the law will remain un-changed but will be more highly revered; (2) there will be a better understanding of, deeper devotion to, and increased ability to keep the old law during the final age; (3) the old law will remain but in a changed, altered, and modified form; (4) the old law and a new law will exist side by side during the final age; (5) the old law will be abolished completely, replaced by a new written law; and, finally, (6) Messiah will reign directly and personally; therefore the word of Messiah alone will be law during the final age. Also un-answered are questions regarding the form the eschatological law was expected to take, its content, and uses (e.g., was it for salvation or something else?). So then, we do not know as much as we would like about the radical changes the arrival of the final age was ex-pected to bring. It is evident, however, that at least some intertes-tamental Jewish groups expected them to touch even to the very heart of Judaism, to covenant and law.

18

Intertestamental Jewish Attitudes toward Gentiles

Jewish Attitudes in General

Jewish attitudes toward Gentiles were complex. In this connection it is significant that in both Hebrew and Greek the same word (*gôy*, *ethnos*) can carry the idea of "Gentile," "the nations," "foreigner," or "heathen." The Scriptures teach that God is the creator of all and that his sovereign power and lordship extend over all. At the same time, the Jews usually viewed the nations of the world as under the control of evil spiritual powers which often used them as tools. Through Gentile nations the evil powers sought to get at God by attacking and persecuting Israel.

Rabbinic literature generally displays deeply hostile feelings against non-Jews.[1] It must be remembered, however, that these

---

1. Summarized by E. G. Hirsch and J. D. Eisenstein, "Gentiles," in *Jewish Encyclopedia*, 12 vols. (New York: Funk and Wagnalls, 1925), 5:614–18; see also Joseph Bonsirven, *Palestinian Judaism in the Time of Jesus Christ*, trans. William Wolf (New York: Holt, Rinehart and Winston, 1964), 64–71; and C. G. Montefiore and H. Loewe, eds., *Rabbinic Anthology* (New York: Schocken, 1974), 556–65.

feelings had been hardened by the experiences of the intertestamental period and the early Christian centuries, including oppression, various anti-Semitic measures, and even the destruction of Jerusalem. These feelings were the result of a long historical process in which particularistic and elitist attitudes and a zeal to protect Jewish privilege had grown. Only to a moderate degree do such attitudes in the later writings capture the sentiments of pre–A.D. 70 Judaism.

In regard to attitudes toward Gentiles we should expect the same diversity that we have frequently noted within many other components of Intertestamental Judaism. This was indeed the case. There was no single uniform attitude toward Gentiles; they were regarded in various ways by individual Jewish groups. Also, Jews made distinctions among Gentiles. Varying degrees of kindness, friendship, and acceptance were accorded Gentiles who were sympathetic or at least not hostile to Jews and Judaism. Respect and honor were usually given those in positions of great power, although feelings of hostility and desire for retribution were evident, especially toward rulers who persecuted or caused hardships for the Jews.[2] Others, perhaps the majority of Gentiles, were the objects of suspicion, contempt, and even animosity.

There is evidence that toward the close of the Old Testament period some Jews had a much less severe attitude than the growing isolationism and scorn for Gentiles evident among many of their race.[3] While the prophet Habakkuk viewed Gentile hostility and brutality toward Israel as opposition by the wicked against the comparatively righteous, other writers like Jeremiah seemed to see the heathen sharing God's love and, ultimately, being objects of salvation. Hence, side by side within Intertestamental Judaism there were a strong separatist movement and a general fearful disdain for Gentiles, but also acceptance of at least some non-Jews and a desire to win them to Judaism.

Numerous elements contributed to developing intertestamental Jewish attitudes toward Gentiles. Prominent among them was a mind-set rising out of Israel's understanding of her special status based on election within the framework of the covenant. Paul's answer to his own question, "What advantage has the Jew?" could have come from many reflective Jews of his day: "Much, in every way. For in the first place the Jews were entrusted with the oracles

2. See, e.g., Philo's treatise against Flaccus and the books of Esther, Maccabees, and Judith.

3. Hirsch and Eisenstein, "Gentiles," 5:616, note that if the conclusions of critical schools are accepted, "the books of Ruth and Jonah are documentary proof that the Hebrew radicalism of Ezra was met with strenuous opposition."

of God. . . . To them belong the adoption, the glory, the covenants, the giving of the law, the worship, and the promises; to them belong the patriarchs, and from them, according to the flesh, comes the Messiah, who is over all" (Rom. 3:1–2; 9:4–5).

It will be useful to attempt to understand just what were the major issues causing the pious intertestamental Jew to recoil from unnecessary contact with Gentiles.[4] Of course some Jews disliked Gentiles simply because they were Gentiles; there are often a suspicion of and a drawing away from peoples and cultures that are different. The dominant force in Israel's negative feelings toward Gentiles was not primarily racial, national, or cultural, however. It was religious. Israel was the people of God, the object of the LORD's special favor, not because of her merits, but simply on the basis of God's free choice and love (Deut. 7:7–8; 26:5–9). Gentiles were outside the covenant; they were the nonelect.

Three specific factors seem to have been especially important in driving many Jews to minimize contact with foreigners. First, Jews abhorred and were suspicious of Gentiles because of their idolatry and all associated with it. Israel's history shows both a revulsion at idolatry and a fascination with it. The exile, it seems, greatly diminished the latter. For the Jew idolatry was the ultimate blasphemy and crime against God. Second, Jews detested the low ethical and moral standards so evident in the Gentile world. Apart from practices associated with pagan worship, there were sexual irregularities, bestiality, abortions, infanticides, murder of slaves, and other acts involving shedding innocent blood. Many Jews recoiled from what they saw as Gentile moral irresponsibility. The pious stayed as far from it as possible. Finally, there was the whole area of ceremonial cleanliness. Gentiles were unclean in both their persons and actions. Intermarriage between Jews and Gentiles would bring pollution into the pure strain of Israel (Ezra 9–10; Neh. 13:23–31).[5] Indeed, any association with Gentiles could bring the Jew into a state of defilement. Unregulated contact with Gentiles might endanger the whole system of ceremonial and ritual observances that were based on Old Testament law, and that during the intertesta-

4. The Midrash *Genesis Rabbah* 31:6 sheds some light on the question, "What are the cardinal sins in Judaism?" The passage comments on Gen. 6:11, which states that God's wrath fell on the world of Noah "because the earth was filled with *ḥāmās* (violence)." Rabbi Levi says that *ḥāmās* means "bloodshed" (proof text Joel 3:19), "sexual abominations" (proof text Jer. 51:35), and "idolatry" (proof text Ezek. 8:17, a quotation of Gen. 6:11). Babylonian Talmud *Sanhedrin* 74a says that every Jew must be willing to be martyred to avoid committing these three sins. For these rabbinic references I am indebted to T. S. Frymer-Kensky, "The Atrahasis Epic and Its Significance for our Understanding of Genesis 1–9," *Biblical Archaeologist* 40.4 (Dec. 1977): 147–55.

5. Bonsirven, *Palestinian Judaism*, 66; Joachim Jeremias, *Jesus' Promise to the Nations*, trans. S. H. Hooke (London: SCM, 1958), 40.

mental period became emblems of national identity and instruments of protective exclusivism within some Jewish groups. So Jewish aversion to table fellowship with Gentiles was based on more than simple fear of nonkosher foods or meats that had been dedicated in a pagan temple. Furthermore, Gentiles frequently disregarded or showed outward animosity for Jewish dietary restrictions and other regulations aimed at racial and ceremonial cleanliness. They sometimes sought to trick or force Jews into compromising situations that would leave them unclean.

Jewish animosity toward Gentiles naturally increased in reaction to periods of national persecution; efforts to stamp out Jews and the Jewish religious distinctives by Haman (of the Book of Esther), Antiochus Epiphanes, and others fed their distrust. High taxation, harsh administrative measures, cruelty, and insensitivity by foreign overlords also stirred up Jewish hatred for foreigners.

Nevertheless, isolation could not be the only stance of Intertestamental Judaism. There was the strong presence of a Gentile culture (Hellenism) and non-Jewish persons resident in the land of Israel, even in the most protected region, the Judean hill country. Jews, particularly in the Diaspora, were deeply involved in Gentile life and culture. In fact, even before the discoveries and reassessments from the middle of the twentieth century onward, one writer could state, "Among all of the ancient peoples none learned as much from the Greeks as the Jews."[6] Particularism was balanced by universalism.

A part of this balance was that the Jewish law extended certain rights and protection to the Gentile.[7] Although these rights and their corresponding applications would not always meet modern standards of equity, their existence indicates a dimension of the intertestamental Jewish attitude toward foreigners that is sometimes overlooked. Even during the rabbinic periods, when some rabbis regarded Gentiles as little better than beasts, there were always some teachers whose outlook was much less severe. This goodwill was especially strong toward Gentiles who attempted to keep the law.[8]

A word needs to be said here about both the provisions for and restrictions on Gentile participation in worship in the Jerusalem

6. I. Heinemann, *Die griechische Weltanschauung bei Juden und Römern* (Berlin: Philo, 1932), cited here from Scot McKnight, *A Light among the Gentiles: Jewish Missionary Activity in the Second Temple Period* (Minneapolis: Augsburg Fortress, 1991), 12.

7. Hirsch and Eisenstein, "Gentiles," 5:616–25.

8. Hence the famous statement of Rabbi Meir (second century), a bitter opponent of Rome, "Therefore the Gentile himself, if he observes the law, is like the high priest" (*Sifra* on Leviticus 18:5).

temple. Here again is an illustration of the mixed attitude toward foreigners. Throughout the Roman occupation, and even during a period of time that Jerusalem was under siege, regular sacrifices were offered for the emperor.[9] The Court of the Gentiles, the area open to Gentile presence and worship, occupied most of the expansive platform built by Herod the Great. However, there was also the wall that warned against Gentile entrance into the temple proper on pain of death.

Scot McKnight has summarized the general features of Jewish attitudes toward non-Jews.[10] Of course, each of these characteristics was more evident in some groups than in others. First there were the positive attitudes: (1) Jewish sources recognize that God is the Lord of all humanity; the Jewish God is the universal God; (2) virtually all Jewish sources indicate that Jews were generally tolerant of and kind to Gentiles; (3) Gentiles were allowed some participation in Jewish religion; and (4) Jews participated in Gentile society in various forms and degrees. There were also strong evidences of negative relations: (1) the Jews were convinced that they were different, and the Gentiles naturally reacted; (2) the Jews maintained a strong consciousness of being God's chosen and holy people to the exclusion of all others; (3) Jews criticized Gentiles because of their pagan religion and the practices to which it led— practices clearly unacceptable for those in covenant relation with the LORD; and, finally, (4) the Gentiles themselves often displayed attitudes of disdain and treated Jews unjustly.

Regulations of Conduct Expected of Gentiles

It was the exceptional Jewish group, like Qumran, which sought complete isolation from Gentiles. From each period of Jewish history comes evidence that at least some Jews were willing to associate with certain Gentiles. In the Old Testament there are laws regulating the *gerim*, the resident aliens, the non-Jews who desired to live in the land of Israel. By searching the Pentateuch we may assemble a list of general regulations for such persons. They were to (1) abstain from blaspheming the name of the LORD (Lev. 24:16, 22); (2) abstain from idols (Lev. 20:2); (3) abstain from sorcery, incest, and other abominations (Lev. 18:26); (4) abstain from working on the Sabbath (Exod. 20:10; 23:12); (5) observe sacrificial ordinances (Lev. 17:8–9; Num. 15:14); (6) observe certain feasts (Deut. 16:11, 14); (7) refrain from eating leavened bread during Passover (Exod. 12:19; they were forbidden, however, to share the

9. Josephus *Jewish War* 2.10.4 (197).
10. McKnight, *Light*, 25–29.

meal [vv. 43–49]); and (8) cease from work on the Day of Atonement (Lev. 16:29).

More compact are the regulations of Leviticus 17 and 18, which provide a safeguard against idolatry by restricting sacrifices to the central sanctuary (Lev. 17:1–9), prohibit eating blood or meat that has not been properly drained (17:10–16), and forbid all sexual perversions (18:6–23). Ezekiel 33:24–26, in a general context condemning idolatry, presents a similar list. There are, for example, prohibitions against eating flesh that contains blood, worshiping idols, shedding blood, and sexually defiling one's neighbor's wife.

In intertestamental Jewish writings the Sibylline Oracles pronounce blessings on Gentiles who (1) recognize the true God, (2) abstain from idolatry and idolatrous sacrifices, (3) abstain from murder, (4) do no violence, (5) abstain from theft, and (6) wash from head to foot in running streams.[11] Josephus notes the Gentiles' awareness of the Jewish expectation that they observe the Sabbath, certain ceremonies, and food laws.[12]

Rabbinic literature details the laws of the sons of Noah.[13] By this is meant those ordinances binding upon all humankind. From a practical viewpoint, however, these regulations could be demanded only of those Gentiles who desired contact and association with Hebrews. The various rabbinic writings offer different lists, numbering from six to more than thirty regulations. The talmudic tractate *Sanhedrin* provides an adequate sample:

---

11. Sibylline Oracles 4:24–34, 162–70: "Happy will be those of mankind on earth who will love the great God, blessing him before drinking and eating, putting their trust in piety. They will reject all temples when they see them; altars too, useless foundations of dumb stones (and stone statues and handmade images) defiled with blood of animate creatures, and sacrifices of four-footed animals. They will look to the great glory of the one God and commit no wicked murder, nor deal in dishonest gain, which are most horrible things. Neither have they disgraceful desire for another's spouse or for hateful and repulsive abuse of a male. . . .

"Ah, wretched mortals, change these things, and do not lead the great God to all sorts of anger, but abandon daggers and groanings, murder and outrages, and wash your whole bodies in perennial rivers. Stretch out your hands to heaven and ask forgiveness for your previous deeds and make propitiation for bitter impiety with words of praise; God will grant repentance and will not destroy. He will stop his wrath again if you all practice honorable piety in your hearts."

12. Josephus *Against Apion* 2.39 (282): "The masses have long since shown a keen desire to adopt our religious observances; and there is not one city, Greek or barbarian, nor a single nation, to which our custom of abstaining from work on the seventh day has not spread, and where the fasts and the lighting of lamps and many of our prohibitions in the matter of food are not observed."

13. Midrash *Genesis Rabbah*, Noah, 34; Babylonian Talmud *Sanhedrin* 56b; see Montefiore and Loewe, eds., *Rabbinic Anthology*, 556–57.

1. Do not worship idols
2. Do not blaspheme the name of God
3. Establish courts of justice
4. Do not murder
5. Do not commit adultery
6. Do not rob
7. Do not eat flesh containing blood or meat not ritually slaughtered

It is not our concern to compare the Old Testament, intertestamental, and rabbinic lists of regulations for Gentiles. What is significant is the evidence that at least some Jews were open to association with Gentiles, but that such contacts were regulated. The regulations both set forth a minimum standard of morality for the non-Jew and offered the Hebrew some protection from unnecessary ceremonial defilement.[14]

The Issue of a Jewish Mission to the Gentiles

There is no conclusive answer to the question whether there was a Jewish mission to the Gentiles.[15] Some writers believe there was vigorous missionary activity aimed at converting Gentiles.[16] McKnight, on the other hand, believes that although Judaism did attract converts, Intertestamental Judaism was not a "missionary religion."[17] Rather than aggressively seeking converts intertestamental "Jews were *a light among the Gentiles* and were more than willing to allow others to partake of that light."[18]

Although McKnight is certainly right, there is evidence, as he acknowledges, that some Jews were indeed concerned to make converts. This is reflected in Jesus' statement, "You [scribes and Pharisees] cross sea and land to make a single convert" (Matt. 23:15). The desire for converts is also shown in Josephus's account of Metilius, a Roman general who, when threatened with death at

14. It is helpful to compare these various lists with the decrees of the Jerusalem Council: Gentile converts would do well to abstain from (1) idolatry, (2) fornication (unchastity), (3) things strangled, and (4) blood (Acts 15:20, 29; 21:25).

15. For a summary of studies of this topic see McKnight, *Light*, 1–4.

16. E.g., Jeremias, *Promise*, 11: "At the time of Jesus' appearance an unparalleled period of missionary activity was in progress in Israel."

17. McKnight, *Light*, 4–5, carefully defines "missionary religion" as "a religion that self-consciously defines itself as a religion, one aspect of whose 'self-definition' is a mission to the rest of the world, . . . [and that] practices its mission through behavior that intends to evangelize nonmembers so that these nonmembers will convert to the religion."

18. McKnight, *Light*, 48.

the hands of Jews, saved his life by promising to submit to circumcision and become a proselyte.[19]

Even without engaging in a formal program of evangelistic missions, Jews did undertake to present themselves in such a way as to gain understanding, goodwill, and even converts from the nations. It appears there were no regularly used methods for reaching non-Jews with the message of Judaism.[20] There were, however, numerous means through which Jewish distinctives, both in beliefs and conduct, gained exposure. The synagogue provided a visible symbol of Judaism and a place from which both the curious and interested could seek information. Embedded in some Jewish literature, such as the Letter of Aristeas, 4 Maccabees, much of Philo, and Josephus's *Jewish War* and *Against Apion*, were apologetic aims. Education (Jewish schools attended by Gentiles) and Jewish lifestyle may have also caught non-Jewish eyes. Awareness of Jews and Judaism sometimes resulted in ridicule and hostility; at other times it gained respect, admiration, and proselytes.

Proselytes and God-Fearers

Proselytes

Some Gentiles were attracted to Judaism and attached themselves to it in varying degrees of commitment.[21] Of these we need concern ourselves only with proselytes (or converts) and God-fearers. The former were Gentiles who fully converted to Judaism. The words of Ruth to Naomi, "Your people shall be my people, and your God my God" (Ruth 1:16), reflect the kind of commitment expected. Converts accepted every area of Jewish life—law, national allegiance, social and cultural customs, and the rest; they became naturalized Jews.[22] Although some may have regarded proselytes as second-class Jews, Jews they were.

Although there is no way to determine the number of proselytes, their existence is certain. The Book of Acts refers to proselytes at Pentecost (2:11), among the seven (6:5), and in Antioch of Pisidia (13:43). They are noted in ancient literature and inscriptions. The best-known converts to Judaism were members of the royal family of Adiabene.[23]

19. Josephus *Jewish War* 2.17.10 (454).
20. McKnight, *Light*, 49–77.
21. Ibid., 90–101; Emil Schürer, *History of the Jewish People in the Age of Jesus Christ*, ed. Geza Vermes et al., 3 vols. (Edinburgh: T. and T. Clark, 1973–87), 3.1:164–72.
22. Tacitus *Histories* 5.5 (281).
23. Josephus *Antiquities* 20.2.1–5 (17–53). Josephus *Jewish War* 2.20.2 (560) also mentions that the wives of the leaders of Damascus had embraced the Jewish religion (though the word for "proselyte" [*prosēlytos*] does not occur here).

It is usually assumed that in addition to committing to observe the whole law, the proselyte candidate was expected to be circumcised (if male), offer a sacrifice, and undergo baptism. Of these requirements Emil Schürer says, "All three are regarded as traditional already in the Mishnah; indeed, they are so much taken for granted in rabbinic Judaism that even in the absence of definite proof they can be considered as prevailing in [the] Second Temple period."[24] This may be so, but some exceptions need be noted and questions asked; it may be too easy to accept later procedures as normative in the earlier period.

None can doubt the importance of circumcision in the Jewish mind. Circumcision was commanded by God as the symbol of membership in the covenant community (Gen. 17:10–14) and has been a mark of the Jew ever since. In the intertestamental period Achior the Ammonite "believed firmly in God. So he was circumcised, and joined the house of Israel" (Judith 14:10). The Roman Metilius assumed circumcision was necessary. Nevertheless, neither Hebrew women nor female converts to Judaism were circumcised.[25] And in Galatians Paul seems to fight against the demand for the circumcision of his converts. Before deciding to submit to the rite, Izates, king of Adiabene, was subjected to conflicting opinions on its necessity.[26] McKnight summarizes: "It seems quite probable . . . that circumcision was seen as an act whereby the male convert demonstrated his zeal for the law and his willingness to join Judaism without reservation. I hesitate to conclude that circumcision was a requirement throughout Second Temple Judaism, because the evidence is not completely unambiguous."[27]

Like circumcision, to make an offering in the sanctuary would seem a natural requirement. Nevertheless, a clear-cut statement is missing from intertestamental sources. There is abundant evidence that Jews, both natural-born and proselytes, did offer sacrifices, but there is no indication that sacrifice was part of a prescribed initiatory rite. Philo affirmed that if "worshippers bring nothing else, in bringing themselves they offer the best of sacrifices, the full and truly perfect oblation of noble living."[28] Diaspora Jews functioned with few or no sacrifices. Moreover, after the destruction of the temple, sacrifices were replaced by (1) reading of

---

24. Schürer, *History*, 3.1:173; see also George Foot Moore, *Judaism in the First Centuries of the Christian Era*, 3 vols. (Cambridge, Mass.: Harvard University Press, 1927–30), 1:331.

25. Female circumcision is practiced in some other cultures to this day. A bill outlawing it in the United States was introduced as recently as early 1994.

26. Josephus *Antiquities* 20.2.4 (38–48).

27. McKnight, *Light*, 82.

28. Philo *Special Laws* 1.50 (272).

the law, (2) fasting, (3) prayer, and (4) deeds of charity and justice. Even after the three requirements had been firmly established by the rabbis, sacrifice was not necessarily a rite for admission into the community. George Moore puts it well: "The offering of a sacrifice is . . . not one of the conditions of becoming a proselyte, but only a condition precedent to the exercise of one of the rights which belong to him as a proselyte, namely, participation in a sacrificial meal. As soon as he was circumcised and baptized, he was in full standing in the religious community, having all the legal rights and powers and being subject to all the obligations of the Jew by birth."[29]

The argument that baptism was a prerequisite for admission into the community also stands on trembling legs. Two facts need to be made clear. First, there were indeed numerous prescribed ceremonial washings for all practicing Jews, both natural-born and proselytes; these washings were a major part of the requirements to become clean after contracting defilement. Second, the particular water ceremony that is usually assumed when one speaks of baptism in connection with the admission of proselytes was different from the regular Jewish cleansing ceremonies in at least one aspect: it was not to be repeated. To assert that baptism was a condition for acceptance into Judaism we need evidence in the form of either an explicit command to that effect or a historical record. We also need assurance that what is in view is something other than the regular ritual washings.

The command in Sibylline Oracles 4:165 ("wash your whole bodies in perennial rivers") is hardly a clear reference to proselyte baptism. Viewed in its context it is at most an injunction to Gentiles wishing to be a part of the Jewish community to indicate their resolve to live a moral life, and so to achieve some acceptance from Jews.

Philo is sometimes discussed in connection with proselyte baptism. In his essay "On the Unchangeableness of God" he says, "If we cultivate the spirit of rendering thanks and honor to Him, we shall be pure from wrongdoing and wash away the filthiness which defiles our lives in thought and word and deed. For it is absurd that a man should be forbidden to enter the temples save after bathing and cleansing his body, and yet should attempt to pray and sacrifice with a heart still soiled and spotted."[30] Philo has just spoken of Hannah's giving Samuel to God and then of thank-offerings and various other gifts to God. These, he says, are the worshipers' return of what God first gave them. There follows the remark that

---

29. Moore, *Judaism*, 1:332.
30. Philo *On the Unchangeableness of God* 1.2 (7–8).

true worship is not performed by gifts and washings, but by the heart. Elsewhere Philo speaks of washing or cleansing in referring to the water mixed with the ashes of the red heifer, a regular part of the rituals of all Jews, including natural-born ones.[31] It is conceivable that in "On the Cherubim" Philo may have in mind a cleansing of proselytes who have continued in a wicked life; however, that is far from clear. His comment that "they pass into the inmost sanctuary" more likely suggests that he is speaking of unworthy priests.[32] In short, it appears that the washings to which Philo refers are rituals for those already in the community, not those about to enter it.

The strongest evidence for baptism as a requirement for proselytes comes from the Mishnah:

> He that mourns his near kindred may, after he has immersed himself, eat the Passover-offering in the evening, but he may not eat of [other] Hallowed Things. If a man heard of the death of one of his near kindred or caused the bones of his dead to be gathered together, he may, after he has immersed himself, eat of Hallowed Things. The School of Shammai say: If a man became a proselyte on the day before Passover he may immerse himself and consume his Passover-offering in the evening. And the School of Hillel say: He that separates himself from his uncircumcision is as one that separates himself from a grave. [*Pesahim* 8:8]

> R. Jose reports six opinions in which the School of Shammai follow the more lenient and the School of Hillel the more stringent ruling. . . . The School of Shammai say: If a man became a proselyte on the day before Passover, he may immerse himself and consume his Passover-offering in the evening. And the School of Hillel say: He that separates himself from his uncircumcision is as one that separates himself from the grave. [*Eduyoth* 5:2]

Both passages refer to the same debate by first-century rabbis. The issue for us is whether the self-immersion of the proselyte in these texts refers to a regular cleansing ritual or to a special, nonrepeatable bath. In *Pesahim* the topic is raised immediately after the question of whether a Jew just now cleansed from a major defilement, contact with the dead, may partake of the Passover meal on the same day. The same question is then asked about a proselyte who has immersed himself on Passover eve. Certainly someone

---

31. Philo *Special Laws* 1.49 (262); idem, *On Dreams* 1.36–38 (209–20).

32. Philo *On the Cherubim* 28 (95): "They cleanse their bodies with lustrations and purifications, but they neither wish nor practice to wash off from their souls the passions by which life is defiled. They are zealous to go to the temple white-robed, attired in spotless raiment, but with a spotted heart they pass into the inmost sanctuary and are not ashamed."

coming from a Gentile culture would have to go through at least as much ritual cleansing as would someone who had contracted defilement by touching a dead body. But is the self-immersion of the proselyte in these passages of the same kind as that of the Hebrew who had come into contact with the dead? That is, is it one of the regular cleansings of someone who is already a recognized part of the community, or is it a special proselyte baptism? A proselyte's initial cleansing might be looked upon as a moment of singular importance by oneself and others. Yet again we ask, in Intertestamental Judaism was the ceremony a special, nonrepeatable act? There is no way to be sure.

McKnight concludes his investigation with the statement that "in the light of the sociological nature of a Jewish community and in light of needed rituals for women, it is more likely (in my opinion) that baptism became a requirement for most Judaism during the Second Temple period." He goes on to dare the suggestion that this still might not mean that proselyte baptism was pre-Christian in origin: "I would like to suggest, then, that the rites in Judaism and Christianity owe their origin to a common Jewish milieu in which water lustrations became increasingly important for converts and that Judaism's rite of baptism may very well have received a decisive impetus from John the Baptist, Jesus, and the earliest Christians. The origins of Jewish proselyte baptism, then, may have been in the entrance requirement of Jewish Christianity."[33]

For our part, we are content to observe that all Jewish washing ceremonies had the same purpose. These rites marked the point at which one who was considered defiled and unacceptable by his coreligionists became acceptable. The act of washing involved recognizing one's unclean status and then utilizing the divinely prescribed procedure for removing ceremonial pollution. This would certainly be expected of a proselyte. The evidence for a distinct nonrepeatable proselyte baptism in Intertestamental Judaism is lacking.

God-Fearers

The New Testament refers to certain individuals as, literally, "fearing God" (*phoboumenos ton theon*), "worshiping God" (*sebomenos ton theon*), or simply "worshiping" (*sebomenos*).[34] These terms are customarily assumed to refer to a class of uncircumcised Gentiles who stopped short of becoming full proselytes, but were permitted (by some Jews) limited participation in Jewish wor-

33. McKnight, *Light*, 85.
34. "Fearing God" is the term used of Cornelius in Acts 10:2, 22; see also 13:26, 43, 50; 16:14; 17:4, 17; 18:7.

ship.[35] Furthermore, it is assumed that they were expected to observe certain basic standards involving monotheism, morality, and ceremony.

The nature and even the existence of this group have been the center of contemporary scholarly controversy.[36] There is a significant volume of evidence to indicate that there were non-Jews who associated themselves with the synagogues.[37] It is likely that they were an unofficial group. This could account for the fact that they are called by various terms and that precisely what was required of them is uncertain.

In general, God-fearers were expected to worship the LORD only, practice imageless worship, attend the synagogue, observe the Sabbath and food laws, abide by Jewish standards of morality, and conform to other basic elements of Jewish law and tradition. It is reasonable to assume that their treatment and status were patterned after that which the Old Testament lays down regarding the resident alien. The various lists of regulations of conduct for all Gentiles (see pp. 339–41) are the likely source and models for that which was expected of God-fearers. It is significant that the Old Testament regulations and intertestamental requirements for Gentile associates provided safeguards against each of the three major aspects of Gentile culture and behavior from which many Jews recoiled (idolatry, immorality, and ceremonial defilement).

Gentiles in the Final Age

In previous chapters we had occasion to make some reference to expectations about the status and fate of Gentiles in the final age. The significance of this issue for the New Testament reader should be obvious. As Jews from divergent backgrounds became believers in Jesus as Messiah, they accepted the reality that the final age was already present. Without any indication to the contrary, they would expect their pre-Christian notions to govern their Christian notions

---

35. See Kirsopp Lake, "Proselytes and God-Fearers," in F. J. Foakes Jackson and Kirsopp Lake, eds., *Beginnings of Christianity*, 5 vols. (Grand Rapids: Baker, 1966), 5:74–96; Karl Georg Kuhn, "*Sebomenoi* or *phoboumenoi ton theon*," in *Theological Dictionary of the New Testament*, ed. Gerhard Kittel and Gerhard Friedrich, trans. Geoffrey W. Bromiley, 10 vols. (Grand Rapids: Eerdmans, 1964–76), 6:743–44; Schürer, *History*, 3.1:165–76.

36. For recent restudy see Max Wilcox, "The 'God-Fearers' in Acts—A Reconsideration," *Journal for the Study of the New Testament* 13 (1981): 102–22; and three articles in *Biblical Archaeologist Review* 12.5 (Sept./Oct. 1986): Robert S. MacLennan and Thomas Kraabel, "The God-Fearers—A Literary and Theological Invention," 47–53; Robert Tannenbaum, "Jews and God-Fearers in the Holy City of Aphrodite," 55–57; Louis Feldman, "The Omnipresence of God-Fearers," 59–63.

37. Schürer, *History*, 3.1:165.

about the status of Gentiles during the final age. Jewish Christian attitudes toward Gentiles in the eschatological period had implications for both the legitimacy of Christian missions to the Gentiles and social contacts with Gentile believers. These issues were behind much of the conflict reflected in Acts 10–15 and in Paul's epistles to the Romans, Corinthians, Galatians, and Ephesians.

Consideration of the question of Gentiles in the final age again confronts us with complex issues, insufficient source material, and a multiplicity of opinions. To my knowledge only Joseph Bonsirven has attempted even a summary statement of Jewish beliefs about Gentiles in the final age.[38] He is forced to draw mainly from rabbinic writings. Thus again we face the question of how to form an accurate understanding of pre–A.D. 70 views. Fortunately, we know that at least a general thread of the rabbinic opinions runs back into the Old Testament; some of these views, in one form or another, are also reflected in intertestamental literature. A survey of Jewish expectations regarding Gentiles will provide, if not precise information, at least an appreciation of the difficulty faced by the first Christians, who were Jewish, as they sought to understand the situation arising from their faith and experiences as followers of Jesus the Messiah.

We begin with a couple of general views which, in one form or another, were widely held. First, it was assumed that in the great battle of the final age some, or all, of the Gentiles would gather around the leaders of hostile spiritual powers and be defeated. Many would be annihilated.[39] The Messiah, says Philo, "leading his host to war . . . will subdue great and populous nations."[40] Psalms of Solomon 17 portrays the Messiah as conqueror of the Gentiles. Similar statements about the defeat of the powers of evil and judgment of their leader occur in other writings.[41]

Second, there was also the conviction that in the final or messianic age the kingdom of God will embrace the whole world.[42] The

---

38. Bonsirven, *Palestinian Judaism*, 220–25; Schürer, *History*, 2:525–47, also has material on this subject, but not in as consolidated a form as does Bonsirven.

39. See, e.g., 1 Enoch 90:18–19.

40. Philo *On Rewards and Punishments* 16 (95). Philo goes on to say (16 [96–97]): "He promises to marshal against them to their shame and perdition, swarms of wasps to fight in the van of the godly, who will win not only a permanent and bloodless victory in the war but also a sovereignty which none can contest, bringing to its subjects the benefit which will accrue from the affection or fear or respect which they feel. For the conduct of their rulers shows three high qualities which contribute to make a government secure from subversion, namely dignity, strictness, benevolence, which produce the feelings mentioned above. For respect is created by dignity, fear by strictness, affection by benevolence, and these when blended harmoniously in the soul render subjects obedient to their rulers."

41. E.g., Isa. 10:25; 2 Baruch 39:7–40:2; 70:2, 6–9; 2 Esdras 12:32–33; 13:26–38.

42. See W. D. Davies, *Torah in the Messianic Age and/or the Age to Come* (Philadelphia: Society of Biblical Literature, 1952), 76–78.

LORD will be king over all the earth,[43] and Messiah a signal for all people.[44] God will establish a kingdom over all humanity (Dan. 2:44; 7:14, 27); either his people as a whole will rule,[45] or at least the prophets will be judges and upright kings.[46]

As we look closer, it is evident that there were two clear, divergent expectations of the state of Gentiles in the final age. First, at least some Gentiles would experience a favorable condition; they would be incorporated into the messianic kingdom. Ezekiel, one of the more particularistic prophets, says, "My holy name I will make known among my people Israel; and I will not let my holy name be profaned any more; and the nations shall know that I am the LORD, the Holy One in Israel" (Ezek. 39:7); and Zechariah declares, "Many nations shall join themselves to the LORD on that day, and shall be my people" (Zech. 2:11).[47]

At the same time there was the strong sentiment that the vast majority of Gentiles will be destroyed or delivered to some form of severe punishment. Later writers associate the destruction of Gog and Magog in Ezekiel 38–39 with destruction of the Gentile nations. In fact, as Bonsirven says, "On the whole, . . . rabbinical texts show little confidence in nations who wish to become attached to the Israelites, and tend to keep them in a state of inferiority and dependence."[48]

The Apocalypse of Baruch gives a good example of the mixed views about the status of Gentiles in the final age:

> After the signs have come of which I have spoken to you before, when the nations are moved and the time of my Anointed One comes, he will call all nations, and some of them he will spare, and others he will kill. These things will befall the nations which will be spared by him. Every nation which has not known Israel and which has not trodden down the

43. Zech. 8:20–21: "Thus says the LORD of hosts: Peoples shall yet come, the inhabitants of many cities; the inhabitants of one city shall go to another, saying, 'Come, let us go to entreat the favor of the LORD, and to seek the LORD of hosts; I myself am going.'"

44. Isa. 11:10: "On that day the root of Jesse shall stand as a signal to the peoples; the nations shall inquire of him, and his dwelling shall be glorious."

45. Jubilees 32:19, "And I shall give to your [Jacob's] seed all of the land under heaven and they will rule in all nations as they have desired. And after this all of the earth will be gathered together and they will inherit it forever."

46. Sibylline Oracles 3:767–82.

47. Note also Ps. 22:27, "All the ends of the earth shall remember and turn to the LORD; and all the families of the nations shall worship before him"; 47:8, "God is king over the nations"; 67:2, "[May God make his face to shine upon us,] that your way may be known upon earth, your saving power among all nations"; 86:9, "All the nations you have made shall come and bow down before you, O Lord, and shall glorify your name"; 102:15, "The nations will fear the name of the LORD, and all the kings of the earth your glory."

48. Bonsirven, *Palestinian Judaism,* 222.

seed of Jacob will live. And this is because some from all the nations have been subjected to your people. All those, now, who have ruled over you or have known you, will be delivered to the sword. [2 Baruch 72:2–6]

This evidence is valuable because it comes from the end of the intertestamental period. At that time the sting of Gentile oppression was strong, but the negative attitude toward Gentiles that is evident in some rabbinic writings had not yet solidified.

The anticipation that some Gentiles will enjoy the benefits of the final age raises the question of their role and status at that time. That they will acknowledge the God of Israel and the supremacy of Israel was expected. They will come to recognize the LORD as the supreme judge (Isa. 2:4; Mic. 4:3; 7:16–17) and submit to the community of his people. In addition, the Testaments of the Twelve Patriarchs assume that through the messianic priest and king the Gentiles will be saved along with Israel.[49]

On the issue of Gentiles honoring Israel[50] and bringing gifts to her, Isaiah says, "Nations shall bring you their wealth" (Isa. 60:11); thus Israel will possess the "wealth of the nations" (Isa. 61:6; 66:12). Sibylline Oracles 3:702–31 indicates that when Gentiles become aware of the peace and quiet of the people of God, they will give praise and honor to the one true God, send gifts to his temple, and obey his laws. Psalms of Solomon 17:31 speaks of the nations bringing a gift, but here the gift is Israel's "children who had been driven out." Isaiah 61:5 declares, "Strangers shall stand and feed your flocks, foreigners shall till your land and dress your vines," which, according to Bonsirven, was later interpreted to mean that in the messianic age Gentiles would become the slaves of Israel.[51]

An important question involved whether Gentiles could be accepted as proselytes in the final age. Some texts assume that the Messiah will be a light to the nations, that is, he will not rule Gentiles by power alone (Isa. 42:6; 49:6; 51:4; 1 Enoch 48:4; see also Luke 2:30–32). Thus some writers believed that at least some Gentiles will be converted to God. Jeremiah 16:19 ("O LORD, . . . to you shall the nations come from the ends of the earth") seems

49. Testament of Simeon 7:1–2: "Be obedient to Levi and to Judah. Do not exalt yourselves above these two tribes, [because from them will arise the Savior come from God]. For the Lord will raise up from Levi someone as high priest and from Judah someone as king [God and man]. He will save all the gentiles and the tribe of Israel."

50. The figurative language of 1 Enoch 90:30 seems to imply that the surviving Gentiles will honor Israel: "Then I saw all the sheep that had survived as well as all the animals upon the earth and the birds of heaven, falling down and worshiping those sheep, making petition to them and obeying them in every respect."

51. Bonsirven, *Palestinian Judaism*, 222.

to anticipate Gentiles becoming worshipers of the LORD (see also Jer. 3:17; Zeph. 2:11; 3:9; Zech. 8:20–23). Bonsirven suggests that predictions of the heathen abandoning their idols (e.g., Isa. 2:20–21) are further evidence.[52] Yet at least one rabbinic text takes the opposite view. It asserts that any Gentile seeking to become a proselyte during the final age will be doing so out of self-interest and therefore should not be accepted.[53]

In summing up we must note that Judaism was concerned with orthopraxy and was concrete as opposed to the abstract approach of Western-type logic. Accordingly, there is little systematic structure of thought to be found in most intertestamental Jewish writings. Only a few sources deal with the issue we are investigating, and most of them come from a late date. This leaves us with less than we could wish for in regard to answering our question, "What were the major intertestamental Jewish views about the state and fate of Gentiles in the final age?"

Any, even tentative, conclusions must partially rest upon inference. Most can be only general in nature. With this in mind we can offer a list of some probable intertestamental Jewish attitudes about the position of Gentiles during the final age:

1. Gentiles will be the enemy, the allies of evil, to be defeated in the final battle; they will be either eliminated or severely punished.
2. Gentiles are beyond God's concern and salvation; therefore it will not be proper to seek to make proselytes of them during the final age.
3. Gentiles are so depraved that, even if given the opportunity to become proselytes during the messianic age, they will resist and reject the LORD.

52. Ibid., 221; other evidence includes *Mekilta de Rabbi Ishmael* in Exodus 15:11, "The idols will perish forever," and Babylonian Talmud *Pesahim* 118b, "The nations will praise God, Egypt and Ethiopia will bring gifts to the Messiah, and since he hesitates to accept them, God commands him to do so" (as quoted by Bonsirven).

53. "R. Isaac had said that the only time when God would laugh would be at the judgment of the nations. R. Yose added that in the future idolators would come to be made proselytes. But can they be accepted, since tradition says they should no more be received at the time of the Messiah than at the time of David and Solomon? They will be insincere converts, even if they wear phylacteries and fringes, and put a mezuzah on their door posts. But when they see the war of Gog and Magog, the former will ask, 'Against whom are you fighting?' And they will answer, 'Against Yahweh and his Messiah.' For it is written (Ps 2:1, 3), 'Why do the nations rage?' They reject the commandments: 'Let us break their fetters and cast their bonds from us.' Then the Holy One, blessed be He, will be sitting in heaven and smiling, as it is written, 'He who is seated in heaven smiles'" (Babylonian Talmud Abodah Zarah 3b, as quoted by Bonsirven, Palestinian Judaism, 221–22).

4. Any Gentiles seeking to become proselytes during the final age will be motivated by self-interest and therefore cannot be accepted into Israel.
5. Some Gentiles will probably come to serve the LORD under the direction of Israel, but not as proselytes.
6. Surviving Gentiles will become slaves to serve Israel.
7. It is the LORD's will that some Gentiles be incorporated into Israel and therefore receive the blessings and salvation; therefore it is proper and desirable to seek proselytes, even during the final age.

One can only imagine the mixed reactions of confusion, satisfaction, joy, and probable anger in the early Jewish church as, for the first time, they heard the proclamation that since the final age has now dawned in Christ, Gentiles "have been brought near by the blood of Christ . . . he has made both groups [Jews and Gentiles] into one and has broken down the dividing wall, that is, the hostility between us. He has abolished the law with its commandments and ordinances, . . . [creating] one new humanity in place of the two, thus making peace . . . through the cross. . . . So then [Gentiles] are no longer strangers and aliens, but . . . citizens with the saints and also members of the household of God" (Eph. 2:13–19). Crises in Intertestamental Judaism, the background for Christianity, had already forced its people to face changes and adjustments. Now, for these Jewish Christians, another crisis, the crisis point in the history of God's salvation, demanded one more change, the ultimate one.

Epilog

Even after years of travel and preaching in the Gentile world, including Roman courts, Paul was most comfortable discussing Christianity within the setting of "the customs and controversies of the Jews." We have sought not only to identify some of the more influential of those customs and controversies, but also to look at forces which brought them into existence. This we have done in order to better equip ourselves to be the "There and Back Again" kind of New Testament readers C. H. Dodd taught us to be: "The ideal interpreter would be one who has entered into that strange first-century world, has felt its whole strangeness, has sojourned in it until he has lived himself into it, thinking and feeling as one of those to whom the Gospel first came, and who will then return into our world, and give to the truth he has discerned a body out of the stuff of our own thought."[1] To do this one needs to practice the art of the historian as much as the science. Thus we have sought to look at the available facts and through them to catch something of the mood and feelings of the time. The historian must strive to present the data objectively and clearly, and thus convey to the modern reader some of the power that lies within the very facts about another time and place.

Our study of Intertestamental Judaism has consisted of surveying the historical framework, looking at some of its important elements—events, institutions, changes, thought and attitudes, customs and controversies. We have seen its kinship with what went before, but also its uniqueness within Hebrew history. It was, we have suggested, profoundly influenced by crises and multiple reactions to them. We have stressed the diversity of the Jewish world. We pondered the nature of the intertestamental Jewish religion, including its nationalism and particularism, its legalistic

---

1. C. H. Dodd, "Cambridge Inaugural Lecture," as quoted by J. A. T. Robinson, "Theologians of Our Time: XII. C. H. Dodd," *Expository Times* 75.4 (Jan. 1964): 102. *There and Back Again* is the title of a series of children's stories in which Professor Dodd depicts the difficulty a group of children had in explaining in their own world a strange "other world" into which they had gained access.

and nomistic outlook, and its character as primarily a religion of orthopraxy. We considered the diversity and uncertainty of Jewish beliefs about the final age, which nonetheless provided the most prominent element of hope in Jewish society. For the final age was the focus of intertestamental Jewish messianic speculations and expectations. We tried to grasp something of the impact that the intertestamental beliefs had upon the early Christian conviction that the final age had dawned.

The intertestamental Jewish world was the home of Jesus during his incarnation. Its geography, people, customs and controversies were the environment in which he was born, grew, carried on his ministry, and died. He knew that world intimately. He, with the scribes, Pharisees, and average Jews of his day, unquestioningly accepted monotheism, the covenant, the law, and the authority of the Hebrew Scriptures. What Jesus questioned or rejected were some of the added traditions, interpretations, and customs about which the Jews themselves had controversies. Even so, he did not necessarily object to these additions as much as he objected to the neglect of what he saw as the real heart of the Hebrew religion, "the weightier matters of the law: justice and mercy and faith. It is these you ought to have practiced without neglecting the others [i.e., some of the minutiae over which controversy raged]" (Matt. 23:23).

For Jesus internal, spiritual, and relational matters were central. The greatest of all the commandments is love, a love that has concrete, specific objects, God and one's neighbor. But love is first the love of God, love which takes seriously the rupture in our relationship with him and is anxious to remove the presence and effects of sin. From the human perspective it is love which accepts and responds to God's prior love by heeding Jesus' call "Come to me . . . follow me."

The stumbling block for intertestamental Jews was not that Jesus accepted some customs and rejected others, or that he took one side and not the other in controversies. They were accustomed to a diversity of opinion on such matters. The stumbling block was his own person and claims—that God was at work and made himself known in Jesus, that the covenant was made new, that both the Law and the Prophets were fulfilled. He came as both Messiah and bearer of the reign of God, but he fitted none of the contemporary models for what those figures would be like. And so "he came to what was his own, and his own people did not accept him" (John 1:11).

The jeering throng at the foot of Jesus' cross included representatives from all segments of Intertestamental Judaism. But representatives of the Gentiles were present as well. Blame for his death rests not on one group but on all. He died that all, Jew and Gentile, might be able to find forgiveness and acceptance before God, and that all peoples, nations, and languages might be one under his rule as sovereign divine king.

Jesus' world was the world of Intertestamental Judaism, but in the preceding half millennium events had made that world a part of the whole world. On the cross he was lifted above the world that he might call all persons to God. In his resurrection and ascension, having accomplished in time and space the will and requirements of God, he soared above to reign as the messianic Son of man–Suffering Servant–Son of David–Savior–King before whom every knee shall bow and every tongue confess.

After the Christ event early Christianity had to clarify its beliefs, practices, and morals. It was aware of doing so under the guidance of the Holy Spirit (see, e.g., Acts 15:28), but also within the context of what had gone before and the dynamics of the societies and cultures within which the Christians found themselves. The milieu of Intertestamental Judaism remained, but the early church could not permit intertestamental customs and culture to determine its nature and response to the world.

Ever since, Christianity as a whole has had to define itself in relation to the customs and controversies of Intertestamental Judaism. Indeed, the task of adapting to and defining itself in unique sociocultural settings, without compromising its essential nature, has followed the church into each succeeding generation. Its successes and failures have been largely determined by how well each generation understood the nature of the struggles of the early church and the basic moral and spiritual principles which Jewish Christians of the first-century world applied in their divergent settings and situations.

Theological and ethical implications should be obvious. But let me mention an area that is less so. Modern missiologists stress the challenge of ministry in unfamiliar settings. The problem is not new. The deportation of Hebrews in the sixth century B.C. and the presence of Hellenism from the fourth century B.C. on forced intertestamental Jews to deal with the same kinds of issues. As the first Christians moved from the Jewish to the Gentile world, they must have been aware of and profited from the fact that Intertestamental Judaism before them had already struggled with cross-cultural challenge. Their rejection of the more particularistic and isolationist responses that some intertestamental Jews had made indicates that the early Christians had learned well.

Intertestamental Judaism still teaches. The responsible, thoughtful reader of the New Testament must be prepared to listen and learn. By more fully understanding its setting, we become better equipped to comprehend the message of the New Testament and to deal with present-day situations that are akin to situations faced by the early church.

Once, twice, maybe four times a year, I used to head my car east out of Decatur, Georgia, down Ponce de Leon Avenue in the direction of Stone Mountain. About a mile from the city limits I turned left onto a narrow road and past a grove of trees. Then I could see the two-storied white house with the big porch. It was set on a hill and showing its age. First I would visit with the two elderly people who lived there. Then I'd walk out back through the yard and the pasture up into the barn. And I'd go through the woods which surrounded the farm on three sides. After visiting the rock outcropping which had looked to a young boy like a camel's humps, I'd move to a twisted old pine tree and into a familiar little clearing surrounded by bramble, vines, and trees growing closely together.

In a few years the old folks were gone. Then I simply walked through the rooms of the vacant house and revisited the outbuildings, woods, and fields. Soon, too soon, it was time to go, to travel again down the familiar driveway. Back on the main road I was conscious, once again, that I didn't live there anymore.

Today, even the possibility of that sentimental journey is gone. A barrier blocks the drive, time and weather have won the war with the barn, the house fell prey to a bulldozer. Even so, I still return, return through memory and mental pictures. Sometimes I go, physically, to two graves beneath a single stone. These trips are important. Although I can't go home again, I need to be reminded of the roots from which I sprang. They remind me of who I am. They give me a greater understanding of both how alike and how different are the farm boy who once was and the college professor who now is. I am grateful for what was, but I can't go home no mo'.

And so it is with Intertestamental Judaism. Christians visit to grasp more fully the spiritual roots from which we sprang, but also the radical difference of what has been built upon the foundation of Jesus the Messiah. We understand more, believe more firmly, and function better as we consciously grasp the nature of and appreciate the roots of Christianity in the customs and controversies of Intertestamental Judaism.

The Apocrypha of the Old Testament

Tobit
Judith
Additions to Esther
The Wisdom of Solomon
Ecclesiasticus, or the Wisdom of Jesus the Son of Sirach
Baruch
3 Ezra (=1 Esdras)
4 Ezra (=2 Esdras)
The Letter of Jeremiah
The Prayer of Azariah and the Song of the Three Young Men
Susanna
Bel and the Dragon
1 Maccabees
2 Maccabees
3 Maccabees
4 Maccabees
Psalm 151

All of these except 4 Ezra (2 Esdras) are present in the Greek translation of the Old Testament (LXX); 2 Esdras is found in the Latin translations of the Old Testament and was used by many early church fathers. While the Greek Orthodox use 3 Maccabees, 4 Maccabees, and Psalm 151, the Roman Catholic Church does not.

Appendix B

The Pseudepigraphal Books

The sixty-three titles listed here appear in *The Old Testament Pseudepigrapha,* ed. James H. Charlesworth, 2 vols. (Garden City, N.Y.: Doubleday, 1983, 1985); those marked with an asterisk also appear in *The Apocrypha and Pseudepigrapha of the Old Testament,* ed. R. H. Charles, 2 vols. (Oxford: Clarendon, 1913), vol. 2.

Apocalypse of Abraham
Apocalypse of Adam
Testament of Adam
* Life of Adam and Eve
* Ahiqar
* Letter of Aristeas
Aristeas the Exegete
Aristobulus
Artapanus
*2 Baruch
*3 Baruch
4 Baruch
Cleodemus Malchus
Apocalypse of Daniel
More Psalms of David
Demetrius the Chronographer
Eldad and Modad
Apocalypse of Elijah
* 1 Enoch
* 2 Enoch
3 Enoch
Eupolemus
Pseudo-Eupolemus

Apocryphon of Ezekiel
Ezekiel the Tragedian
* 4 Ezra
Greek Apocalypse of Ezra
Questions of Ezra
Revelation of Ezra
Vision of Ezra
Fragments of Pseudo-Greek Poets
Pseudo-Hecataeus
Hellenistic Synagogal Prayers
* Martyrdom and Ascension of Isaiah
Ladder of Jacob
Prayer of Jacob
Jannes and Jambres
Testament of Job
Joseph and Aseneth
History of Joseph
Prayer of Joseph
* Jubilees
3 Maccabees
* 4 Maccabees
Prayer of Manasseh
Syriac Menander
* Testament of Moses (Assumption of Moses in Charles)
Orphica
Philo the Epic Poet
Pseudo-Philo
Pseudo-Phocylides
The Lives of the Prophets
History of the Rechabites
Apocalypse of Sedrach
Treatise of Shem
* Sibylline Oracles
Odes of Solomon
* Psalms of Solomon
Testament of Solomon
Theodotus
Testaments of the Three Patriarchs
* Testaments of the Twelve Patriarchs
Apocalypse of Zephaniah

Sedarim and Tractates of the Mishnah, Talmud, and Tosephta

The rationale behind the organization of the Mishnah is not known. Sometimes it appears that the material has been organized in such a way as to facilitate memory. There are six major sections *(sedarim)*: (1) *Zeraim* (Seeds); (2) *Moed* (Set Feasts); (3) *Nashim* (Women); (4) *Nezikin* (Damages); (5) *Kodashim* (Hallowed Things); (6) *Tohoroth* (Cleannesses).

Each *seder* is divided into *massektoth* (tractates). *Sedarim* are generally concerned with only one topic or two closely related topics. Each tractate is divided into *perakim* (chapters). Individual tractates or chapters may deal with topics which appear to be unrelated to the general subject of the *seder* in which they are found. Each chapter is divided into paragraphs called *mishnah* or *halakah* (individual teachings).

The reader should be aware that transliterations vary. The translations given here are from *The Mishnah*, trans. Herbert Danby (Oxford: Oxford University Press, 1933). Because of most readers' lack of familiarity with this material and the difficulty of locating a particular tractate, we have included an index (the first number represents the section, the second number the tractate within the section).

The Mishnaic Divisions

1. *Zeraim* (Seeds)
   1. *Berakoth* (Benedictions)
   2. *Peah* (Gleanings)
   3. *Demai* (Produce not certainly tithed)
   4. *Kilaim* (Diverse kinds)
   5. *Shebiith* (The seventh year)
   6. *Terumoth* (Heave offerings)
   7. *Maaseroth* (Tithes)

8. *Maaser Sheni* (Second tithe)
9. *Hallah* (Dough offering)
10. *Orlah* (The fruit of young trees)
11. *Bikkurim* (First-fruits)

2. *Moed* (Set Feasts)
   1. *Shabbath* (Sabbath)
   2. *Erubin* (The fusion of Sabbath limits)
   3. *Pesahim* (Feast of Passover)
   4. *Shekalim* (The shekel dues)
   5. *Yoma* (The Day of Atonement)
   6. *Sukkah* (The Feast of Tabernacles)
   7. *Yom Tob* or *Betzah* (Festival-days)
   8. *Rosh ha-Shanah* (Feast of the New Year)
   9. *Taanith* (Days of fasting)
   10. *Megillah* (The scroll of Esther)
   11. *Moed Katan* (Mid-festival days)
   12. *Hagigah* (The festal offering)

3. *Nashim* (Women)
   1. *Yebamoth* (Sisters-in-law)
   2. *Ketuboth* (Marriage deeds)
   3. *Nedarim* (Vows)
   4. *Nazir* (The Nazarite-vow)
   5. *Sotah* (The suspected adulteress)
   6. *Gittin* (Bills of divorce)
   7. *Kiddushin* (Betrothals)

4. *Nezikin* (Damages)
   1. *Baba Kamma* (The first gate)
   2. *Baba Metzia* (The middle gate)
   3. *Baba Bathra* (The last gate)
   4. *Sanhedrin* (The Sanhedrin)
   5. *Makkoth* (Stripes)
   6. *Shebuoth* (Oaths)
   7. *Eduyoth* (Testimonies)
   8. *Abodah Zarah* (Idolatry)
   9. *Aboth* (Fathers)
   10. *Horayoth* (Instructions)

5. *Kodashim* (Hallowed Things)
   1. *Zebahim* (Animal offerings)
   2. *Menahoth* (Meal offerings)
   3. *Hullin* (Animals killed for food)
   4. *Bekhoroth* (Firstlings)
   5. *Arakhin* (Vows of valuation)
   6. *Temurah* (The substituted offering)
   7. *Kerithoth* (Extirpation)

8. *Meilah* (Sacrilege)
9. *Tamid* (The daily whole-offering)
10. *Middoth* (Measurements)
11. *Kinnim* (The bird offerings)

6. *Tohoroth* (Cleannesses)
1. *Kelim* (Vessels)
2. *Oholoth* (Tents)
3. *Negaim* (Leprosy-signs)
4. *Parah* (The red heifer)
5. *Tohoroth* (Cleannesses)
6. *Mikwaoth* (Immersion pools)
7. *Niddah* (The menstruant)
8. *Makshirin* (Predisposers)
9. *Zabim* (They that suffer a flux)
10. *Tebul Yom* (He that immersed himself that day)
11. *Yadaim* (Hands)
12. *Uktzin* (Stalks)

Alphabetical List of Individual Tractates

Two numbers follow each name. The first is the number of the *seder* and the second is the number of the tractate within that *seder*. Thus, *Aboth* 4:9 indicates that this is the ninth tractate within the fourth *seder* (*Nezikin*). This list and these references provide a map of the rabbinic material to facilitate finding a particular tractate.

Abodah Zarah 4.8
Aboth 4.9
Arakhin 5.5

Baba Bathra 4.3
Baba Kamma 4.1
Baba Metzia 4.2
Bekhoroth 5.4
Berakoth 1.1
Betzah 2.7
Bikkurim 1.11

Demai 1.3

Eduyoth 4.7
Erubin 2.2

Gittin 3.6

Hagigah 2.12
Hallah 1.9
Horayoth 4.10
Hullin 5.3

Kelim 6.1
Kerithoth 5.7
Ketuboth 3.2
Kiddushin 3.7
Kilaim 1.4
Kinnim 5.11

Maaseroth 1.7
Maaser Sheni 1.8
Makkoth 4.5
Makshirin 6.8
Megillah 2.10
Meilah 5.8
Menahoth 5.2
Middoth 5.10
Mikwaoth 6.6
Moed Katan 2.11

Nazir 3.4
Nedarim 3.3
Negaim 6.3
Niddah 6.7

Oholoth 6.2

Orlah 1.10

Parah 6.4

Peah 1.2

Pesahim 2.3

Rosh ha-Shanah 2.8

Sanhedrin 4.4

Shabbath 2.1

Shebiith 1.5

Shebuoth 4.6

Shekalim 2.4

Sotah 3.5

Sukkah 2.6

Taanith 2.9

Tamid 5.9

Tebul Yom 6.10

Temurah 5.6

Terumoth 1.6

Tohoroth 6.5

Uktzin 6.12

Yadaim 6.11

Yebamoth 3.1

Yoma 2.5

Yom Tob 2.7

Zabim 6.9

Zebahim 5.1

Appendix **D**

Crucifixion

Crucifixion involved elevating the condemned upon a pole, some form of frame or scaffolding, or a natural tree.[1] This exposed the victim to public view and derision. In many cases the individual was executed by some other means, and then all or a part of the body (usually the head) was elevated. In other circumstances crucifixion was the actual means of execution. Usually crucifixion was a means of punishment, but there is evidence that in some areas it may have also been associated with religious human sacrifice.

Because of the effects upon the body and the lengthy period of time before death occurred, crucifixion was the most painful, cruel, and barbaric form of execution. Its roots are lost in history. Known to have been used in one form or another by many different groups, it is most closely associated with the Persians, Carthaginians, Phoenicians, Greeks, and especially the Romans.[2] In the land of Israel crucifixion was a Roman form of execution; the Jewish method was stoning.

Crucifixion gave executioners opportunity to use their most cruel and sadistic creativity; victims were sometimes hanged in grotesque positions by a variety of means. The earliest forms of crucifixion probably involved impaling the condemned on a single pole or suspending him by wedging the head between the prongs of a Y-shaped structure. By New Testament times several different types of crosses were commonly used by the Romans. Most involved at least two separate pieces of wood to construct a frame. The two forms most likely used for the execution of Jesus are the T-shaped

1. This appendix is an adaption of J. Julius Scott, Jr., "Cross/Crucifixion," in *Evangelical Dictionary of Theology,* ed. Walter A. Elwell (Grand Rapids: Baker, 1984), 286–88. See also Martin Hengel, *Crucifixion in the Ancient World and the Folly of the Message of the Cross,* trans. John Bowman (Philadelphia: Fortress, 1977); and William D. Edwards, Wesley J. Gabel, and Floyd E. Hosmer, "On the Physical Death of Jesus Christ," *Journal of the American Medical Association* 255.11 (March 21, 1986): 1455–62.

2. Among the other groups practicing crucifixion were the Indians, Scythians, Celts, Germani, Britanni, and Taurians.

Saint Anthony's cross and the Latin cross, the vertical piece of which rose above both the horizontal crossbar and the head of the victim.[3]

Detailed descriptions of crucifixions are few; the ancient writers seem to have avoided the subject. Recent archaeological discoveries, including the skeletal remains of a man crucified in first-century Jerusalem, have added considerably to our knowledge. It seems that the Gospel accounts of the death of Jesus indicate the standard Roman procedure for crucifixion. At some point the victim was flogged, an experience from which some died. The condemned was required to carry the horizontal piece to the site of execution, always a prominent place outside the city. The leader of the four-man execution squad bore a sign detailing the reason for the execution.

The condemned was stripped; nudity added to the shame. The victim's outstretched arms were affixed to the crossbar either by nails or ropes. The crossbar was then raised and secured to the perpendicular pole, which in some areas was left in place permanently, both for convenience and as a warning. The sign identifying the crime was also secured to the cross. A small board or peg may have been provided as a seat to bear some of the body's weight. The feet were secured in a manner that forced the knees into a bent position. Contrary to popular modern opinion, crosses were not high; the feet were probably only a few inches above the ground.

Death came slowly; it was not unusual for persons to survive for days on the cross. The precise cause of death could be exposure, hunger, shock, or exhaustion. Some recent medical studies suggest that if the crucified did not have some sort of seat for support or was unable to use his feet to push his body upward, he would be unable to breathe properly and would soon die of suffocation. Occasionally death was "mercifully" hastened by breaking the legs of the condemned. This increased bodily shock and induced suffocation by making it impossible for the feet to push the body upward. An additional disgrace was that the bodies of the crucified were usually left unburied and eaten by carnivorous birds and beasts.

The social stigma and disgrace associated with crucifixion in the Roman world can hardly be overstated. It was a punishment usually reserved for slaves, criminals of the worst sort from the lowest levels of society, military deserters, and especially traitors. In only rare cases, such as military desertion, were Roman citizens crucified. The stigma of crucifixion extended to the family and friends of the victim; to be known as an associate of one who had been crucified was a mark of utmost shame. In the Jewish world, crucifixion bore an additional disgrace. According to Deuteronomy 21:23, "anyone hung on a tree is under God's curse"—the very method of death brought a divine curse upon the crucified.

---

3. Both the statement in Matt. 27:37 (Luke 23:38) that the inscription was placed "over his head" and most ancient traditions suggest that Jesus was crucified on a Latin cross.

The Jewish Daily Prayer and the Exclusion of Jewish Christians

Sometime in the first century the wording of the twelfth petition of the Jewish daily prayer (the *Shemoneh 'Esreh*) was altered to include a condemnation of Jewish Christians. Thus the difference in wording between the common version and that of the Cairo genizah (the Palestinian version):

Babylonian Version
And for informers let there be no hope; and let all who do wickedness quickly perish; and let them all be speedily destroyed; and uproot and crush and hurl down and humble the insolent, speedily in our days. *Blessed art thou, Lord, who crushest enemies and humblest the insolent.*

Palestinian Version
And for apostates let there be no hope; and may the insolent kingdom be quickly uprooted, in our days. And may the Nazarenes and the heretics perish quickly; and may they be erased from the Book of Life; and may they not be inscribed with the righteous. *Blessed art thou, Lord, who humblest the insolent.*

The word translated "Nazarenes" is the modern Hebrew word (*Naṣorim*) for Jewish Christians; the word translated "heretics" (*minim*) is a broader term for heretics in general.[1] The wording from the Cairo version, usually assumed to come from the end

---

1. Five suggestions have been offered to explain the etymology of *minim*: (1) a contraction from the Hebrew word for "believers"; (2) an acrostic from the Hebrew for "believers [in] Jesus the Nazarene"; (3) a derivation from the name Manes, founder of the Manichean system; (4) a derivation from the root meaning "to deny"; and (5) a derivation from the common and original meaning of *min*, "sort" or "kind," designating an unfaithful Jew. The last suggestion seems the most likely. See R. Travers Herford, *Christianity in Talmud and Midrash* (Clifton, N.J.: Reference Book, 1966), 362–81, and 161; George Foot Moore, *Judaism in the First Centuries of the Christian Era*, 3 vols. (Cambridge, Mass.: Harvard University Press, 1927–30), 3:68–69. Par-

of the first century, calls to mind John 9:22; 12:42; and 16:2, which speak of exclusion of Jesus' followers from the synagogue (in contrast to persecution in the synagogues [Mark 13:9; Luke 12:11]). The inclusion of this wording in the daily prayer uttered in the synagogues of Israel became the instrument for excluding Jewish Christians from continued participation in the service—their enthusiasm for joining in corporate prayer would be severely undercut by the petition asking for their own damnation.

It should be noted that modern versions do not contain specific references to the Nazarenes and the heretics. The version of Simeon Singer (*Authorised Daily Prayer Book*) says, "And for slanderers let there be no home, and let all wickedness perish as in a moment; may all Thine enemies be soon cut off, and the dominion of arrogance do Thou speedily root out and shatter, cast down, and humble speedily in our days. Blessed art Thou, O Lord, who shatterest enemies and humblest the arrogant."

---

ticularly helpful are Herford's (p. 366) distinctions between four terms in Tosephta *Sanhedrin* 12:4–5: *masoroth* (delators, political betrayers), *epiqurosin* (free thinkers, Jew or Gentile), *meshummadim* (those who willingly transgress some part of the ceremonial law and thereby proclaim their apostasy from the Jewish religion), and *minim* (those who are false at heart, but do not necessarily proclaim their apostasy). He sees here a series of four terms which are on the same footing.

Appendix **F**

Apocalyptic Literature and Inspired Scripture

Apocalyptic literary form is foreign to most contemporary Christians, especially in the Western world. Its strangeness often creates an atmosphere of mystery which suggests to some readers a special degree of spiritual significance. There is a tendency to assume that the presence of the apocalyptic form automatically indicates not only a general eschatological content, but also predictions about the events immediately preceding and accompanying the return of Christ and the end of the world. Such assumptions fail to recognize that apocalyptic was (and is) a recognizable human literary form used by writers for a variety of purposes. Its special quality for Christians comes not from something inherent in its nature, but from its use by inspired writers in Scripture. Furthermore, just as the biblical writers both used and adapted other ancient literary forms (such as narrative, poetry, prophecy, epistle), so did they both use and adapt the apocalyptic form.[1]

Persons who hold to a traditional view of the nature of the Bible have seldom addressed several issues regarding how that view relates to the apocalyptic phenomena. It is of particular importance that apocalyptic appeared elsewhere in the ancient world at approximately the same period at which Jewish apocalyptic was coming into prominence and being incorporated into biblical literature. In short, how do assumptions regarding the origin of apocalyptic affect claims for the divine inspiration of Scripture? Persons who approach Scripture with an antisupernaturalistic bias assume that biblical apocalyptic, like other parts of Scripture, is of human origin. Even if they grant that the vision or dream through which the apocalyptist enters the other world is more than a literary device, they see here the workings of a mystical or highly subjective psychological orientation or a literary symbol for an existential experience.

---

1. An example of adaptation is that the Christian apocalyptists' view of the period of salvation history in which they live is different from the view of the Jewish writers (see p. 190 n. 14).

On the other hand, those who accept the divine origin of Scripture assume that the process of inspiration utilized the apocalyptic literary form just as naturally as it did other genres. Hence the visions and dreams are taken to be but two of the modes through which the Spirit spoke to biblical writers. Consequently, apocalyptic literature, like other genres, must be interpreted in accordance with its nature and by appropriate interpretive principles.

Another issue involving apocalyptic and Scripture has to do with the dating of the origin of apocalyptic and of certain biblical books. Contemporary scholars often assume that certain canons of criticism may be used by themselves to determine the limits for the dates of a document. Thus, on the assumption that biblical apocalyptic is the result of Israel's exposure to a particular influence, such as Zoroastrianism or Hellenism, the biblical books containing apocalyptic sections must, according to this logic, be dated after the Hebrews came in contact with that influence. Hence parts of Isaiah, Daniel, Joel, and other sections of the Old Testament must be postexilic. Another canon has to do with historical allusions. Biblical statements referring to a historical person, event, or institution cannot be predictions, but must have been written after the fact (*ex eventu*).

This is not the forum for a full discussion of such issues. Nevertheless, a few observations are in order. First, within the shifting sands of scholarly opinion, assumptions about the origin and development of apocalyptic are subject to revision. Recent uncertainty about precisely which features identify a document as apocalyptic clouds the issue of its nature and date of origin. Is, for example, Isaiah 24–27 apocalyptic or preapocalyptic? Although 24:21–23 and other passages speak of eschatological judgment (note the phrase "on that day" in 24:21; 25:9; 26:1; 27:1–2, 12–13), there is no clear-cut dualism. There is now some acceptance of the possibility that the roots of apocalyptic are much earlier than previously thought. The question "Who borrowed from whom?" is no longer automatically answered that the Hebrews must have been the borrowers.[2]

Second, it is important to reach conclusions on the issues we have raised, but they should not be used as tests for either traditional or critical orthodoxy. Neither side is free from circular reasoning, special pleading, and the like. There is need to acknowledge bravely our presuppositions and their influence, to separate data from assumption and interpretation, and to look again and again at the facts and where they lead. Such an approach will not diminish the influence of presuppositions, but it will enable us to distinguish between differences of opinion which rest on factual evidence alone and those which are rooted in philosophical assumptions and commitments.

2. P. Gignoux, "Apocalypses et voyages extra-terrestres dans l'Iran Mazdéen," in *Apocalypses et voyages dans l'Au-delà*, ed. C. Kappler (Paris, 1987), 355, raises the possibility of Jewish influence on Persian apocalypticism.

Appendix **G**

Interpreting Apocalyptic Literature

For whatever reason, the apocalyptic writers used language that was difficult for all but their own group to understand. The modern reader stands not only outside the writer's group, but in a different geographical location, period of history, culture, and linguistic framework. The apocalyptic literary form is foreign to most of us. The difficulty of understanding it is demonstrated by the variety of interpretive schemes for the Book of Revelation alone.[1] Many books on hermeneutics or biblical interpretation give suggestions for interpreting apocalyptic.[2] Here we offer only a few observations to help readers of this literary form.

1. Although there are almost as many different interpretations of Revelation as there are interpreters, they may be categorized under four broad types:
   1. *Idealist:* The Book of Revelation depicts the continual struggle between good and evil, God and Satan, the church and paganism, and the eventual triumph of Christianity. Hence it contains no prediction of the future.
   2. *Preterist:* The Book of Revelation depicts the persecution of Christianity by ancient Rome during the author's own time; there is also some indication of what he expected to happen in the immediate future. Thus the book was written during one of the two first-century empirewide persecutions: (a) during the reign of the emperor Nero (54–68), who persecuted Christians from 64 to 68; or (b) during the reign of Domitian (81–96), who persecuted Christians in 95–96.
   3. *Historicist:* Revelation is a symbolic presentation of church history from apostolic times until the end of history. The book depicts either successive stages of church history or cycles which have constantly recurred throughout church history and will continue until the second coming of Christ.
   4. *Futurist:* The Book of Revelation depicts only times and conditions immediately prior to the second coming of Christ and the end of both the world and history. Hence, from the writer's perspective, it deals with events that were in the distant future. Most of those who take this interpretive stance assume that they are living in the last days and that the book describes their own times.

2. For example, A. Berkeley Mickelsen, *Interpreting the Bible* (Grand Rapids: Eerdmans, 1963); Gordon D. Fee and Douglas Stuart, *How to Read the Bible for All Its Worth* (Grand Rapids: Zondervan, 1982).

First, it is essential to understand the distinctives of the genre. The definitions given in chapter 10 should be of some assistance. Nevertheless, we can never become acquainted with a literary form, especially one so alien to our own experience, by secondary definitions alone. To understand any literary genre we must read widely in that form; to understand novels, we must read many novels. We become familiar with apocalyptic by reading as many apocalypses as possible.

Second, the wide variety of interpretations of apocalypses is in large measure the result of using methods that are inappropriate for the genre. That the writers had specific people, events, and situations in mind does not mean that every detail of their imagery is to be searched for hidden meanings. The modern reader is not in a position to understand fully the writer's figures or, at times, even the writer's intent.

Third, the better the interpreter's knowledge of the history, culture, society, and thought of the writer's time, the more likely one is to be able to catch allusions, innuendoes, and oblique references. Again, the modern reader must proceed with caution. Although historical study provides much necessary and helpful information, we can never know and feel all that the writer and his original readers experienced.

Fourth, it is helpful to recognize that the apocalyptist focuses on the big picture, the whole sweep of history. Even the details of the present are seen as parts of the gigantic mosaic; each piece is important, but its importance is evident only when the whole is in view. The apocalyptic scribe insists that past and present persecutions, reversals, and disasters suffered by God's people be seen in the light of God's ultimate victory and the future glory of his people. The interpreter has missed the mark unless one seeks and appreciates at least the outline of the apocalyptist's total work.

Fifth, the interpreter must allow the writer to speak to the emotions as well as the mind. The scribe desires to draw the readers into the other world so they can feel its utter strangeness and then, with an enlarged point of view, reenter their own world and life.

Finally, the question of the relevance of apocalyptic to the modern world must be considered. The apocalyptists dealt with problems and issues which are continuing concerns within the human drama. Sin and suffering, the prosperity of the wicked, the meaning of history, the nature and relevance of a supernatural world, and the final destiny of the universe and those in it are ever-present issues. The apocalypses, like the Book of Job, provide, if not answers, at least a way to cope with such issues.

Those of us who believe the Bible to be divine revelation face the additional question of how its apocalyptic writings can be normative in our own time and place. From at least the second century onward, this question has led to many attempts to find exact parallels between the images of the apocalyptists and the reader's world. Obviously, those in previous generations who predicted the return of Christ and the end of the world in their day were wrong. What is clear is that biblical apocalyptic, especially that in the New Testament, deals with eschatology. Its general message is consistent with that of many nonbiblical apocalyptic scribes, yet it has a distinctive Christian message as well. God's people are the church, the new Jerusalem, the bride of Christ (Rev. 2–3; 19:7; 21:2, 9–10). The various powers that have persecuted God's people are the beasts or Satan (Rev. 12–19). Christians are redeemed by and conquer through the blood of the Lamb; Christ is the slaughtered Lamb who is the ultimate agent of victory (Rev. 1:5; 5:9; 7:14; 12:11).[3] The second coming of Christ will signal the defeat of evil, judgment, rewards for God's people and punishment for the wicked, and the new heaven and earth.

How much of the detail of biblical apocalyptic is applicable beyond the writer's own time is a most difficult question. The history of interpretation chronicles the disagreements on this point. We hope our comments will be of assistance. In addition, the reader must beware of interpreting in isolation from others of like faith, for Christianity is communal! We need help from our brothers and sisters, both in person and through their writings. The more the better. It is dangerous to permit one individual or small group to do our interpreting for us. We need to profit from, as much as possible, the accomplishments and mistakes of the past and our contemporaries.

3. The identification of Christ with the Lamb is confirmed by the reference to "the twelve apostles of the Lamb" in Rev. 21:14.

How Scholarship Works

It is important that those interested in biblical and related studies understand something about the process for dealing with a newly discovered body of information. The first step is the reporting of the facts. This includes what was found, where, by whom, and the present location of what was discovered. It is important that the material be made available for all to see and interpret. In the case of manuscripts this means furnishing reproductions and transcriptions to the scholarly public as a whole. Herein lies the first area of difficulty and controversy. Individuals controlling such material want to reserve first crack at it for themselves. Thus the content of manuscripts may be withheld for a reasonable period of time. Debate continues over what is a "reasonable" period.

The process of transcription of manuscripts is difficult and often subject to question. By "transcription" we mean copying the actual letters into a modern medium for study or publication. Not infrequently some letters will be difficult to identify because of the handwriting of the scribe, fading of the writing, deterioration or mutilation of the manuscript. Because manuscripts are both valuable and fragile, they cannot be routinely shipped from one place to another. Hence it is customary to publish photographs. Sometimes modern photographic techniques assist in determining what is on the manuscript, but often photographs are not as good as working with the original. There may be justifiable debate among scholars as to the reading of a particular passage (that is, as to precisely what are the letters in the original).

From transcription the process moves to translation and interpretation. The influence of the subjective increases. It is impossible to translate from one language, even a modern one, to another with a complete accuracy that will convey not only the meaning of words but also nuances. With a language like ancient Hebrew, translation is even more difficult. Ancient Hebrew was written without vowels, the proper pronunciation being passed on orally. Its grammatical constructions are different from English and often involve subtleties to which the modern Western mind is unaccustomed. Moreover, modern scholars simply do not know the meaning of some words. In documents like the Dead Sea Scrolls the problem is compounded because parts of the manuscripts are missing; indeed the majority of the scrolls are only small fragments. Needless to say, in such a situation there will be legitimate disagreements over the proper translation.

Even more controversial is the area of interpretation: What do the words and sentences signify? What are the historical events and ideas to which they refer? Is the Wicked Priest mentioned in some scrolls, for example, the Commentary (or *Pesher*) on Nahum, Jonathan Maccabeus (160–143), Simon Maccabeus (143–134), John Hyrcanus (134–104), Alexander Jannaeus (103–76), or someone else? Is the verb represented by the consonants *WHMYTW* in fragment 4Q285 a causative (translated "they caused to be killed") or indicative ("they killed")? Do the regulations of the Manual of Discipline (1QS) and the Covenant of the Damascus Community (CD) indicate an Essene community or some other group?

Scholarship works for a consensus. Once the raw data—the letters, words, and sentences of the scrolls—are made available, different individuals begin making and publishing their own translations and interpretations. Their findings are evaluated and debated by others working in the field. The impossible will quickly be exposed and eliminated. Other options will continue to be studied and evaluated. Sometimes it is impossible to judge between alternative opinions.

Unfortunately, sensation seekers often rush into print with ideas designed to catch the public fancy, sell books, and gain celebrity for the writer. An early publication about the Dead Sea Scrolls claimed that every word of the Isaiah manuscript from Qumran differs from the text currently used by Jews and Christians. The author was correct—the Dead Sea manuscript did not and could not include the vowels, for they were not a part of the original writing, but were added by Jewish scholars five hundred to six hundred years after the Qumran Isaiah scroll was copied. The true scholarly process is much slower, more painstaking, and less dramatic than the precipitate offerings of sensation seekers.[1]

1. Shortly before the publication of the so-called long-secret Dead Sea material in the fall of 1991, I warned a class that if the documents were made available, there would be wild interpretations almost beyond imagination. Before the semester was over, I brought to class a supermarket tabloid which claimed that the newly published scrolls proved that Elvis Presley was alive and living in Israel, and that a cure for cancer was available from a certain plant that grows in Palestine.

Bibliography

Primary Sources

The Apocrypha and Pseudepigrapha

The Apocrypha and Pseudepigrapha of the Old Testament. Edited by R. H. Charles. 2 vols. Oxford: Clarendon, 1913.

The Apocryphal Old Testament. Edited by H. F. D. Sparks. New York: Oxford University Press, 1984.

The Old Testament Pseudepigrapha. Edited by James H. Charlesworth. 2 vols. New York: Doubleday, 1983, 1985.

Philo and Josephus

Josephus. *Works.* Translated by H. St. J. Thackeray, Ralph Marcus, Allen Wikgren, and Louis H. Feldman. 9 vols. Loeb Classical Library. Cambridge, Mass.: Harvard University Press, 1926–65.

_____. *The Works of Josephus.* Translated by William Whiston. Peabody, Mass.: Hendrickson, 1987.

Philo. *Works.* Translated by F. H. Colson, G. H. Whitaker, and Ralph Marcus. 10 vols. with two supplements. Loeb Classical Library. Cambridge, Mass.: Harvard University Press, 1929–62.

_____. *The Works of Philo.* Translated by C. D. Yonge. Peabody, Mass.: Hendrickson, 1993.

Dead Sea Scrolls

The Dead Sea Scrolls in English. Translated by Geza Vermes. 3d ed. New York: Viking-Penguin, 1990.

Dupont-Sommer, André. *The Essene Writings from Qumran.* Translated by Geza Vermes. Cleveland: World, 1962.

Rabbinic Writings

The Babylonian Talmud. Edited by Isidore Epstein. 35 vols. London: Soncino, 1935–52.

Midrash Rabbah. Translated and edited by Harry Freedman and Maurice Simon. 3d ed. London: Soncino, 1983.

The Mishnah. Translated by Herbert Danby. Oxford: Oxford University Press, 1933.

Montefiore, C. G., and H. Loewe, eds. *Rabbinic Anthology.* New York: Schocken, 1974.

Bibliography

The Targum of Isaiah. Edited by J. F. Stenning. Oxford: Clarendon, 1949.

The Targums of Onkelos and Jonathan ben Uzziel. Edited by J. W. Etheridge. New York: Ktav, 1968.

Non-Jewish Writers

Eusebius. *Ecclesiastical History.* Translated by Kirsopp Lake et al. 2 vols. Loeb Classical Library. Cambridge, Mass.: Harvard University Press, 1959.

Greek and Latin Authors on Jews and Judaism. Edited by Menahem Stern. 3 vols. Jerusalem: Israel Academy of Sciences and Humanities, 1989.

Hippolytus. *Refutation of All Heresies.* In *Ante-Nicene Fathers,* edited by Alexander Roberts and James Donaldson, 5:9–153. Grand Rapids: Eerdmans, 1978.

Justin Martyr. *Dialogue with Trypho.* In *Ante-Nicene Fathers,* edited by Alexander Roberts and James Donaldson, 1:194–270. Grand Rapids: Eerdmans, n.d.

Juvenal. *Satires.* Translated by G. G. Ramsay. Rev. ed. Loeb Classical Library. Cambridge, Mass.: Harvard University Press, 1940.

Pliny the Elder. *Natural History.* Translated by E. H. Warmington. 10 vols. Loeb Classical Library. Cambridge, Mass.: Harvard University Press, 1938–62.

Tacitus. *The Histories* and *The Annals.* Translated by Clifford Moore. 4 vols. Loeb Classical Library. Cambridge, Mass.: Harvard University Press, 1973.

Secondary Sources

Abegg, Martin. "Paul, 'Works of the Law' and MMT." *Biblical Archaeology Review* 20.6 (Nov.-Dec. 1994): 52–56.

Adam, Alfred. *Antike Berichte über die Essener.* Kleine Texte 182. Berlin: Walter de Gruyter, 1961.

Aharoni, Yohanan. *The Land of the Bible: A Historical Geography.* Rev. ed. Philadelphia: Westminster, 1979.

Anderson, Robert T. "Samaritans." In *Anchor Bible Dictionary,* edited by David Noel Freedman, 5:945–46. New York: Doubleday, 1992.

Applebaum, S. "Economic Life in Palestine." In *The Jewish People in the First Century,* edited by S. Safrai, M. Stern et al., 2:631–700. Philadelphia: Fortress, 1976.

Arnold, Brian. "The Messianic Woes in Jewish and Christian Apocalyptic Literature." Wheaton College Graduate School, 2 December 1985.

The Asatir: The Samaritan Book of the "Secrets of Moses." Translated by Moses Gaster. London: Royal Asiatic Society, 1927.

Baeck, Leo. "The Faith of Paul." *Journal of Jewish Studies* 3 (1952): 93–110.

_____. *The Pharisees.* New York: Schocken, 1947.

Balchin, J. A. "Life after Death in the Psalms." *Theological Students Fellowship Bulletin* 29 (Spring 1961): 1–4.

Baron, Salo W., and Joseph L. Blau. *Judaism: Postbiblical and Talmudic Period.* New York: Liberal Arts, 1954.

Barr, James. *Biblical Words for Time.* Naperville, Ill.: Allenson, 1962.

Becker, Joachim. *Messianic Expectation in the Old Testament.* Translated by David E. Green. Philadelphia: Fortress, 1980.

Bevan, Edwyn R. "Hellenistic Judaism." In *The Legacy of Israel,* edited by Edwyn R. Bevan and Charles Singer, 29–67. Oxford: Clarendon, 1927.

_____. *Jerusalem under the High-Priests.* London: Edward Arnold, 1918.

_____, and Charles Singer, eds. *The Legacy of Israel.* Oxford: Clarendon, 1927.

Bickerman, Elias. *From Ezra to the Last of the Maccabees: Foundations of Post-Biblical Judaism.* New York: Schocken, 1962.

Black, Matthew. *The Essene Problem.* London: Dr. Williams's Trust, 1961.

_____. *The Scrolls and Christian Origins.* New York: Thomas Nelson, 1961.

Boccaccini, Gabriele. *Middle Judaism: Jewish Thought, 300 B.C.E. to 200 C.E.* Minneapolis: Fortress, 1991.

Bokser, Baruch M. "Unleavened Bread and Passover, Feasts of." In *Anchor Bible Dictionary,* edited by David Noel Freedman, 6:760–65. New York: Doubleday, 1992.

Bonsirven, Joseph. *Palestinian Judaism in the Time of Jesus Christ.* Translated by William Wolf. New York: Holt, Rinehart and Winston, 1964.

Bousset, Wilhelm. *The Antichrist Legend.* Translated by A. H. Keane. London: Hutchinson, 1896.

_____. *Die Religion des Judentums im späthellenistischen Zeitalter.* 3d ed. Edited by Hugo Gressmann. Tübingen: Mohr, 1926.

Bowker, John W. *Jesus and the Pharisees.* New York: Cambridge University Press, 1973.

_____. *The Targums and Rabbinic Literature.* New York: Cambridge University Press, 1969.

Bronner, Leah. *Sects and Separatism during the Second Jewish Commonwealth.* New York: Bloch, 1967.

Bruce, F. F. *The Acts of the Apostles.* 3d ed. Grand Rapids: Eerdmans, 1990.

_____. *Biblical Exegesis in the Qumran Texts.* London: Tyndale, 1959.

_____. *The Book of the Acts.* Rev. ed. Grand Rapids: Eerdmans, 1988.

_____. "Eschatology." In *Evangelical Dictionary of Theology,* edited by Walter A. Elwell, 362–65. Grand Rapids: Baker, 1984.

_____. "Inter-testamental Literature." In *What Theologians Do,* edited by F. G. Healey, 85–102. Grand Rapids: Eerdmans, 1970.

_____. *Israel and the Nations.* Grand Rapids: Eerdmans, 1963.

_____. *New Testament History.* Garden City, N.Y.: Doubleday, 1972.

_____. "Paul on Immortality." *Scottish Journal of Theology* 24.4 (Nov. 1971): 458–61.

_____. *Second Thoughts on the Dead Sea Scrolls.* 2d ed. Grand Rapids: Eerdmans, 1961.

Brueggemann, Walter. *The Land.* Philadelphia: Fortress, 1977.

Buehler, William W. *The Pre-Herodian Civil War and Social Debate: Jewish Society in the Period 76–40 B.C. and the Social Factors Contributing to the Rise of the Pharisees and Sadducees.* Basel: Friedrich Reinhardt, 1974.

Bultmann, Rudolf. "History of Salvation and History." In Rudolf Bultmann, *Existence and Faith,* translated by Schubert M. Ogden, 226–40. New York: Meridian, 1960.

_____. "The New Testament and Mythology." In Rudolf Bultmann, *The New Testament and Mythology and Other Basic Writings,* translated by Schubert M. Ogden, 1–43. Philadelphia: Fortress, 1984.

Burrows, Millar. *Burrows on the Dead Sea Scrolls.* Grand Rapids: Baker, 1978.

Callaway, Phillip R. *The History of the Qumran Community.* Sheffield, Eng.: Sheffield Academic Press, 1988.

Cambridge History of Judaism. Edited by W. D. Davies and Louis Finkelstein. Vol. 1, *Introduction; The Persian Period;* vol. 2, *The Hellenistic Age.* New York: Cambridge University Press, 1984, 1989.

Charlesworth, James H. *The Pseudepigrapha and Modern Research.* Missoula, Mont.: Scholars, 1976.

_____, ed. *The Messiah: Developments in Earliest Judaism and Christianity.* Minneapolis: Augsburg Fortress, 1992.

Chilton, Bruce D. *The Glory of Israel: The Theology and Provenience of the Isaiah Targum.* Sheffield: JSOT, 1982.

Cohen, Shaye J. D. "The Political and Social History of the Jews in Greco-Roman Antiquity." In *Early Judaism and Its Modern Interpreters,* edited by Robert A. Kraft and George W. E. Nicklesburg, 33–56. Atlanta: Scholars, 1986.

Collins, John J. *The Apocalyptic Imagination.* New York: Crossroad, 1984.

_____. "Apocalyptic Literature." In *Early Judaism and Its Modern Interpreters,* edited by Robert A. Kraft and George W. E. Nicklesburg, 345–70. Atlanta: Scholars, 1986.

_____. "Dead Sea Scrolls." In *Anchor Bible Dictionary,* edited by David Noel Freedman, 2:85–101. New York: Doubleday, 1992.

_____. "Early Jewish Apocalypticism." In *Anchor Bible Dictionary,* edited by David Noel Freedman, 1:282–88. New York: Doubleday, 1992.

_____, ed. *Apocalypse: The Morphology of a Genre.* Semeia 14. Missoula, Mont.: Scholars, 1979.

Compendia Rerum Iudaicarum ad Novum Testamentum. 7 vols. Philadelphia: Fortress, 1974–92.

Cook, Edward M. *Solving the Mysteries of the Dead Sea Scrolls: New Light on the Bible.* Grand Rapids: Zondervan, 1994.

Corpus Papyrorum Judaicarum. Edited by Victor Tcherikover and Alexander Fuks. 3 vols. Cambridge, Mass.: Harvard University Press, 1957–64.

Cowley, A. E. *Aramaic Papyri of the Fifth Century B.C.* New York: Oxford University Press, 1929.

Crenshaw, James L. "Education in Ancient Israel." *Journal of Biblical Literature* 104.4 (Dec. 1985): 601–15.

Cross, Frank Moore. *The Ancient Library of Qumran.* 2d ed. London: Duckworth, 1961.

Cullmann, Oscar. *Christ and Time: The Primitive Christian Conception of Time and History.* Rev. ed. Philadelphia: Westminster, 1964.

_____. *The Christology of the New Testament.* Translated by Shirley C. Guthrie and Charles A. M. Hall. Philadelphia: Westminster, 1959.

_____. *The New Testament: An Introduction for the General Reader.* Translated by Dennis Pardee. Philadelphia: Westminster, 1968.

Dalman, Gustaf H. *The Words of Jesus.* Edinburgh: T. and T. Clark, 1902.

Daniel-Rops, Henri. *Daily Life in the Time of Jesus.* Translated by Patrick O'Brian. New York: Hawthorn, 1962.

Daube, David. *The New Testament and Rabbinic Judaism.* New York: Arno, 1973.

Davies, W. D. *Christian Origins and Judaism.* London: Dalton, Longman and Todd, 1962.

_____. *The Gospel and the Land: Early Christianity and Jewish Territorial Doctrine.* Berkeley: University of California Press, 1974.

_____. *Paul and Rabbinic Judaism.* 2d ed. London: SPCK, 1955.

_____. *The Setting of the Sermon on the Mount.* New York: Cambridge University Press, 1964.

_____. *The Territorial Dimension of Judaism*. Berkeley: University of California Press, 1982.

_____. *Torah in the Messianic Age and/or the Age to Come*. Philadelphia: Society of Biblical Literature, 1952.

Dictionary of Jesus and the Gospels. Edited by Joel B. Green, Scot McKnight, and I. Howard Marshall. Downers Grove, Ill.: Inter-Varsity, 1992.

Dodd, C. H. *According to the Scriptures: The Sub-Structure of New Testament Theology*. New York: Scribner, 1952.

_____. *The Old Testament in the New*. Philadelphia: Fortress, 1963.

Dupont-Sommer, André. *The Jewish Sect of Qumran and the Essenes*. Translated by R. D. Barnett. London: Valentine, Mitchell, 1953.

Edersheim, Alfred. *The Life and Times of Jesus the Messiah*. 8th ed. 2 vols. New York: Longmans, Green, 1907.

Edwards, William D., Wesley J. Gabel, and Floyd E. Hosmer. "On the Physical Death of Jesus Christ." *Journal of the American Medical Association* 255.11 (March 21, 1986): 1455–62.

Ellis, E. E. "Jesus, the Sadducees, and Qumran." *New Testament Studies* 10 (1963–64): 274–79.

Ellison, H. L. *From Babylon to Bethlehem: The People of God between the Testaments*. Grand Rapids: Baker, 1984.

Eskenazi, Tamara C. "Sheshbazzar." In *Anchor Bible Dictionary*, edited by David Noel Freedman, 5:1207–9. New York: Doubleday, 1992.

Evangelical Dictionary of Theology. Edited by Walter A. Elwell. Grand Rapids: Baker, 1984.

Farmer, William R. *Maccabees, Zealots, and Josephus*. New York: Columbia University Press, 1956.

Fee, Gordon D., and Douglas Stuart. *How to Read the Bible for All Its Worth*. Grand Rapids: Zondervan, 1982.

Feldman, Louis. "The Omnipresence of God-Fearers." *Biblical Archaeologist Reader* 12.5 (Sept./Oct. 1986): 59–63.

Finkelstein, Louis. "The Men of the Great Synagogue (*circa* 400–170 B.C.E.)." In *Cambridge History of Judaism*, edited by W. D. Davies and Louis Finkelstein, 2:229–44. New York: Cambridge University Press, 1989.

_____. *The Pharisees: The Sociological Background of Their Faith*. 3d ed. 2 vols. Philadelphia: Jewish Publication Society of America, 1962.

Fitzmyer, Joseph A. "Did Jesus Speak Greek?" *Biblical Archaeology Review* 18.5 (Sept.-Oct. 1992): 58–63.

Foakes Jackson, F. J., and Kirsopp Lake, eds. *The Beginnings of Christianity*. 5 vols. Grand Rapids: Baker, 1966.

Foerster, Werner. *From the Exile to Christ*. Philadelphia: Fortress, 1964.

_____. "*Sōtēr*." In *Theological Dictionary of the New Testament*, edited by Gerhard Friedrich, translated by Geoffrey W. Bromiley, 7:1003–14. Grand Rapids: Eerdmans, 1971.

Freyne, Sean. *Galilee from Alexander the Great to Hadrian, 323 B.C.E. to 135 C.E.* Wilmington, Del.: Michael Glazier, 1980.

Frymer-Kensky, T. S. "The Atrahasis Epic and Its Significance for Our Understanding of Genesis 1–9." *Biblical Archaeologist* 40.4 (Dec. 1977): 147–55.

Fujita, Neil S. *A Crack in the Jar: What Ancient Jewish Documents Tell Us about the New Testament*. Mahwah, N.J.: Paulist, 1986.

Gaster, Moses. *Samaritan Oral and Ancient Traditions.* Vol. 1, *Eschatology.* London: Search, 1932.

_____. *The Samaritans: Their History, Doctrines and Literature.* Schweich Lectures. London: Oxford University Press, 1925.

Gaster, Theodor H. *Festivals of the Jewish Year: A Modern Interpretation and Guide.* New York: Sloane, 1952.

Gignoux, P. "Apocalypses et voyages extra-terrestres dans l'Iran Mazdéen." In *Apocalypses et voyages dans l'Au-delà,* edited by C. Kappler, 351–74. Paris, 1987.

Ginzburg, Louis. *The Legends of the Jews.* 7 vols. Philadelphia: Jewish Publication Society of America, 1909–38.

Goodenough, E. R. *An Introduction to Philo Judaeus.* 2d ed. New York: Barnes and Noble, 1963.

Goodman, Martin. *Ruling Classes of Judaea: The Origins of the Jewish Revolt against Rome, A.D. 66–70.* New York: Cambridge University Press, 1987.

Grabbe, Lester L. *Judaism from Cyrus to Hadrian.* 2 vols. Minneapolis: Augsburg Fortress, 1991–92.

Greenhut, Zvi. "Burial Cave of the Caiaphas Family." *Biblical Archaeology Review* 18.5 (Sept.-Oct. 1992): 28–44.

Guignebert, Charles. *The Jewish World in the Time of Jesus.* Translated by S. H. Hooke. London: Kegan Paul, Trench, Trubner, 1939.

Hagner, Donald A. "Paul and Judaism—The Jewish Matrix of Early Christianity: Issues in the Current Debate." *Bulletin for Biblical Research* 3 (1993): 111–30.

Hanson, Paul D. "Apocalypse, Genre." In *Interpreter's Dictionary of the Bible,* suppl. vol., edited by Keith Crim et al., 27–28. Nashville: Abingdon, 1976.

_____. "Apocalypses and Apocalypticism, The Genre." In *Anchor Bible Dictionary,* edited by David Noel Freedman, 1:279–80. New York: Doubleday, 1992.

_____. *The Dawn of Apocalyptic.* Philadelphia: Fortress, 1975.

_____. *Old Testament Apocalyptic.* Nashville: Abingdon, 1987.

Heinemann, I. *Die griechische Weltanschauung bei Juden und Römern.* Berlin: Philo, 1932.

Hengel, Martin. *Crucifixion in the Ancient World and the Folly of the Message of the Cross.* Translated by John Bowman. Philadelphia: Fortress, 1977.

_____. *Judaism and Hellenism: Studies in Their Encounter in Palestine during the Early Hellenistic Period.* Translated by John Bowden. 2 vols. Philadelphia: Fortress, 1974.

Herford, R. Travers. *Christianity in Talmud and Midrash.* Clifton, N.J.: Reference Book, 1966.

_____. *The Ethics of the Talmud: Sayings of the Fathers* [Pirke Aboth]. New York: Schocken, 1962.

_____. *The Pharisees.* Boston: Beacon, 1962.

Hillyer, Norman. "*Hērōdianoi* (Herodians)." In *New International Dictionary of New Testament Theology,* edited by Colin Brown, 3:441–43. Grand Rapids: Zondervan, 1978.

Hirsch, E. G., and J. D. Eisenstein. "Gentiles." In *Jewish Encyclopedia,* 5:614–18. New York: Funk and Wagnalls, 1925.

Hoehner, Harold W. *Herod Antipas.* Grand Rapids: Zondervan, 1980.

Horsley, Richard. "The Zealots." *Novum Testamentum* 27 (1986): 159–92.

_____, with John S. Hanson. *Bandits, Prophets, and Messiahs: Popular Movements at the Time of Jesus.* New York: Harper and Row, 1985.

Isaac, E. "1 (Ethiopic Apocalypse of) Enoch." In *Old Testament Pseudepigrapha*, edited by James H. Charlesworth, 1:5–12. Garden City, N.Y.: Doubleday, 1983.

Jagersma, H. *A History of Israel from Alexander the Great to Bar Kochba.* Translated by John Bowden. Philadelphia: Fortress, 1986.

Jellicoe, Sidney. *The Septuagint and Modern Study.* Oxford: Clarendon, 1968.

_____. *Studies in the Septuagint: Origins, Recensions, and Interpretations.* New York: Ktav, 1974.

Jeremias, Joachim. *Jerusalem in the Time of Jesus.* Translated by F. H. and C. H. Cave. London: SCM, 1973.

_____. *Jesus' Promise to the Nations.* Translated by S. H. Hooke. London: SCM, 1958.

Jones, A. H. M. *The Greek City from Alexander to Justinian.* Oxford: Clarendon, 1940.

Kampen, John. *The Hasideans and the Origin of Pharisaism: A Study in 1 and 2 Maccabees.* Atlanta: Scholars, 1988.

Kidner, Derek. *Ezra and Nehemiah: An Introduction and Commentary.* Tyndale Old Testament Commentaries. Downers Grove, Ill.: Inter-Varsity, 1979.

Klausner, Joseph. *The Messianic Idea in Israel.* Translated by W. F. Stinespring. New York: Macmillan, 1955.

Knox, Wilfred L. *St. Paul and the Church of the Gentiles.* New York: Cambridge University Press, 1939.

Koch, Klaus. *The Rediscovery of Apocalyptic.* Studies in Biblical Theology, 2d series, vol. 22. Naperville, Ill.: Alec R. Allenson, 1972.

Kohler, Kaufmann. "The Pharisees." In *Jewish Encyclopedia*, 9:661–66. New York: Funk and Wagnalls, 1925.

Kraft, Robert A. "The Multiform Jewish Heritage of Early Christianity." In *Christianity, Judaism, and Other Greco-Roman Cults: Studies for Morton Smith at Sixty,* edited by Jacob Neusner, 174–99. Leiden: Brill, 1975.

_____. Review of *Les Testimonia dans le christianisme primitif: L'Epitre de Barnabé I–XVI et ses sources*, by Pierre Prigent. *Journal of Theological Studies*, n.s., 13 (1962): 401–8.

_____, and George W. E. Nickelsburg, eds. *Early Judaism and Its Modern Interpreters.* Atlanta: Scholars, 1986.

Kuhn, Karl. "*Sebomenoi or phoboumenoi ton theon.*" In *Theological Dictionary of the New Testament*, edited by Gerhard Friedrich, translated by Geoffrey W. Bromiley, 6:743–44. Grand Rapids: Eerdmans, 1968.

_____. "The Two Messiahs of Aaron and Israel." In Krister Stendahl, ed., *The Scrolls and the New Testament*, 54–64. New York: Harper and Row, 1957.

Ladd, George E. *A Theology of the New Testament.* Rev. ed. Grand Rapids: Eerdmans, 1993.

Lake, Kirsopp. "Proselytes and God-Fearers." In *The Beginnings of Christianity*, edited by F. J. Foakes Jackson and Kirsopp Lake, 5:74–96. Grand Rapids: Baker, 1966.

Lane, William L. *The Gospel According to Mark.* New International Commentary on the New Testament. Grand Rapids: Eerdmans, 1974.

Levey, Samson H. *The Messiah: An Aramaic Interpretation; The Messianic Exegesis of the Targum.* Cincinnati: Hebrew Union College–Jewish Institute of Religion, 1974.

Liebermann, Saul. *Greek in Jewish Palestine.* New York: Jewish Theological Seminary of America, 1942.

_____. *Hellenism in Jewish Palestine.* 2d ed. New York: Jewish Theological Seminary of America, 1962.

Lohse, Eduard. *The New Testament Environment.* Translated by John E. Steely. Nashville: Abingdon, 1976.

Macdonald, John. *The Theology of the Samaritans.* London: SCM, 1964.

MacGregor, G. H. C., and A. C. Purdy. *Jew and Greek: Tutors unto Christ.* Rev. ed. Edinburgh: Saint Andrew, 1959.

McKnight, Scot. *A Light among the Gentiles: Jewish Missionary Activity in the Second Temple Period.* Minneapolis: Augsburg Fortress, 1991.

MacLennan, Robert S., and Thomas Kraabel. "The God-Fearers—A Literary and Theological Invention." *Biblical Archaeologist Reader* 12.5 (Sept./Oct. 1986): 47–53.

McNamara, Martin. *Palestinian Judaism and the New Testament.* Wilmington, Del.: Michael Glazier, 1983.

McRay, John. *Archaeology and the New Testament.* Grand Rapids: Baker, 1991.

_____. "High Priest Caiaphas' Tomb Found South of Jerusalem." *Messianic Times* 3.2 (Fall 1992): 10.

Malina, Bruce J. *The New Testament World: Insights from Cultural Anthropology.* Atlanta: John Knox, 1981.

Manson, T. W. *The Servant-Messiah.* New York: Cambridge University Press, 1953.

_____. "The Son of Man in Daniel, Enoch and the Gospels." In T. W. Manson, *Studies in the Gospels and Epistles,* 123–45. Philadelphia: Westminster, 1962.

Marcus, Ralph. "The Pharisees in the Light of Modern Scholarship." *Journal of Religion* 32 (1952): 153–64.

Marshall, I. Howard. *The Gospel of Luke: A Commentary on the Greek Text.* New International Greek Testament Commentary. Grand Rapids: Eerdmans, 1978.

Metzger, Bruce M. *An Introduction to the Apocrypha.* New York: Oxford University Press, 1957.

_____. *The New Testament: Its Background, Growth, and Content.* New York: Abingdon, 1965.

Meyer, Rudolf. "*Saddoukaios.*" In *Theological Dictionary of the New Testament,* edited by Gerhard Friedrich, translated by Geoffrey W. Bromiley, 7:35–54. Grand Rapids: Eerdmans, 1971.

Mickelsen, A. Berkeley. *Interpreting the Bible.* Grand Rapids: Eerdmans, 1963.

Mielziner, Moses. *Introduction to the Talmud.* 5th ed. New York: Bloch, 1968.

Milik, J. T. *The Books of Enoch.* New York: Oxford University Press, 1976.

_____. "Problèmes de la littérature hénochique à la lumière des fragments araméens de Qumrân." *Harvard Theological Review* 64 (1971): 333–78.

Miller, Madeline S., and J. Lane Miller. *Harper's Encyclopedia of Bible Life.* Revised by Boyce M. Bennett, Jr., and David H. Scott. San Francisco: Harper and Row, 1978.

Montgomery, James Alan. *The Samaritans: The Earliest Jewish Sect.* Philadelphia: John C. Winston, 1907.

Moore, George Foot. "The Am Ha-Areṣ (the People of the Land) and the Ḥaberîm (Associates)." In *The Beginnings of Christianity*, edited by F. J. Foakes Jackson and Kirsopp Lake, 1:439–45. Grand Rapids: Baker, 1979.

———. "Christian Writers on Judaism." *Harvard Theological Review* 14.3 (July 1921): 199–254.

———. *Judaism in the First Centuries of the Christian Era*. 3 vols. Cambridge, Mass.: Harvard University Press, 1927–30.

Mowinckel, Sigmund O. P. *He That Cometh*. Translated by G. W. Anderson. New York: Abingdon, 1956.

Murphy, Frederick J. *The Religious World of Jesus*. Nashville: Abingdon, 1991.

Murphy-O'Connor, Jerome. "The Judean Desert." In *Early Judaism and Its Modern Interpreters*, edited by Robert A. Kraft and George W. E. Nickelsburg, 139–41. Atlanta: Scholars, 1986.

Myers, Jacob M. *I and II Esdras: A New Translation with Introduction and Commentary*. Anchor Bible 42. Garden City, N.Y.: Doubleday, 1974.

Neusner, Jacob. *Formative Judaism: Torah, Pharisees, and Rabbis*. Chico, Calif.: Scholars, 1983.

———. *From Testament to Torah: An Introduction to Judaism in Its Formative Age*. Englewood Cliffs, N.J.: Prentice Hall, 1988.

———. *Messiah in Context*. Philadelphia: Fortress, 1984.

———. *The Rabbinic Traditions about the Pharisees before 70*. 3 vols. Leiden: E. J. Brill, 1971.

———, ed. *Christianity, Judaism, and Other Greco-Roman Cults: Studies for Morton Smith at Sixty*. Leiden: E. J. Brill, 1975.

———, et al., eds. *Judaisms and Their Messiahs at the Turn of the Christian Era*. New York: Cambridge University Press, 1987.

———, et al., eds. *The Social World of Formative Christianity and Judaism*. Philadelphia: Fortress, 1988.

New Bible Dictionary. Edited by J. D. Douglas. 2d ed. Downers Grove, Ill.: InterVarsity, 1982.

Nickelsburg, George W. E. *Jewish Literature between the Bible and the Mishnah*. Philadelphia: Fortress, 1981.

———. *Resurrection, Immortality, and Eternal Life in Intertestamental Judaism*. Cambridge, Mass.: Harvard University Press, 1972.

Perowne, Stewart. *The Later Herods*. Nashville: Abingdon, 1958.

———. *The Life and Times of Herod the Great*. Nashville: Abingdon, 1956.

Pfeiffer, Robert H. "Canon of the OT." In *Interpreter's Dictionary of the Bible*, edited by George A. Buttrick et al., 1:498–520. New York: Abingdon, 1962.

———. *History of New Testament Times*. London: Adam and Charles Black, 1949.

Porten, Bezalel. *Archives from Elephantine: The Life of an Ancient Jewish Military Colony*. Berkeley: University of California Press, 1968.

Porton, Gary G. "Diversity in Postbiblical Judaism." In *Early Judaism and Its Modern Interpreters*, edited by Robert A. Kraft and George W. E. Nickelsburg, 57–80. Atlanta: Scholars, 1986.

———. "Sadducees." In *Anchor Bible Dictionary*, edited by David Noel Freedman, 5:892–95. New York: Doubleday, 1992.

Purvis, James D. "The Samaritans and Judaism." In *Early Judaism and Its Modern Interpreters*, edited by Robert A. Kraft and George W. E. Nickelsburg, 81–98. Atlanta: Scholars, 1986.

Qimron, Elisha, and John Strugnell. *Discoveries in the Judaean Desert.* Vol. 10, *Qumran Cave 4.* New York: Oxford University Press, 1994.

Reicke, Bo. *The New Testament Era: The World of the Bible from 500 B.C. to A.D. 100.* Translated by David E. Green. Philadelphia: Fortress, 1968.

Rhoads, David. "Zealots." In *Anchor Bible Dictionary,* edited by David Noel Freedman, 6:1043–54. New York: Doubleday, 1992.

Riggan, George A. *Messianic Theology and Christian Faith.* Philadelphia: Westminster, 1967.

Rivkin, Ellis. *A Hidden Revolution: The Pharisees' Search for the Kingdom Within.* Nashville: Abingdon, 1978.

Robinson, J. A. T. "Theologians of Our Time: XII. C. H. Dodd." *Expository Times* 75.4 (Jan. 1964): 100–102.

Rost, Leonhard. *Judaism outside the Hebrew Canon: An Introduction to the Documents.* Translated by David E. Green. Nashville: Abingdon, 1976.

Rowland, Christopher. *The Open Heaven.* New York: Crossroad, 1982.

Rowley, H. H. *The Relevance of Apocalyptic.* 3d ed. London: Lutterworth, 1963.

Russell, D. S. *Between the Testaments.* London: SCM, 1960.

_____. *From Early Judaism to Early Church.* Philadelphia: Fortress, 1986.

_____. *The Method and Message of Jewish Apocalyptic.* Philadelphia: Westminster, 1964.

Safrai, S. "Education and the Study of the Torah." In *The Jewish People in the First Century,* edited by S. Safrai, M. Stern et al., 2:945–69. Philadelphia: Fortress, 1976.

_____. "Home and Family." In *The Jewish People in the First Century,* edited by S. Safrai, M. Stern et al., 2:748–91. Philadelphia: Fortress, 1976.

_____. "The Synagogue." In *The Jewish People in the First Century,* edited by S. Safrai, M. Stern et al., 2:908–44. Philadelphia: Fortress, 1976.

Saldarini, Anthony J. "Pharisees." In *Anchor Bible Dictionary,* edited by David Noel Freedman, 5:289–303. New York: Doubleday, 1992.

_____. *Pharisees, Scribes and Sadducees in Palestinian Society.* Edinburgh: T. and T. Clark, 1988.

Sanders, E. P. *Jewish Law from Jesus to the Mishnah: Five Studies.* Philadelphia: Trinity Press International, 1990.

_____. *Paul and Palestinian Judaism.* Philadelphia: Fortress, 1977.

_____. *Paul, the Law, and the Jewish People.* Philadelphia: Fortress, 1983.

Schiffman, Lawrence H., ed. *Archaeology and History in the Dead Sea Scrolls: The New York University Conference in Memory of Yigael Yadin.* Sheffield, Eng.: Sheffield Academic Press, 1990.

Schmithals, Walter. *The Apocalyptic Movement: Introduction and Interpretation.* Translated by John E. Steely. Nashville: Abingdon, 1975.

Scholem, Gershom G. *Jewish Gnosticism, Merkabah Mysticism and Talmudic Traditions.* New York: Jewish Theological Seminary, 1965.

_____. *Major Trends in Jewish Mysticism.* 3d ed. New York: Schocken, 1961.

Schürer, Emil. *The History of the Jewish People in the Age of Jesus Christ.* Edited by Geza Vermes et al. 3 vols. Edinburgh: T. and T. Clark, 1973–87.

_____. *The History of the Jewish People in the Time of Jesus Christ.* Translated by J. MacPherson et al. 5 vols. Edinburgh: T. and T. Clark, 1897–98.

Scott, J. Julius, Jr. "*Archēgos* in the Salvation History of the Epistle to the Hebrews." *Journal of the Evangelical Theological Society* 29.1 (March 1986): 47–54.

_____. "Crisis and Reaction: Roots of Diversity in Intertestamental Judaism." *Evangelical Quarterly* 64.3 (1992): 197–212.

_____. "Cross/Crucifixion." In *Evangelical Dictionary of Theology*, edited by Walter A. Elwell, 286–88. Grand Rapids: Baker, 1984.

_____. "Josephus." In *Dictionary of Jesus and the Gospels*, edited by Joel B. Green, Scot McKnight, and I. Howard Marshall, 391–94. Downers Grove, Ill.: Inter-Varsity, 1992.

_____. "Sadducees." In *New International Dictionary of New Testament Theology*, edited by Colin Brown, 3:439–41. Grand Rapids: Zondervan, 1978.

Sherwin-White, A. N. *The Roman Citizenship*. 2d ed. New York: Oxford University Press, 1973.

_____. *Roman Society and Roman Law in the New Testament*. Oxford: Clarendon, 1963.

Silva, Moisés. "The Pharisees in Modern Jewish Scholarship." *Westminster Theological Journal* 42 (1979–80): 395–405.

Simon, Marcel. *Jewish Sects at the Time of Jesus*. Translated by James H. Farley. Philadelphia: Fortress, 1967.

_____. "Saint Stephen and the Jerusalem Temple." *Journal of Ecclesiastical History* 2 (1951): 128–33.

_____. *Verus Israel: A Study of the Relations between Christians and Jews in the Roman Empire (A.D. 135–425)*. Translated by H. McKeating. New York: Oxford University Press, 1986.

Smith, George Adam. *The Historical Geography of the Holy Land*. New York: Harper and Row, 1966 reprint.

Smith, Morton. *Palestinian Parties and Policies That Shaped the Old Testament*. New York: Columbia University Press, 1971.

_____. "Zealots and Sicarii: Their Origins and Relation." *Harvard Theological Review* 64 (1971): 1–19.

Stambaugh, John E. *The Ancient Roman City*. Baltimore: Johns Hopkins University Press, 1988.

Stendahl, Krister, ed. *The Scrolls and the New Testament*. New York: Harper and Row, 1957.

Stern, Menahem. "Aspects of Jewish Society: The Priesthood and Other Classes." In *The Jewish People in the First Century*, edited by S. Safrai, M. Stern et al., 2:602–3. Philadelphia: Fortress, 1976.

_____. "The Greek and Latin Literary Sources." In *The Jewish People in the First Century*, edited by S. Safrai, M. Stern et al., 1:18–35. Philadelphia: Fortress, 1974.

Stone, Michael E. *Scripture, Sects and Visions*. Philadelphia: Fortress, 1980.

Strack, H. L., and Paul Billerbeck. *Kommentar zum Neuen Testament aus Talmud und Midrasch*. 6 vols. in 7. Munich: C. H. Beck, 1922–61.

Strack, H. L., and G. Stemberger. *Introduction to the Talmud and Midrash*. Translated by Markus Bockmuehl. Edinburgh: T. and T. Clark, 1991.

Strathmann, Hermann. *"Polis."* In *Theological Dictionary of the New Testament*, edited by Gerhard Friedrich, translated by Geoffrey W. Bromiley, 6:516–35. Grand Rapids: Eerdmans, 1968.

Talmon, Shemaryahu, ed. *Jewish Civilization in the Hellenistic-Roman Period*. Philadelphia: Trinity, 1991.

Tannenbaum, Robert. "Jews and God-Fearers in the Holy City of Aphrodite." *Biblical Archaeologist Reader* 12.5 (Sept./Oct. 1986): 55–57.

Taylor, Stephen. "Pharisees." In *Evangelical Dictionary of Theology,* edited by Walter A. Elwell, 849–51. Grand Rapids: Baker, 1984.

Tcherikover, Victor. *Hellenistic Civilization and the Jews.* Translated by S. Applebaum. Philadelphia: Magnes, 1961.

Teeple, Howard M. *The Mosaic Eschatological Prophet.* Philadelphia: Society of Biblical Literature, 1957.

Thomas, Joseph. *Le Mouvement baptist en Palestine et Syrie.* Gembloux: J. Duculot, 1935.

Tödt, H. E. *The Son of Man in the Synoptic Tradition.* Translated by Dorothea M. Barton. Philadelphia: Westminster, 1965.

Tov, Emanuel. "Jewish Greek Scriptures." In *Early Judaism and Its Modern Interpreters,* edited by Robert A. Kraft and George W. E. Nickelsburg, 223–37. Atlanta: Scholars, 1986.

van der Horst, Pieter W. "Jewish Funerary Inscriptions." *Biblical Archaeology Review* 18.5 (Sept.-Oct. 1992): 46–57.

VanderKam, James C. *The Dead Sea Scrolls Today.* Grand Rapids: Eerdmans, 1994.

van der Ploeg, J. *The Excavations at Qumran: A Survey of the Judean Brotherhood and Its Ideas.* Translated by Kevin Smyth. New York: Longmans, Green, 1958.

Vermes, Geza. *The Dead Sea Scrolls: Qumran in Perspective.* Cleveland: Collins and World, 1978.

Volz, Paul. *Jüdische Eschatologie von Daniel bis Akiba.* Tübingen, 1903.

Waltke, Bruce K. "Samaritan Pentateuch." In *Anchor Bible Dictionary,* edited by David Noel Freedman, 5:932–40. New York: Doubleday, 1992.

Weiss, H. F. *"Pharisaios."* In *Theological Dictionary of the New Testament,* edited by Gerhard Friedrich, translated by Geoffrey W. Bromiley, 9:11–48. Grand Rapids: Eerdmans, 1974.

Weiss, Johannes. *Earliest Christianity.* Translated by F. C. Grant. New York: Harper, 1959.

Wilckens, Ulrich. *"Sophia."* In *Theological Dictionary of the New Testament,* edited by Gerhard Friedrich, translated by Geoffrey W. Bromiley, 7:498–505. Grand Rapids: Eerdmans, 1971.

Wilcox, Max. "The 'God-Fearers' in Acts—A Reconsideration." *Journal for the Study of the New Testament* 13 (1981): 102–22.

Wiseman, D. J. "Siloam." In *New Bible Dictionary,* edited by J. D. Douglas et al., 2d ed., 1113–14. Downers Grove, Ill.: Inter-Varsity, 1982.

Yadin, Yigael. *The Message of the Scrolls.* New York: Grosset and Dunlap, 1962.

Yamauchi, Edwin M. *Persia and the Bible.* Grand Rapids: Baker, 1990.

Yarbro Collins, Adela. "The Origin of the Designation of Jesus as Son of Man." *Harvard Theological Review* 80 (1987): 391–407.

Zimmerli, Walther, and Joachim Jeremias. *The Servant of God.* Translated by Harold Knight. Naperville, Ill.: Allenson, 1957.

Index of Scripture and Jewish Writings

Subject Index

J. Julius Scott, Jr. (Ph.D., University of Manchester) is emeritus professor of biblical and historical studies at Wheaton College, where he
taught from 1977–2000. Scott has contributed numerous articles to
scholarly journals. He resides in Wheaton, Illinois and Franklin, North
Carolina.